Fodor's EXPLORING
PROVENCE

FODOR'S TRAVEL PUBLICATIONS

NEW YORK • TORONTO • LONDON • SYDNEY • AUCKLAND

WWW.FODORS.COM

Please note:

In January 2006, the French government transferred the administration and maintenance of approximately 18,000km (11,200 miles) of National roads to local authorities (*départements*), resulting in an extensive re-classification and re-numbering programme which will take several years to complete. You may find, therefore, that some of the road numbers used in this book do not match those appearing on current road signs.

Important Note

While every care has been taken to ensure the accuracy of the information in this guide, time brings changes, and consequently the publisher cannot accept responsibility for errors that may occur. Prudent travelers should call ahead to verify prices and other perishable information.

Published in the United States by Fodor's Travel, a division of Random House, Inc., and simultaneously in Canada by Random House of Canada Limited, Toronto. Published in the United Kingdom by AA Publishing.

Fodor's and Fodor's Exploring are registered trademarks of Random House, Inc.

ISBN: 978-1-4000-1837-6

Fifth Edition

Fodor's Exploring Provence

Author: **Nick Hanna**
Updated by: **Donna Dailey**
Revision Editor: **Bookwork Creative Associates Ltd**
Original Copy Editor: **Lynn Bresler**
Original Photography: **Adrian Baker**
Cartography: **The Automobile Association**
Cover Design: **Tigist Getachew, Fabrizio La Rocca**
Front Cover Silhouette: **Catherine Karnow**
Front Cover Top Inset: **AA Photo Library**

Special Sales

Fodor's Travel Publications are available at special discounts for bulk purchases (100 copies or more) for sales promotions or premiums. Special editions, including personalized covers, excerpts of existing guides, and corporate imprints, can be created in large quantities for special needs. For more information, contact your local bookseller or write to Special Marketing, Fodor's Travel Publications, 1745 Broadway, New York, NY 10019. Inquiries from Canada should be directed to your local Canadian bookseller or sent to Random House of Canada Ltd., Marketing Department, 2775 Matheson Blvd., Mississauga, Ontario L4W 4P7.

A03259

Printed and bound in Italy by Printer Trento S.r.l.
10 9 8 7 6 5 4 3 2 1

How to use this book

ORGANIZATION

Provence Is, Provence Was
Discusses aspects of life and culture in contemporary Provence and explores significant periods in its history.

A–Z
Breaks down the region into chapters, and covers places to visit, including walks and drives. Within this section fall the Focus On articles, which consider a variety of subjects in greater detail.

Travel Facts
Contains the strictly practical information vital for a successful trip.

Hotels & Restaurants
Lists recommended establishments throughout Provence, giving a brief summary of their attractions.

ADMISSION CHARGES
An indication of an establishment's admission charge is given by categorizing the standard, adult rate as:
Expensive (over €8)
Moderate (€4–8), or
Inexpensive (up to €4).

ABOUT THE RATINGS
Most places described in this book have been given a separate rating:

▶▶▶   **Do not miss**

▶▶   **Highly recommended**

▶   **Worth seeing**

MAPS
Every main entry has a map reference, such as 54A2. The first number (54) refers to the page on which the map can be found. The letter (A) and the second number (2) pinpoint the square in which the place is located. The maps on the inside front cover and inside back cover are referred to as IFC and IBC, respectively. A red square denotes a point of interest.

Contents

5

A–Z

IMPORTANT NOTICE

In January 2006, the French government transferred the administration and maintenance of approximately 18,000km of National roads to local authorities (Départements), resulting in an extensive re-classification and re-numbering programme which will take several years to complete.
You may find, therefore, that some of the road numbers used in this book do not match those appearing on current road signs.

My Provence

Nick Hanna has travelled in and around Provence by every conceivable means—car, train, bicycle, hitch-hiking, and on foot—for over 20 years, and although he has written guidebooks to numerous other destinations, Provence remains one of his favourites. He has journeyed across vast distances, criss-crossing a region that now feels like his second home and which, despite its familiarity, continues to delight and astonish him, as it has generations of visitors.

On my most recent trip back to Provence, I was in the tiny municipal museum of a remote Haut Var village when I came across some fascinating photographs. The record of a local archaeology dig, the pictures revealed some unusual facts about the neolithic people who had dwelt in the caves behind the village. Along with clear evidence of human cannibalism, the photographs showed that these people had discovered trepanning. The technique, now medically obsolete, involves removing a portion of the skull. The fact that these cave-dwellers had used it as a form of surgery 300,000 years ago and that the "patient" had survived is extraordinary.

Obscure though this discovery may be, it is just one example of the richness of Provence's multi-layered history, and its capacity to surprise even the most knowledgeable visitor. The region of Provence-Alpes-Côte d'Azur is famous for the splendour of its Roman antiquities (at Arles, Nîmes and St.-Rémy), for its unbelievably photogenic medieval *villages perchés*, and steamy port cities (Marseille and Nice) founded by the ancient Greeks. However, Provence is also a dynamic, forward-looking region, and the combination of respect for its heritage and a vision of its future has sparked off numerous innovative projects in recent years, such as Nîmes' striking modern Carré d'Art complex, and the Musée de Préhistoire des Gorges du Verdon at Quinson.

Thus Provence is continually reinventing itself, drawing upon the texture of the past to create a heritage for the future. At the same time, I am always reassured whenever I go back by the unchanging patterns of daily life: the quiet "clonk" of *boules* being played beneath the plane trees in village squares; the queues of tractors waiting to disgorge their glistening loads at the local co-operative during the grape harvest; the lively village markets, with their eye-catching displays of seasonal produce; and the obligatory lunchtime closure of almost everything except restaurants, during which you might as well forget whatever it was you were trying to achieve and succumb to the temptation of the *plat du jour* and a glass of Côtes-de-Provence rosé in the nearest bistro. *Bon appetit!*
Nick Hanna

Provence Is

Despite the picture-postcard images of mellow landscapes, in reality Provence is rugged and mountainous, with arid, wind-blown terrain alternating with the lush river valleys.

MOUNTAINS, RIVERS, GORGES In the northeast corner of Provence the craggy peaks of the Alpes de Haute-Provence tower above glaciated valleys, such as the Vallée de l'Ubaye, the dramatic mountain passes often cut off by deep snow in winter. To the south, these alpine heights adjoin the Mercantour *massif* on the border with Italy and lead down into the upper valleys of the Var, Tinée, Roya and Vésubie rivers. On the way to the coast these torrents have created chasms through the pre-Alps, which shelter the hinterland and the Riviera resorts.

To the west, the Verdon River has carved out of the limestone of the Plateau de Valensole one of the great natural wonders of the region, the Grand Canyon du Verdon. The Plateau de Valensole and the Plan de Canjuers to the south of the Verdon are

Spring blossoms on the slopes of the Dentelles de Montmirail

amongst the least-populated regions in Provence; desolate, wild areas dominated by *garrigue* (scrubland).

The River Durance loops down from the Alps through the heartland of Provence before disgorging into the Rhône. During the summer its stony bed is all but dried out, but in the spring the melting snow transforms it into an impressive, foaming torrent.

Above the broad curve formed by the Durance are the Petit and Grand Luberon ranges, reaching their peak at the Mourre Nègre (1,125m/3,690ft). The wide-open, arid plains of the Plateau de Vaucluse beyond the Luberon are fractured by chasms and fissures that lead down to a vast network of subterranean rivers through which rainwater is carried to spectacular resurgent springs such as the Fontaine-de-Vaucluse.

Rising up to the north of the Plateau de Vaucluse is the imposing Mont Ventoux, with its barren summit at 1,909m (6,263ft) dominating the

surrounding landscapes. Flanking it to the east is the Montagne de Lure, with the unusual mini-peaks of the Dentelles de Montmirail displaying a jagged profile to the west.

To the south of the Durance's leisurely arc lie the southern Provençal ranges—Ste.-Victoire above Aix, Ste.-Baume behind Marseille, and Mont Faron over-shadowing Toulon harbour.

The western boundary of Provence closely follows the Rhône, a major artery for communication and transportation in Provence since antiquity. Alluvial deposits built up on either side of the river have created the fertile valleys of the Comtat Venaissin and the plains of la Crau and Petite Crau near its delta. Separating the Crau and the Petite Crau is the rugged Alpilles chain.

On either side of the delta, the Grand Rhône and Petit Rhône embrace the marshy wilderness of the Camargue; along with the rest of the Rhône valley, the Camargue is subject to periodic flooding, which can have devastating effects.

Three of the most distinctive geographical features of the present-day coastline are the Cap Canaille (which has the highest cliffs in France) and the unusual *massifs* of the Esterel and the Maures.

THE "MUD-EATER" *MISTRAL*

Provence has many winds but the most famous is the *mistral*, its course shaped by the mountains and rivers of the region. Originating in the north or northwest, the *mistral* is channelled down the Rhône valley and blasts across mid-Provence and the coast before dissipating on the Alpes-Maritimes. The *mistral* (in Provençal, the *mangio fango* or the "mud-eater") has a profound effect, drying out the soil and clearing up the atmosphere, creating luminous blue skies in its wake. It knocks off roof tiles and sets doors banging, getting on everyone's nerves. Folklore claims that it blows in cycles of three days (a *mistral* blowing for nine days is not unknown) if it starts up by day, although if it begins at night it may last only "as long as it takes to bake bread." Generally, it blows for between 100 and 150 days in the year.

11

View of the Camargue (top)
Canoeists work their way through the Ardèche gorges (below)

The people of Provence are mostly Mediterranean in temperament and looks, but they also have their own distinct character based on a strong regional identity and sense of independence. After decades of neglect the Provençal language, a symbol of a shared identity, is undergoing a modest revival.

12

THE PROVENÇALS Who are the real Provençals, and what are they like? Generations of writers and travellers have tried to provide answers and more often than not come up with patronizing generalizations. Victor Hugo considered them typically Mediterranean and hot-blooded ("in Paris one quarrels, in Avignon one kills"), while almost everyone from Stendhal to Lawrence Durrell thought they embodied the *mañana* attitude—lazy, unhurried, ready to put off work until *demain* or (more likely) *après demain*. This reputation is no doubt partly due to the difficulties some newcomers experience when getting locals to work on their houses, a storyline that has been mined from the days of Lady Fortescue (who settled near Grasse in the 1930s) through to Peter Mayle in the 1980s.

Dual French—Provençal road signs are now common

Alphonse Daudet was first responsible for portraying the Provençals as whimsical, comic characters through his *Tartarin* novels, and the enormously popular books and films of Marcel Pagnol have reinforced this stereotype of the light-hearted, playful Provençal who spends all day doing nothing more serious than playing *boules* and drinking *pastis*.

There may be a grain of truth in these caricatures but in reality Provençals are far more serious and hard-working, although they do know how to enjoy themselves. They also have a reputation for surliness and distrust of outsiders (natural enough, one would think, in a region that has seen so many invasions, including invasion by tourism), but once the ice is broken they become welcoming and hospitable.

In rural areas, villages are bound together by a strong sense of community and old-fashioned values (among the older generation, at least) combined with a profound respect and love for the Provençal countryside. Although regular church-going is no longer universally observed, Catholicism is deeply ingrained. Alongside their religious beliefs, the Provençals have retained many customs and rituals, some dating back centuries, and a healthy dose of superstitious belief.

THE PROVENÇAL LANGUAGE
Although Provençal is no longer widely spoken, the distinctive accent is easily recognizable and tells you that you are conversing with a true Provençal, if you can understand what he or she is saying behind the thick nasal twang (where *vin* becomes *ving*, *demain* becomes *demang* and so on), which is often

rendered even more incomprehensible by high-speed delivery.

The Provençal language has been in decline since the 16th century, despite the efforts of the poet Mistral, who collated his giant Provençal dictionary and published a popular journal, *L'Aïoli*, in an attempt to revive it in the late 19th century. Today, however, there are signs that the sense of regional identity is becoming stronger once more, and Provençal is a study option in many schools. Nearly every rural village now has its name on the road sign in both French and Provençal.

In the post-war years the younger generation deserted many of the old ways, lured away from the traditional lifestyle by the bright lights (and prospect of work) in the big cities. But now another generation is taking a far greater interest in their linguistic heritage. Curiously, one of the strangest manifestations of young Provençals seeking out their roots has emerged from Marseille, where learning Provençal has become the latest craze among second-generation

A disappearing lifestyle: fisherman in Bandol

immigrants. Local folklore has become a way of asserting their identity and sense of belonging, a trend which has developed hand in hand with the rise of ragamuffin music—a blend of reggae and rap interwoven with old Provençal songs. One local band even starts off its performances with the symbolic rallying cry of "Aïoli!" Mistral would have been both horrified and delighted.

Drinking pastis all day long—the whimsical image of the Provençaux

13

In contrast to the futuristic ambitions of public buildings in Nice, Marseille or Nîmes, in rural areas of Provence one architectural form remains supreme—the Provençal country house. Although it has some elements in common with an Italian villa or a Spanish hacienda, the Provençal country house is as different from these as it is from a Normandy farmhouse.

PERFECT ADAPTATION The Provençal house has evolved to cope with the often harsh extremes of the climate in this part of France—the strong sunlight of summer and the bitingly cold winter winds. Its thick walls, sometimes buttressed, merge into the terrain and usually have no windows on the north side and just enough openings on the other three sides to let in light. A perfect example of thermal insulation, the house is well designed to stay cool in summer and warm in winter.

In regions where the *mistral* predominates (most of Provence between the Alps, the sea and the Rhône) the house is usually orientated north–south with a slight turn to the east so that the front of the house is sheltered from the north-westerly *mistral*.

TILED ROOFS The characteristic curved roof tiles of the Provençal house are Greek in origin. Their shape (which is tapered at one end) probably comes from being moulded on the thigh of the potter. Traditionally made by hand, tiles were fired in the kilns at Aubagne, Biot, Moustiers, Vallauris and Apt. The Provençal roof is usually finished off with a *génoise*, a double or triple row of tiles embedded under the eaves.

DEFINITIONS First of all there is the *mas*, which could mean anything from a country house to a farm or even a barn. Typically, the Provençal *mas* is a large, low-lying farmhouse that sprawls outwards and encompasses stables, storerooms, dovecots and even sheep pens under one roof. It has evolved and been added to over many generations. In the Camargue and the Crau, the *mas* was often built around an enclosed courtyard, again, for protection from the *mistral*.

Then there is the *bastide*, which could also be a farm but was more likely to be a country house, with decorative elements such as balconies, exterior stone staircases, and sculpted lintels. It was usually two floors high, with a third floor adorned by oval "eyebrow windows" (in Provence known as *oeils de boeuf* or bull's eyes). Unlike the long, low, sloping roof of the *mas*, the *bastide* roof had four slopes.

The *bastidon* ("little *bastide*") preserved the same proportions on a smaller scale.

INTERIORS Years ago, the *mas* was often divided in two by a corridor, with one side for the owner and the other for the *bayle* (farmer or steward). Terracotta tiles were used on the floors, with roof beams made from whole tree-trunks—left round in *mas*, squared off in the *bastides*.

> ❏ "In August, in our region, just before evening, a powerful heat sets the fields ablaze. The whitewashed, beaten soil radiated against the low wall of the abandoned sheepfold. The heart of the house remained cool, however. There remained in this retreat some reserves of shade and freshness that were fed at night and which, during the heat of the day, were a great resource." Henri Bosco, *Le Mas Théotime.* ❏

A typical example of a mas *(below) and (top) a close-up view of its roof*

As well as wall ovens and open hearths, kitchens nearly always had their *pétrins* (wooden trunks which were used for leavening bread dough) and *panatières* (wooden cages hung on the wall, used for storing bread), both of which might be elaborately carved in the Arlesian style. Another distinctive Provençal feature, found in the drawing-room, was the *radassie*, a three- or four-seater settee with armrests between the seats.

Farming and forestry still play an essential role in modern Provence. Fields and forests cover more than two-thirds of the region and support a remarkably varied agricultural profile assisted by local geography, which ranges from Alpine pastures to the Rhône plains and marshy Camargue.

A BOUNTIFUL HARVEST One of the strengths of agriculture in Provence is the enormous diversity of the produce grown, a cornucopia that includes lavender from the mountains, chestnuts from the forests, flowers from the greenhouses of the Côte d'Azur, rice from the Camargue, *les primeurs* (early crops of fruits and vegetables) such as cherries, strawberries, asparagus, melons and peaches from the fertile plains...not to mention olives, sunflowers, grapes, apples and tomatoes.

CHANGING PATTERNS Despite the relatively buoyant state of local agriculture at present, some forecasts predict that within a generation the peasant lifestyle will have all but disappeared. Pressures from developers, particularly in coastal areas, have forced many farmers off the land. High land costs are another contributing factor, with prices climbing dramatically in recent years, notably in the Var.

The influx of wealthy Parisians and foreigners keen to find a second home in the sun, at prices the local inhabitants cannot hope to match, is also changing the face of centuries-old agricultural communities, and their effect on local culture is not altogether benign.

ADAPTATION Agriculture in Provence is having to adapt to competition within the European Union, and to modernize. Greater emphasis is now being placed on food processing, better marketing, new varieties of fruit and vegetables (there are several applied plant-breeding stations in the region) and on other innovations such as biological pest control to reduce crop losses, and new irrigation schemes.

Other farmers are moving in different directions, many of which are connected to tourism and the realisation that the rural environment is a valuable attraction in its own right. Some are restoring old olive oil mills, not only so that they can process oil but also to draw visitors. Others are developing "gourmet routes" through their localities, with farms selling food products (*produits fermiers*), from fragrant lavender, honey and goats' cheeses to freshly-picked fruits and vegetables. In the Alps, they are even studying the possibility of introducing bison; not only would they be a great attraction, but their meat sells at a premium.

HORTICULTURE The main centres for horticulture in Provence are the Var and the Alpes-Maritimes, where tracts of poly-tunnels (plastic covered greenhouses) are a familiar sight, and which between them grow over 300 varieties of ornamental plants and cut flowers including mimosa, tulips, roses, carnations, and 30 different types of palm tree.

❏ Traditional Provençal delicacies include *herbes de Provence* (mixed thyme, rosemary, savory, oregano, bay and lavender) and truffles ("black gold"). ❏

VITICULTURE The patchwork of vineyards that gives the Provençal countryside its characteristic appeal is also undergoing change, notably the upgrading of vine stocks to produce better-quality wines. In the Bouches-du-Rhône, for instance,

> ❏ The largest area of vineyards in Provence is found in the Vaucluse, home to such famous names as Châteauneuf-du-Pape, Gigondas and Beaumes-de-Venise. ❏

rough-and-ready *vin de table* accounted for nearly 70 per cent of production in the 1970s; now it is less than a quarter, with many more vineyards having gained the coveted *Appellation d'Origine Contrôlée* (AOC) status (see also Regional Wines, pages 94–95). Another phenomenon is overseas winemakers buying vineyards in Provence. Though this development has not always been greeted with enthusiasm by the old regime, overall outside investors are making a vital contribution, injecting new capital and new ideas into this important sector of the economy.

17

Lavender is one of many crops that Provence produces in abundance

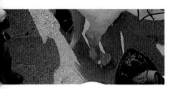

With some 500 festivals encompassing around 4,000 separate events, Provence in the summertime is justifiably called "The Land of Festivals." The following is but a sample of the cultural riches the region has to offer.

TRADITIONAL FESTIVALS Many of the traditional village festivals revolve around the natural calendar and the bounty of the earth and the sea. Others have their roots deep in Provençal folklore. Whatever the reason, the day will usually involve a procession of some sort in traditional costumes, accompanied by pipes and drums, culminating in a vast feast with *pastis* and wine flowing freely, when a good time is had by one and all.

> ❏ In the St. Eloi processions, horses with their bridles and Saracen-style harnesses ablaze with ribbons and pompoms pull chariots piled high with wheat, followed by men and boys on horseback and women and children in horse-drawn carts in Provençal costumes. ❏

On 1 May the cowboys of the Camargue, the *gardians*, put on a rodeo in the arena at Arles for the *Fête des Gardians*, while at Whitsun the old sheep migrations between

Nice's famous carnival dates back to the 13th century

the mountains and the plains are celebrated in the *Fête de la Transhumance* in St.-Rémy. St.-Tropez has its noisy and ebullient *bravades* on 16 May (in honour of St. Tropez or St. Torpes himself) and 15 June (to celebrate seeing off the Spanish fleet in 1637), while on 24 and 25 May gypsies from all over Europe arrive for the *pèlerinage* (pilgrimage) to les Stes.-Maries-de-la-Mer.

In June the atmospheric *procession dai limaca* (in thanksgiving for the olive harvest) takes place in Gorbio, and the highly colourful Tarasque festival (last weekend in June) unrolls in Tarascon. The Feast of St. John, 24 June, is widely celebrated throughout Provence.

St. Eloi is one of the most popular saints in Provence, and festivities in his honour (or those fêting St. Roch, another popular saint) take place between June and early September in dozens of villages (see box).

August sees the *Fête de la Lavande* in Sault, the *Fête du Muscat* in Beaumes-de-Venise, and the *Fête de la Véraison* with medieval pageantry to celebrate the grapes maturing in Châteauneuf-du-Pape. In September the Camargue rice harvest is celebrated in Arles, the apple harvest in Peyruis, and the *vendange* (wine harvest) is a prime excuse to party in the wine regions.

CULTURAL FESTIVALS Provence has numerous outstanding venues that resonate during summer evenings to the classics, jazz and folk music, or simply act as a superb backdrop to theatre and dance performances. What better stage could there possibly be than the grand arenas of Arles and Nîmes, the forecourt of the

Palais des Papes in Avignon, or the exquisite Roman theatre in Orange? And then there are smaller, more intimate locations—the charming medieval tower that gave Simiane-la-Rotonde its name, the cloisters of the various churches or cathedrals, the enchanting *théâtres de verdure* (open-air "green theatres") set among ruins in Draguignan, Villefranche and elsewhere. Another dramatic venue is the ruined château in la Tour-d'Aigues, which plays host to the Sud-Luberon summer festival. Add to this a line-up that includes performers of international calibre and the stage is set for a creative

❏ Over 300 towns and villages have some kind of festival in the summer. Complete information is available from regional tourist offices and is on their websites (see pages 269–270). ❏

The gardians *of the Camargue parade on their famous white horses*

extravaganza that lasts right through the summer season.

July and August are the busiest months, with jazz festivals in Nice, Toulon and Aix; an international folklore festival in Cavaillon; theatre, jazz and classical music in Gordes; music, dance and theatre at Fontaine-de-Vaucluse and l'Isle-sur-la-Sorgue; folklore in Marseille; classical music at the Organa festival in St.-Rémy-de-Provence and Cassis; and early music in Entrevaux and Simiane-la-Rotonde. In Orange, *Les Nuits d'Été du Théâtre Antique* encompasses everything from pop to jazz, with the renowned *Chorégies* (opera and classics) taking place in the same superb setting.

And then there is the big festival in Avignon (with literally hundreds of theatre performances, films and concerts from mid-July onwards) as well as a festival of dance and photography in Arles.

Tourism plays an essential part in the Provençal economy, as it has done since the 19th century, when foreigners first started holidaying on the Côte d'Azur. Today, around 36 million visitors descend on the Provence-Alpes-Côte d'Azur region annually.

EARLY TOURISM Tourism on the Riviera started in the 1830s when the British aristocracy began building luxury mansions in which to escape the winter fog of England. In the inter-war years Coco Chanel popularized sunbathing, and the season switched to the summer, a phenomenon that intensified after World War II with the emergence of mass tourism. By the mid-1970s millions of people were holidaying on the coastline, but inland Provence still remained largely unspoiled, discovered only by more adventurous visitors.

TOURISM TODAY The Var has become the most popular destination for holi-daymakers, and together with the two other coastal *départements*, Alpes-Maritime (which includes the Côte d'Azur) and Bouches-du-Rhône, attracts three-quarters of all visitors to the region. They are followed by the Hautes-Alpes, Vaucluse and Alpes de Haute-Provence. The vast majority of visitors favour the summer season, though a significant proportion choose springtime. Skiing boosts the winter figures to just above the levels for autumn, the quietest season of all.

The Provence-Alpes-Côte d'Azur region boasts:
- 883km (548 miles) of coast
- 135 marinas with 60,000-plus berths
- 3 national parks; 4 regional natural parks
- 2,000 notable or historic sites
- 100 classified museums
- 60 ski/winter sports destinations
- 66 golf courses

   Tourism generates an annual revenue, which results in billions of euros comfortably lining the coffers of the Provence-Alpes-Côte d'Azur (PACA) region. One in five local people are employed in the tourism industry and the future looks rosy over the region as a whole. However, tourism on the coast is suffering from a noticeable overcapacity of hotel rooms, and the changing patterns of international tourism are also having an effect. Due to increased awareness of the dangers of sunbathing, fewer people are taking beach holidays. No longer content simply to get a tan (*bronzer à idiot* as the French say),

Harbourside lido, Monte-Carlo

visitors want more things to do, they want better value for money, and they want to experience the real Provence.

Cultural tourism is now being more heavily marketed, emphasizing the extraordinary artistic legacy of the Côte d'Azur, for instance, which is blessed with dozens of museums, running the gamut from Impressionist paintings to Picasso and Chagall, perfume and honey to wine and wildlife. Many of the existing facilities have been upgraded and refurbished, while new attractions are being opened on a regular basis throughout the region.

As mentioned earlier, however, the tourist industry does suffer from a significant seasonal imbalance. Business tourism is seen as part of the solution for a more uniform year-round visitor pattern, augmented by state-of-the-art conference facilities

Tourism is now a big money-spinner in coastal resorts

such as the Acropolis in Nice and the massive Centre de Congrès Auditorium in Monte-Carlo.

The rich natural and cultural heritage has always been the main drawcard in inland Provence, but with increasing numbers of people now wanting to hike, cycle or simply do their own thing and discover the mountains and valley byways, the authorities are keen to tap into this market and promote activity holidays in rural areas. They have embarked on a coordinated scheme that includes supplying management expertise for rural communities that want to diversify into tourism. It also provides grants to upgrade hotels and restaurants and for renovating houses in historic villages.

Initiatives such as these are good news for rural communities but also point the way forward for better quality tourism and a sustainable future for this important sector of the Provençal economy.

21

Horror stories of the polluted Côte d'Azur were once commonplace but the seas are now again safe to swim in. The challenge is managing conflicting demands on the coastline, such as recreation, aquaculture and development, and maintaining the health of marine ecosystems. At the same time, Provence is mobilizing its marine industries to place itself at the forefront of global developments in undersea technology.

22

THE COAST Huge efforts have been made to clean up beaches in recent years and the quality of bathing water has improved enormously, although, given the fact that the Mediterranean is an enclosed sea, Provence is still dependent on neighbouring countries taking similar action. A large proportion of beaches on the coast have been awarded the European Blue Flag. To achieve this, they must not only pass the strictest water quality controls but also meet required standards in 25 other areas (such as having safe access, life guards, first-aid posts and so on). The prime Côte d'Azur beaches around Cannes, Antibes and Nice have generally scored well on the Blue Flag ratings, but if the big public beaches are not really your thing there are plenty of secluded coves to be discovered where the water quality is also excellent.

❏ The first experimental fish farm was at the Paul Ricard Oceanographic Institute on the Île des Embiez, founded in 1966, and a noted aquacultural facility today. The Institute was the first to develop microbacteria that eat crude oil; this knowledge was put to good use in the *Exxon Valdez* disaster in Alaska in 1989. ❏

Mussels and some types of fish are now farmed extensively

If you were expecting sandy beaches on the Riviera be prepared for disappointment. A few resorts lie on man-made sand strands, but for the most part it is large flat rocks from Cannes to Menton. Real sand beaches begin to the west, around Fréjus, and continue along the coast past the glories of St.-Tropez to the popular resorts of Bandol and Cassis, interspersed with rocky inlets known as *criques*.

AQUACULTURE AND FISHING The picture-postcard cliché of the weather-beaten old fisherman mending

Clean seas have become a major priority for Provençal authorities

his nets on the quayside is in danger of becoming just that, a snapshot of the past, given the decline in the coastal fishing in Provence. In the Var, for instance, there are now only a few hundred fishing boats left to trawl for increasingly slim pickings. Overfishing, lack of investment, and EU directives to reduce fishing fleets

❏ Provence is one of the world's leading research centres for ocean engineering. Local enterprises are involved in projects ranging from the manufacture of remote-control deep-sea robots, catamarans or passenger submarines, to submarine cable maintenance and the development of pollution-control techniques. ❏

have all had an impact. Faced with declining catches, many fishermen are now turning to fish farming. There is enormous potential for aquaculture in Provence, with plenty of suitable coastal sites. The most popular species are sea bass and sea bream (neither of which tastes different from their "wild" cousins) and mussels.

MARINE RESERVES Since 1989, 10 Mediterranean marine species that were in danger of extinction have been protected under French law, and the 300ha (74-acre) Côte Bleue marine reserve lies off Carry-le-Rouet, west of Marseille. Provence also has the Parc National de Port-Cros, which protects both the islands of Port-Cros and the Porquerolles (opposite Hyères) and the surrounding seas. However, many more such reserves are needed to act as nurseries to replenish declining fish populations.

The intense light and rich palette of the Mediterranean, with its blue skies and water, sunbaked hills, olive groves and orchards, have drawn artists to the south of France for generations. Their legacy is displayed in a collection of superb art museums—a must-see on any cultural itinerary.

SIGNAC IN ST.-TROPEZ Paul Signac led the 19th-century artistic invasion of Provence when he took refuge in St.-Tropez during a storm while sailing along the coast in 1892. The artist was so taken by the beautiful bay that he delayed his departure in order to stay and paint, and eventually settled in the charming fishing village on the shore. Matisse and Bonnard, Dunoyer de Segonzac, Dufy and the Fauvist painters Derain and Van Dongen all followed in his wake, and many of their local scenes are on show at the fascinating Musée de l'Annonciade.

Detail from a Chagall mosaic (top). St.-Tropez pinewood, captured by Signac

> ❏ "My complexion has changed from green-greyish-pink to greyish-orange...I live in a little yellow house with a green door and green blinds...and over it an intensely blue sky, and...the shadows in the middle of the day much shorter than in our country." Vincent Van Gogh, in a letter to his sister Wilhelmina, Arles (1888). ❏

ARLES AND AIX In western Provence there are two important stops on any artistic tour of the region: Arles and Aix-en-Provence. In 1888,

24

Paul Cézanne (above) was inspired by the Provençal countryside around his home

Vincent Van Gogh came to Arles, where he worked furiously recording his impressions in vivid, passionate oils, continuing through his incarceration in the mental asylum at St.-Rémy-de-Provence.

Paul Cézanne, born in Aix-en-Provence in 1839, threw his artistic talent into depicting the familiar Provençal surroundings of his home town. Cézanne's studio has been carefully preserved and several of his works are in Aix's Musée Granet.

THE RIVIERA Two giants of the art scene are celebrated in museums dedicated to their work in Nice. Matisse first visited the city in 1914 and stayed on the Riviera for most of the rest of his life, working from a studio a stone's throw from the Musée Matisse. Another gem not to be missed on the Matisse trail is the enchanting Chapelle du Rosaire in Vence.

Also in Nice, the Musée Chagall contains the luminous, dreamlike canvases of the Russian-born painter's *Biblical Message* series, which he completed between 1954 and 1967.

Other artistic highlights include Jean Cocteau's elaborate fantasies in the Musée Cocteau and the Salle des Mariages in Menton, as well as Picasso's paintings and ceramics in Antibes' Château Grimaldi. Also of interest is the Musée Fernand Léger in Biot; a visit to Renoir's home in Cagnes-sur-Mer; and the superb modern art collection containing works by Braque, Miró, Kandinsky, Arp, Calder and Giacometti at the Fondation Maeght in the hills behind St.-Paul-de-Vence.

❏ If you are planning to hit the art museums of the Côte d'Azur, it is worth investing in a *Carte Musées Côte d'Azur*. For a one-off fee, one-, three- and seven-day passes offer unlimited access to 62 museums, monuments and gardens in the region. ❏

Dances such as the farandole *are an important part of the Provençal identity, and not just something staged for visitors' cameras. Similarly, the folk art of making* santons *(little saints) is rooted in ancient traditions.*

DANCES AND COSTUMES

Traditional costumes are often worn during village fêtes and festivals. For women, the costume consists of a full skirt and a long-sleeved, black blouse over which a pleated shirt or lace shawl is worn. There are several different types of headgear (usually embellished with lace, velvet or delicate embroidery), always worn on top of a high bun. For men, a white shirt is set off by a lace tie or ribbon and a velvet waistcoat, with canvas trousers supported by a wide woollen belt. They can wear either black felt hats with raised brims or straw hats.

The best-known Provençal dance is the *farandole*, which is performed by young men and women in traditional costume at village festivals. It is accompanied by a six-beat rhythm on the *tambourin*, a small drum made from calf-skin and decorated with coloured ribbons or cords. The *tambourinaire* hangs the tambourine on his right side and with his left hand he holds a small three-holed flute known as the *gaboulet* with which he plays a piercing tune.

Santons Nativity scenes with small figures known as *santons* (little saints) first appeared in Provence in the 17th century and were originally made from wood, wax or cork. When churches were closed after the Revolution, a potter from Marseille, Jean-Louis Lagnel, conceived the idea of mass-producing *santons* in clay, so that every family could have a Christmas crib. Soon the range of figurines produced came to include Provençal characters (the innkeeper, the shepherd, the baker and so on) bringing their gifts to the Christ child, with the nativity setting transposed to a typical Provençal village. Today, *santonniers* still make these traditional figures, usually in clay (sometimes in wood), often with hand-painted finishes or dressed in miniature costumes.

Santons are a Provençal tradition

Provence Was

The first traces of human habitation in Provence have been found in some of the Côte d'Azur's most sophisticated resorts—this coastal area must have appealed as much to Cro-Magnon man as it does to visitors today.

❏ There are no cave paintings in Provence to compare with those at Lascaux in the Dordogne, but in 1991 a local diver discovered a partially submerged cave in one of the *calanques* near Cassis with a number of paintings (depicting horses, bison, deer, fish and other marine life species) thought to be around 27,000 years old—see panel, page 123. The entrance to the caves, named after their discoverer, Henri Cosquer, lies safely concealed 37m (121ft) below sea level. ❏

EARLY HUNTERS The earliest evidence of settlements in Provence dates back 400,000 years and comes from the site known as *Terra Amata*, just behind the old port in Nice. Unearthed in 1966, *Terra Amata* revealed several encampments built by Cro-Magnon man. These nomadic hunters had found the perfect spot for a camp at the mouth of the Vallée de Paillon, where there was a freshwater spring next to a small, sheltered beach. Primarily hunters of deer and elephant, they built small, circular huts from branches, each with its own central hearth. Palaeolithic remnants have also been found near Menton, notably the skull of "Menton man" which is believed to date back around 30,000 years. The skeletons were covered in sea shells and necklaces, coinciding with the first use of burial grounds in the late palaeolithic period.

FROM HUNTERS TO SHEPHERDS
During the neolithic era, from around 6000 BC, there was a shift towards growing crops and the domestication of wild sheep. Those who lived in

The first Greek settlers landed at Massalia (Marseille) in 600 BC

tribes began descending on Provence, bringing with them iron tools and building the first of their fortified hilltop settlements known as *oppidi*. By intermarrying with the local Ligurians, the Celts started to build up powerful alliances and gradually the trading links across the Mediterranean region began to blossom, particularly those with Asia Minor.

❏ Greek traders from the island of Rhodes are attributed with having given Provence's greatest river its current name: *Rhodéenne* is an adjective still in use to describe the plains alongside the Rhône. ❏

Driven by the desire to establish new trading colonies, and by the depletion of their agricultural lands, Phocaeans (they came from Phocis in Asia Minor) set up their first Greek settlements at Massalia (Marseille) around 600 BC, providing a bridgehead for the arrival of Greek civilization on the European mainland. The Celto-Ligurians welcomed the Greeks as trading partners, exchanging metals (such as copper, gold, tin and silver) and foodstuffs for Greek vases and other artefacts.

The Greeks introduced the cultivation of cherries, olives, figs, walnuts and vines (although vines and olives were both already present in Provence, neither had been cultivated to yield fruit). The Greeks confined themselves to trading up the Rhône and the Durance and along the coast, setting up a series of ports such as Antipolis (Antibes), Athenopolis (St.-Tropez), Citharista (la Ciotat), Nikaia (Nice), and Olbia (Hyères).

Ligurian legacy: carving in Vallée des Merveilles and (top) bories

Provence at this time are known as the Ligurians, although their origins are uncertain. Some say they arrived from the east, others from the Iberian peninsula. Either way, during the neolithic and the Bronze Age, the Ligurians started to build villages, constructing drystone huts known as *bories* and trading with the outside world. Although none of the *bories* that survive today date back so far, the Ligurians left huge standing stones (dolmens) and the impressive rock engravings of the Vallée des Merveilles.

ARRIVAL OF THE CELTS AND THE GREEKS

Some time between the 8th and the 4th centuries BC the Celtic

The peaceful arrival of the Greeks was not to be repeated when the Romans descended on Provence with full military force in the second century BC. They stayed for around 600 years and their legacy is a series of monuments that are unparalleled elsewhere in Northern Europe outside Italy.

THE COHORTS MARCH IN

After Rome had conquered Spain in 206 BC, securing the land-route across Provence was the next priority. They were given the perfect excuse in 124 BC when the Greeks of Massalia appealed for help against the Celto-Ligurian Salyens, who were threatening them from their base at Entremont. The Romans came in force, with Sextius Calvinus leading a whole army to pacify the Salyens. Once that had been achieved, the Romans decided to stay permanently, founding their first settlement in Provence at *Aquae Sextiae*, the present city of Aix-en-Provence.

THE ROMAN "PROVINCIA" In 118 BC

Narbonne was founded and became the capital of the Roman territory, which extended from the Pyrenees to the Alps and north as far as Lyon. Only the Alpes-Maritimes were left

A Roman bust, Vaison-la-Romaine

more or less under Phocaean control. This new province (or Provincia, from where the present-day name of Provence derives) was known as Gallia Narbonensis.

THE BARBARIAN INVASIONS

Rome's stranglehold on southern Gaul was not yet complete. From 115 BC onwards the region was subject to attacks by several northern tribes, most notably the Teutoni. They were finally defeated by Marius in a battle below Montagne Ste.-Victoire near Aix in 102 BC.

THE DOWNFALL OF MASSALIA In the
civil wars that followed the conquest

❏ After the defeat of the Teutoni, pockets of local resistance to Roman rule continued through until 14 BC, when the last of the Alpine tribes were subdued. This final subjugation of Provincia was marked by the building of the *Trophée des Alpes* at la Turbie, a monumental symbol of Roman power. ❏

of Gaul by Julius Caesar in 51 BC, the inhabitants of Massalia made a huge mistake in not taking the side of Caesar against Pompey. In 49 BC Caesar took his revenge by laying siege to the city and ruining its trade, stripping Massalia of its territory along the coast below the Alpes-

Roman remains at St.-Rémy-de-Provence

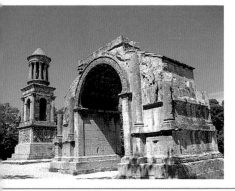

Maritimes. Caesar promoted Arelate (Arles) in its place, and before long Massalia was also eclipsed by Aix, Nîmes and Fréjus.

❑ The main settlements during this era developed alongside the major Roman roads (the *Via Agrippa*, which went north through Avignon and Orange from Arles, and the *Via Aurelia*, which linked Italy with Arles via Cimiez, Fréjus and Aix) and in the Rhône valley. ❑

PAX ROMANA The next 400 years saw the blossoming of Roman civilization in Provence, particularly under the Emperor Augustus, Caesar's great-nephew. Augustus established colonies, ruled by veteran legionnaires, at Apt, Arles, Avignon,

Carpentras, Digne, Fréjus, Glanum, Riez and Vaison. These settlements grew into prosperous cities with baths, theatres, arenas, aqueducts, temples and bridges. The arts and culture thrived, and Provence paid its way by supplying the Roman Empire with grain, oil and even ships.

EARLY CHRISTIANITY Legend has it that Christianity arrived on the shores of Provence with the "boat of Bethany" (see page 141), and St. Trophimus is also said to have arrived in Arles at around the same time. Christianity received a major boost under the Emperor Constantine and the first Church council was held in Arles in AD 314. Around a hundred years later, the great monasteries of the Îles de Lérins and St.-Victor in Marseille were founded.

31

Pont du Gard (top). The theatre at Vaison-la-Romaine (below)

After the collapse of the western Roman empire in the 5th century, Provence suffered from numerous invasions and went through a period of anarchy and decline. Once the invaders had been driven out, a period of stability followed, during which troubadours roamed between the powerful courts of the local seigneurs and Romanesque architecture flourished. The feudal squabbles continued, however.

WARS AND BLOODSHED Since the beginning of the 5th century the Visigoths had been making raids on Arles, and by the time the Roman empire disintegrated they were in control of all the land south of the Durance. At the same time the Burgundians had established their domination to the east and north. Neither of these new overlords lasted long, since they were ousted by the Ostrogoths from Italy. In turn, they were succeeded in AD 536 by the Franks, who carved up the territory into semi-autonomous regions.

The time of the troubadours was a golden age for Provence

During these troubled times life was hard in Provence, with land being appropriated and populations declining through bloodshed, famine and disease.

SARACEN INVASIONS The 8th century saw the emergence of the Islamic powers, with Arab armies sweeping up through Spain and over the Pyrenees into France. The Arabs (or Saracens, as they became generally known) got as far north as Poitiers before being defeated by the Frankish general Charles Martel in 732. Martel took advantage of the Saracen retreat to drive down through Provence between 736 and 740 and reassert Frankish control, mercilessly sacking Avignon, Marseille and Aix. Provence was once more under Frankish rule, and by the end of the century had been integrated into the empire of Charlemagne.

With the demise of Charlemagne's empire in 843, Provence passed through the hands of various rulers before being made in 855 into a king-dom, which also encompassed terri-tory farther north in the Rhône basin (such as Lyon). This was of little help to the Provençals, who still had to contend with invasion by the Normans in 859 and the constant threat from the Saracens.

THE COUNTS OF PROVENCE A new age of stability and prosperity dawned in Provence when Guillaume le Libérateur (William the Liberator) finally expelled the Saracens in 1032. Provence began to develop its inde-pendence during the years which followed, with the local lords

❏ After their rout by Martel, the Saracens switched tactics. They harassed Provence from the coast, successfully establishing several outlaw bases (notably at La Garde-Freinet in the Massif des Maures, from where they terrorized the surrounding countryside for around 200 years) and laid siege to Marseille in 838 and Arles in 842. ❏

(*seigneurs*) controlling their own fief-doms. The country began to emerge from the Dark Ages, helped along by the Benedictine monasteries, which became centres of learning, and agriculture and vineyards thrived. With the Mediterranean no longer controlled by the Saracens, trade links grew (particularly with Spain, Italy and the Orient) and the Rhône became a major artery for commerce with northern Europe, leading to increased wealth for Marseille, Arles, Avignon and Orange. Commerce on the coast benefited enormously from the Crusades, which started in 1095. In the courts of the feudal barons, the troubadours made their first appear-ance. These roaming entertainers were welcomed in the baronial castles, where they performed popular songs of the day, usually about love.

In 1125 Occitania was divided up between the counts of Toulouse (who ruled west of the Rhône and north of the Durance) and the counts of Barcelona (who controlled most of the land south of the Durance). However, the never-ending game of shifting alliances and squabbles

between fiefdoms continued. The counts of Forcalquier fought on, as did the notorious *seigneurs* of Les Baux.

Les Baux was a powerful feudal stronghold in the 12th century

❏ Linguists call the language spoken between the Alps and the Pyrenees at this time the *langue d'oc*, to distinguish it from the *langue d'oïl*, which was the dialect in the north of France (*oc* and *oïl* were the words for "yes" in each region). The *langue d'oc* spread across the whole of southern France, an area dubbed Occitania. Provençal was one of many regional dialects spoken within Occitania. ❏

Under the House of Anjou, Provence drew closer to France but was still largely autonomous. During the 14th century the popes settled in Avignon, but by the beginning of the 15th century they had gone and in 1481 the last of the Angevins bequeathed his kingdom to France, heralding the end of independent Provence.

THE HOUSE OF ANJOU Count Raymond-Bérenger V of Barcelona managed to bring some degree of stability to the warring fiefdoms in Provence during the 13th century, and imposed a unified system of law and administration based on Catalan practice. Several of his daughters made illustrious marriages. The most important was the union in 1246 of his youngest daughter, Beatrice, to Charles of Anjou, brother of the French king (later St. Louis). Charles became Count of Provence when Beatrice inherited the region from her father, and this ushered in nearly 200 years of Angevin rule.

At the beginning of the 13th century the French had embarked on a crusade against the Cathars (a heretical Christian sect otherwise known as the Albigensians) in Languedoc, sacking Avignon into the bargain as punishment for loyalty to Toulouse (see page 52). The counts of

René of Anjou's castle at Tarascon

❏ Under Angevin rule the boundaries of Provence changed. Sault, Gap, Les Baux and Marseille were brought into the fold, while Nice, Puget-Théniers and Barcelonnette became part of the Duchy of Savoy (and remained so for nearly 500 years). ❏

Toulouse were forced to turn over their territories north of Avignon, the Comtat Venaissin, to placate King Louis IX. In 1274 France handed over the Comtat Venaissin to the Holy See in Rome, an event which was to lead to an extraordinary era in Provençal history.

THE AVIGNON POPES In 1309 Pope Clement V decided to shift the centre of papal power away from strife-torn Italy closer to his native France. He moved to Carpentras in the Comtat Venaissin, and his successor, Pope John XXII, moved the papal court to

34

Avignon in 1316, beginning more than 100 years of what the Italians called "the Babylonian Captivity." It was indeed a time of avarice and debauchery but the city also witnessed a flowering of the arts and culture, the founding of the university, and the construction of dozens of churches and chapels as well as the grandiose Palais des Papes. Founded by the third pope, Benedict XII, this was greatly expanded by his successor, Clement VI, who was also responsible for buying Avignon from Queen Joan. Altogether seven popes presided over this glittering court before the papacy reverted to Rome.

THE LAST OF THE ANGEVINS While the popes at Avignon feuded with Rome, the rest of the country was suffering a succession of disasters, notably the first great plague (1348) and political instability and wars brought about by the death of Queen Joan in 1382. A semblance of normality returned under Louis II of Anjou, and on his death in 1434 sovereignty was transferred to René of Anjou, who passed into popular legend as Good King René.

❑ One of the greatest blows to Provençal cultural autonomy was the hated Edict of Villers-Cotterêts, passed by François I in 1539. This decreed that French would henceforth be the official language in schools, churches and the administration. It dealt a deathblow to the Provençal language and is still railed against today by Provençal nationalists. ❑

Pope Benedict XII (above)
Detail, Palais des Papes, Avignon (top)

UNION WITH FRANCE René's heir, his nephew Charles III, inherited the throne in 1480 but died a year later without an heir, bequeathing Provence to Louis XI of France. In 1482 the *parlement* in Aix approved the union, but the French monarch immediately set about eroding the powers of the Provençal *États-Généraux* (States General), beginning a process of assimilation that signalled the end of an independent Provence.

In the face of Provençal opposition, the French crown was forced to take a more conciliatory line because the region was still a crucial buffer zone with Italy. In 1486 a treaty was signed, designed to ensure the autonomy of Provence and its legal institutions and local customs. This was gradually weakened by successive edicts, however, and Provence surrendered its autonomy to the centralized state. Union swiftly became unification.

During the 16th century the reformist ideas of John Calvin took hold in Provence; Protestantism became a symbol of rebellion against royal control as much as it was a protest against the old Catholic order. Repression was followed by greater loss of autonomy for Provence, and the third and deadliest outbreak of the plague.

THE VAUD HERESY The Vaudois were the first sect to suffer the wrath of the established church against Protestantism. They lived quietly in the villages of the Petit Luberon until the 1540s, when the *parlement* at Aix ordered a crackdown. During five days in April 1545, blood ran through the village streets as 3,000 people were massacred and a further 600 were sent to the gallows.

This was the beginning of half a century or more of bloodshed and mayhem as the Catholic church resisted the "heretical" ideas of the Reformation.

THE SPREAD OF PROTESTANTISM Calvin's doctrines appealed to the Provençals not only as a reaction to the bloated Church hierarchy but also as an expression of opposition to the French state. Reformers sacked the cathedral in Orange, destroyed the abbey at St.-Gilles, and pillaged churches throughout Haute-Provence. The backlash brought more violence (with massacres at Barjols, Sisteron and Orange) and atrocities continued until the arrival of the plague in 1580 put a temporary stop to hostilities.

Trouble continued to ferment when the Huguenot Henri de Navarre became heir to the French crown in 1584. The traditionalist Catholic League was formed to counter Protestant influence, seizing Paris and eventually murdering Henri III. After Henri de Navarre's conversion and accession to the

Fort St.-Nicolas, symbol of Louis XIV's power over Marseille

throne (as Henri IV) he issued the Edict of Nantes, in 1598, which guaranteed freedom of worship to Protestants.

> ❏ Outside the cities and ports, Provence stagnated. In the countryside the peasantry eked out a living based on cereals, sheep, vines and the recently introduced art of raising silkworms, which provided the raw material for a nascent textile industry. ❏

LOUIS XIII AND LOUIS XIV With the assassination of Henri IV in 1610, Louis XIII came to the throne and the influence of the French state increased under the stewardship of Cardinal Richelieu, who further whittled away the powers of the regions. Richelieu overrode the *parlement* in Aix by imposing his own agents, the *intendants*, who collected taxes and had control over military and fiscal affairs. The *États-Généraux* (States General), having resisted contributing to the royal purse, were

> ❏ The Vaudois' beliefs originated with Pierre Valdo, who had founded a sect in Lyon as a reaction against the excesses of the avaricious papacy. Drawing on elements of Manichaeism (which had also been central to the Cathar heresy), they preached poverty and a rejection of the ecclesiastical hierarchy. ❏

simply banned from holding parliamentary assemblies.

Dissension continued, notably in Marseille, which rebelled in 1659: Louis XIV quickly repressed the uprising, and built the Fort St.-Nicolas so he could monitor what he called *"ce peuple violent et libertin."* In 1685 Louis XIV revoked the Edict of Nantes, and thousands of Protestants fled fearing reprisals.

Victims of the 1720 plague (above)
Members of Louis XIV's family (top)

EARLY 18TH CENTURY Despite his hostility towards Marseille, Louis XIV made it a free port, and at the beginning of the 18th century it prospered on trade with the Near East. Unfortunately this also led to the third and worst outbreak of the plague in 1720, carried by a ship from the East, during which 100,000 died in Provence—50,000 from Marseille alone, half the population of the city.

Maritime commerce also led to the creation of great wealth and the construction of some of the magnificent *hôtels particuliers* (private mansions) in Avignon, Aix and Marseille. A boom in shipbuilding (principally in Marseille, Toulon and la Ciotat) led to massive deforestation of areas such as Mont Ventoux.

The upheavals of the Revolution and its after-math were as keenly felt in Provence as they were elsewhere in France. Despite hopes to the contrary, under the First Republic ancient "Provence" disappeared as an entity in its own right as new départements *were created.*

DISCONTENT AND REVOLUTION The decadence of the Sun King's court, followed by corruption and the abuse of privileges under Louis XV and Louis XVI, led to widespread discontent throughout France, where the economic gap between rich and poor was creating hardship, unemployment and famine. Provence was no exception, particularly since the loss of the silk harvest and a steep drop in the price of wine in 1787. The following year, a heavy frost wiped out a large percentage of the olive groves in the region, and in 1789 there was widespread rioting over the price of bread. As the Bastille was being stormed in July 1789, the people of Provence followed suit and looted and pillaged châteaux

❏ In 1792 the *Féderés* (National Guard) from outlying regions were summoned to Paris to defend it from counter-revolution-aries. Five hundred Marseillaise marched to the capital singing Rouget de Lisle's *Hymn to the Army of the Rhine* (composed for the war against Germany several months earlier). This stirring song instantly became known as the *Marseillaise*, France's national anthem. ❏

and churches. Guillotines were set up in the streets of Marseille, and aristocrats were lynched in Aix.

THE AFTERMATH The enthusiastic reception for the Revolution in Provence was partly due to the Provençals' hope of regaining privileges lost during the preceding centuries. However, the Jacobin-dominated National Assembly proved to be even more centralist than the *ancien régime*. In 1790, local government was dissolved and the region was divided into three *départements:* the Bouches-du-Rhône (capital, Aix, and after 1800, Marseille); the Var (capital, Toulon); and the Basses-Alpes (capital, Digne). A year later the Vaucluse was created, and in 1793 the annexation of Nice led to the addition of the Alpes-Maritimes.

In the White Terror, unleashed in 1795 following the execution of Robespierre, thousands of people

Napoléon (left) brought defeat to the English fleet in Toulon (top) when it came to the aid of the Royalists

died in Provence, as elsewhere.

After Napoléon's surprise *coup d'état* in 1799 order was restored, but Provençals showed little enthusiasm for the Napoleonic wars that followed. With the defeat of Napoléon in his Russian campaign, Provence also lost much of the Alpes-Maritimes *département,* which was ceded to Sardinia at the Congress of Vienna in 1814.

A year later, Napoléon escaped from exile on Elba and marched up through Provence, before being conclusively defeated at Waterloo and sent farther afield, to remote St.-Helena. The restoration of the Bourbons after Waterloo led to further bloodshed between royalists and republicans in Provence, but the eventual replacement on the French throne in 1830 by the "Citizen King,"

France's national flag, originally from Martigues

Thousands died in Provence after Robespierre's execution

Louis-Philippe, created little interest in the south, which had endured its share of civil unrest and tumult.

THE 1848 REVOLUTION Continuing discontent over economic conditions led to the overthrow of Louis-Philippe and the creation of the Second Republic in 1848. This was supported in Provence, but the election of Louis-Napoléon in 1850 and his coronation as emperor was bitterly contested. Many areas, particularly in the Provençal Alps, turned once more to armed revolt. In the reprisals that followed thousands were shot or deported.

❑ As well as the national anthem, France also acquired its national flag from Provence during the Revolution. The red, white and blue tricolour adopted by the revolutionaries had previously been the flag of the small town of Martigues, west of Marseille. ❑

Improved communications and economic growth began to transform Provence as it emerged from isolation in the 19th century and the discovery of the Riviera coastline placed it firmly on the international map. Although development was brought to a halt by two world wars, the pattern had been set for the 20th century.

RURAL DEPOPULATION In the second half of the 19th century the foundations were laid for profound changes in the pattern of life in Provence. Marseille rose to become France's premier port, largely due to a booming trade with the newly acquired colonies (such as Algeria) and the Far East after the opening of the Suez Canal in 1869. Traditional industries, such as sugar refining and the manufacture of "Marseille soap," expanded alongside new activities such as shipbuilding.

Although Provence remained essentially rural in nature, increased economic activity was already starting to affect village life. Migrations to the cities began, and land was turned over, for example, to horticulture in

❑ The arrival of the railway along the coastline in the 1860s, connecting Paris with Marseille and Italy, marked the real beginning of the winter tourist season on the Côte d'Azur. ❑

the Var and orchards in the Rhône valley. Extensive vineyards were planted, although the devastating onslaught of phylloxera in the 1870s destroyed vast areas. The development of light industries signalled the end of many traditional rural activities such as silk production, tanning and dyeing.

WRITERS AND ARTISTS Provence also witnessed a linguistic and literary revival under the auspices of the Félibrige, founded by Frédéric Mistral and a group of like-minded poets and writers in 1854. Harking back to the "golden age" of the troubadours, the Félibrige mounted a spirited defence of Provençal culture in the face of constant erosion by the French state.

EARLY 20TH CENTURY This saw an acceleration of demographic changes, such as rural depopulation and the arrival of immigrants from around the Mediterranean to work in the coastal cities. The economic gap between the booming coastal region and deprived inland areas increased.

A second generation of artists (amongst them Matisse, Dufy, Bonnard, Derain and Vlaminck) arrived on the coast, exchanging grey northern skies for the dazzling Mediterranean light. The *belle époque*

W. Somerset Maugham, one of the postwar crowd

40

mansions of the Côte d'Azur marked a new era in architecture, financed by the thriving tourism industry. The effects of World War I were largely felt in the north of France but conscription drained Provençal villages of their already dwindling manpower. After the war, tourism was quickly re-established and a new wave of talent (in the form of writers and *literati* such as Gertrude Stein, Anaïs Nin, Somerset Maugham, Katherine Mansfield and others) discovered the joys of the Riviera high life. Picasso and Jean Cocteau also spent time on the coast.

WORLD WAR II During World War II, Provence was part of the "free" zone controlled by the Vichy government in the south, but once the Allied counter-offensive began in 1942, the Germans marched on Marseille and Toulon. Resistance groups were particularly active in the Vaucluse and the Provençal Alps, where reprisals and deporta-tions followed their courageous harassment of enemy forces.

Two months after the D-Day land-ings on the beaches of Normandy, the Allied forces landed on the beaches between St.-Raphaël and St.-Tropez. Within a month they had swept the Germans back and by 15 September most of Provence had been liberated.

Cézanne's house and studio, Aix

❏ In the 1890s Provence's greatest artist, Paul Cézanne, was painting the landscapes around his home town of Aix or on the coast at l'Estaque near Marseille. Van Gogh came south to capture the brilliance of the southern light on canvas—and eventually to lose his mind and be hospitalized, first in Arles and then in St.-Rémy. ❏

Provence was slow to recover from World War II. With the arrival of mass tourism on the Riviera and the establishment of heavy industries near Marseille, the economy picked up, but growth was still largely confined to the coast. Mass immigrations led to the emergence of extreme right-wing political groups.

POST-WAR YEARS World War II had taken a heavy toll on the infrastructure of Provence, most notably in cities such as Toulon, Marseille and Avignon. In the Alpes-Maritimes, where there had been heavy fighting, particularly along the Italian border, whole communities were devastated. Towns such as Breil, Sospel and Lantosque lost almost half their populations; Castillon lost all but 47 of its 300 inhabitants.

Recovery after the war was slow, and the task of rebuilding cities such as Marseille was jeopardized by a decline in international trade. Nice airport opened in 1946 (with flights to Paris, Brussels and Stockholm), but tourism did not pick up again until two years later, partly because the beaches had to be cleared of mines and the concrete blocks put there by the Germans as obstacles to the Allied landings.

❑ The delineation of the boundaries of Provence-Alpes-Côte d'Azur (PACA) in the 1950s created one of the largest regions in France, covering nearly 6 per cent of the country's total land mass. ❑

EXPANSION AND GROWTH In the 1950s work began on the *autoroute* Esterel–Côte d'Azur, and the right-wing Médecin dynasty rose to power in Nice, heralding the end of socialist politics in the south. When Algeria regained its independence in 1962, hundreds of thousands of colonists returned to France. Derisorily known as the *pieds noirs*, they brought with them racist attitudes that were fuelled by the French government's

policy of encouraging immigration from North Africa.

The 1960s saw massive expansion of the petro-chemical industries around the Étang de Berre and Fos-sur-Mer, west of Marseille. Oil refineries sprang up thanks to the South European oil pipeline and huge tanker terminals were built. Coincidentally, the first marina opened in Cannes in 1964.

In inland Provence massive irrigation schemes such as the Canal de Provence and the development of hydroelectric power helped to slow the decline in the agricultural and industrial economy, although rural depopulation continued to accelerate. This trend was reversed to some extent by an influx of bohemian newcomers who rebuilt old village houses in their quest for the rural idyll.

The first purpose-built ski resort, Isola 2000, opened in the 1970s in the Alpes-Maritime. Tourism on the coast, meanwhile, went into overdrive, and the seaside became overrun with concrete. Tower blocks, such as the controversial Marina Baie-des-Anges, were built along the coast and rapidly became a byword for insensitive development on the Riviera.

The regional administration of Provence-Alpes-Côte d'Azur (PACA,

❑ The population of Provence escalated dramatically in the post-war years: from 1.5 million inhabitants in 1870 it grew to 2 million by 1950, to 3 million by 1960 and nearly 4 million by 1982. Today it stands at approximately 4.5 million. ❑

42

which includes the Hautes-Alpes), originally established in 1956, was put on a new footing in the 1970s with the creation of the *Conseil Régional* (Regional Council), which held its first assembly in 1974. In 1982, power was decentralized to the *Conseil Général* (General Council) of each *département*, with responsibilities covering education, transportation, economic development, the environment and social and cultural affairs.

In the 1980s Jean-Marie Le Pen's fascist *Front National* party started to gain a foothold in the south, swept along by a tide of anti-immigrant sentiments and economic recession. Its particular stronghold has been

The autoroute at Marseille (top)
A townscape (Bollène) that reflects the changes of recent years (above)

around Marseille, which is home to a large and highly visible North African immigrant population. During the 1990s, the *Front National* consolidated its hold in the region, but since then internal feuding has split the party and slightly weakened its grip. Today Provence's fortunes are on the rise, with increasing numbers of visitors and investors attracted by its location. With nearly 10 million passengers in 2006, Nice's Cote d'Azur International Airport has overtaken Marseille and Lyon as France's third-busiest airport.

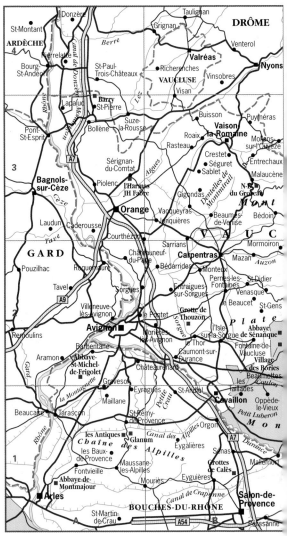

44

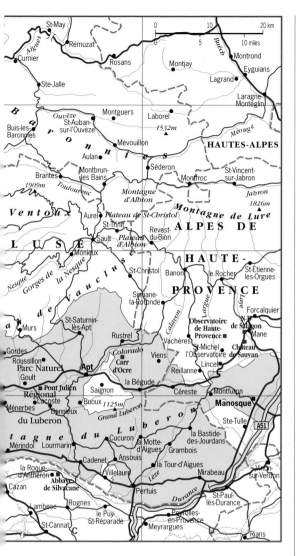

A view over Bonnieux and the Luberon region (left, below)

VAUCLUSE Despite being one of the smallest *départements* in France, Vaucluse can boast attractions that range from grand Roman monuments to sleepy wine villages, from the red ochre cliffs of Roussillon and Rustrel to mighty Mont Ventoux.

MONT VENTOUX AND THE NORTH Rising like a sentinel at the northern gateway to the Vaucluse, Mont Ventoux is the highest peak between the Alps and the Pyrenees. The ascent to the top is one of the most awesome in Provence and the views can take the breath away, sometimes almost literally, since the winds come from all directions of the compass. The *mistral*, howling down from the north, has reached record levels of 230kph (143mph) at the summit. Legend has it that this is the origin of the mountain's name (from *ventour*, the Provençal for windy)

Lavender, sage, rosemary and thyme, some of the constituents of herbes de Provence, *are on sale in a variety of packages and containers throughout the Vaucluse*

46

VAUCLUSE TRUFFLES
"Proust conjures up Combray, its panorama and its good people from a teacake dipped in a cup of herb tea," says the famous chef Curnonsky. "An exiled citizen of Carpentras could call into being his native town, with its monuments and all the resources of its country-side, as in a dream, from a truffle stew." The Vaucluse is the country's top truffle region, account-ing for 74 per cent of all truffle sales in France. This highly prized fungus (known in Provence as *rabasse*) grows around the root of the downy oak, a small tree that is planted in rows in fields called *truffières*. They are harvested from November to March and sold in the markets (usually on a Saturday morning) in Carpentras, Valréas and, to the west, Richerenches and Grillon.

but it may also be that the barren limestone summit, often covered in snow, gave rise to *ven top*, meaning "white mountain" in Celtic.

To the west of Mont Ventoux lies the jagged curtain of peaks known as the Dentelles de Montmirail, with enchanting wine villages such as Gigondas, Rasteau and Beaumes-de-Venise nestling under the flanks of the Dentelles. On the other side of the Dentelles, the town of Vaison-la-Romaine straddles the Ouvèze River. On the right bank of the Ouvèze are the remains of a pros-perous Roman settlement, partly built over by the 18th-century town, which is now the heart of Vaison. On the left bank of the river, the medieval village encircles a dramatic ruined castle, which further enhances the appeal of this popular spot.

Roman ruins are much in evidence in the historic town of Orange, sprawling beneath the St.-Eutrope hill, whose northern slopes accommodate the multiple tiers of an ancient theatre. Its magnificent backstage wall, one of the best preserved in Europe, provides a dramatic setting for summer choral performances. Orange, too, has its *arc de triomphe*, another imposing legacy from the time when the town was an important staging post on the Roman high-way up through the Rhône valley to northern Gaul.

From Orange it is a short hop to Châteauneuf-du-Pape, rising amid a sea of vineyards, which produce the full-bodied Rhône wines that have earned this small village an international reputation.

AVIGNON AND THE PLATEAU DE VAUCLUSE Heading south again, Avignon presents an unpromising facade, girded by industrial suburbs, unless you arrive by river steamer (as did Dickens and Robert Browning) and witness the ramparts, with the Palais des Papes rising behind them like a medieval tableau. Within the ramparts is a different city, a feisty, lively place infused with cultural riches during the summer season and always full of fascination. Even if some are disappointed by the famous bridge, no one can fail to be awed by the Palais des Papes, part-church, part-fortress, and undoubtedly one of the most extensive feudal castles in the world.

Across the river Villeneuve-lès-Avignon has consider-able charm, as does the attractive town of l'Isle-sur-la-Sorgue farther to the east of Avignon. The river which runs through it rises at Fontaine-de-Vaucluse on the edge of the Vaucluse plateau. The funnel-shaped cavern, out of which the spring rises, lies at the foot of towering cliffs over 200m (650ft) high, with the river running down a beautiful valley through the village and on down to the Rhône. The site was originally known as *Vallis Clausa* ("the closed valley"), which later became Vaucluse and eventually gave its name to the entire *département*.

This enchanted valley cast a spell on the great humanist poet Petrarch, but to experience it as he did you would be wise to avoid the peak summer months, especially as the source itself is at its most dramatic out of the main tourist season, during the winter and spring.

Fluorescent traces added to rivers far away have shown that the source has a huge catchment area, cover-ing over 120sq km (46sq miles) from Mont Ventoux to the eastern extremes of the Vaucluse plateau.

On the southern escarpment of the plateau, to the east of the *fontaine*, the village of Gordes is perched some 300m (985ft) above the Coulon valley in a spectacular setting that also attracts considerable crowds. Hidden away behind the village in a lavender-scented valley is the 12th-century Abbaye de Sénanque, whose pure silhouette, stripped down to the essentials, echoes the spirituality of the Cistercian monks who built it.

Another way of life, another bewitching testament to the past, is reflected in the remarkable Village des Bories behind Gordes. In Provence there are at least 5,000 to 6,000 *bories* (drystone huts), the majority of which can be found in the Vaucluse.

THE LUBERON And so to the Luberon, where the renovation of old houses has turned this corner of Provence into one of the most fashionable addresses for foreigners and Parisians. No matter, since there are many wild and unspoiled corners, secret valleys and lovely villages still to be explored. Most of the region is part of the Parc Naturel Régional du Luberon.

On the southern flanks of the Luberon the vegetation becomes more Mediterranean in character, hinting at the coastal hinterlands that start below the Durance, the natural boundary that marks the southernmost extent of the Vaucluse.

Some of the drystone huts in the extraordinary Village des Bories near Gordes. The reason for their construction is still debated

47

The Sabran family home, commanding the hilltop above Ansouis village

▶▶ **Ansouis**   *45C1*

Ansouis is built on a rocky spur dominated by the keep of its **Château**▶▶ (*Open* Easter–Oct daily 2.30–6; Nov–Easter Sun only. Closed Jan. *Admission: moderate*), home of the Sabran family for the last 800 years. From the north the château displays an impregnable exterior—part of the original fortress—but, as you circle it, it changes to reveal an 18th-century mansion facade with gardens and terraces shaded by chestnut trees. The interior of the château is furnished in a way that reflects this dual identity: The ground floor displays a collection of arms and armour, while upstairs Flemish tapestries and Italian Renaissance furniture predominate. From the upstairs balcony you get a good overview of the elegant garden (closed to visitors). The 18th-century Provençal kitchen (still in use today) features several very fine hand-crafted pieces.

Adjoining the château, the church of St. Martin contains busts of St. Delphine and St. Elzéar (see panel).

Down at the end of the village, veteran diver Georges Mazoyer has assembled his **Musée Extraordinaire**▶ (*Open* afternoons. *Admission: moderate*) featuring minerals, fossils, shells and paintings of underwater life, and a little "Blue Grotto" built into the vaults.

▶ **Apt**   *45C2*

A busy market town proclaiming itself not only capital of the Luberon but also world capital of crystallized fruits, Apt has been a prosperous urban centre since Roman times.

Its principal monument is the old **Cathédrale Ste.-Anne**▶ (*Open* Tue–Sat), famous for its ancient crypt, on two levels, which is said to house the bones of Ste. Anne. The saint is depicted in a fine set of 14th-century stained-glass windows at the end of the apse; her shroud is displayed among the reliquaries in the *trésor*.

Next door is the 16th-century **Tour de l'Horloge**, which straddles the rue des Marchands. On Saturday mornings this old shopping street and all the neighbouring thoroughfares overflow with the stalls of Apt's lively **market**. Other sights include the **Musée d'Histoire et d'Archéologie** (*Open* Jun–Sep Mon–Sat 10–12, 3–6.30, Sun 3–7; Oct–May Mon–Sat 10–12, 2–5.30. *Admission: inexpensive*) and the **Maison du Parc du Luberon**▶ (*Open* Apr–Sep Mon–Sat; Oct–Mar Mon–Fri and Sat morning), which houses an information centre for the Parc Naturel Régional (see page 49).

Created in 1977, the Parc Naturel Régional du Luberon covers around 140,000ha (345,940 acres) in the Vaucluse and the Alpes de Haute-Provence, the greater part of it in the Vaucluse.

The natural setting Between Manosque and Cavaillon, the Durance River, flowing westwards towards the Rhône, takes a mighty loop within which the Luberon range lies. Stretching 65km (40 miles) from east to west, the mountains are divided in two by a wooded valley, the *combe de Lourmarin*. To the west is the Petit Luberon, while to the east the Grand Luberon reaches its summit of over 1,000m (3,280ft) at the Mourre Nègre.

One of the most striking features of the Luberon *massif* is the contrast: To the south, the rich agricultural land sloping gently down to the Durance is characteristically Mediterranean; to the north the steep ravines and abrupt cliff faces are cooler and forested with Downy oaks.

Wildlife The variety of natural features in the Luberon has created a species-rich environment where plants such as the fragrant Etruscan honeysuckle, aspic lavender and downy rockroses thrive. Predators that have all but disappeared in the rest of Europe, such as Bonelli's eagle, the white Egyptian vulture, the eagle owl and the migratory eagle Circàete Jean Le Blanc, manage to retain a precarious foothold here.

The human impact The most startling evidence of early habitation are the curious *bories*, or drystone huts, which can be seen dotted about the countryside. Although some were built as recently as the 18th century, many date back to the Iron Age.

The Middle Ages left the Luberon with numerous *villages perchés* (perched villages), strategically positioned high above the valley floors. Surrounded by an intricate network of cultivated land, many of these villages (particularly those on the northern slopes) went into a decline with the changing agricultural patterns of the 19th century.

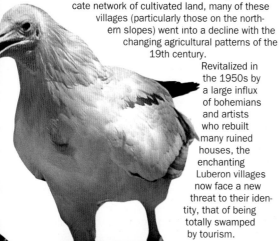

Revitalized in the 1950s by a large influx of bohemians and artists who rebuilt many ruined houses, the enchanting Luberon villages now face a new threat to their identity, that of being totally swamped by tourism.

ON THE MULE TRAIN Walking tours off the beaten track, through some of the most evocative scenery in the Parc Naturel Régional du Luberon, are organized in conjunction with the *Maison du Parc* as part of their *Voyages au Naturel* trips. Your luggage is transported by mule on these seven-day tours, which take place from May through to September. Contact Les Muletiers, tel: 04 76 95 02 21; www.les-muletiers.com; e-mail: lesmuletiers@yahoo.fr

49

LIVING PROJECTS As well as conducting scientific studies on the natural environment and publishing information for visitors, the *Maison du Parc* (which administers the park from Apt) carries out restoration projects in rural areas and has created nature trails and other attractions (tel: 04 90 04 42 00). In particular, you can visit the Sentier du Conservatoire des Terrasses en Culture (Open Air Terrace Museum) at Goult (see page 75), the botanic trail through the Forêt des Cèdres (near Bonnieux), and the Sentier des Ocres (Ochre Trail) at Roussillon (see page 83).

Rockroses (top) Unmistakable but rarely seen, the white Egyptian vulture (left)

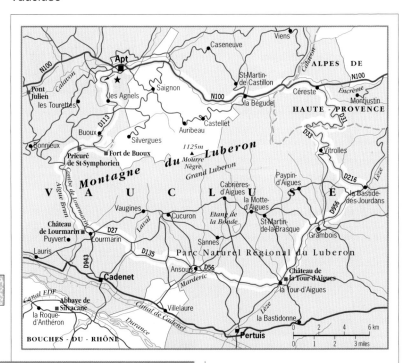

Drive

Grand Luberon

This 80km (50 mile) drive encompasses one of the most beautiful valleys in the Luberon as well as the principal châteaux of the Sud-Luberon, before traversing the *massif* to return to Apt. Allow a whole day if you plan to make stops.

From Apt, take the D113 to the tiny hamlet of Buoux, which is surrounded by fields of lavender. Continue on into the wild and beautiful **Vallon de l'Aigue Brun**▶▶. The **Fort de Buoux**▶▶, reached via a steep footpath, commands a magnificent view of the Vallon de l'Aigue Brun, hence its strategic importance, since this was once the main pass across the Luberon. First occupied by the Ligurians, then the Romans, the site was fortified in the 13th century.

Back on the D113, the elegant bell tower of the 12th-century **Prieuré de St.-Symphorien** (not open to visitors) rises above the tree-tops on your left.

Follow the D943 through the *combe de Lourmarin* until you come to **Lourmarin**▶ itself at the mouth of the valley. This lively town was once the home of Albert Camus, who moved here after winning the Nobel Prize for Literature in 1957 and is buried in the cemetery. On the edge of the town is the imposing **Château**▶▶ (*Open* Feb–Dec, daily; Jan, Sat–Sun afternoons only. *Admission: moderate*). The older part of the château was built between 1495 and 1525, while the "new" part was begun in 1540.

Abandoned in the 19th century, the château was salvaged in the 1920s by a wealthy Lyonnais industrialist, Robert Laurent-Vibert, who hired a team of 40 artisans for the four years which it took to complete the restoration. At his untimely death in 1925 the château was bequeathed to the Academy of Arts, Agriculture, Science and Belles Lettres at Aix, and a foundation set up to encourage talented youngsters. The older part now houses both an arts library and accommodation. The Renaissance wing contains a collection of old Provençal and Spanish furniture as well as souvenirs from Laurent-Vibert's travels in Egypt, Indonesia, Morocco and Russia.

Leaving Lourmarin behind, take the D27 and then the D135 to Ansouis (see page 48), passing through the Côtes du Luberon vineyards flanking the foothills of the Luberon *massif*. From Ansouis, take the D56 and then follow signs to **la Tour-d'Aigues**.

In the middle of this large market town is one of the most astonishing Renaissance ruins in Provence: the remains of the **Château de la Tour-d'Aigues**▶▶, built in the latter half of the 16th century. Early engravings show it to have been an ambitious palace. In 1780 it was damaged by fire, and then finally torched during the Revolution in 1792. Now, the

The southern slopes of the Luberon massif, overlooking the Durance valley

ruins accentuate the dimensions and make a spectacular backdrop for the dance, theatre and musical performances held here as part of the Festival du Sud-Luberon in summer. The cellars of the château contain exhibitions (*Open* Jul to mid-Aug, daily 10–1, 2.30–6.30; Apr–Jun, mid-Aug–Oct closed Sun, Mon, Tue mornings; Nov–Mar 10–12, 2–5, except Sun, Mon, Tue mornings. *Admission: moderate*) including the **Musée de la Faïences du Pays d'Aigues**.

From la Tour-d'Aigues follow the D956 towards la Bastide-des-Jourdans and turn left on the D216 for the sleepy hamlet of Vitrolles. The road then becomes the D33 as it winds up over a pass in the Grand Luberon and then down to the old Roman village of Céreste. In contrast to the valley of the Aigue Brun, the mountain here is cloaked in *garrigue* scrub and oak forests. Return along the N100 to Apt.

51

THE AVIGNON FESTIVAL
Founded as a drama festival in 1947 by Jean Villar, the festival brief was widened in 1967 to include cinema, music, and dance, and at the same time fringe events (*le festival off*) became increasingly popular. Today, around 120,000 people descend on Avignon for this sell-out arts extravaganza, which starts in July and continues for one month. For details contact the Bureau du Festival d'Avignon, Cloître St.-Louis, 20 rue du Portail Boquier, 84000 Avignon (tel: 04 90 27 66 50; www.festival-avignon.com).

▶▶▶ **Avignon** 44A2

Avignon has always evoked rather extreme reactions from visitors. On the one hand it is a major centre for art and culture, a lively, innovative city, which over the centuries served as a channel for the influence of the Italian Renaissance on the rest of France, nurtured the Provençal literary group the Félibrige (see pages 60–61), and gave birth to one of the country's most celebrated cultural events, the annual Festival of Dramatic Arts. It is an inevitable "must see" on every tourist itinerary.

On the other hand, Avignon has not always been a likeable city, provoking detestation from many a traveller since medieval times. Petrarch called it a living hell, "the sewers of the earth"; Henry James loathed it at first sight, and Lawrence Durrell railed against it in his novel *Monsieur*. In the summer months the place is full of outsiders who flock here to mine the gold dust of tourism with no care for the city and its rich heritage.

And yet, unlovable though it can be, Avignon has a magnetism that was recognized long ago in the Provençal proverb, *"Quau se lèvo d'Avignoun, se lèvo de la resoun"* ("He who takes leave of Avignon takes leave of his senses").

The Rocher des Doms, overlooking the confluence of the rivers Rhône and Durance, was occupied in neolithic times but, despite flourishing as a river port, the settlement was eclipsed by Arles and Nîmes in the Roman period and sank into relative obscurity. By the 12th century it had grown into a large town and, surrounded as it was by feuding baronies, Avignon declared itself a sovereign state and ruled its own affairs. The first ramparts were erected and trade prospered largely thanks to the rebuilding of the bridge over the Rhône, which was then the only route between Italy and Spain upriver from the sea.

Avignon made a strategic mistake in allying itself with the Albigensians (followers of the heretical Cathar sect) in the 13th century, as a consequence of which Louis VIII razed the city in 1226 and destroyed its defences. However, it was also as a result of the Albigensian Crusade that the papacy acquired a large slice of Provençal territory that became known as the Comtat Venaissin. The French pope Clement V, under pressure

Standing forlornly on the last remaining arches of Avignon's famous bridge, the Chapelle St.-Nicolas is part Romanesque, part Gothic

Trompe-l'oeil paintings on the east side of the place de l'Horloge depict scenes from the city's past

53

from his king, agreed to reside in Avignon, where the papal court moved in 1309.

Avignon in this period was a thriving city of between 30,000 and 40,000 people, a large proportion of whom were clergy and religious orders occupying the numerous convents, churches and chapels. The university, founded in 1303, housed thousands of students, and the best Sienese artists were summoned to embellish the pontifical palaces. Avignon became a refuge for exiles, including a sizeable Jewish community, but its open doors also attracted criminal outcasts and adventurers, and the city's name became a byword for filth, debauchery, overcrowding and vice. The Italian hierarchy, envious at the loss of the papal court, declared it the "second Babylonian Captivity."

In 1377 St. Catherine of Siena persuaded the seventh Avignon pope, Gregory XI, to return to Rome, where he soon died. With Francophobia rife, the cardinals (most of them French) elected an Italian pope. But within months the same cardinals, back in Avignon elected another pope, Clement VII, thus setting off the Great Schism, which saw pope and anti-pope struggle for universal acknowledgment for the next 40 years.

After this issue was finally resolved with the election of Martin V in 1417, Avignon remained papal property and was ruled by the cardinal legates until 1791, when the Comtat Venaissin became part of France during the Revolution.

Before the Revolution, Avignon had been an important publishing centre, thanks to freedom from French censorship laws, and the printing presses continued to roll through the 1800s, helping to foster the growth of the nascent Félibrige movement. Its cultural influence was firmly re-established in recent times with the creation in 1947 of the annual Avignon Festival (see panel opposite).

The many steeples defining Avignon's skyline led Rabelais to call it la ville sonnante (the ringing city)

Walk

Avignon

Around the periphery of the town centre there are numerous interesting back streets with fine old mansions, churches and other sights. Allow 2–3 hours for this circular walk from place de l'Horloge.

From place de l'Horloge, head west towards rue St.-Étienne. At the beginning of this street are some of the few Roman relics from early Avignon, stone blocks dug up from what was the place du Forum (now place de l'Horloge) and part of a Roman arcade. At No. 18, the ironwork balconies of the house are discreetly embellished with balloons to mark the place where Joseph de Montgolfier invented the hot-air balloon.

Follow the street down to place Crillon, where the lovely facade of the old **Théâtre Comédie**▶▶ (built in 1734, restored in 1979) faces the Porte de l'Oulle. Take a small passageway (rue Mazan, beside the theatre) to reach rue Joseph Vernet. Along the street there are several impressive 18th-century facades, as well as the **Chapelle de l'Oratoire** (now an exhibition centre), the **Musée Calvet** (see page 58) and the **Musée Requien** (see page 59).

Cross over the cours Jean-Jaurès into rue Henri Fabre. Continue down the rue des Lices, where, on your left, is the immense, unusual **Almône Générale**▶ (General Almshouse), built between 1546 and 1557. Only the central portion remains, a three-storey arcade with a fine sundial (1789) on the top floor. The imposing building is now part of the neighbouring École des Beaux Arts.

Turn right onto the **rue des Teinturiers**▶▶, one of Avignon's oldest and most picturesque streets. Immediately on your right are the remains of the Chapelle des Cordeliers. Just past here is the **Chapelle des Pénitents Gris**▶. Towards the end of the street there are several derelict waterwheels, which were used to power the textile

Carved door panel, Église St.-Pierre

factories after which the street is named. Retrace your steps and turn left onto rue de la Masse, then onto rue du Roi René. On the left is the **Chapelle Ste.-Claire**, supposedly the location of the first meeting between Petrarch and Laura (see panel on page 58). Towards the end of rue du Roi René there is a cluster of lovely old mansions, including the **Hôtel d'Honorati de Jonquerettes** (No. 12), the **Hôtel Fortia de Montreal** (Nos. 8 and 10) and the elegant Italianate **Hôtel Berton de Crillon** (No. 7).

Backtrack briefly and turn down rue Collège de la Croix; cross two pedestrianized shopping streets through the arches of rue Bernheim-Lyon, to arrive at place Jerusalem. This was the heart of the old Jewish ghetto, once encircled by walls, although now only the synagogue remains. A little farther on from place Jerusalem is place Carnot, which links directly onto place St.-Pierre, dominated by the Gothic facade of the **Église St.-Pierre►**; the magnificent carved walnut doors date from 1551.

Head up rue Banastèrie until you reach the **Chapelle des Pénitents Noir►►**. Nestling incongruously alongside the walls of Avignon's present-day prison, the delightful baroque facade is ornamented with a relief showing cherubs holding the head of John the Baptist, encircled by rays of sunshine piercing through the clouds.

Take rue Migrenier and then a series of steps which lead up to the **Rocher des Doms►►**, one of the most peaceful parks in the city, scattered about with fountains and statues, and with a sundial that tells the time by your shadow. From the belvedere, there are views across the Rhône to Villeneuve-lès-Avignon.

Steps lead back down the other side of the park past the Palais des Papes to place de l'Horloge.

If you have still got the energy to visit one more sight, just south of the place, on rue Collège du Roure, the 15th-century **Palais du Roure** (guided tours Tue 3pm or by appointment, tel: 04 90 80 80 88) has a lovely courtyard and collections of Provençal arts, crafts, costumes and literature, plus Frédéric Mistral's coach.

Fountain, Rocher des Doms

55

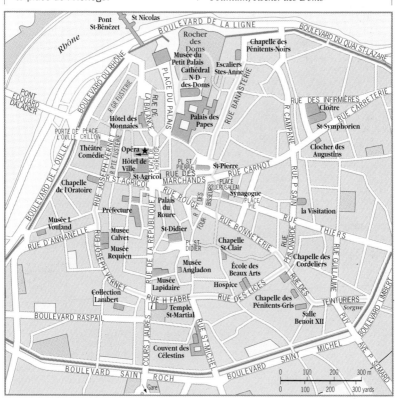

THE SHEPHERD BOY'S BRIDGE

In 1177 a shepherd boy called Bénézet was told by a voice from the sky to leave his sheep and go and build a bridge over the Rhône. Initially hesitant, Bénézet set off for Avignon with an angel disguised as a pilgrim. The bishop laughed at him, and sent him to the provost who, equally derisory, told him that if he could lift a huge stone he could build the bridge. This Bénézet did, hefting it down to the river bank. The awestruck crowd started donating money for the bridge. It was completed in 1185.

WHAT TO SEE The central core of Avignon lies within its 14th-century walls, although this represents just a small part of the city, which sprawls some distance eastwards towards the *autoroute de soleil*. The walls are over 4km (2.5 mile) long but unfortunately only one small section of the rampart (adjacent to the Porte du Rhône) is accessible.

Projecting from the city wall by the Porte du Rhône is one of Avignon's most photographed landmarks, the **Pont St.-Bénézet**▶▶ (*Open* daily. *Admission: inexpensive*; or joint ticket with the Palais des Papes). On the second pier, the Chapelle St.-Nicolas is part Romanesque, part Gothic. Since it was first built, the bridge has been swept away several times by the Rhône; in the 17th century the people of Avignon finally abandoned it to fate.

At the heart of the city is the **place de l'Horloge**▶, a huge square shaded by plane trees and overrun with cafés. Towards late afternoon it comes alive with a pageant of buskers, jugglers and portrait painters. An antique carousel spins round in front of the **Hôtel de Ville** (the clock tower gave the square its name). To the south is the **Église St.-Agricol**▶ (not open for visits), the oldest church in Avignon after the cathedral.

North of place de l'Horloge is the **place du Palais**▶, once a densely populated area, which was cleared on the orders of Benedict XII, who feared that his enemies would be able to sneak up to the palace walls through the houses.

Looming above the square is the gigantic **Palais des Papes**▶▶▶ (tel: 04 90 27 50 00. *Open* daily, Jul–Sep, 9–8; mid-Mar to Jun, Oct, 9–7; Nov to mid-Mar, 9.30–5.45; late Mar, 9.30–6.30. *Admission: expensive*. Guided tours in English available). Inside this veritable fortress there is a maze of rooms, galleries, passageways and chapels; as it was pillaged of all its furnishings during the Revolution, you need a great deal of imagination to envisage the decadent, luxurious lifestyle that once existed inside. In 1810 it was converted into a barracks and the soldiers hacked off many of the murals to sell to collectors. Turned over to the Historic Monuments Board in 1906, it has been under continuous restoration ever since.

Passing through the reception area in the old guardroom, you emerge into the Cours d'Honneur. On the left

Decorative panelling brightens up the antique carousel in place de l'Horloge

is Benedict XII's austere, military-style Vieux Palais and, on the right, Clement VI's Gothic-style Palais Neuf.

The usual route through the building goes first to the Consistoire in the Vieux Palais, where ambassadors and dignitaries were received. The original frescoes were destroyed by a fire in 1413 and replaced with fragments of Simone Martini's frescoes (dated c. 1340) from the cathedral porch. Leading off this room is the Chapelle St.-Jean, with frescoes by Matteo Giovanetti. On the floor above is the Grand Tinel, or banqueting hall, a huge, 45m (148ft) long room with beautifully restored panelling in the shape of an inverted ship's keel on the ceiling.

Past here is the papal Antechamber, hung with Gobelin tapestries, and then the papal Bedchamber, decorated with murals. Next is one of the loveliest rooms in the palace, the Chambre du Cerf, which was the pope's private study. The frescoes depict scenes of hunting and fishing against a forest background: most likely painted by Giovanetti, the frescoes were commissioned by Clement VI. Lastly, the route leads through to the Grande Chapelle (or Chapelle Clementine), bigger even than the banqueting hall.

At the top end of the place du Palais is the **Musée du Petit Palais**▶▶▶ (tel: 04 90 86 44 58. *Open* Jun–Sep, Wed–Mon 10–1, 2–6; Oct–May, Wed–Mon 9.30–1, 2–5.30. *Admission: moderate*). Once a cardinal's residence, it was converted in 1958 to house two important collections—medieval works formerly in the Calvet Museum and those from the Campana collection in the Louvre. The former consist of 600 sculptures and around 60 paintings, including important works by the 15th-century Avignon school, particularly the Requien Altarpiece by Enguerrand Quarton. More valuable, however, are the 13th- to 16th-century Italian paintings from the Campana collection.

Busy outdoor cafés overflow into the place de l'Horloge

BENEATH THE BRIDGE
Only four of the 22 original arches remain of the bridge that is immortalized in a popular song as the Pont d'Avignon. The bridge once spanned two branches of the Rhône (and the Île de la Barthelasse between them) to connect with Villeneuve-lès-Avignon. Although the song, as it has been remembered through the ages, celebrates dancing *"sur le pont,"* in reality it was *"sous"* (beneath) the bridge on the island, where there were once dance halls.

Dragons and eagles on the facade of the Hôtel des Monnaies come from the coat of arms of Cardinal Borghèse, who built it in 1619

THE MYTH OF LAURA
Petrarch was born in Arezzo but his family was exiled in 1302 and eventually came to Avignon in 1314. It was outside the Chapelle Ste.-Claire in 1327 that he first caught sight of Laura, who was to become his muse for the next 15 years: he continued to pour his heart out long after she died in 1348. Laura was Laure de Noves, who was already married to Hugo de Sade at the time Petrarch met her.

Next to the palace is the **Cathédrale Notre-Dame-des-Doms▶**, built between 1140 and 1160 but added to many times since. Worth noting inside is the Romanesque dome and the tomb of John XXII, attributed to the English sculptor Hugh Wilfred. Opposite the Palais des Papes is the **Hôtel des Monnaies▶** (the old mint, now the music conservatory), with its flamboyant 17th-century facade.

Avignon has a number of smaller museums, displaying some engrossing exhibits. Housed in one of the grandest mansions of the city at 65 rue Joseph Vernet is the **Musée Calvet▶▶** (*Open* Wed–Mon 10–1, 2–6. *Admission: moderate*), its beautifully displayed collections encompassing Dutch, French, Italian and Flemish paintings, sculpture, porcelain and furniture from the 16th to the 20th centuries. The Calvet's Greek, Roman, Etruscan and Egyptian antiquities are displayed in the **Musée Lapidaire▶▶** (*Open* Wed–Mon. *Admission: inexpensive*), which is housed in a converted 17th-century Jesuit chapel on rue de la République.

The delightful **Musée Angladon▶▶** (*Open* Wed–Sun 1–6. *Admission: moderate*), at 5 rue Laboureur (behind the Musée Lapidaire), houses the 19th-century collections of Parisian couturier and patron of the arts, Jacques Doucet (1853–1929). Works by Degas, Cézanne, Picasso, Modigliani and Van Gogh are among the highlights, and there are fascinating photographs of Doucet's chic 1920s house in the Paris suburb of Neuilly, plus 16th- to 18th-century treasures amassed by his heirs, the Avignat artists Jean and Paulette Angladon-Dubrujeard.

Avignon is also indebted to art dealer Yvon Lambert for the **Collection Lambert**, 5 rue Violette (*Open* Jul–Aug daily 11–7; Sep–Jun Tue–Sun 11–6. *Admission: moderate*). Works spanning the 1960s to the present day are exhibited in the handsome 19th-century Hôtel de Caumont.

Superb examples of Provençal faience and 18th-century furniture are displayed in the **Musée Louis Vouland▶** (*Open* May–Oct Tue–Sat 10–12, 2–6 and Sun afternoons; Nov–Apr Tue–Sun 2–6. *Admission: inexpensive*). Finally, there is the **Musée Requien** (*Open* Tue–Sat. *Admission free*), with its small natural history collection.

NEARBY Just over the river from Avignon is the town of **Villeneuve-lès-Avignon▶▶**. In the 14th century the cardinals at the papal court built houses here to escape the noise and bustle of Avignon; it still maintains a peaceful, village-like atmosphere and has several interesting and worthwhile places to visit. Foremost among these is the **Chartreuse du Val de Bénédiction▶▶▶** (*Open* Apr–Sep, daily 9–6.30; Oct–Mar, daily 9.30–5.30. *Admission: moderate;* or joint ticket also covering all the sites below), which was the largest and most important Carthusian monastery in France until the Revolution, when art treasures were sold off and the outlying properties taken over by homeless families. Since the beginning of the 20th century the buildings have been gradually repurchased and restored. Of its former treasures, all that remain are the 14th-century frescoes by Matteo Giovanetti in the refectory chapel. Also worth noting is the ornate tomb of Innocent VI in the church.

On the hill above the Chartreuse is the **Fort St.-André▶**, a massive citadel flanked by watch towers (*Open* daily. *Admission: moderate*). Inside the twin-turreted gateway there is a series of vaulted barrack rooms, including one with a bread oven.

On the right of the gateway are the ruins of the **Abbaye St.-André**, destroyed during the Revolution and set in lovely gardens. Apart from the small Romanesque chapel of **Notre-Dame-de-Belvezet**, the rest of the fort's interior is a jumble of ruined houses, but from several vantage points there are fine views of Avignon, Mont Ventoux and the Rhône Valley.

A similar panorama unfolds from the top of the 39m (128ft) **Tour Philippe le Bel▶** (*Open* Tue–Sun. *Admission: inexpensive*), also built to keep watch on Avignon and to protect the French end of the Pont-St.-Bénézet.

In the town centre, the **Église Collégiale Notre-Dame▶** (*Open* Apr–Sep 10–12.30, 2–6.30; Oct–Mar 10–12, 2–5. *Admission: moderate*) has a well-conserved cloister (used as a summer festival venue) and once housed a 14th-century *Madonna and Child* carved out of ivory. This rare work is now in the nearby **Musée Pierre-de-Luxembourg▶▶** (*Open* as Église-Collégiale above).

An ancient vase provides a focal point in the lovely gardens of the abbey of St.-André

THE COWBOY BARON
The eccentric Marquis Folco Baroncelli-Javon left his native city of Avignon in 1890 to lead the life of a *gardian* in the Camargue (see page 119). In 1905 he went to Paris to see Buffalo Bill Cody's Wild West Show, and invited Cody and his Native American companions down to the Camargue. The visitors pitched their camp around Baroncelli's home and a lassoing competition took place between Buffalo Bill's cowboys and the *gardians*. Some of the Native American gifts given to Baroncelli can be seen in the Musée Baroncelli in les Saintes-Maries-de-la-Mer (see page 141).

Cypresses and pines protect the elegant rose parterre in the St.-André gardens

You can't go far in Provence without coming across the name of Frédéric Mistral, the region's most famous poet. Plaques inscribed with his verses are found everywhere from remote beauty spots to bustling town centres, and many a street or park is named in his honour. But Mistral was more than just a poet; he helped spark off what was to become a major revival of Provençal language and literature in the 19th century.

The patrician figure of Frédéric Mistral at the age of 76, pictured with his family

CLOSE TO HOME
"Frédéric Mistral neither sought nor wished for metropolitan success, and was content to spend his long life quietly and happily in Provence, in the very village community in which he had been born. Occasionally he would visit Paris but Mistral was not happy away from Provence, and there he lived out his dedicated life...there are few lives of great writers, perhaps few recorded lives of human beings, as fortunate and enviable as that of Frédéric Mistral, voluntarily circumscribed within the limits of the halcyon landscape into which he had the superlative good fortune to be born."
James Pope-Hennessy, *Aspects of Provence*

Early talent Frédéric Mistral was born on 8 September 1830 in the Mas de la Juge, his parents' farm just outside the village of Maillane near St.-Rémy-de-Provence. He went to school at the abbey of St.-Michel-de-Frigolet and then in Avignon, where his interest in his native language (his mother was a Provençal-speaker) was awakened by Joseph Roumanille.

After finishing law studies in Aix, Mistral moved back to Maillane to help his father with the farm and devote himself to poetry. At the age of 21 he had already embarked on what was to become his most famous work, the epic poem *Miréio*.

The founding of the Félibrige Soon afterwards Mistral joined together with a group of like-minded poets to form the Félibrige, an association dedicated to the rebirth of Provençal (the name itself comes from *félibre*, meaning doctor, although why they chose this name remains a mystery). The seven (Roumanille, Mistral, Brunet, Giera, Aubanel, Mathieu and Tavan) had their first meeting in the Château Fort-Segugne on 21 May 1854. A year later Roumanille and Mistral launched the

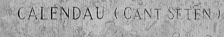

CALÉNDAU (CANT SETEN)

AQUELO NESCO S'ENCAFOURNO
DINS UNE COUMBO AREBRO E SOURNO
E VEN PIEI UN MOUMEN QUE LA ROCO SUBRA
S'ENARCO AMOUNT QU'ES PAS DE DIRE
VOUS PARLE DOU ROUCAS DOU CIRE:
NI CAT NI CABRO NI SATIRE
N'EN RESPONDE SEGUR JAMAI L'ESCALARAN

F. MISTRAL

CENTENARI DE CALENDAU
1866   1966
LOU S I LOU MUNICIPE DE SAUT
E LI FELIBRE

Mistral was the only poet in a minority language ever to be awarded the Nobel Prize

annual *Armanan Provençau*, the first journal to be written in Provençal.

Mistral's cause was helped enormously by the publication of *Miréio* in 1859, which made him instantly famous. This tragic poem tells the story of a beautiful young girl who falls in love with a man whom her parents consider unsuitable; she runs away to seek help from the Holy Marys at les Stes.-Maries-de-la-Mer in the Camargue but dies on the beach from a broken heart.

By now established as the region's greatest writer, Mistral began work on a monumental encyclopedia, *Le Trésor de la Félibrige*, which was to become the most important reference work on Provençal culture ever published. He also published the second of his major epics, *Calendau*, which tells the story of a young fisherman from la Ciotat who falls in love with a water-nymph. In 1876 Mistral married and moved into a house opposite his mother's in Maillane (where he lived until his death in 1914).

In the 1890s Mistral and the Félibrige founded a museum in Arles devoted to Provençal arts and culture (the Museon Arleten) and started a new, more popular journal called *L'Aïoli*. In 1904 Mistral became one of the first recipients of the Nobel Prize for Literature.

Provençal revival The romanticism and nostalgia of the Félibrige for the chivalrous days of the troubadours was embodied in their poetry and their impassioned defence of a lifestyle which they saw being gradually eroded by progress and the imposition of the French language by the central state in Paris.

The greatest achievement of the Félibrige was to create a huge revival of interest in Provençal traditions, legends and folklore, which has ensured their continuance today. However, they never engaged on the political level (unlike their cousins the Basques) and eventually "Occitania" was eclipsed yet again by French culture (see page 33).

Mistral has been almost deified by his admirers since his death; when he was alive he attended the unveiling of a bronze statue of himself in the Forum at Arles. Showing that his feet were still firmly planted on the ground despite the veneration bestowed on him, Mistral commented that the statue looked like a passenger waiting for a train to come into the station. "All he needs is a suitcase!" said the man who will always be remembered with honour and gratitude in Provence.

THE COUNTRYSIDE
"There are gardens of beans, orchards with apples, pears and peaches, cherry trees that catch your eye, fig trees that offer you their ripe figs, round-bellied melons that beg to be eaten, and beautiful vines with bunches of golden grapes—ah, I can almost see them!" *The Memoirs of Frédéric Mistral*

61

Mistral, aged 62, soon after he began his Provençal journal, L'Aïoli

Vaucluse

MUSCAT FESTIVAL
The best time to visit Beaumes is during the annual Wine Festival (July/August), when all the local vineyards set up stalls at various points around the village and everybody wanders, glass in hand, happily trying out one after the other. To soak it all up, other stalls sell goats' cheeses, *foie gras* pâté and local delicacies such as melon or melon sorbet with Muscat.

▶▶ Beaumes-de-Venise   44B3

Best known for the subtly flavoured Muscat wines that bear its name (see panel), Beaumes has been producing this nectar since the Middle Ages; the popes at Avignon owned a 70ha (173-acre) vineyard here in the 14th century and Anne of Austria, visiting in 1660, presented the church with a set of liturgical vestments in recognition of the villagers' winemaking skills.

Built around a rocky cliff at the southern flank of the Dentelles range, Beaumes-de-Venise is named after the grottoes that dot the hillside where the first inhabitants lived (the Provençal word for grotto is *"baume"*). The suffix "de-Venise" refers to the fact that the village was part of the ancient territory of the Comtat Venaissin.

Above the village, the ruins of the 12th-century **château** loom over the ancient streets. These are now private property, but follow the Grand Rue up through the village to come across some of the old grottoes which riddle the rocks beneath the castle walls.

▶ Bollène   44A3

Once one of the richest possessions of the Avignon popes, this unassuming town has grown rapidly from a mere market garden centre to a major conurbation with the development of the nuclear facilities on the nearby Donzére-Mondragon canal. Climb up to the viewpoint next to the parish church of St.-Martin and this huge industrial conglomeration is all too easily visible to the north of town. Beyond the church is a park dedicated to Louis Pasteur, who discovered an inoculation against swine fever while staying here (in a house on avenue Pasteur) in 1882. There are some fine old houses with beautifully decorated doors in the old town around the church. And from the upper town you can see out across the Rhône Valley and off to the Cevennes and pre-Alps.

Built on the site of an ancient priory, St.-Martin dates from the 11th century

NEARBY The extraordinary cave-village of **Barry▶▶** is one of the best preserved in Provence. The origins of the *village troglodytique* lie back in the prehistoric Celto-Ligurian era, and successive generations of stone

quarriers, from Gallo-Roman times through the medieval period and right up to the early 20th century, have left their mark on its stony surroundings. From the parking area, a track leads past a series of houses that look as though someone has attached the front half of a stone cottage onto a cave dwelling: which is exactly what did happen, since the inhabitants didn't need to build a whole house, or even a roof, and simply adapted the caves to their needs by carving most of the internal rooms out of the rock-face. Once the basic living space was prepared, the cave dwellers then began the laborious task of fashioning home comforts.

Nevertheless, they were at constant risk from rock-slides. After several villagers had been killed in the 19th century, the entire population abandoned Barry and moved down the hill to St.-Pierre on the plain. The last inhabitant moved out in 1925.

The inhabitants of this troglodyte village at Barry made their living smuggling salt and matches into neighbouring Dauphiné during the 18th century

▶▶ Bonnieux 45C1

Hugging the northern flank of the Luberon, Bonnieux is a large and lively terraced village which rises up steeply towards the 12th-century church and cemetery at its summit. From the terrace surrounding the church there are sweeping views across the valley and neighbouring *villages perchés*.

Half-way up Bonnieux's main street, rue de la République, an ancient bakery has been converted into the unusual **Musée de la Boulangerie▶** (*Open* Apr–Jun, Oct, Wed–Mon 10–12.30, 2.30–6; Jul–Aug 10–1, 3–6.30. *Admission: inexpensive*). The museum covers every aspect of bread-making from harvesting the wheat onwards.

Just near Bonnieux on the D149 heading northwards is the **Pont Julien▶▶**, one of the best-preserved Roman bridges in Provence. The triple-arched bridge was thought to have been built around 300 BC and named after the nearby town of *Apta Julia* (now Apt).

An ancient bread oven in the Musée de la Boulangerie at Bonnieux

▶ Buoux 45C1

See page 50.

Characteristic blue-and-white faience, which contained herbal remedies, in the old pharmacy of Carpentras's Hôtel-Dieu

64

CARPENTRAS' PATRON SAINT

The patron saint of Carpentras is St. Siffrein (after whom the cathedral is named), who was thought to be a monk from the Îles de Lérins, sent by the abbot to evangelize in Venasque (12km/7.5 miles to the south of Carpentras) in the 6th century. He died in Venasque but since no one is sure of the exact date, his saint's day was set as 12 July, which was the anniversary of his remains being moved to Carpentras in AD 980. This was later changed to 27 November to coincide with a major pilgrimage and fair, inaugurated in 1525 (and still celebrated today). St. Siffrein was famed for healing possessed souls, and legend has it that his mystical powers reached out from beyond the grave. His tomb was robbed and his robes stolen, but as the thieves set out on the road to Carpentras they were suddenly struck blind and forced to abandon their spoils.

▶▶ Carpentras   44B2

Carpentras has been famous as a market centre since the 5th century BC, when a Celtic tribe known as the Meminiens set up their stalls on a busy crossroads just outside the present town. Later, Greeks and Phoenicians came upriver from Marseille to buy wheat, honey, goats, sheep and skins. Under the Romans the town prospered, although little remains from this period except a small triumphal arch. In the 14th century, Clement V, having been proclaimed Pope by King Philippe, chose Carpentras as his second main residence outside Avignon.

From the 14th century onwards Carpentras was one of the four main refugee centres in the Comtat Venaissin (the others were Cavaillon, Avignon and L'Isle-sur-la-Sorgue) for Jews fleeing persecution under Philippe le Bel in France. Despite the best efforts of a succession of bishops in later centuries (notably Monseigneur d'Inguimbert, who commissioned the Hôtel-Dieu), Carpentras went into economic decline. Its fortunes were only revived with the building of a canal from the Durance in the 19th century. The desert-like *garrigue* around the town blossomed into fruit and vegetable gardens, which today supply early season produce such as grapes, cherries and strawberries for the tables of France.

Every Friday there is a huge market that spreads throughout the town; from November to April, truffles change hands at enormous prices in the **place Aristide Briand**; and the town is well known for *berlingots* (mint-flavoured caramels).

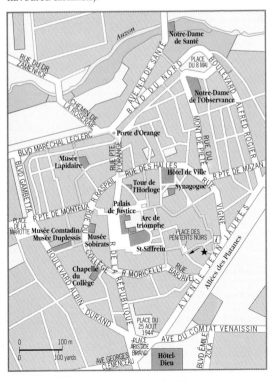

Stallholder in the market

Walk

Carpentras

Allow around two hours for this walk, which delves into some of the town's hidden corners.
See map opposite.

Start at the tourist office and follow the rue Vieux Juiverie onto rue de la Fornaque. Directly opposite you will find a magnificent, carved doorway, typical of the Provençal style of the period. The two Atlas-type figures supporting the portico are from the school of Pierre Puget.

Turn back up the rue des Marins, at the top of which is the disused old chapel of the Pénitents Noirs in the place des Pénitents Noirs. Turn down rue Moricelly, where there are many fine old mansions, in particular those at Nos. 71–83 and at No. 57.

The rue Moricelly leads you into the place Ste.-Marthe, with a pretty fountain in the middle; to one side of the square is an even more ancient fountain embedded in a stone post.

Continue down rue du Collège, with the college itself on your left. The mid-17th-century chapel is now used for art exhibitions.

Weave your way left onto rue Eysseric et Pascal, right onto rue Joseph Fornery (around the back of the Musées Comtadin and Duplessis) and onto rue Piquepeyre. On your right, the immensely tall, misshapen wall forms part of an old Carmelite monastery. Make your way through the backstreets to the Porte d'Orange (see page 67).

From the gateway, walk up rue Porte d'Orange and turn left onto rue Place de l'Horloge. Almost immediately on your right is a small passageway leading into a courtyard: The attractive ceiling here was discovered as recently as 1990. It dates from the 14th century and traces of a fire that took place in the 18th century can still be seen. Inside the courtyard, look up to admire the intricate ironwork of the 16th-century Bell Tower.

Continue down rue Place de l'Horloge and then turn right; at the end take rue Gaudibert-Barret and then turn left down rue Serpentine, one of the city's oldest and smallest streets, to return to the tourist office.

The vivid colouration of the stained glass in Carpentras cathedral shows it to have been heavily restored since the 15th century

Rebuilt many times over the centuries, the cathedral lacks a unifying style

WHAT TO SEE In the middle of the pedestrian zone of the city centre the **Cathédrale St.-Siffrein** is no great beauty to behold, mixing together as it does architectural styles from many different periods. The interior contains work by Mignard, Parrocel and Duplessis, and, most notably, gilded wooden sculptures by Jacques Bernus.

Next to the cathedral is the **Palais de Justice** (ask at the tourist office for details of guided tours), formerly the Archbishop's Palace, commissioned by Cardinal Bichi in 1640. Tucked away behind the cathedral and the Palais de Justice is a **Roman arc de triomphe▶** that was built under Augustus in the 1st century AD to commemorate victory over the Franks. Constructed at the same time as the triumphal arch in Orange, it is not nearly as tall and only one span of the original three remains. However, the smaller scale allows you to get a much closer look at the bas-relief sculptures of the enslaved captives on the east and west faces. It is a pity that this arch, the only Roman relic in Carpentras, is so hemmed in and concealed by the buildings around it.

Another monument that is remarkable for being so inconspicuous is the **Synagogue▶** (*Open* Mon–Fri) on the place de l'Hôtel de Ville. The original synagogue was built in the 14th century but eventually became too small to serve the population of over 2,000 Jews who lived in the surrounding ghetto. When the synagogue was rebuilt in 1741 Monseigneur d'Inguimbert (Bishop d'Inguimbert) gave permission only on the condition that it was no higher than the cathedral—hence its position today, almost dwarfed by the surrounding houses. This is the oldest synagogue in France, and the richly decorated interior of the *salle de culte* (restored in 1954) testifies to the wealth of the Jewish community.

Carpentras has a handful of museums (*Open* Wed–Mon) of no great distinction, but on a rainy day you can take your choice between the municipal collections which are displayed in the **Musée Comtadin** (folkloric mementoes), with the **Musée Duplessis** (local 16th- and 17th-century paintings) on the floor above. Nearby are the **Musée Lapidaire** (prehistoric and Gallo-Roman finds), housed in the former Convent of the Visitation, and the **Musée Sobirats** (a furnished 18th-century mansion).

On the south side of the tree-lined boulevard that encircles the city centre is the imposing **Hôtel-Dieu▶**, a former hospital built in the 18th century by Monseigneur d'Inguimbert, now housing a tourist office. Once inside, the most delightful part of the Hôtel-Dieu is the historic **pharmacy▶▶** (*Open* by appointment, check with tourist office. *Admission: inexpensive*). Almost unchanged since it was created, this is one of the best-preserved antique pharmacies in the whole of France. It contains an excellent collection of faience as well as pestles and mortars, brass scales and all the other paraphernalia of the apothecary's trade. The room is decorated with landscape panels painted by Duplessis.

On the other side of town is the impressive **Porte d'Orange▶▶**, the last remaining tower of the ramparts, which were built between 1357 and 1395 on the orders of Pope Innocent IV. The fortifications originally consisted of 32 towers and four gates but they were nearly all demolished from 1840 onwards in the name of "urban expansion." This huge, 27m (90ft) high tower is unusual in that it is *ouverte à la gorge* ("open-throated"), which means that it was open at the back so that troops could be easily replenished from the town. From the top there are views across Mont Ventoux and the Plateau de Vaucluse (guided tours from the tourist office; tel: 04 90 63 00 78).

THE *BOULE AUX RATS*
On the southern side of the cathedral is a flamboyant Gothic doorway that was known as the Porte Juive, through which Jews entered in order to be baptized. Above the doorway is one of the cathedral's most famous curiosities, the *boule aux rats*. The symbolism of this globe covered with rats has never been satisfactorily explained: it may be a play on the town's name in Latin, *carpere ras* (the nibbling rat); it may represent the Christian world being overrun with sin and hereticism; or it may be connected with the dreaded plague that swept the country in the 14th century.

67

Family values, as portrayed on a poster in the synagogue

The view from Colline St.-Jacques, where Cavaillon was founded by the Celto-Ligurians before it moved down to the plains in the Roman era

CAVAILLON MELONS
In 1864 the writer Alexandre Dumas, who was very fond of melons, heard that the library at Cavaillon couldn't afford to stock his books, so he agreed to supply them with copies in exchange for an annual rent of 12 melons, which were sent to him in Paris. The melons he so enjoyed were the heavy, oval-shaped Cantaloupe melons. Since then many new varieties have been introduced, the most popular being the small Charentais melon, which *aficionados* consider to be absolute nectar.

▶ **Cavaillon** 44B1

Surrounded by market gardens irrigated by the Durance and the Coulon rivers, Cavaillon is one of the biggest agricultural towns in France. By the end of your stay you will be left in no doubt that this is the melon capital of France; there is even a Brotherhood of the Knights of the Order of the Melon. This prosperous town also grows an enormous quantity of prime fruit and vegetables, something for which it has been known since Roman times.

The only relic of the Roman era is a small **triumphal arch▶**, built in the 1st century AD. It was moved stone-by-stone to its present position at the foot of the Colline St.-Jacques in 1880. The town's other main monument is the **Cathédrale St.-Véran▶**, an elegant Romanesque structure dating from the 12th century with a charming cloister on the south side.

Nearby on rue Hébraïque is the old **Synagogue▶** (*Open* Apr–Sep, Wed–Mon 9.30–12.30, 2.30–6.30; Oct–May, Mon, Wed–Fri 9–12, 2–5. *Admission: inexpensive*), sole remnant of the large Jewish population that lived in the surrounding ghetto prior to the Revolution. The ornate interior is masterly; beneath the Worship Room the ancient bakery has been converted into a small museum.

Cavaillon also has a modest **archaeological museum** (joint ticket with Synagogue) inside the chapel of the old Hôtel Dieu on Grand Rue.

▶ **Châteauneuf-du-Pape** 44A2

The fame of this small town revolves around the wines that bear its name. The first vineyards were planted here in the 14th century by the Avignon popes, one of whom, Jean XVII, also built a castle at the summit of the village as a summer residence. The **Château des Papes▶** was burned in 1562 during the Wars of Religion and then finally blown up by the retreating Germans in 1944. The two remaining walls give a good idea of the scale of the original château, and from its hilltop vantage point there are fabulous views down the Rhône Valley.

At the bottom of the village, in the **Musée du Père Anselme▶** (*Open* daily. *Admission free*), there is an interesting display on winemaking through the centuries.

The relatively small area of just over 3,000ha (7,410 acres) of vineyards that surround Châteauneuf-du-Pape on the left bank of the Rhône produces one of the world's most prestigious and well-known wines.

Hot rocks As you approach the vineyards you will notice something curious—there is no soil visible at all, only a sea of smooth pebbles between the vines. This alluvial shingle has a beneficial effect, magnifying the heat of the sun on the grapes by day and keeping them warm long into the night. This superheated microclimate and the wide spacing between the vines produce a wine with the highest minimum strength (12.5 per cent alcohol) of any French wine.

The first *appellation contrôlée* Châteauneuf's most distinguished grower was the late Baron Le Roy de Boiseaumarie, who initiated a series of quality controls in 1923 that later became the standard for the national system of *appellations contrôlées*.

Unlike most Côtes du Rhône winegrowers, whose product uses just one variety of grape, growers here can choose from up to 13 different types. The result may differ slightly from grower to grower but is a characteristically deep red, full-bodied wine with a strong bouquet. There are plenty of opportunities for visiting vineyards in the region, among the best-known of which are the Château Le Nerthe, the Château de Beaucastel, the Château Rayas, the Château de la Gardine and the Domaine des Fines Roches. The annual production of Châteauneuf is around 97,000 hectolitres, but only 6.5 per cent are white; this elegant, pale wine with a subtle bouquet is something of a rarity and well worth trying while you are here.

Festive tastings The annual *Fête de la Véraison* (which is held to celebrate the grapes achieving maturity) takes place at the beginning of August, when all the producers set up their stalls in the streets of the village. The business of winetasting is much easier and more fun during the festival, accompanied as it is by dancing, processions and a medieval pageant.

QUAFFING CARDINALS Such was the fame of Châteauneuf wines at the time of the Avignon popes that when Urban X suggested moving the papacy back to Rome he met with deep opposition from his cardinals, who were reluctant to leave an area producing such exquisite vintages. On hearing this, Petrarch commented that "the princes of the church value the wines of Provence and know that French wines are rarer at the Vatican than Holy Water."

69

Opportunities for tasting the famous wines are never far away in Châteauneuf-du-Pape

▶ Crestet
44B3

This charming little village, which derives its name from the rocky crest on which it is built, is one of the most unspoiled perched villages in the region. With no shops or cafés, there is little to do except enjoy a leisurely stroll through the cobbled alleyways and admire the ancient wooden doorways of the old houses. There is a minuscule square with a bubbling fountain and a 12th-century church, behind which a path leads up between rocks and wild fig trees to an old **château** (no visitors). Above the village, the Centre International d'Art et de Sculpture provides an interesting diversion (see page 72).

▶ Cucuron
45C1

The village of Cucuron lies on the southern flank of the Grand Luberon and is the starting point for the 10km (6 mile) trail to the Sommet du Mourre Nègre.

A short distance from the church on the rue de l'Église is the **Musée Marc Deydier**▶▶ (*Open* Wed–Mon 9–12, 3–6. *Admission free*). Apart from the usual displays of Gallo-Roman finds and old agricultural tools, the prize exhibits are photographs of the village taken at the beginning of the 20th century by Marc Deydier, the town clerk after whom the museum is named. The graphic quality and extraordinary clarity of these superb photographs (reprinted from some of the 2,618 negatives in store) is matched only by their value as a vivid ethnographic record of everyday life in Cucuron, depicting charcoal-making, harvesting with steam tractors, and street scenes.

▶▶ Dentelles de Montmirail
44B3

See pages 72–73.

▶▶ Fontaine-de-Vaucluse
44B2

In the summer months this little village is swamped with thousands of visitors drawn to the fabled fissure where the River Sorgue rises from the depths and disgorges at a rate that makes it one of the most powerful resurgent springs in the world. People used to come to pay homage to Petrarch, who lived here between 1337 and 1353, but now it is the source itself that exerts such a strong fascination, pouring forth in the peak months at a rate of between 100 and 200cu m (330 and 660cu ft) per second.

PROBING THE DEPTHS
The first attempt to explore the Fontaine de Vaucluse was made in 1878, when a pot-holer reached 23m (75ft). Jacques Cousteau sent the remote control *Télenaute* down to 106m (350ft) in 1967, and in 1983 a second probe, the *Sorgonaute*, reached 245m (805ft) but exploded on another attempt a year later. The bottom was finally reached in August 1985, when the mini-sub *Modexa* settled on the sandy bed at 308m (1,010ft). A high-performance probe, the *Spélénaute*, went down in 1994 to venture into the passageways that disappear back into the mountain.

There is little to disturb the peace in Crestet apart from the sound of running water

The source is around 2km (1 mile) from the centre of the village and is reached by a path along the river bank. Once a blissful walk, it is now a circus of buskers and T-shirt and souvenir sellers, with numerous restaurants and bars built out over the water (even in the 1950s the writer James Pope-Hennessy complained that "all has been commercialized and made vulgar...I confess to feeling beside Petrarch's fountain, as I have felt in Venice, that here was one place to which I had come a hundred and fifty years too late").

A handful of museums and exhibitions have sprung up along this path, among which are the **Musée du Santon** (*Open* daily. *Admission: inexpensive*) with its massed pottery figurines, and **Le Monde Souterrain de Norbert Casteret►** (*Open* daily. *Admission: moderate*). Guided tours here focus on the history of caving and the specimens collected over the years by France's most celebrated speleologist. At the exit you will find yourself in a vast underground concrete souvenir centre, leading to the **Moulin à Papier Vallis Clausa►**, which displays the ancient paper-making equipment that was once powered by waterwheels on the banks of the Sorgue.

On the other side of the path the excellent **Musée d'Histoire 1939–1945 l'Appel de la Liberté►►** (*Open* Apr–Oct, Wed–Mon; Nov–Dec, Mar, Sat and Sun. *Admission: inexpensive*) is an evocative tribute to the men and women of the Resistance and to the hardships of life in wartime France. Back in the village, take time out for the 11th-century Provençal Romanesque church of **Notre-Dame** and the **Musée-bibliothèque F. Pétrarque►** (*Open* Apr–Oct, Wed–Mon. *Admission: inexpensive*). The stone column in the village centre was erected in 1804 to celebrate the 500th anniversary of Petrarch's birth.

A riverside view of Fontaine-de-Vaucluse

PETRARCH AND THE SOURCE
"Here I have the Fountain of the Sorgue, a stream that must be numbered among the fairest and coolest, remarkable for its crystal waters and its emerald channels. No other stream is like it; none other is so noted for its varying moods, now raging like a torrent, now quiet as a pool...I would speak of this more at length, were it not that the rare beauties of this secluded dale have already become familiar far and wide through my verses." Petrarch, 1347

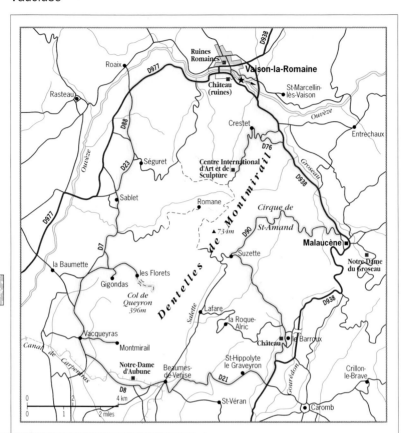

Drive

Dentelles

This round tour from Vaison-la-Romaine skirts the jagged limestone pinnacles of the Dentelles and encompasses hill villages (several are known for their wines). Allow 5–6 hours.

Leave Vaison-la-Romaine by the D938 towards Malaucène. After about 4km (2.5 miles) turn right to **Crestet** (see page 70), then follow the signs for the **Centre International d'Art et de Sculpture►►**. Surrounded by dense woods, the centre is housed in the former studio of sculptor François Stahly, and is where artists explore the theme of art and nature. The *Chemin de Sculptures* is a magical mystery tour through the pine and oak trees, where sculptures in stone, wood and iron appear as if growing from the ground on either side of the marked trail.

Return to the main road and continue on to **Malaucène** (see page 76). Follow the boulevard back in the direction of Vaison but take a left turn on the D90 signposted Suzette.

After passing through vineyards and fields of sunflowers the road begins to wind up through the forest towards the Dentelles.

At the tiny hamlet of Suzette, you can turn right for **Beaumes-de-Venise** (see page 62). A summer season alternative is a left turn for **le Barroux** and its imposing **château►** (*Open* Apr–May Sat–Sun; Jul, Aug and Sep daily; Jun and Oct, afternoons only. *Admission inexpensive*), which was founded in the 12th century, but sacked during the Revolution and abandoned until restoration work began in 1929. Set

alight by the Germans in 1944, it burned for 10 days and the long struggle to restore it again began in the 1960s. The château is well worth visiting, particularly the curious dog-leg shaped chapel—impenetrable rock forced a change of building direction. For Beaumes-de-Venise, take the D78 down to the main road, turn right onto the D938 towards Carpentras for 3km (2 miles) then right again to **Beaumes-de-Venise**. From here take the Vacqueyras road and turn right just outside Beaumes to **Notre-Dame d'Aubune▶**. This small Romanesque chapel lies on the southern slopes of the Dentelles beneath a series of terraces cultivated for centuries.

Continue to **Vacqueyras**. Its claim to fame (apart from its wines) used to be a statue of Rambaud de Vacqueyras, a famous Provençal troubadour. His statue was stolen, alas, and has never been replaced. However, from here you can detour to the sulphur springs at **Montmirail**, fashionable enough to warrant a casino next to the *station thermal* in the 19th century, when over 1,000

Serrated pinnacles of the Dentelles

guests a year took the waters.

Take the D7 on to **Gigondas** (see page 74). Turning right out of the village, follow signs for the **Dentelles de Montmirail**. The road becomes an unmetalled track, at the top of which is a parking area with signs for the footpath to the pass, the **Col de Queyron▶**, at the centre of the Dentelles' peaks.

Return to Gigondas and continue, via Sablet, to **Séguret▶▶**. This lovely village was almost in ruins by the 1950s, but les Amis de Séguret set about breathing life back into it by restoring many of the monuments and reinvigorating local crafts and culture. There is a Provençal folklore festival here in August.

Return to Vaison via the D88/D977.

Vineyards shelter in the shadow of the Dentelles

*An old château
dominates Gigondas*

HILLSIDE TERRACING
Many of the labour-inten-
sive terraces, once found
throughout the Provençal
hills, have fallen into
disuse, largely due to the
mechanization of farming.
However, terracing has
unique qualities as a
growing environment:
resistance to erosion and
fire, and a microclimate
beneficial to plants. Now,
attempts are being made
to grow specialized crops
(such as kiwi fruits, rasp-
berries and Japanese artichokes) on terraces, and
traditional plantations of
apricot, almond, olive,
peac and fig trees
are being irrigated to
increase yields.

*The thick drystone walls
of the* bories *near Gordes*

▶ **Gigondas** *44B3*

A small village with a reputation for strong, full-bodied
red wines, Gigondas has little in the way of sightseeing
but plenty of opportunities for the serious imbiber to try
what many consider to be one of the best wines in
Provence. Around the main square there are at least half a
dozen *caves* within weaving distance of each other,
including the Caveau de Gigondas, which stocks bottles
from 40 different Gigondas *domaines*.

▶▶▶ **Gordes** *45C2*

Seen from afar, houses seem to cling precariously to the
hillside terraces that lead up steeply to the centre of
Gordes. In the heart of the village is a 15th-century
château whose profile is visible from some distance.

Gordes was set to become yet another victim of rural
depopulation and decline until 1938, when the Cubist
painter André Lhote gave it a new lease of life. The
village's future as a centre for art and tourism was sealed
in 1970, when Hungarian artist Victor Vasarély bought
the château and installed an exhibition of his famous
geometric works (later transferred to Fondation Vasarély
in Aix, which closed in 1997). Today, the château houses
the pop art works of the Musée Pol Mara. Be sure to visit
the first floor, where the Grande Salle (which is part of the
Mairie) has a magnificently decorated Renaissance fire-
place. Built in 1541, its pediments and pilasters are ornamented with flowers and shells.

In an area as rich in historical relics as Provence, perhaps
none is as curious and compelling as the fascinating
Village des Bories▶▶▶ (*Open* daily, 9–dusk. *Admission:
moderate*), 1km (0.5 miles) west of Gordes. Reached down
a narrow, winding lane enclosed on either side by stone
walls and *garrigue* scrub, the *bories* seem to grow out of the
landscape around them; the thick walls of the enclosures
merge into the dwelling houses, and are joined by yet
more walls to other, smaller huts.

The *bories* were built using an ingenious technique
whereby each layer of flat stone slightly overlapped the
next to create a corbelled vault, which was then topped off
with flagstones. No mortar was used in the construction
of these sturdy dwellings. Similar drystone huts exist
elsewhere in Europe, some of them dating back to neolithic
times. In Provence there are probably between 5,000 and

6,000, with the majority found in this part of Vaucluse. It takes around 200,000–300,000 stones to build a *borie* and they can weigh from 30–200 tonnes. Often seen in fields (where they are used as shepherds' huts), some have been converted into modern homes.

The integration of architecture and the environment is complete, but what is astonishing is that although some of the *bories* gathered here date back as far as the 14th and 15th centuries, making them contemporary with the Renaissance château in the village, others may have been constructed as recently as the 19th century.

Also in the vicinity of Gordes is the **Abbaye de Sénanque**▶▶▶ (*Open* for guided tours only Feb to mid-Nov daily except Sun mornings; mid-Nov to Jan afternoons only. For times see www.senangue.fr. *Admission: moderate*). One of three Cistercian monasteries in Provence, the 12th-century abbey makes an extraordinary impression rising from the lavender fields in a valley 4km (2.5 miles) north of the village. The honeyed stone monastery complex has been occupied for over 850 years save for a 60-year break after the French Revolution and between 1969 and 1988, when the monastery served as a cultural complex. Off the central courtyard, a long dormitory block leads directly into the abbey church, its unadorned austerity marginally softened by Romanesque rounded pillars and arches. There is some strikingly simple modern glass, and the acoustics are superb. Outside, the pillars are adorned with carved capitals in stylised flower and foliage designs.

▶ **Goult**   *45C2*

Just off the N100, which runs parallel to the Luberon range, Goult is the site of the unusual **Sentier du Conservatoire des Terrasses en Culture**▶ (Open Air Terrace Museum), where you can ramble around a signposted trail explaining the nature and function of ancient hill terraces and the intricate techniques of drystone walling (*Open* daily. *Admission free*). Alongside the traditional shelters and cabins many old, and increasingly rare, varieties of olives and almonds have been planted here.

75

The serene Abbaye de Sénanque, set among oak trees and lavender

ANTIQUES TO GO

L'Isle-sur-la-Sorgue has a reputation as the antiques capital of Provence. This is partly because of its large antiques market, which has been held every Sunday since 1967 on the avenue des Quatre Otages alongside one of the canals. There are now nearly 200 permanent bric-à-brac and antiques dealers spread throughout seven "villages" (often in converted warehouses and the like) around the town centre. There are two annual antiques fairs, lasting four days: at Easter and in mid-August.

Treasure-hunting at the antiques markets of L'Isle-sur-la-Sorgue

▶▶ l'Isle-sur-la-Sorgue 44B2

Soon after the start of its journey from Fontaine-de-Vaucluse down to the Rhône at Avignon, the River Sorgue briefly divides around an island on which sits l'Isle-sur-la-Sorgue, a charming town that has built its fortunes on the river that runs through it.

No one is sure when the inhabitants of the village decided to dig three canals through their island estate, but in the Wars of Religion they put their mastery of the river to good use by flooding the surrounding plains so that they were out of reach of cannon fire. Later the villagers built a whole series of waterwheels across the canals, their paddles powering what was to become a hive of industry including grain, oil and paper mills, tanneries and textile and silk works.

The wealth these enterprises brought to the town is evident in the riches displayed in the baroque **Notre-Dame-des-Anges**▶▶ in the town centre. The magnificent interior is mostly the work of 17th-century artists of the Avignon school. Also worth seeing is the 18th-century **Hôtel-Dieu**▶ with its intricate wrought-iron gates and antique pharmacy (ask for the concierge at the main gate if you want to go inside), and the **Hôtel Donadú de Campredon**▶ (*Open* daily during exhibitions. *Admission: moderate*). The latter hosts an impressive schedule of temporary art exhibitions; in the past these have included works by Miró, Matisse, Dufy and Poliakoff.

Unless you are hunting for antiques (see panel), the main pleasure in visiting l'Isle-sur-la-Sorgue lies in strolling through the streets, watching the soothing waters running beneath small ironwork bridges and past terraces and balconies replete with flowering plants. Of the 64 waterwheels that once existed, only a handful remain. On the **quai des Lices** and **quai Berthelet** three of these magnificent wheels have been restored, and alongside **rue Jean-Theophile** and **rue Jean Roux** some of the remaining moss-encrusted paddlewheels still revolve slowly and steadily to the rhythm of the waters.

▶ Lacoste 45C1

This hilltop village on the northern flank of the Luberon is still a fashionable address for Parisian *residences secondaires* despite (or perhaps because of) its heritage as the home for many years of the notorious Marquis de Sade (see panel opposite). Dating back to the 11th century, the **château**▶ used to be one of the grandest in the region. Pillaged in the Revolution, it fell into ruins and stayed that way until the current owner, a retired teacher called André Bouër, began his lifelong and quixotic task of restoring it; 40 years on, the project is no nearer completion (the interior cannot be visited).

▶ Lourmarin 45C1

See pages 50–51.

▶ Malaucène 44B3

An attractive town encircled by a boulevard of plane trees, Malaucène is the major base for hiking, riding and cycling expeditions up nearby Mont Ventoux (see page 93). Four **fortified gates** mark the entrances into the old town: Follow rue St.-Étienne and rue du Château up past

Still slowly turning under their mossy burdens, the paddlewheels of L'Isle-sur-la-Sorgue are nearly 200 years old

the crumbling old clock tower (used as a look-out point during the Wars of Religion) to reach the belvedere created from the ruins of the ancient château.

▶▶ Mazan   44B2

Mazan, 7km (4.5 miles) east of Carpentras, is the sort of town you could easily pass by without giving it a second glance. However, behind its solid gateways, the centre of the town (which mostly dates from the 16th and 17th centuries) is a delight to explore and there are many architectural details such as statues in niches, fountains, and ancient doorways, to savour as you wander around the streets. Opposite the church, a bell tower marks the Chapelle des Pénitents Blancs, which now houses the **Musée de Mazan▶** (*Open* mid-Jun to mid-Sep, Wed–Mon 3–7). Although there is little that is dramatic here (apart from a chilling skeleton from the 4th century of a young woman who was killed by a stone from a catapult, which left a gaping hole in the front of her skull), it is clear that the people of Mazan have raided their attics: their treasures seem to speak to us from across history in a way that a grand museum could never do.

THE MISCREANT MARQUIS
The Marquis de Sade, author of *120 Days of Sodom* and *Justine*, was born in Paris in 1740. When he was 31, his debaucheries forced him to leave the city for Lacoste, where he spent much of his wife's money embellishing the château. His sexual preferences have come to be called sadistic after his name and also earned him the death sentence in 1772, from which he fled to Italy in the company of his wife's sister. The Marquis lived at Lacoste between his numerous prison sentences until 1814, when he died in a lunatic asylum at Charenton.

*Stonework merges
into the natural
surroundings in
Oppède-le-Vieux*

►► Ménerbes   45C1

The layout of this village on the northern flank of the
Luberon is inevitably compared with the shape of a ship,
due to its narrow promontory projecting like a prow out
over the valley. Walking up through the village towards
the promontory you pass the Mairie and a 17th-century
bell tower on your right, with the archway between them
framing a picture-postcard view of the Luberon. Past here
there is a 14th-century church (with more lovely views
from the old cemetery) and the ruins of an ancient **citadel**.

Just outside Ménerbes (along the D3), the **Musée du Tire-
Bouchon►►** (*Open* Apr–Oct Mon–Sat 10–12, 2–7;
Nov–Mar 10–12, 2–5. *Admission: inexpensive*) has a fascinating collection of over a thousand corkscrews from all
over the world, displaying every conceivable variation
and elaboration on this humble utensil. The museum is
part of the Domaine de le Citadelle, and admission
includes a tour of the winery and cellars. The winery is
well worth a visit; it has a high-tech control panel with so
many lights it looks like it could launch a space shuttle.

►► Oppède-le-Vieux   44B1

Built on a limestone pinnacle set against the dramatic
backdrop of the steep north-facing slopes of the Petit
Luberon, this evocative village is still partly in ruins and
not (as yet) overrun by the trinket trade.

Oppède-le-Vieux was once a thriving community
clustered around the base of the castle, but the castle was
pillaged during the Revolution and the village itself went
into a decline after the Comtat Venaissin was handed
back to France, finally being abandoned altogether in
1910 when the remaining inhabitants moved down the
hill to Oppède-les-Poulivets.

Recolonized by artists during the 1940s, some houses
have been restored, but in the upper half of the village it is
sometimes difficult to tell where houses end and ruins
begin. Overgrown pathways wind up between ancient
archways to the summit, where there is an old **church**
with massive flying buttresses and, farther on, the ruins of
the **château** itself (take great care because there are many
dangerous unprotected drops).

▶▶▶ Orange   44A3

Once an important Roman city, Orange has always been considered the gateway to Provence, initially as a major settlement on the Via Agrippa, which followed the Rhône valley and, later, as the first stop on the railway lines and roads that led south into the sunshine.

Despite the construction of the *autoroute du soleil* just to the west, traffic on the N7 still thunders past one of Orange's most famous monuments, the Arc de Triomphe, before engulfing the city and making navigation around the outer boulevards somewhat hazardous. Thankfully almost the entire city centre is semi-pedestrianized, creating a pleasant environment with many squares linked together where you can wander from café to café under the shade of the plane trees.

After the Roman era the town passed through the hands of various feudal lords, including the House of Baux from 1173 to 1530. It was then inherited by René de Nassau, whose strongly Protestant family turned Orange into a refuge for dissenters amid the surrounding sea of Catholicism. Maurice de Nassau fortified the town in the early 1600s but to no avail, since it was then razed by Louis XIV after war had broken out between the king and Maurice de Nassau's nephew, William of Orange, who led The Netherlands to victory against Spain and secured Dutch independence in 1648. In 1678 the House of Orange regained the town, but it was ceded back to France under the treaty of Utrecht in 1713.

Whether the town of Orange gave its name to the Dutch royal family or vice versa is by no means clear, but what is certain is that the Dutch connection was bad news for the town's heritage, since Maurice de Nassau pulled down the Roman monuments to use the stone for his fortifications. Only by chance did the theatre survive, because its massive rear wall was needed as part of the defences.

The top-heavy Arc de Triomphe in Orange celebrates Rome's victory over the Celtic tribes

RESISTING ROME
Once a Celtic settlement, Orange's downfall came when the inhabitants defeated the Roman legions in a huge battle in 105 BC. Three years later the legions returned under General Marius to exact their revenge, virtually wiping out the town. It was not inhabited again until 35 BC, this time by veterans of the Second Gallic Legion, who were given the territory in return for their part in Caesar's conquest of Gaul. They set about building a prosperous, well-ordered town, complete with theatre, gymnasium, temples and of course the Arc de Triomphe, which personified their victory over the barbarians.

The fully restored tiers of seating in Orange's Théâtre Antique can hold up to 10,000 spectators

CLOSED FOR 300 YEARS
The last recorded performance in the theatre during the Middle Ages was the *Farce de Clin Bérnard*, performed by travelling players in 1514. Less than 50 years later, the Wars of Religion were causing devastation across the region, and Orange was sacked in 1562. The population took refuge in a series of caves in the Colline St.-Eutrope behind the theatre, and constructed small houses and cabins in the theatre itself, some of them on the tiers of seating. Fortifications and watchtowers were also built, and the princes of Orange installed a prison in the western wings which was later put to infamous use during the French Revolution. Work began on clearing the theatre in 1834, and the reconstruction was completed by 1856.

Today Orange is an industrial and market garden centre and a strategic base for the French Air Force, who have been established at Caritat, east of the town, since 1936. Tourism has formed part of the economy since amateur historians started coming here in the 20th century to see two of the finest Roman monuments in Provence.

The first of these is the superb **Théâtre Antique► ► ►** (tel: 04 90 51 17 60; *open* Apr–Sep, daily 9–7; Oct–Mar, daily 9–6; guided tours in summer. *Admission: moderate* includes entry to the Musée Municipal). Considered to be one of the best preserved theatres in the Roman world, its main focus of interest is the impressive stage wall.

Standing 36m (118ft) high and measuring 103m (338ft) from end to end, the grandeur of the wall testifies to the important role that the theatre must have played in the lives of the citizens of the colony. Decorated with columns, marbles, statues and mosaics, it is said to have been described by Louis XIV as "the finest wall in my kingdom." Hidden passageways within the wall allowed the stagehands and actors to move about unseen, and the huge wooden stage was fitted out with traps so that actors and props could disappear and reappear at will. A statue of Augustus, reconstructed from fragments, dates from the 1st century and stands above the central "Royal door."

The semicircular auditorium (or *cavea*) is built into the slope of the St.-Eutrope hill and could hold up to 10,000 spectators, graded according to rank, as shown by the inscription found on one of the lower tiers "EQ. G III," or *Equus Gradus III*, "third row for knights."

Outside the main theatre, excavations have uncovered a number of other structures that may have been part of a forum or a temple complex.

The second important monument is the magnificent **Arc de Triomphe► ►**. Like its counterpart in Paris, it has also

FROM ORGIES TO OPERAS
Roman theatres were used for a wide variety of entertainments, including anything from circus performances to lottery competitions. Drama, however, was the main focus, with Roman comedies proving more popular than heavyweight Greek tragedies. In the Middle Ages mystery plays were performed, but it was not until the end of the 19th century that the theatre at Orange regained its prominence with the staging of a festival of choral music and opera that became known as the *Chorégies*. The festival (which traditionally features popular opera) continues today, with the addition of a repertoire of pop, jazz and classical music throughout the summer months (tel: 04 90 34 24 24; www.choregies.asso.fr).

been left stranded in the middle of a roundabout—in this case, on the N7 (which follows the route of the Via Agrippa from Arles to Lyons) just to the west of town.

Built about 20 BC to commemorate the Second Gallic Legion's victories, the triple archway is one of the oldest of its kind in existence and, despite the erosion of some features, one of the best preserved. The three arches are flanked by columns and echoed by the three horizontal planes, including the unusual double attic. On the north face of the arch the reliefs depicting captured trophies and Roman naval supremacy (prows of galleys, oars, anchors, and tridents) are easily visible, although you will need either binoculars or exceptional eyesight to interpret details of the battle scenes on the topmost attic, which is about 20m (65ft) from ground level. Originally topped off with a bronze chariot drawn by four horses, the archway was dedicated to Tiberius some time after it was built.

In the first-rate **Musée Municipal**▶▶ (*Open* Jun–Aug daily 9–7; Apr–May, Sep 9–6; Mar, Oct 9.30–5.30; Nov–Feb 9.30–4.30), the airy rooms on the ground floor trace the history of Orange and display fragments and friezes from the theatre. Old engravings and prints show the theatre before it was restored, neglected, overgrown and sprouting houses inside and around the periphery, many of them built from the stones of the theatre itself.

Outside the museum, the rue du Pontillac passes beneath an archway set in a large chunk of Roman wall that may once have encircled the forum. In the middle of town is the Romanesque **Cathédrale Notre-Dame**, with the grand **Hôtel de Ville** just next to it.

The best views of Orange are from the **Colline St.-Eutrope**, reached either by car or on foot. In front of the ruined foundations of a fortress there is an orientation table with views of the city and the Rhône valley beyond.

Roman legionnaires battle it out against the Celts in a detailed frieze on the Arc de Triomphe

▶▶ Pernes-les-Fontaines
44B2

Like its neighbour l'Isle-sur-la-Sorgue, 11km (7 miles) to the south, Pernes-les-Fontaines has achieved prominence thanks to the harnessing of water. In Pernes's case, the languid stream of the Nesque was channelled from the 15th century onwards into a series of fountains that today give the town its own particular appeal. There are now 36 in all, ranging from the ancient (**la fontaine Reboul**, over 400 years old) to the sublime (**la fontaine de Cormoran**, dating from 1761) to the ridiculous (**la fontaine Villeneuve**, built in 1952 and reputedly so hideous that moss has been allowed to grow all over it; only the old villagers can remember what's underneath).

Apart from the fountains, Pernes ("les-Fontaines" was added only in 1936) has one or two outstanding sights worthy of a stop. The first is the lovely 16th-century **Porte Notre-Dame**▶▶ which has a small chapel, **Notre-Dame-des-Graces**, built onto one of the piles of the bridge. Stepping down to the walkway beside the Nesque, you will discover a photogenic cameo of the bridge, the chapel and the keep framing the town's clock tower.

A visit to the interior of the **Tour Ferrande**▶▶ (accessible only on guided tours from the tourist office. *Admission: inexpensive*) is a must. Inside the tower is a series of frescoes depicting religious and historical scenes, thought to date from around 1285 (possibly the oldest in France), although their origins are a mystery.

The eroded cliffs of the Chausée des Géants (Giants' Causeway) display the many hues of the ochre upon which Roussillon was built

The Sentier des Ocres (Ochre Trail) at Roussillon passes through old mine workings and quarries

83

▶ Rasteau   44B3

The vineyards that slope downwards from the village produce a naturally sweet wine similar in taste to the Muscat wineries of the Beaumes-de-Venise. Rasteau is also one of the leading villages in the *Côtes du Rhône* appellation, with a famous wine route, the Route Orange, passing close by. The **Musée du Vigneron** (*Open* Jul–Aug, Mon, Wed–Sat 11–6; Apr–Jun and Sep daily 2–6. *Admission: inexpensive*), on the main road, also attracts visitors and there is a ruined 12th-century church.

▶▶▶ Roussillon   45C2

It is hard to walk around this photogenic hill village without obscuring someone's video lens or tripping over art students sketching in the streets and alleyways.

Roussillon owes its unusual aesthetic appeal to the many different shades of ochre (17 in all, we are told) that have been used as if from an artist's palette to tint the village houses in intense colours ranging from golden yellow to blood red. Of course the villagers didn't plan it that way; they simply used the nearest available materials—the ochre rocks that for many centuries formed the basis of an important mining industry here.

Ochre has been used for colouring since prehistoric times, and when the Romans occupied nearby *Apta Julia* they were quick to spot the potential of the extensive deposits around Roussillon. Commercial exploitation began in earnest in 1780, with ochre powders shipped all over the world from Marseille. At the beginning of the 20th century over a thousand people were employed here and nearly everyone in the village was an *ocrier*. The decline set in with the discovery of synthetic dyes and by 1930 the industry had all but collapsed.

Ochre was mined either in tall, underground galleries or in the open air. The underground galleries are now closed but you can visit the disused quarries of the **Sentier des Ocres**▶▶ (*Open* Mar to mid-Nov daily; mid-Nov to Feb Tue–Sun. *Admission: inexpensive*) with information boards.

▶ Rustrel   45C2

Rustrel shares a common heritage of ochre mining with nearby Roussillon. Today, the village's main claim to fame is its position as a starting point for exploring the old quarries on the southern side of the Doua valley, known as the **Colorado Provençal**▶ (see panel).

THE COLORADO WALK
To reach the ochre quarries, head back from Rustrel towards Apt and take the D22 to Gignac: Shortly you will see a signpost on the left for Colorado. From the main parking area there is a slightly confusing network of footpaths leading off through the woods, but just head away from the road and within a few minutes you will arrive at the quarries, a fantastic landscape of richly toned colours. Bear eastwards in order to reach the towering red pillars known as the *cheminées des fées* (chimneys of the fairies).

Lavender honey, scented sachets, essential oils and dried lavender are among the many products made from this aromatic plant on sale at a roadside stall near Sault

▶ Saignon 45C2

Way above the Calavon valley, Saignon is slung like a hammock between two rocks—the remains of an old castle on one and, on the other, the parish church. Approaching Saignon from the direction of Apt, it is easy to see why it has been a natural fortress since Celto-Ligurian times: The towering rocks on which the village is built would be enough to dissuade any attacker. Today it is a typically peaceful Provençal village with nothing more demanding of your attention than an old clock tower, a pretty square with a fountain in the middle and washing-troughs off to one side, and an unusually broad-beamed, 12th-century church.

▶ St.-Didier 44B2

Lined with plane trees, the main street in St.-Didier ends at a medieval gateway and church, behind which a small square leads into the **Château de Thézan▶**. This 15th-century building was converted in 1863 into a hydrotherapy centre, which today is renowned for the treatment of nervous diseases; it isn't open to the public but you can peek into the courtyard to see the Renaissance doorways and windows of the main facade.

The power of healing is also at the centre of the nearby **Hermitage of St.-Gens▶**, past the neighbouring village of le Beaucet on the D39 (see panel).

▶ St.-Saturnin-lès-Apt 45C2

Set on the southern slopes of the Vaucluse plateau, the village today is mostly known for its cherries, olive oil, asparagus, honey and truffles. Its violent past, however, is all too evident in the ruins of the 11th-century **château** that sprawls across the rocks above the village; at the top of these atmospheric ruins is a small Romanesque **chapel**, from where there are magnificent views across the surrounding countryside (the chapel itself is closed). Back down in the village, the remnants of past fortifications are evident in the **Portail Ayguier** (1420) and later additions such as the **Tour du Portalet**, the **Porte de Rome** and **Porte de Roque**.

ST.-GENS

On the right-hand side of the nave in the Hermitage of St.-Gens is the rock in which St.-Gens was apparently buried after his death, with numerous crutches and walking sticks propped up nearby as testimony to the efficacy of his miracles. Behind the hermitage a path leads up to a spring which St.-Gens caused to gush out of the rock. As he is the patron saint of farmers, a procession is held in his honour here every May.

►► Sault *45C3*

Set on a rock spur on the edge of the Vaucluse plateau, Sault, the ancient capital of the Comté de Sault, makes a good base for excursions to Mont Ventoux or the wilder corners of the Baronnies and Lure mountains to the north and northeast. Only vestiges remain of its château, but the *vieille ville* features several medieval and Renaissance houses. The parish church, dating from the 12th to 14th centuries, is remarkable for its barrel-vaulted nave supported by unusually slender columns.

The municipal museum, **Musée de Sault** (tel: 04 90 64 02 30; *open* Jul–Aug, Mon–Sat 3–6, otherwise by appointment. *Admission free*) contains prehistoric and Gallo-Roman artefacts as well as an Egyptian mummy. The **Maison de la Chasse et de l'Environment** (*Open* Wed–Mon. *Admission: inexpensive*) has exhibitions covering the flora and fauna of the Vaucluse and the role of hunting.

NEARBY South of Sault is the Plateau d'Albion, which houses a massive French Air Force base together with underground bunkers concealing the country's strategic nuclear missiles. From Sault to Carpentras the D942 runs westwards through the Gorges de la Nesque, a deep canyon that cuts through the calcareous rock of the Vaucluse plateau. Perhaps the most dramatic point is the 300m (985ft) high **Rocher du Cire** (the Wax Rock), 11km (7 miles) from Sault, inspiration for Mistral's epic poem *Calendau.*

COUNTRY TREATS
The products of the surrounding countryside play a prominent role in the economy of Sault. First, there are the rare mushrooms and truffles from the oak woods (*saltus*) that gave the village its name. Then there is nougat, a Provençal delicacy made here by the Boyer family for generations. Add to this lavender honey (a lavender festival is held here in August) and a highly regarded local *saucisson* (sausage), and you will realize why the Wednesday markets are patronized by people from far and wide.

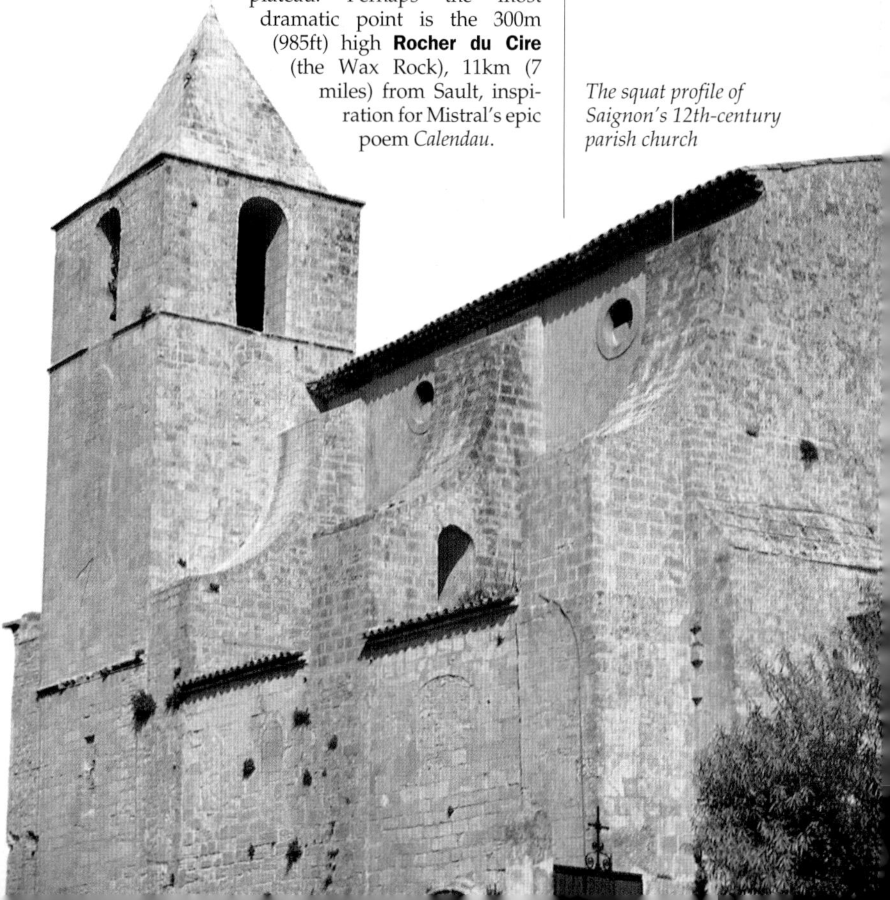

The squat profile of Saignon's 12th-century parish church

▶ ▶ **Séguret** 44B3

See page 73.

▶ **Sérignan-du-Comtat** 44A3

The principal attraction of this small village, 8km (5 miles) from Orange, is the **Museum National d'Histoire Naturelle Harmas de J-H Fabre**▶▶ (*Open* Mar–Oct Wed–Mon 10–12.30, 2.30–6). Jean-Henri Fabre was the son of a Languedoc peasant who rose to become one of the most eminent entomologists of the 19th century. Fabre's prodigious output of over 100 published works (which encompassed algebra, chemistry, astronomy and geology as well as entomology) includes the famous *Souvenirs Entomologiques*, which earned him the nickname of the "Virgil of Insects."

   When he bought a house on the outskirts of Sérignan-du-Comtat, he built a high wall around the garden and planted thousands of species of herbs and flowers, creating a botanical wilderness where he could study insects and plants to his heart's content. He christened it the *Harmas*, from the old Provençal word *herme*, meaning a plot of untended land. He lived here until his death in 1915 at the age of 92.

   Although Fabre was primarily an entomologist, a visit to the Harmas is about much more than just bugs and butterflies: On the ground floor, for instance, there is a selection from the 700 wonderfully delicate watercolours he painted of the fungi of the Vaucluse. Alongside editions of his published works (translated into more than a dozen languages) are letters from Mistral and Darwin, and his collection of coins. Upstairs in his study the glass cabinets that line the wall contain shells, fossils and minerals, while on top, his colossal herbarium of France and Corsica contains some 325,000 specimens. Fabre's minute desk, with his collecting satchel nearby, gives the

CAMUS AT LE THOR

Notre-Dame-du-Lac had a powerful effect on Albert Camus; the building's massive solidity conjured in his mind a bull at bay: "The bull sinks his four hooves into the sand of the arena. The church of Le Thor moves no more, by the force of stone: But reflected in the waters of the Sorgue this strength is purified, and becomes intelligence: It embraces the sky at the same time as anchoring itself in a bed of rocks near the stomach of the earth. On the Thor bridge I sometimes felt the fleeting taste of an unmerited happiness. Sky and earth were reconciled at that point." *La Postérité du Soleil*

THE LEGEND OF THOUZON

On the hill above the Grotte de Thouzon, there are the ruins of a medieval château, which featured in an endearing legend. In 1207 Count Raymond VI of Toulouse wished to marry his daughter off to a powerful neighbour, but instead she eloped with a penniless troubadour. The lovers sought refuge in the Thouzon château, and although Count Raymond sent his emissaries to capture and kill the hapless poet, every time they searched the castle the couple were nowhere to be found. A woman's silhouette was glimpsed at the ramparts but she always vanished at the first alarm, so the tale goes, disappearing down a secret passageway into the cave.

Harvest time in the vineyards surrounding Suze-la-Rousse

impression that he just stepped out yesterday.

The gardens, with home-made insect traps, are still much the same as Fabre left them and are best in April or May.

► Suze-la-Rousse   44A3

This village near Bollène has become the Provençal capital of wine studies thanks to the conversion of part of its 12th-century castle into the **Université du Vin** (*Open* daily, conferences permitting). The oenological institute runs courses on all aspects of wine, from marketing to tasting, mostly aimed at professionals. The huge library contains books on every subject related to wine.

House walls merge with quarry walls in the upper village of les Taillades

► les Taillades   44B1

It is worth a quick detour off the Apt–Cavaillon road to see the upper half of this village, a rather bizarre assemblage of rocks and houses that has arisen because the old village was built on top of a quarry. Park in the square next to the post office and walk up to the old church at the top, passing by the Théâtre des Carrières (summer performances) and a number of dwellings where it is difficult to distinguish between house and rock.

On the D31 in the modern village, there is a lovely paddlewheel on the Canal de Carpentras, which once powered a flour mill.

► le Thor   44B2

Apples and the white dessert grape Chasselas were once the traditional mainstays of this modest market town in the Sorgue valley. On the banks of the Sorgue is one of the most impressive Romanesque churches in the Comtat, **Notre-Dame-du-Lac►►** (see panel opposite).

Completed at the end of the 12th century, it marks the transition between the Romanesque and the Gothic, with the Gothic influence evident in the vaulting of the nave (one of the earliest examples of its kind in Provence). The west portal is finely detailed and shelters a wooden statue of the Virgin with what is locally described as a "Provençal haircut."

Surrounded by vineyards, the Université de Vin is housed in a 12th-century château

NEARBY Three kilometres (2 miles) north of le Thor, the **Grotte de Thouzon►►** (*Guided tours* Apr–Oct, daily; Nov and Mar, Sun afternoons; *closed* Dec–Feb. *Admission: moderate*) is one of the prettiest cave systems in Provence. Discovered in 1902 while a quarry was being excavated in the side of the Thouzon hill, its 230m (755ft) long gallery was almost immediately opened up to visitors. It is easy to walk on the reasonably level gallery where you can see near-perfect examples of fistulous stalactites or "macaronis," thin and transparent "draperies," and small internal pools called "gours."

►► la Tour-d'Aigues   45D1

See page 51.

87

The intensity of the Mediterranean sun beating down on the hillsides of Provence forces wild, aromatic herbs to increase their yield of essential oils, thus making them more pungent and more efficacious in the many herbal remedies and recipes for which the region is celebrated.

88

Herbs in all their various forms provide an aromatic souvenir of Provence

Shepherd sorcerers The Provençal shepherd has long been considered a kind of sorcerer, a plant magician who was thoroughly conversant with the wild herbs of the hills and their healing properties. He knew that the sap from marsh mallow was good for healing cuts, that the juice of snails could strengthen rotten nails. He would cure the wounded foot of a sheep by transferring the illness to a patch of turf, at sunset. His knowledge of plants, of where they were to be found and when they should be picked, was legendary.

Many country people in Provence still cure themselves with age-old remedies such as "red oil," which is made from the flowers of St. John's wort (hypericum) mixed with olive oil and used in the treatment of wounds and burns. Sage is a popular cure-all and is used for everything from hangover cures (in sage soup) to steam baths for acne.

Garlic is a well-known antiseptic (cut a clove in half and rub it on the skin as an antidote to bee stings) and useful for "cleansing the blood." It is also used as a remedy for corns, worms and warts. Thyme can be used to protect against respiratory infections and coughs; it is also supposedly an aphrodisiac.

Many of these cures are now being revived thanks to the current fashion for treatments such as herbalism, aromatherapy and other forms of natural healing.

The Plant Magic Man In the early 1970s the writer Lawrence Durrell was passing through Arles market when he came across a stall selling fresh herbs and herbal cures run by a local man called Ludo Chardenon. Driven to desperation by eczema, Durrell bought a herbal tea and was astonished when his painful condition cleared up in 10 days: the infusion had succeeded where the top doctors of London and Paris had failed.

Durrell befriended Ludo Chardenon, and wrote a feature on his life story for the *International Herald Tribune* in 1972, christening him "the Plant Magic Man." A decade later Durrell persuaded Chardenon to write a book of his recipes, which is still in print today: *In Praise of Wild Herbs—Remedies and Recipes from Old Provence* (Century Publishing) is a fascinating compendium containing cures for everything from acne to worms, covering

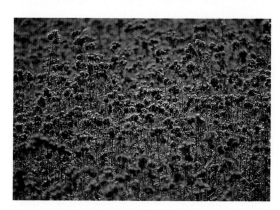

ageing, baldness, cellulite, obesity, rheumatism, stress and much more in between.

Lavender and lavandin The scent of lavender is one of the most characteristic aromas of Provence; rare is the souvenir shop that does not have bundles of scent bags stuffed with its fragrant flowers. The Romans treasured it for its soothing qualities, and added it to their baths (hence the name, from *lavare*, "to wash" in Latin). Today it is used in everything from soaps to expensive perfumes.

The main growing area for lavender in Provence is the so-called "mauve triangle" between Sault, Banon, and Séderon, which accounts for 46 percent of national lavender essence production (the other main growing area is on the other side of Mont Ventoux, north of Nyons in the *département* of the Drôme).

The first lavender distillery started up in the 1880s to supply lavender essence for the apothecaries of Apt and Carpentras. After World War I, systematic cultivation began in response to demands from the *parfumeurs* of Grasse and by 1929 there were 47 stills around Sault, producing 10,000kg (22,045 pounds) of essential lavender oil. Only a handful of distilleries now remain.

Most bouquets and other products that you buy in the shops are made using lavandin, a hybrid lavender that grows prolifically at low altitudes. The most highly scented and highly prized lavender is *lavande fine*, which grows at higher altitudes and carries its own *Appellation d'Origine Contrôlée* (AOC) like wine. Maps of *Les Routes de la Lavande* (see panel) are available from all local tourist offices for a self-guided tour of lavender-scented sights and scenery.

THE LAVENDER ROUTES
The official Lavender Routes guide details five suggested drives through lavender-growing areas from the Drôme to Mont Ventoux and the Montagne de Lure. The height of the lavender-growing season lasts from June through to August, and each route offers a selection of additional attractions along the way, such as picturesque villages, mountain scenery, vineyards and olive groves. For the fit, there are suggestions for cycle tours and there is a day-by-day calendar listing all sorts of stops along the route including botanical gardens, essential oil distilleries, farm shops and festivals.

The Roman legacy is highly visible in Vaison-la-Romaine

▶▶▶ Vaison-la-Romaine
44B3

Over the centuries, the inhabitants of Vaison have moved backwards and forwards between the two banks of the River Ouvèze. The first settlement was the Celtic stronghold on top of the hill when Vaison was the regional capital of the Voconces people. Conquered by the Romans in the 2nd century BC, the inhabitants moved down to the more fertile plains on the other side of the river and lived alongside the Romans in what then became Vasio Vocontiorum. Accorded the status of a federated city, the town prospered and its population grew to 10,000: Luxurious villas, a theatre, baths, an aqueduct and a bridge were constructed.

Vaison became a bishopric in the 4th century and the building of the cathedral began in the 6th century; the latter was one of the casualties of the Frankish invasions that devastated much of the town. In the 12th century Count Raymond of Toulouse built a castle on the site of the old Celtic fortress and gradually people moved away from the Roman town to the greater safety of the *Haute Ville*.

Vaison became part of the Comtat Venaissin in the 1300s, remaining papal property until the Revolution. In the 19th century the people of Vaison were on the move again, drifting back down to the left bank and leaving the *Haute Ville* to fall into ruins. As they started to rebuild the town they uncovered parts of the Roman town, although it was not until 1907 that excavations began in earnest.

Spread over an area of 13ha (32 acres), the **Roman ruins▶▶** (*Open* Jul–Aug daily 9–12.30, 2–6.45; Sep–Jun Mon–Sat 9–12, 2–5.45. *Admission: moderate;* joint ticket includes museum and cathedral cloister; see opposite), lie in two halves on either side of the place Abbé Sautel and the tourist office in the centre of town. To the east is the Quartier de Puymin, built around the base of a hill. On entering, you immediately find yourself in the middle of a huge villa, the Villa des Messii; next door is the Portique du Pompée, a public courtyard with gardens and a pool. Built into the north slope of the hill, the **theatre▶** held around 6,000 people and was probably constructed about the 1st century AD. Restored in the last century, it yielded several fine statues which are now in the **Musée Archéologique Théo Deplans▶▶**. Alongside superb mosaics and other important archaeological finds, some of the joys of the museum's collections are the small details from daily life, from dolphin doorknockers to domestic utensils.

On the other side of the road excavations are still going on in the Quartier de la Villasse. A Roman street leads down to the city baths and another huge villa. This has become known as the Maison au Buste d'Argent, after the silver bust of the owner which was found here, and includes mosaic floors and two gardens with pools. Next door is the Maison au Dauphin, also with private gardens and baths.

As you leave the Quartier de la Villasse at the exit next to the baths, a pathway alongside the excavations

*Vaison's colourful
market spreads over the
lower town every
Tuesday*

will take you to **Notre-Dame-de-Nazareth▶▶**, the former cathedral which many consider to be one of the finest Romanesque monuments in Provence. On the north side, there is a lovely 12th-century **cloister▶** (*Admission: inexpensive*), which has several finely carved pillars.

The two halves of Vaison are connected by a 17m (55ft) Roman bridge, from where a road leads up through a fortified gateway into the narrow streets of the **Haute Ville▶▶**. Many of its houses have been carefully restored and a handful of discreet craft shops and art galleries can be found among the cobbled streets and fountains. There are views back down to the town and across to Mont Ventoux from the ruins of the 12th-century château.

GOURMET DAYS
Every November, Vaison hosts *Les Journées Gourmandes*—"five days in the Provençal autumn dedicated to the most subtle of pleasures"— which brings together winemakers, restaurateurs, bakers, cheesemakers and growers in an extravaganza of eating and drinking. The best of local food and wines are displayed, tasted, discussed and simply enjoyed. Full details are available from the Maison du Tourisme et des Vins, place du Chanoine Sautel, 84110 Vaison-la-Romaine (tel: 04 90 36 02 11).

*The cobbled streets of
the* Haute Ville *lead
up to the ruins of an
old château*

Memorial to British cyclist Tommy Simpson, Mont Ventoux

PETIT-ST.-JEAN
Valréas is the setting for a spectacular and colourful festival on 23 June each year, when the town celebrates *La Nuit du Petit-St.-Jean*. Some 400 participants in full costume march through the streets by torchlight up to the Château de Simiane for the enthroning of "petit St.-Jean," represented by a four-year-old child who becomes the protector of Valréas for the following year. The spectacle dates back many centuries and was originally a pagan ceremony in honour of the Sun, Water and Fire, later to be transformed by the church into a summer solstice celebration.

▶ **Valréas** 44B4

Valréas sometimes appears with *"l'Enclave des Papes"* tacked on after its name, a description that harks back to when Pope Jean XXII acquired this territory with the aim of expanding the Comtat Venaissin northwards. Unfortunately, King Charles VII heard of this plan and forbade the sale of further land, leaving Valréas and the surrounding villages isolated. When the *départements* of France were created in the 18th century, Valréas opted to remain part of the Vaucluse (and hence part of Provence) even though it was then, as it is now, encircled by the *département* of the Drôme.

Valréas today is a pleasant town ringed by a boulevard of plane trees, its economy mostly dependent on the cardboard industry, which has spawned an unusual but surprisingly interesting packaging and printing museum, the **Musée du Cartonnage et de l'Imprimerie** (*Open* Apr–Oct Mon, Wed–Sat 10–12, 3–6; Nov–Mar Mon, Wed–Sat 10–12, 2–5, Sun 2–5. *Admission: moderate*), and the production of Côtes du Rhône wine, asparagus and lavender. Within the medieval town centre, the most imposing monument is the mainly 18th-century **Château de Simiane▶**, housing the town hall and contemporary art shows in the summer. There are several fine old mansions in Valréas, as well as the Romanesque church of **Notre-Dame-de-Nazareth▶**.

The village of **Richerenches**, 7km (4.5 miles) southeast, is famous for its Saturday truffle market (November–March).

An old fountain in the quiet streets of Venasque

▶ Venasque 44B2

Overlooking the Carpentras plain, Venasque is another village whose strategic position is immediately obvious: in this case, dominating the only route through the mountains between Carpentras and Apt. Occupied since Celtic times, it later became a refuge for the bishops of Carpentras during the barbarian invasions. For reasons unknown, this small village gave its name to the entire territory of the Comtat Venaissin.

Alongside this honour, it also possesses one of the oldest religious buildings in France, the **baptistery**▶▶ (*Open* Mon–Tue, Thu–Sat, and Sun afternoons. *Admission: inexpensive*) next to the church. Dating from around the 6th century AD, it may originally have been a pagan temple dedicated to Diana, Venus or Mercury. There are many curiosities inside: fragments of a sarcophagus dating from AD 420; the elegant columns that bear evidence of usage in Roman times; an octagonal font set in the floor; and a strange arrangement of holes bashed in the walls of the north apse, designed to improve the acoustics.

At the opposite end of the village is a huge medieval curtain wall with three turrets, which barred the entrance to this once formidable stronghold.

▶▶▶ Ventoux, Mont 45C3

The highest peak between the Pyrenees and the Alps, Mont Ventoux (literally the "windy mountain") dominates the Vaucluse plateau and the Rhône valley, marking the northern entrance to Provence.

From Malaucène the D974 winds up past **Notre-Dame du Groseau** (an octagonal chapel which is the only surviving part of a 12th-century monastery) and the **Source du Groseau**, a spring that the Romans channelled in an aqueduct to Vaison. As you continue to climb, the views become increasingly spectacular, and nearer the summit, the vegetation thins out until only rocks remain. Once at the top, turn your back on the radar towers and radio masts and soak up one of the most astounding views in Provence, extending from the Alps down to the Mediterranean.

Mont Ventoux was once covered in dense forests of oak, cedar and pine. By the beginning of the 19th century the forest had all but disappeared (cut down to build warships in Toulon), but in the late 1900s a reforestation scheme began, with extensive plantings of Austrian pine and cedar of Lebanon; these now provide a habitat for wild boar, deer and over 100 bird species including owls and rare eagles. Mont Ventoux is also home to 950 species of plants.

In 1990 a large part of the mountain was designated a UNESCO Biosphere Reserve and research into its unique flora and fauna continues today at the forest ecology laboratory in Malaucène.

CONQUERING MONT VENTOUX
The first recorded ascent of "the Provençal Giant" was by the poet Petrarch, who climbed it in 1336 with his brother. From the 18th century onwards there were many scientific expeditions, which led to the building of an observatory in 1882. Later, when a road was built, the steep climb became a proving ground for cars—a de Dion-Bouton made it in 2 hours 15 minutes in 1909—and bicycles. It is one of the most demanding stages of the Tour de France; a monument to British cyclist Tommy Simpson, who died on the way up in 1967, can be seen on the roadside.

93

The summit of Mont Ventoux

MOUNTAIN SPORTS
Many sporting activities take place on, and above, the slopes of Mont Ventoux, such as skiing, paragliding, and mountain biking; plus daytime and night-time walks (you reach the summit at dawn) in the summer from Malaucène tourist office (tel: 04 90 65 22 59).

With the exception of a few notable vineyards, wines from Provence used to be sniffed at by connoisseurs, but in recent years the quality has improved enormously, adding to the pleasures of the sunny south.

WINE TO GO

Walk into almost any *cave cooperative* and you can sample local wines and buy them direct by the bottle or case, usually at much better value than at other outlets. You can also buy your wine *en vrac* (in bulk), which is what most locals do. Simply turn up at the *cave*, pay at the cash desk, and your container is filled from a petrol-pump type nozzle from the vats below. You can buy old-fashioned *bonbons* (wicker-covered glass jars) in hardware stores or inexpensive plastic containers, which hold up to 33 litres (7 gallons) in the *cave* itself.

Although said to have been enjoyed by the kings of France in the 17th and 18th centuries, Provençal wines did not enjoy a glowing reputation in the 19th and early 20th centuries and many have only recently acquired the coveted AOC (*Appellation d'Origine Contrôlée*) status. Hugh Johnson's definitive *World Atlas of Wine*, published at the beginning of the 1970s, is typically dismissive: "An optimistic description of Provence wines always mentions the sun-baked pines, thyme and lavender and claims that the wine takes its character from them. This is true of some of the best of them…others get by on a pretty colour and a good deal of alcohol. 'Tarpaulin edged with lace' is a realistic summing up of one of the better ones."

However, in the last couple of decades the quality of Provençal wines has improved significantly and this is reflected in Johnson's more recent comments ("rock hills of limestone and shale, and in some cases a cool breeze off the sea, can give considerable distinction to certain eras"). You will certainly find plenty of reasonably priced, highly drinkable bottles on your travels.

In addition to the main appellations listed below there are numerous wines designated VDQS (*Vin Delimité de Qualité Supérieur*) which, while unlikely to be memorable, are at least good value. *Pichets* (carafes) of very quaffable Côtes-de-Luberon and Côtes-du-Ventoux are offered in most local resturants.

Côtes du Rhône Although not generally considered a Provençal wine, there are several Côtes du Rhône vineyards in the Vaucluse. Most are made from a blend of grape varieties, resulting in a robust, full-bodied flavour that develops considerably in depth and subtlety if left to mature, preferably for at least five or six years.

The *appellation* Côtes du Rhône Villages is much more restricted and produces a superior wine, more complex and firmer than the normal AOC. Within the area covered by this guide, the Côtes du Rhône Villages *appellations* come from Beaumes-de-Venise, Cairanne, Rasteau, Roaix, Sablet, Séguret, Valréas, and Visan. In addition, vintage wines (Grand Crus) are produced by Gigondas (rosé and red), Vacqueyras (red, white, and rosé), Rasteau

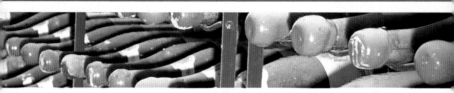

(Grenache sweet apéritif wine) and Beaumes-de-Venise (Muscat sweet apéritif wine).

The best-known wine from this area, right in the heart of the Côtes du Rhône district, is that of Châteauneuf-du-Pape (see page 69).

Bandol Covering some 1,300ha (3,200 acres), the territory of the AOC Bandol (one of the earliest in the region, designated in 1941) also encompasses neighbouring vineyards in Sanary, la Cadière, le Castellet and, to a lesser extent, le Beausset, Evenos, and Ollioules.

These fine wines owe their unusual characteristics to a high percentage of Mourvèdre grapes blended with Grenache and Cinsault varieties. The reds are made using up to 80 per cent of Mourvèdre grapes and are soft and dark, with undertones of spice, vanilla and blackberry. They keep exceptionally well—10 to 15 years for the reds.

Cassis The small area where AOC Cassis wines can be grown (covering just 200ha/495 acres) means that they can be pricey since output is limited. The calcareous soil around this little port produces a light, dry white with a freshness that seems to come from the sea.

Côtes-de-Provence Classified an AOC area in 1977, the Côtes-de-Provence specializes in those dry, fruity rosés that slip down all too easily on a hot summer's day when served well chilled. Seventy-five per cent of production is rosé, with just 20 per cent red and 5 per cent white. One very special wine to look out for here is the red from the tiny Palette district around Aix-en-Provence.

95

Vineyards in Provence are now producing some highly palatable wines

Bouches-du-Rhône

96

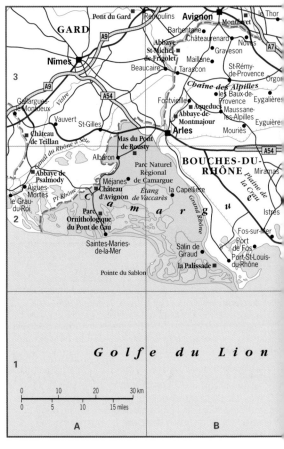

*The Espace Van Gogh in
Arles, a town that has
played a significant role
in the story of Provence
since the 6th century* BC

The Bouches-du-Rhône is one of the oldest inhabited regions in Provence, its roots reaching deep into history and tapping the sources of early civilization. It has some of the best monuments from Roman and medieval times and it was later the cradle of Provençal culture, the home of the troubadours, and the inspiration for great artists such as Cézanne and Van Gogh and writers such as Mistral and Marcel Pagnol.

Bordered by the Durance to the north and the Rhône to the west, the Bouches-du-Rhône is mostly low-lying (below 300m/985ft) although at Cap Canaille it has the highest cliffs in France. It is the most densely populated and heavily industrialized *département* in Provence and yet has more protected areas (covering over 200,000ha/494,200 acres) than any *département* in France.

MARSEILLE AND THE EAST The "capital" of the Bouches-du-Rhône is Marseille, the oldest city in Provence and nowadays almost as well known for organized crime as for its famous fish soup, the *bouillabaisse*.

Marseille's one million inhabitants live at the heart of an industrialized coastline that expands westwards around the nearby Étang de Berre, and yet within a short distance in the other direction there is a sublime

Bouches-du-Rhône

SHEEP ON THE GRANDE CRAU

Irrigated by canals, the plains of the Petite Crau yield crops in abundance. The Grande Crau, by contrast, is relatively barren, mostly comprising a vast sea of stones that was deposited by the Durance before it changed course to disgorge itself into the Rhône farther north. Between the stones, tufts of grass (known as *coussous*) support a large sheep population, which grazes here between mid-October and early June. In the summer, the sheep are taken to their Alpine pastures: This *transhumance*, as it is known, is now done by lorry, but the ancient procession is still celebrated in the *Fête de la Transhumance* in St.-Rémy-de-Provence.

coastline of pine-covered cliffs gashed by deep inlets, the famous *calanques*. Nestling beneath the cliffs is the port of Cassis, its streets crowded with gastronomic pilgrims in search of the renowned seafood and delicate white wines.

East of Marseille are the hilliest parts of the Bouches-du-Rhône, with the crest of the Massif de la Ste.-Baume marking the boundary with neighbouring Var. Beneath the wooded slopes of Ste.-Baume, the town of Aubagne is a major ceramics centre that produces, among other things, the small clay figures known as *santons* that are used in Christmas cribs.

Running parallel to the Ste.-Baume massif are the limestone ridges of the Montagne Ste.-Victoire, which dominate the landscape around Aix-en-Provence.

LA CRAU At the centre of the Bouches-du-Rhône is the vast plain known as la Grande Crau, or just la Crau, divided in two by the jagged peaks of the Chaîne des Alpilles, which culminates in a modest summit at la Caume (387m/1,230ft). To the north of the Alpilles are the fertile plains of the Petite Crau, where the abundant harvests of soft fruit and vegetables are well protected from the dreaded *mistral* by long rows of cypress and poplar. The man after whom the wind was named was born here in the small village of Maillane, and the legends and customs of the Petite Crau were some of the primary sources of inspiration for Frédéric Mistral.

Sheltering beneath the northern flank of the Alpilles is the delightful town of St.-Rémy-de-Provence, with the ancient ruined city of Glanum on the slopes above it. West of St.-Rémy, the Renaissance castle at Tarascon stands guard on the banks of the Rhône, symbol of the centuries-old mistrust between Provence and the Kingdom of France.

On the south face of the Alpilles the windswept heights of les Baux dominate the Grande Crau, stretching away down to the Rhône delta. Now drained, the Grande Crau was once swampland with settlements on isolated outcrops: One of these was the former Abbaye de Montmajour, whose ruins still dominate the surrounding countryside.

Bordering the Grande Crau, the lively town of Arles has more than its share of historic monuments, testimony to its role as the Roman capital of Provence. To the west, Nîmes shares much of the same heritage and is part of a popular Provençal "tourist triangle" that also includes Arles and Avignon, even though Nîmes itself is in the Languedoc-Roussillon region.

THE CAMARGUE Finally, there is the domain of flamingos, white horses, cowboys and bulls—not to mention mosquitoes—down in the Camargue, a marshy triangle of hazy sea and sky that has been created by the joint efforts of man and the mighty River Rhône.

MIGHTY BOUCHES-DU-RHÔNE
Of all the *départements* in Provence, the Bouches-du-Rhône has the highest population at 1.8 million, mostly accounted for by the two major cities, Marseille and Aix. It also has the highest proportion of farmland, sells the most fish, has the greatest number of industrial enterprises and the largest number of hotels and restaurants. However, at just over 5,000sq km (1,930sq miles), it is in fact smaller in size than either the Var or the Alpes de Haute-Provence.

99

One of the wonders of the Roman world, the Pont du Gard

The Tour de Constance rises above the impressive fortifications of Aigues-Mortes

THE TOUR DES BOURGUIGNONS
Alongside the canal at the southwest corner of Aigues-Mortes' fortifications is the Tour des Bourguignons, which gained its name after a gruesome incident during the Hundred Years' War. Thanks to the treachery of the town governor, the Bourguignons captured Aigues-Mortes in 1421 but the Royalist troops swiftly recaptured it, massacring hundreds in the process. There were so many corpses that they were all thrown into this tower and, in order to avoid an outbreak of the plague, covered in salt until they could be buried.

► ► ► **Aigues-Mortes**
96A2

The western half of the Camargue is dominated by the imposing fortified walls of Aigues-Mortes. Although it is actually in the *département* of the Gard and not the Bouches-du-Rhône, Aigues is an essential part of the tourist circuit around the delta.

In the 13th century the land around Aigues-Mortes was owned by the monks of the powerful Abbaye de Psalmody near by, but when Louis IX (St. Louis) began building a port here in 1241 they agreed to exchange their territories for the Château de Villevieille near Sommières. Louis IX was desperate for a French port on the Mediterranean, since the coast on either side was controlled by the Counts of Provence and the Kings of Aragon, and without this base he would have been unable to launch his long-dreamt-of crusades to the Holy Land.

By 1248, the port was complete and Louis IX and his 30,000 knights set off in an armada of 1,500 ships to liberate Jerusalem. This Seventh Crusade was a disaster for the king, but he survived and came home to prepare for the Eighth Crusade to North Africa. This time, Aigues-Mortes was to be his last glimpse of French soil, for he died of typhoid at the gates of Tunis in 1270.

Two years after the death of Louis IX, his successor Philip III began construction of the town's remarkable

ramparts, which took nearly 30 years to complete. The fortifications, which extend for over 1.5km (1 mile) around the town, contain no less than 15 towers and 10 gates and have been preserved almost entirely intact to this day. The reason for this is that Aigues-Mortes soon went into decline, left high and dry by the retreating waters in the middle of the 14th century. The unappealing name of Aigues-Mortes (which means "dead waters") was given to the port to distinguish it from the nearby town of Aigues-Vives ("living waters"), 20km (12.5 miles) farther to the north.

The most impressive of the towers is the massive **Tour de Constance**▶▶▶ (*Open* May–Aug daily 10–7; Sep–Apr daily 10–5.30; ticket office closed 1–2pm. *Admission: moderate*), which is reached via the Logis du Gouverneur, start point for a tour of the ramparts. The impregnable tower was soon put to use as a prison: Philippe le Bel imprisoned 45 Templars here in 1307, but its most notorious period was in the 17th century when hundreds of women, all of them Protestants rounded up in the Cévennes, were incarcerated in the tower in appalling conditions. One of these women, Marie Durand, was kept here for 38 years because she refused to renounce her faith (you can still see where she carved the one word *register*—"resist" in her local dialect—into the stone wall).

From the top of the 52m (170ft) high tower there is a terrific view across the town and the Camargue.

Unlike most medieval towns, Aigues-Mortes is laid out in a neat grid pattern with the streets converging on the tidy central square, **place St.-Louis**, where there is a statue of Louis IX by Pradier, commissioned in the 19th century to commemorate the Seventh and Eighth Crusades. On the corner of rue Jean-Jaurès is the attractive church of **Notre-Dame-des-Sablons**▶ (Our Lady of the Sands), where sunlight streaming through the modern stained-glass windows colours the simple, airy interior.

The town has a handful of hotels and restaurants, and in the latter you might like to try the local delicacy, *taureau à la gardienne*, which is a beef and olive stew.

SALT AND WINE TOURS
Aigues-Mortes is an important salt-production centre (rivalling the Salin de Giraud at the other extremity of the Camargue) and is famous for its local wine grown entirely in sandy vineyards, the *Vin du Listel*. Tours of both the wine cellars and salt pans are organized by the tourist office (reservations required, tel: 04 66 53 73 00).

101

Over half of French salt production comes from the Salins de Midi outside Aigues-Mortes

▶▶▶ Aix-en-Provence 97D2

Aix owes its origins and even its name to the thermal springs discovered here in pre-Roman times. A Celto-Ligurian tribe, the Salyens, built a fortified camp at Entremont (3km/2 miles north) around the 2nd or 3rd century BC, but their harassment of the local population led the Greeks of Massalia (Marseille) to turn to their allies in Rome for military might. In 124 BC Sextius Calvinus duly razed Entremont, and later set up his own camp (see page 30). Twenty years later 200,000 Teutoni barbarians arrived, to be defeated by the Roman general Marius. Montagne Ste.-Victoire was named after this great victory.

Under Roman rule, many monuments and aqueducts were built, later destroyed in the Dark Ages. During the 12th century Aix became the capital of the Counts of Provence and the university was founded in 1409. The town's golden age came under the reign of Good King René (1434–1480).

After René's death in 1480 Aix endured many centuries of plague, war and religious disputes before blossoming in the 17th century into a wealthy, bourgeois city with considerable political and cultural influence in the region.

The town declined somewhat from 1880 onwards, when regional power was transferred to Marseille.

102

Above and right: just two of Aix's many fountains

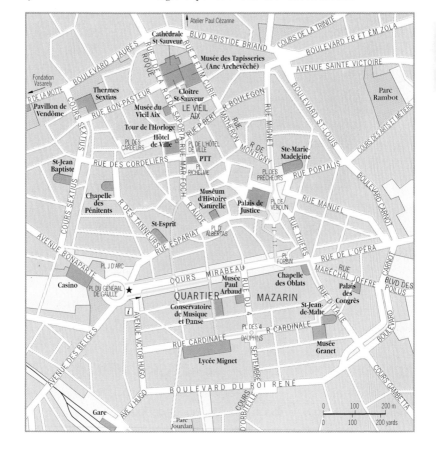

Walk

Fountains and fine mansions

This walk covers the best of Aix's fountains and fine mansions, as well as the contrasting areas of the Quartier Mazarin and the old quarter. Allow 2–3 hours. *See map opposite.*

From place Général de Gaulle walk up the right-hand side of the busy, café-lined cours Mirabeau.

Turn down rue Joseph Cabassol opposite the Fontaine des 9 canons. On your left farther down is the **Hôtel de Caumont**, built for the Marquis de Cabannes in the 18th century, now the Conservatoire de Musique et Danse. At the end of the road is the **Lycée Mignet**, once the Collège Bourbon.

Go left down the rue Cardinale to the **place des Quatres Dauphins▶**, which has a 17th-century dolphin fountain. Continue on (with a possible detour to the Musée Paul Arbaud in rue du 4-Septembre) to the place St.-Jean de Malte for the **Église St.-Jean-de-**

Malte and the Musée Granet (see page 105).

Turn left and left again back to the cours Mirabeau, briefly acknowledging King René before crossing the boulevard to see the old advertisement for the Chapellerie du Cours Mirabeau at No. 55, where Cézanne grew up in his father's hat shop.

Follow the small passageway beside the shop through to the place de Verdun, which is dominated by the 18th-century **Palais de Justice**. There is a regular flea market (*marché aux puces*) here and the neighbouring **place des Prêcheurs** has a food market on Tuesday, Thursday and Saturday mornings. Above the square is the **Église Ste.-Marie-Madeleine▶** with works by Rubens and Van Loo.

Continue up rue Mignet, which has several fine 18th-century buildings and the crumbling facade of the ancient Monastère de la Visitation. Turn left down rue Boulegon, continuing onto the **place de l'Hôtel de Ville** (see page 105). From here, either detour northwards up rue Gaston de Saporta towards the **Musée du Vieil Aix**, the **Musée des Tapisseries** and the **Cathédrale-St.-Sauveur** (see page 106), or return through the **Vieil Aix** backstreets to the cours Mirabeau.

104

Architectural details such as this wood carving enliven Aix's many belle époque mansions

Dried flowers make a colourful display in one of Vieil Aix's many street markets

WHAT TO SEE To feel the pulse of Aix take a preliminary stroll down the **cours Mirabeau►►**, a wide boulevard with a canopy of huge plane trees that shield the passersby from the sun as they flit from café to café, socializing and checking out everybody else's outfits and partners in what is essentially centre stage for smart Aixois society. Locals call it simply *le cours*. Apart from one or two bookshops, the north side is lined almost entirely by cafés and *pâtisseries*, with tempting ice creams, cakes and cocktails on offer, inviting you to sit and watch the parade. One of the most elegant cafés (with prices to match) is the *fin-de-siècle* **Les Deux Garçons**, with its interior a riot of gilded mirrors and antique lights. The more restrained south side of the boulevard is characterized by splendid 17th- and 18th-century mansions with facades of honey-coloured stone ornamented with fine wrought-iron balconies and carved doorways.

Running down the middle of the cours Mirabeau is a series of fountains, including the moss-covered **Fontaine Chaude** with bubbling hot spring water, and the **Fontaine du Roi René**. At the lower end, the roads from Avignon and Marseille meet at the roundabout (rotary) in place Général de Gaulle, with its spouting jets from the fountain of **La Rotonde**.

To the south of cours Mirabeau are the orderly streets of the **Quartier Mazarin►►**, created in 1646 by Michel Mazarin, archbishop of Aix, specifically for the lawyers and nobles attending parliament. At 2a rue du 4-Septembre is the **Musée Paul Arbaud** (*Open* Mon–Sat 2–5. *Admission: inexpensive*), which houses a fine collection of faience from Moustiers-Ste.-Marie and Marseille, works by Puget and Fragonard, sculptures and an enormous collection of manuscripts, rare editions and books on Provence. Once the home of collector and bibliophile Paul

Arbaud, the house itself is fairly remarkable, with hand-crafted ceilings and fireplaces, silk wallpaper and carved wooden doorways.

Nearby is the **Musée Granet▶▶** (*Open Wed–Mon 10–noon, 2–6. Admission: inexpensive*), devoted to art and archaeology. It reopened in 2007 after a major renovation which added a new group of modern works, some by Picasso, Kleee and Mondrian, to the collection of 18th- and 19th-century paintings. Cézanne is represented by eight paintings, donated in 1984 by the French government to remedy the total absence of his works in his native city. The archaeology museum displays finds from the ancient *oppidum* of Entremont. The Celto-Ligurian sculptures (unearthed in the 1940s) rank amongst the oldest known pre-Roman works in France and include some fascinating ritual masks, statues and torsos.

Next door to the museum is the 13th-century **church of St.-Jean-de-Malte**, with its elegant fortified Gothic facade.

The harmonious urban planning of the Quartier Mazarin seems a world away once you cross into the chaotic, busy streets of **Vieil Aix▶▶**, on the other side of the cours Mirabeau. Wander at a leisurely pace, stopping to admire the lovely old buildings or fountain-splashed *places* and soaking up the lively atmosphere of people milling around the markets, shops and restaurants.

At the centre of the old town is the **place de l'Hôtel de Ville**, which is at its best when filled with the colours and scents of the flower market on Tuesday, Thursday and Saturday mornings. The square was built in 1741 to create space in front of the classical Italianate **Hôtel de Ville▶**, which was rebuilt in the late 17th century by Pierre Pavillon. Tacked onto a corner of the town hall is the 16th-century **Tour de l'Horloge▶**, which has an astronomical clock as well as one defining the seasons. On the south side of the square, the old **Corn Exchange** (now the central post office) boasts a massive pediment statue by Chastel. Around the back, the **place Richelme** has a daily fruit and vegetable market and is one of the city's main hang-outs for buskers and students.

Old Aix has a variety of museums, including the **Musée des Tapisseries▶** (*Open Wed–Mon 10–6. Admission: inexpensive*) inside the grand old Archbishop's Palace. Most of the whimsical Beauvais tapestries were collected by archbishops in the 17th and 18th centuries; costumes from the opera festival are also featured.

Another fine old mansion, the Hôtel Boyer d'Eguilles, now contains the **Museum d'Histoire Naturelle** (*Open daily 10–noon, 1–5. Admission: inexpensive*), which has all the usual fossils and bones as well as an astronomy section, and a clutch of rare dinosaur eggs.

105

The whimsical Tour de l'Horloge, a landmark of Vieil Aix

THE GOOD KING RENÉ

René d'Anjou (1408–80) inherited the titles of Duke of Anjou, Duke of Lorraine, Count of Provence and King of Sicily, Naple and Jerusalem in 1434. During the first half of his reign he flitted between his various kingdoms, unsuccessfully playing at diplomacy and politics, until he settled in Aix in 1471 and devoted himself to patronage of the arts instead. He was a poet, musician, painter and linguist (he spoke six languages fluently). He introduced Muscat grapes and silkworms to Provence, but it was probably not the general populace who coined the term "Good King René" since he taxed them heavily to pay for his indulgences.

MIRABEAU'S MISFORTUNES

Later to achieve fame as a political leader during the Revolution, at the age of 23 the penniless Count Mirabeau decided to marry the aristocratic Émilie de Covet Marignane. Although his suit had already been rejected, he sneaked into her house, leaving his carriage outside the door for all to see in the morning. Her virtue compromised, the marriage had to take place but his father-in-law cut off the young couple's allowance. Mirabeau promptly ran up debts all over Aix and was imprisoned in the Château d'If. Once released, he eloped to Amsterdam with a married woman but was summoned back to Aix for the divorce case, which he lost.

An elegant door-knocker is just one detail on Pierre Puget's classic Hôtel de Ville

Just north of the Tour de l'Horloge in rue Gaston de Saporta you'll find the **Musée du Vieil Aix** (*Open* Oct–Mar Tue–Sun 10–12, 2–5; Apr–Sep, 10–12, 2.30–6. *Admission: inexpensive*) with an assortment of curiosities that includes a set of masks and mechanized marionettes portraying characters in the ancient *Fête-Dieu* ceremonies. This religious festival, once celebrated throughout Provence, was originally initiated in the 13th century by Pope Urban IV; King René revived it in the 15th century and turned it into a massive, popular procession with costumed groups and festivities lasting up to five days. The celebrations were abandoned after the Revolution, though several attempts were made to revive them.

At the top of the same street is the **Cathédrale-St.-Sauveur▶▶** (*Open* daily 9–12, 2–5) whose charm largely derives from its curious hotchpotch of styles from different periods. The west face, for example, combines a Romanesque doorway from the 12th century, a flamboyant Gothic facade from the early 16th century and a belfry from the 15th century. Inside, the 5th-century octagonal **baptistery▶** is one of the oldest in France; the Roman columns supporting a Renaissance cupola above the pool were originally part of a temple to Apollo which stood on this site.

The cathedral is full of art treasures, including a series of 16th-century tapestries originally woven for Canterbury cathedral, and Nicolas Froment's *Triptyque du Buisson*.

Just outside the old city centre on rue Célony is the **Pavillon de Vendôme▶** (*Open* Wed–Mon. *Admission: inexpensive*). Built in 1665 as a summer house, it was the last work of Pierre Pavillon and now houses collections of *grand siècle* furniture and art.

Cézanne in Aix

Paul Cézanne was a lonely genius, struggling for most of his life against the incomprehension, and often ridicule, of the public. Driven by an inner conviction, he remained aloof and unsociable, painting feverishly until the very end, intolerant of the bourgeois Aix society into which he was born.

Early years Born on 10 January 1839, Paul Cézanne received a classical schooling in Aix. His father, first a milliner and then a successful banker, made him study law, but it soon became clear that the young Cézanne preferred painting.

Parisian sojourn Cézanne went to live in Paris in 1862 at the urging of his friend Zola, and there he fell in with Monet, Sisley, Renoir, Manet and other young painters. He exhibited with the early Impressionists but their work met with derision and sarcasm.

Return to Aix Rebuffed, Cézanne took no further part in Impressionist exhibitions. He retreated to Aix, painting in solitude in his attic studio in the rue Boulegon or in the Provençal countryside, where his work took on a new richness that went beyond the analytical vision of Impressionism. His mastery of the underlying geometric structure of landscapes grew, and he returned repeatedly to the hilltop village of Gardanne, near Aix, as well as to the Jas de Bouffan and the banks of the Arc River.

Fame at last In the final decade of his life, from 1895 onwards, Cézanne completed over 300 paintings, many of which are among his masterpieces. It was only then that he began to achieve some recognition, although it was in Paris, Berlin and Vienna rather than Aix itself.

Final days When his mother died in 1897 Cézanne built himself a Provençal-style house, Les Lauves, on a hill above the cathedral: He painted in this studio from early morning onwards, stopping only for lunch before setting off to work on landscapes in the afternoon. In 1906, aged 67, he was still painting in the open countryside every day despite ill health and fatigue. On 15 October that year he was caught in a rainstorm and collapsed walking home. He died a few days later, on 22 October, from pneumonia.

IN THE FOOTSTEPS OF CÉZANNE
The Office du Tourisme in Aix (2 place Général de Gaulle; tel: 04 42 16 11 61) produces an excellent leaflet called *Sur les Pas de Cézanne*. The first part guides you step by step around locations within Aix where Cézanne lived, studied and worked. The second part describes a round tour in the environs of Aix to see the locations which he immortalized in his paintings, including the Arc valley, the Pont des Trois Sautets, and the views of Montagne Ste.-Victoire from the D17 (now the *Route Cézanne*).

107

Still life with apples, bottle and chairback, *1900–1906 (pencil and gouache)*

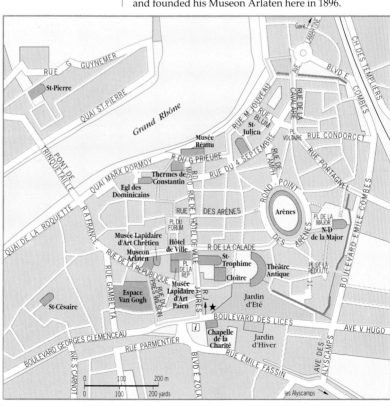

*Reliquaries in the Église
St.-Trophime, Arles*

▶▶▶ Arles

96B3

Strategically positioned at the northern tip of the Rhône
delta, Arles was the Roman capital of Provence, then an
important religious centre in the Middle Ages, and later
became a focal point for the Provençal renaissance of the
19th century. Today it is the unofficial capital of the
Camargue. First a Celto-Ligurian settlement on the banks
of the Rhône, just where the river divides into its Petit and
Grand branches, Arles became a major centre for trade
between the Greeks of Massalia (Marseille) and the inland
tribes in the 6th century BC. Its future was assured when
the town built a fleet of 12 boats to help Julius Caesar
conquer Marseille in 49 BC.

For five centuries the city thrived at the crossroads of
trade routes between Italy and Spain (the Domitian
Way) and between the Mediterranean and Northern
Gaul, and was a significant centre for the early Christian
church, hosting several major synods. Arles went into
decline from the 13th century onward, when it was overtaken in political and economic importance by Aix and
Marseille.

In the 19th century Arles re-emerged as a major focus
for Provençal folk traditions, furniture and crafts. Its
women, who still wore the distinctive Provençal costume,
inspired Daudet's famous play *L'Arlésienne* (1866), later
turned into an opera by Bizet. Frédéric Mistral (see pages
60–61) thought Arles the embodiment of old Provence
and founded his Museon Arlaten here in 1896.

Walk

Roman remains and ramparts

This walk will allow you to see most of Arles' major monuments in one circular route, as well as the remains of the Roman and medieval ramparts. Allow 3–4 hours. *See map opposite.*

From the boulevard des Lices head down rue Jean Jaurès to the place de la République. In the far corner, turn right up the rue de la Calade, past the *sous-préfecture* housed in a 17th-century mansion, to reach the Roman **Théâtre Antique** and, just past here, the **Arènes**.

After visiting the arena, climb the steps on the east side to the place de la Major, where there is a viewpoint next to the **Église Notre-Dame de la Major**. Built on the foundations of a palaeo-Christian sanctuary (itself built on top of a pagan temple dedicated to Cybele), the church has

elements from several different epochs and contains, inside, a wooden statue of St. Georges, patron saint of the *gardians* of the Camargue.

Head down rue Madeleine to place de la Redouté, where two round towers mark the old **Porte de la Redouté** (or Porte d'Auguste) in the Roman ramparts, where the Aurelian Way once led into the city.

Follow around the outside of the ramparts, turning in again down rue Portagnel, across place Voltaire, and down rue de la Cavalerie to the Porte de la Cavalerie. Walk through the gardens next to the remains of the medieval ramparts to reach the banks of the Rhône. Turn left and walk down the riverbank until you come to the **Musée Réattu** and the **Thermes de Constantin**.

Head up the sinuous rue du Sauvage, at the end of which is the **Hôtel d'Arlaten** and then the **place du Forum**.

Continue to walk up to rue de la Calade, turning right past the old lapidary museum, left around the corner to the **Museon Arlaten**, and then right down rue President Wilson back to the boulevard des Lices.

St.-Trophime cloister and tower

Cooling water flows from a streetside fountain

WHAT TO SEE Most of the sights in Arles are within 1sq km (0.4sq miles) of the city centre, which is bordered on one side by the Rhône and on the other by the **boulevard des Lices**. On Les Lices are the tourist office and several cafés in which to sit and watch the world go by (most enjoyable when the Saturday market is on).

At the heart of the town is the **place de la République▶** with its landmark obelisk (dug up in 1675, it was once part of the Roman forum). Facing the square is the **Église St.-Trophime▶▶▶** (*Open* daily. *Admission free*), one of the most glorious monuments to the Provençal–Romanesque style, built on the site of a 5th-century church during the 11th and 12th centuries. The most striking aspect of St.-Trophime is the great portal, a masterpiece of classical decoration possibly inspired by the triumphal arches of Glanum and Orange. Behind St.-Trophime is the equally famous and beautiful **cloister▶▶▶** (*Open* May–Sep daily 9–6.30; Oct, Mar–Apr daily 9–6; Nov–Feb daily 10–5. *Admission: inexpensive*).

On rue de la République the **Museon Arlaten▶▶** (*Open* Jun–Aug daily 9–1, 2–6.30; Apr–May, Sep daily 9.30–12.30, 2–6; Oct–Mar Tue–Sun 9.30–12.30, 2–5. *Admission: moderate*) focuses on traditional Provençal life, ranging from costumes and furniture to the

CONTEMPORARY FESTIVALS
Throughout the summer there are contemporary events and exhibitions in Arles, the most important of which are *Rencontre des Suds* in July (with a busy schedule of dance, drama, music and opera) and the renowned *Rencontres Internationales de la Photographie* (Aug), which features numerous photographic shows and workshops with top international photographers. Art exhibitions are held in the Espace Van Gogh, a multimedia centre installed in the former Hôtel-Dieu, where Van Gogh was treated after he cut off part of his own ear.

Alfresco eating is de rigueur *in the lively place du Forum*

Camarguais *gardians*. It was founded by Mistral in 1896.

Arles' social hub is the attractive **place du Forum▶**, with busy cafés and restaurants presided over by a statue of Mistral. Down towards the river is the 14th-century priory of the Knights of Malta, which now shelters the **Musée Réattu▶** (*Open* May–Sep daily 10–12, 2–7; Oct daily 10–12.30, 2–5.30. *Admission: moderate*). The museum houses a collection of 57 ink and crayon drawings by Picasso, which the artist donated in 1972 as a gift to the people of Arles because he had enjoyed the bullfights so much here.

Arles' star attraction is undoubtedly the amphitheatre, the **Arènes▶▶▶** (*Open* as cloister at Église St.-Trophime. Closed Oct–Apr 12–2. *Admission: inexpensive*), which was probably built around the end of the 1st century AD. It is only just bigger (by 3m/10ft) than the amphitheatre at Nîmes, although slightly less well preserved; the latter retains its attic. It was turned into a fortress during the Saracen invasions, and a village was later built inside the arena (which also happened at Nîmes). You can climb up one of the three remaining towers for a view over the arena and the city, with the Rhône in the background.

The **Théâtre Antique▶** (*Open* as cloister at Église St.-Trophime. Closed Oct–Apr 12–2. *Admission: inexpensive*), just to the south, was built during the reign of Augustus, but was pillaged for stone in the 5th century by Christians eager to build churches. Although a mere shadow of its former self, the theatre is still a suitably impressive venue for the annual *Fête du Costume* (dance and drama), which takes place in July. Between the theatre and the boulevard des Lices is the Jardin d'Été (*Open* daily) with its lovely cedars and a bust of Van Gogh.

Another Roman monument, which merely hints at past glories, is the **Thermes de Constantin▶** (*Open* as cloister at Église St.-Trophime. Closed Oct–Apr 12–2. *Admission: inexpensive*), near the riverfront. This huge bathhouse is the largest in Provence and once formed part of Constantine's palace on the waterfront.

The Roman cemetery in Arles was at the **Alyscamps▶** (*Open* as cloister at Église St.-Trophime. *Admission: moderate*), to the southeast of the town centre. Many of the hundreds of elaborately carved sarcophagi were given away to visiting nobles in the 16th century, and the huge necropolis was carved up by railway lines and workshop buildings in the 19th century. The 12th-century **Église St.-Honorat▶** is the only one left of 19 chapels that once studded the Alyscamps.

The old Pagan and Christian art museums have now been combined into the excellent **Musée de l'Arles Antique▶▶** (*Open* Mar–Oct, daily 9–7; Nov–Feb, daily 10–5. *Admission: moderate*) on the Presqu' île de Cirque Romain. Housed in a superb modern building, the museum offers an evocative insight into the prehistory of the region and Roman Arles, with scale models of all the town's major monuments as they once were.

TRADITIONAL FESTIVALS
Arles has a lively calendar of traditional festivals including the *Feria Pascale* at Easter which marks the beginning of the bullfight season, the *Fête des Gardians* in May with the Camargue "cowboys" parading on horseback through the streets, and the *Fête d'Arles* in late June, with torchlight processions where everybody wears local costume. Another festival, revived at the beginning of the 1980s, is the *Fêtes des Prémices du Riz,* which takes place in September to celebrate the rice harvest from the Camargue.

111

The Hôtel de Ville overlooks Arles' place de la République

BILLET GLOBAL
If you are planning to visit several of the monuments and museums in Arles, buy a *billet global* (global ticket) from the tourist office or any participating site. The tourist office organizes various themed walking tours throughout the summer.

Alongside Cézanne (see page 107), Van Gogh is another towering genius whose work will forever be linked with the light-filled landscapes of Provence and the brilliance of the southern skies.

112

Self-Portrait with Bandaged Ear, *one of two self-portraits painted by Van Gogh early in 1889 while convalescing in Arles after cutting off a piece of his right ear*

Arrival in Arles Van Gogh took up painting at the age of 27, having previously been an art dealer, a teacher and an evangelical preacher. He moved to Paris in 1886, where he fell under the spell of the Impressionists. He moved to Arles in 1888 and, although he wrote that the town had "a worn and sickly look" about it, he nonetheless stayed, captivated by the vivid colours around him. The artist mostly lived on place Lamartine, where he rented a cheap room opposite the Café de l'Alcazar, which he painted as the *Café de Nuit.* He also painted *La Maison Jaune* and the famous drawbridge of the *Pont de Langlois* (few of the locations he painted remain today).

Confrontation with Gauguin Van Gogh dreamed of setting up an artists' colony in Arles, and implored Gauguin to come down and join him. This Gauguin eventually did, but he hated Arles. Van Gogh's dreams were shattered: He threatened Gauguin with an open razor. Later, in a fit of remorse, Van Gogh went home and cut off part of his left ear, which he gave to a prostitute. Gauguin took the first train back to Paris.

Move to St.-Rémy Van Gogh was hospitalized in the Hôtel-Dieu but the townspeople petitioned the mayor to get rid of him. He finally left of his own accord in May 1889, checking in as a voluntary patient at the sanatorium of St.-Paul-de-Mausole in St.-Rémy. While there he worked feverishly, producing over 100 drawings and 150 canvases, including some of his most famous paintings such as *Les Blès Jaunes* and *Les Oliviers.*

Final days A year later Van Gogh left the sanatorium (supposedly "completely cured") and went to stay in Auvers near Paris; he had convinced himself that the southern sunshine was contributing to the agony of his mental illness. After only two months in Auvers, in July 1890, he shot himself, and died two days later.

▶ Aubagne 97D1

Once a small market town for fruit and vegetables grown in the surrounding Huveaune valley, Aubagne is now effectively a suburb of Marseille, surrounded by *autoroutes*, industrial zones and home of the French Foreign Legion. It is also the birthplace of Marcel Pagnol, who set many of his works in the town and surrounding countryside. Characters from his books have been made into *santons*, which are displayed in **Le Petit Monde de Marcel Pagnol** (*Open* daily) next to the tourist office, and the town is well-known for its *santonniers* and ceramicists (see panel) whose workshops are found in the tightly knit streets of the *vieille ville*.

▶ Barbentane 96B3

Barbentane's main attraction is the classic **Château de Barbentane▶▶** (*Open* Jul–Aug, daily 10–noon, 2–6; Easter–Jun, Sep–Oct, Thu–Tue. *Admission: moderate*). Founded by the Marquis of Barbentane in 1674 and finished over a hundred years later, its style owes much to the great châteaux of the Île de France. The house is still occupied by the Barbentane family and its rich furnishings are the result of over 400 years of antique collecting. The interior, which is often used for magazine shoots, is dripping with 18th-century tapestries, Aubusson carpets, porcelain, statues, chandeliers and priceless furniture. On the outskirts of Barbentane is the **Parc Floral Provence Orchidées** (*Open* Mar–Nov, daily. *Admission: moderate*), which has an "exotic garden" with tropical plants, orchids and butterflies.

NEARBY On the D35E, 5km (3 miles) south of Barbentane, is the **Abbaye St.-Michel-de-Frigolet▶▶** (*Open* daily for guided tours 7–12, 1.30–6. *Admission moderate*), established by monks from Montmajour. Surrounded by hillsides of fragrant herbs, the abbey got its name from the Provençal word for thyme, *ferigoulo*. This is one of the ingredients in the monks' liqueur, **Le Frigolet**, which you can buy in the abbey shop. In the 11th-century **chapel of Notre-Dame-du-Bon-Remède** the sumptuous gilt panels were donated by Anne of Austria, who came here in 1632 to pray for a son; in 1638 she gave birth to Louis XIV.

POT LUCK
Aubagne is a major production centre for traditional Provençal ceramics, which have been made here since the 16th century. Local potters specialize in *santons* and beautiful decorative pots, vases, plates and so on, which can be bought from artisans' shops in the old town or during the annual fairs of ceramics and *santons* in July and August, and *santons* in December. Every two years, in summer, Aubagne hosts France's largest ceramics fair, the *Argilla* (from the Latin for clay, *argile*). Every other December over 50 artisans specializing in *santons* gather for the *Biennale de l'Art Santonnier*.

113

Untouched during the Revolution, the Château de Barbentane has been lived in by the Barbentane family for over 300 years

RED "BAUXITE" ROCKS
In 1821, geologists discovered that the red rock from the hills surrounding les Baux could be smelted to create aluminium. They christened it bauxite in honour of the village.

▶▶▶ **les Baux-de-Provence**   96B3

On the D27, 19km (12 miles) northeast of Arles

Les Baux is one of the classic sights of Provence, a powerful evocation of the feudal dynasties that once ruled the country. It is also a classic case of tourist over-crowding, with over 1 million annual visitors; come out of season if you can.

Perched on a barren rock plateau jutting out southwards from the Alpilles chain, les Baux had been a stronghold since Ligurian times, but it first achieved notoriety in the 10th century when it became the power base for the ambitious *seigneurs* of Baux, who claimed to be descended from Balthazar of Bethlehem, one of the three kings who attended Christ's Nativity. They put the Star of Bethlehem on their coat of arms and waged war incessantly, eventually gaining control over 79 surrounding towns and villages, secure in the knowledge that their eagles' eyrie at les Baux was impregnable.

The last of this troubled family was the Princess Alix of Baux, and on her death in 1426 les Baux became the property of the Count of Provence, Louis III d'Anjou. Later, King René gave it to his second wife, Jeanne de Laval, and a temporary peace reigned, until les Baux became a Protestant stronghold under the Manville family, and more troubles beset the fiefdom during the Wars of Religion. They then made the fatal mistake of siding with the Duke d'Orleans in a rebellion against Louis XIII in 1632, who retaliated by besieging the citadel.

Tired of their bothersome overlords (and partly prompted by Cardinal Richelieu), the inhabitants of les Baux asked Louis XIII to demolish the citadel and the castle and ramparts were pulled down in 1633.

For nearly two centuries les Baux became a ghost town until the 1940s, when Raymond Thuilier opened his famous hostelry, L'Oustaù de Baumanière, which attracted celebrities and politicians. Gradually the forgotten village was restored and the tourist trickle turned into a torrent, engulfing les Baux in souvenir shops, *crêperies*, art galleries, ice cream parlours and boutiques.

If you can stand this overload there are some interesting places to visit within the village, such as the 16th-century **Hôtel de Manville▶**, which now houses the town hall, just across from the tourist office (tel: 04 90 54 34 39), and is arranged around a beautiful Renaissance courtyard.

TROUBADOURS
Despite their warring habits, some of the *seigneurs* of Baux were fond of more refined pastimes. In the 13th century their citadel became famous for its court, with troubadours visiting from far and wide to compose passionate odes to the daughters of Baux.

The cafés and souvenir shops in this once-deserted village are, in the high season, packed with visitors

On the other side of the village, on place l'Église, is the **Église St.-Vincent►**, which was partly hewn out of the rock in the 12th century. On Christmas Eve the famous pastoral festival (see panel) takes place here. Across the square is the 17th-century **Chapelle des Penitents Blancs**, decorated by Yves Brayer in 1974.

Rue du Château leads through the middle of the village to the **Château►►** (*Open* Mar–Oct, daily 9–6.30, to 8 in Jun–Aug; Nov and Feb, daily 9–6, Dec–Jan daily 9–5. *Admission: moderate*), where the **Musée d'Histoire des Baux** is laid out inside the Hôtel de la Tour du Brau. Strewn across the arid plateau there are about a dozen buildings still standing, interspersed by an assortment of reconstructions of medieval siege machines. A map directs you around the sites, including the 13th-century *donjon*, an olive museum, a chapel and a pigeon house cut out of the rock. The views are fantastic.

To the north of les Baux is a valley, the **Val d'Enfer** (the Valley of Hell) which leads into the Alpilles. Its tortured-looking rock formations were supposedly the inspiration for Dante's *Inferno*. Jean Cocteau shot scenes from *Orphée* in the deserted quarries here in 1950 and one of these huge underground caverns has now been converted into the extraordinary **Cathédrale d'Images►►** (*Open* Mar–Sep, daily 10–7; Oct to early Jan daily 10–6. *Closed* mid-Jan to Mar. *Admission: moderate*). Thirty-five projectors beam powerful, themed images across the vast space within the enclosed quarry.

CHRISTMAS FESTIVITIES
In a chapel on the right-hand side of the Église St.-Vincent is the *charette de l'agneau* (lamb's cart), which plays a key role in the *fête du pastrage* on Christmas Eve, in a tradition dating back to the 16th century. During midnight mass, an angel hidden behind the altar announces the Nativity to shepherds at the back of the church. The shepherds come forward, dancing and singing traditional Christmas songs, accompanied by shepherdesses with flowers and fruits strung about them. They are followed by the chariot bearing a new-born lamb.

115

Les Baux is perched romantically on a rocky outcrop

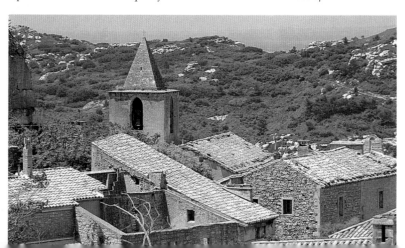

A DUCK TRAP
Duck-hunting is big business in the Camargue, and many of the large estates have flooded huge areas to create freshwater marshes. The movement of the ducks, morning and evening, between the salt-water marshes in the reserve (where they rest in the daytime) and the private freshwater marshes (where they feed at night) makes them easy pickings for hunts-men. This is causing prob-lems not only because of excessive hunting, but also because over a period of years the shot used is killing other aquatic birds through lead poisoning.

▶▶▶ The Camargue　　96B2

Approaching the Camargue from Marseille, the road skirts the Étang de Berre and passes through the industrial nightmare of the Port de Fos complex, a wasteland of oil terminals, cranes and chimneys, criss-crossed by a web of roads, railway lines and electricity pylons.

Then all of a sudden, once you have crossed the Rhône on the Bac de Barcarin ferry, a transformation takes place: Here are groups of pink flamingos elegantly picking their way through the shallow lagoons in search of food, while birds of prey stand sentinel on the fence posts by the road-side. The space around you seems infinite as the horizons of the marshes, lagoons and the sea stretch away into the distance. The silence is almost total apart from the honk-ing of geese as they migrate in ever-changing, fluttering ribbons across the open sky.

All the more extraordinary for its proximity to indus-trial civilization, the Camargue is a rich tapestry of many different ecosystems, a haven for wildlife and a joy for anyone seeking tranquillity or long, wild walks amid its watery landscapes.

The Camargue is a vast delta formed by the two branches of the Rhône (the Grand Rhône to the east and the Petit Rhône to the west) where they meet the sea. In the Middle Ages communities of monks settled on the edge of this swamp to collect valuable salt and reclaim the land, but by the 17th century they had been replaced by ranchers, whose primary purpose was the raising of the

The neat little cabanes that dot the Camargue were the traditional homes of the gardians

famous white horses and the black, longhorn bulls that thrive on the saline pastures. Sheep were also grazed here in the winter, before being moved up to Alpine pastures during the annual *transhumance*. It may appear to be a wilderness but in fact it is an environment shaped by

An avenue of plane trees shades a quiet Camargue back road

FLOODED
The vulnerability of the Camargue was highlighted in 1993 when the Rhône burst its banks and flooded some 12,000ha (4,940 acres) of the delta; over 5,000 bulls, horses and sheep were evacuated by helicopter and lorry while frantic efforts were made to fill the breaches in the dike. A vast amount of fresh water flooded into the system, altering the salinity of the lagoons and marshes dramatically. Many mammals died. Although floods have occurred previously (principally in 1960 and 1978) they have never caused such a sudden change in salinity, resulting in possible long-term damage to the entire ecosystem.

human activities with several overlapping zones. The conflict between different users of the Camargue is graphically illustrated by the problem of duck-hunting (see panel opposite).

The whole of the delta is part of the Parc Naturel Régional de Camargue, created in 1970, which covers 86,300ha (213,250 acres) and aims to achieve a balance between traditional activities, the interests of local inhabitants and nature conservation. At the core of the park the most sensitive areas have been classified as nature reserves; the most important is the Réserve Nationale Zoologique et Botanique de Camargue, covering 13,500ha (33,360 acres) around the Étang de Vaccarès.

On average, visitors spend less than half a day in the Camargue and in this time you can only see the "postcard Camargue," the bulls, horses and flamingos. To appreciate it fully, you have to put in some effort; walk, rent a bicycle, ride a horse or go on safari to get the most from this wonderful region.

The hardy horses of the Camargue are well adapted to the salty marshlands

ROSY PINK FLAMINGOS
The most spectacular and photogenic of the delta's residents are the flamingos, one of the three "icons" of the Camargue (bulls and horses are the other two). These beautiful birds are easily seen at any time of year, although the greatest numbers (up to 50,000) are present during the spring and summer. Most migrate to Africa or Spain for the winter, but around 5,000 to 6,000 stay on. During March and April their pink plumage is shown off to best effect in spectacular courtship displays. Flamingos feed mostly on small invertebrates, and have been known to live for up to 34 years.

DOS AND DON'TS
Not all wildlife in the Camargue is as charming as the flamingos: The mosquitoes, for instance, are voracious and ever-present; they breed prolifically in the marshes. Never venture out without adequate protection, except perhaps on windy days in winter when you should be OK. The wind (specifically the all-powerful *mistral*) can also be a hazard if you are cycling or walking long distances. Lastly, don't go marching off down the beaches or the *digue-à-la-mer* without an adequate supply of water.

WHAT TO SEE Apart from **Arles** (see page 108), which is within easy reach of the Camargue, the main accommodation and tourist centres are at **les Saintes-Maries-de-la-Mer** (see page 141) and **Aigues-Mortes** (see page 100). From les Saintes-Maries you can hike part or all of the way along the *digue-à-la-mer*, a sea wall that divides the unspoiled beaches and lagoons around the southern perimeter of the Étang de Vaccarès. The reserve of the Étang de Vaccarès itself is open only to visitors with a special permit, but you can still find many vantage points on the surrounding roads (principally the D37), from where you can watch birdlife.

The reserve headquarters are on the eastern side of the Étang de Vaccarès, where the **Centre d'Information Nature▶▶▶** (tel: 04 90 97 00 97. *Open* Apr–Sep, daily 9–1, 2–6; Oct–May, Wed–Mon 9–1, 2–5. *Admission: inexpensive*) at **la Capelière** has one of the best and most up-to-date displays on the Camargue. There are three observatories close to the Centre and a 1.5km (1 mile) walking trail.

Continuing on past la Capelière, you will arrive at **Salin de Giraud**, a quaint town that was created at the turn of the 20th century by a Belgian company to house factory workers: hence the neat streets, shaded by plane trees and acacias, which are laid out in a strict grid pattern. Most of the employment now is with the Salins du Midi, who manufacture salt in the massive lagoons south of town: After the "harvest" in late summer the huge salt mounds are a startling sight, gleaming in the sun and lining the edge of the lagoons in long, serried ranks. There is a viewpoint just off the D36D south of Salin de Giraud for an overview of this rather unusual production process.

Farther down the same road is **la Palissade▶** (*Open* daily. Closed Nov–Feb Mon–Tue). *Admission: inexpensive*). This former private hunting estate was bought by a private conservation group in 1976 and is unusual in that it is one of the few areas in the Camargue not controlled by dikes. The waters of the Rhône mix with sea water in the lagoons, giving rise to fauna and flora typical of the lower Camargue before it was altered. Inside la Palissade are audio-visual displays, a herbarium and an aquarium. Walking trails criss-cross the 702ha (1,735-acre) estate, with guided tours on request (tel: 04 42 86 81 28).

Back on the west side of the Étang de Vaccarès there are two more observation points on the edge of the reserve. The **Centre d'Information Ginès▶▶** (*Open* Apr–Sep daily; Oct–Mar Sat–Thu), 4km (2.5 miles) north of **les Saintes-Maries-de-la-Mer**, has environmental displays, including a 15-minute video, and huge plate-glass viewing windows. To get in close to the birdlife, go to the **Parc Ornithologique du Pont de Gau▶▶** (*Open* daily until dusk. *Admission: moderate*), nearby, which has signposted trails around the Étang de Pont de Gau (a half-hour walk), or the more extensive Étang de Ginès sanctuary, where bulls graze in the summer. Large aviaries near the entrance to the park house predators such as buzzards, black kites, Egyptian vultures and eagle owls. The bird park also looks after injured predators sent here from all over Europe.

If you've overdosed on avian antics, you could visit the **Château d'Avignon▶** (tel: 04 90 97 58 60. *Guided tours* Apr–Oct, Wed–Mon. *Admission: inexpensive*), 13km (8 miles) north of les Saintes-Maries, an 18th-century mansion converted into a luxurious hunting lodge by the Marseille industrialist Louis Prat-Noilly in the 19th century. The interior has fine Gobelins and Aubusson tapestries as well as paintings and carved woodwork.

Dotted about the countryside you will see many vast farmhouses (or *mas*), often surrounded by trees and nearly always built with their backs to the biting north-westerly *mistral*. Many of the *mas* were originally owned by wealthy Arlesians and managed on their behalf by a *bayle* (steward), while the *gardians* had their own traditional homes, little *cabanes* with thatched roofs that you can also see by the roadsides.

The *gardians* were at the heart of the romantic image of the Camargue conjured up by Mistral and the Félibrige, and they still play a major part in the Provençal tradition of the *cocardes* (see page 132), travelling from village to village throughout the summer with their bulls and horses.

A good introduction to the traditions of the Camargue is the inspirational **Musée Camarguais▶▶** (*Open* Apr–Sep, daily; Oct–Mar, Wed–Mon. *Admission: moderate*), in an old barn at the Mas du Pont de Rousty, which was until recently a working sheep and cattle ranch. As well as exhibits on the geology and history of the Camargue there are sections on the *gardians* and farmhouse life in the last century. The 3.5km (2 mile) walking trail crosses pastures and the swamps of the Marais de la Grand Mar.

To see the *gardians* in action you can head down to the **Domaine de Méjanes▶** 4km (2.5 miles) south of Albaron on the D37. This ranching spread is an offshoot of the Paul Ricard *pastis* empire and has been turned into a popular entertainment centre with bullfights and *ferrades* in the stadium, horse-rides and even a *petit train* that does a 20-minute circuit of the marshes. There are various events throughout the year and *spectacles taurins* (bull-baiting) daily in summer (tel: 04 90 97 10 10).

Jeep safaris of the Camargue and boat tours of the canals operate from les Saintes-Maries-de-la-Mer, or you can hire mountain bicycles or go horse-riding.

SAVED BY TOURISM
You still sometimes see old graffiti that proclaims *"tourisme—mort au Camargue"* ("tourism—death to the Camargue"), but it is now recognized not only that tourism brings economic benefits but also that it does not have a detrimental effect on the birdlife. In fact, park managers say the ducks have learnt that landing near a tourist coach is the safest option. Those ducks that don't learn this quickly are likely to be shot dead by hunters outside the reserve.

119

Looking towards the Camargue from the bell tower of the church in the centre of les Saintes-Maries-de-la-Mer

The marshes, canals and lagoons of the Camargue delta provide a wide diversity of habitats for an enormous number of wildlife species, including the greatest variety of aquatic birds (some 400 different species) found in one place in the Mediterranean.

THREATENED DUNES
The beaches and sand dunes are one of the most threatened areas in the Camargue, partly due to rising sea levels and partly because the Rhône has too many dams on it and no longer carries enough silt downstream to replenish the delta. Dikes and sea groynes have had to be built to protect the beach, and wooden fencing erected to stop the dunes disappearing.

120

Salty zones Starting at the coast, the first and most obvious ecosystem encompasses the beaches and sand dunes. In the winter months, rainwater accumulates beneath the surface of the dunes and nourishes spring plants such as perfumed *Helichrysum* and sea wormwood, elegant sand lilies and delicate sea rocket and sea stock. Once the supply of water is exhausted other species appear that are better adapted to survive the summer heat, such as sea holly and sea spurge.

Also on the coast are the salt pans, centre of a vast salt-production industry since the 19th century. Sea water is pumped across a series of lagoons between April and September, gradually increasing in density until it finally reaches the settling beds completely saturated with salt. Between August and October the salt starts to crystallize and it is then raked up into giant mounds (known as *camelles*) over 20m (65ft) high before being washed, dried and crushed.

The constant water levels of the salt pans throughout the summer months, as well as the wealth of

Eagle owl nestlings—rarely seen but part of the prolific birdlife here

invertebrates living there, make them very attractive to colonies of flamingos, terns and black-headed gulls, as well as solitary species such as the oystercatcher, shelduck and redshank.

The third type of habitat in the lower half of the Camargue is the *sansouire*, huge, flat expanses of

saltmarsh between the sea and the lagoons covered in scrubby vegetation: Flooded in winter, they become mudflats in the spring and autumn and a salty desert in the summer. These wide open spaces are typical of the Camargue, their role changing with the seasons. On the higher ground of the *sansouire*, where only sea lavender and glasswort can survive the changing water levels, skylarks thrive all year round. When it is flooded in winter, tens of thousands of duck use the *sansouire* as a daytime resting place. From February onwards the water level drops and thousands of waders stop here on their long journey from northern Europe down to Africa.

In the summer months, herds of cattle and horses, no longer free to roam, graze behind the endless barbed wire fences.

Freshwater zones The freshwater marshes with their extensive reed beds provide ideal conditions for many species of bird that you can easily see from the roadside, such as herons, moorhens, coot, mallards and egrets.

Another inhabitant of the freshwater marshes that you are likely to see is the enchanting coypu, which makes a curious burbling noise as it swims across the surface in search of aquatic plants (it is particularly fond of bulrushes) to nibble on. The coypu is often mistaken for a beaver, but it is part of an entirely different family (it was introduced from South America); there are beavers, mostly along the banks of the Rhône, but they are nocturnal and rarely spotted.

On slightly higher ground are the remains of the grasslands, which provide a vital habitat for the colourful bee-eater as well as rollers and hoopoes; the grasslands are a particularly beautiful sight in the spring, when they are covered in white daisies, and again in the autumn, when they are a mass of purple sea lavender.

Agriculture has also taken its toll on the woodlands, remnants of the riverine forest that used to cover most of the northern part of the delta. The predominant species are white poplar, willow, ash and elm, and there are still narrow belts along the banks of the Rhône that provide nesting sites for owls, woodpeckers, tits and starlings. Herons and egrets also nest here, feeding in the daytime in the freshwater marshes.

RICE PADDIES
Cattle, horses and sheep once used to graze on the richer pastures of the grasslands, but huge areas of this productive ground were converted to rice paddies in the 1950s. In the 1960s the Camargue was growing nearly a third of France's rice requirements, but since 1970 production has dropped dramatically. Instead, other crops such as fruit and vegetables have taken over, thanks to the fact that the paddies cleansed the soil of salt.

Wading birds such as storks find rich feeding grounds in the Camargue marshes

The attractive port of Cassis was a favourite of the Fauve artists a hundred years ago

THE ROUTE DES CRÊTES
One of the wildest coastal roads in Provence is the 17km (10.5 miles) long Route des Crêtes between la Ciotat and Cassis. Take avenue Camusso out of la Ciotat and follow the twisting road as it dips and plunges along the clifftops, with spectacular views from the many stopping places *en route*. From the heights of Cap Soubeyran and Cap Canaille you can peer over the edge of the highest cliffs in France, with the sea pounding the rocks nearly 400m (1,130ft) below. The hillsides behind the cliffs have been planted with neatly curving rows of pines.

▶▶▶ Cassis 97D1

Squeezed into a little bay between the cliffs of the Gardiole (which conceal the famous *calanques*) to the west and Cap Canaille to the east, this photogenic fishing port has long been popular with visitors. It is also a great favourite with the Marseillais, who flock here throughout the year to eat delicious seafood meals, washed down with copious quantities of the excellent local *vin blanc*, in one of the many restaurants that line the dockside.

Presiding over the port is a rambling château built by the *seigneurs des Baux* at the beginning of the 13th century, now privately owned by the Michelin family. In the centre of town is the small **Musée d'Arts et Traditions Populaires** (*Open* Apr–Sep Wed–Sat 10.30–12.30, 3.30–6.30; Oct–Mar 10.30–12.30, 2.30–5.30. *Admission free*), with local paintings, amphorae, coins and other relics.

Apart from seafood restaurants, the main attraction of Cassis is its proximity to the magnificent **calanques**▶▶, long, narrow inlets eroded from the limestone cliffs of the Gardiole. There are several ways to see them: there are regular passenger boat departures from the quayside, with tours that vary in length according to how many *calanques* you want to visit. You can also hire kayaks, small motorboats and windsurfing equipment; or you can set out on foot (see *calanques* walk, page 124).

Hemmed in as it is on all sides by high hills, there isn't much space around Cassis for vineyards, so the annual production from its 200ha (495 acres) of vines is highly prized: the light, fruity whites go admirably with local seafoods and *bouillabaisse*. If you want to take some home, some of the best *caves* are the Clos Ste.-Magdeleine (tel: 04 42 01 70 28), the Domaine Caillol (tel: 04 42 01 05 35), the Domaine du Paternel (tel: 04 42 01 77 03) and the Clos Val Bruyère (tel: 04 42 73 14 60).

▶ la Ciotat 97D1

Entering la Ciotat from any direction, you can't miss the industrial architecture that symbolizes its maritime past—the massive, gaunt gantries, now immobilized, that dominate the small harbour at the centre of the town. La

Ciotat has been a port since the 4th century, when the Greeks from Marseille set up an anchorage here, and in the 17th century the local mariners invented a system (called *la caravanne*) to get the most from their ships by never sailing empty from one port to the next; today, every modern shipping line operates a similar back-to-back cargo system.

The first boats were built here in 1836 and the first dry dock opened in 1936, but the dockyards were finally shut down in April 1990. Exhibitions on the town's maritime history are housed in the **Musée Ciotaden▶** (*Open Wed–Mon afternoons*) in the Ancien Hôtel de Ville on quai Ganteaume.

With the derricks now standing idle above the fishing boats and pleasure craft in the harbour, la Ciotat has turned to tourism for its survival, with glossy brochures extolling the virtues of the beaches of the "Golfe d'Amour" and the "Ville des Lumières." The appropriately named Lumière brothers gave the first ever public showing of motion pictures here (see panel). Capitalizing on this connection, there has been an annual film festival since 1981 and, more recently, an annual jazz festival.

Behind the dockyards to the west of town, in the shadow of the 70m (230ft) high Bec de l'Aigle (eagle's beak) promontory, is a small wilderness area now protected as the **Parc Naturel du Mugel▶ ▶** (*Open daily. Admission free*). There is a little rocky beach on the creek and pathways lead through typically Mediterranean vegetation to a viewpoint beneath the Cap. The oaks, chestnuts, aleppo, umbrella and maritime pines are all neatly marked. There is an underwater nature trail in the Calanque du Petit Mugel.

THE COSQUER CAVE

In 1991 a local diver, Henri Cosquer, discovered an underwater fissure in one of the *calanques* that led to a cave containing hundreds of wall paintings, similar to the famous ones at Lascaux, depicting bison, horses and over 50 human hands in charcoal. Declared a historic monument in 1992, the cave has since been walled up to prevent public access; several divers have lost their lives attempting to see it.

123

LUMIÈRE BROTHERS

By inventing the simple technique of piercing the edge of a roll of film with holes and running it through a toothed mechanism attached to a projector, Auguste and Louis Lumière gave birth to modern cinema. In 1895, they showed the first ever moving picture images to a private audience in la Ciotat. Three months later these same films were shown to a public audience in Paris, where spectators almost jumped out of their seats as a train approached them on the screen in *L'Arrivée d'un train en Gare de la Ciotat*. The film festival (now encompassing photography and art exhibitions) takes place in la Ciotat in June.

Fishing boats tied up at the Cassis quayside, their catches by now being prepared in the waterfront restaurants

The *calanques*

The soaring limestone cliffs known as *les calanques* are a dramatic coastal feature, which can be explored by boat trips or on foot. Walkers have the advantage of time to stop and enjoy the diverse flora (more than 900 hardy

124

species cling to the sun-baked rock) and the multitude of seabirds that make their home here. From the Calanque de Port-Miou just outside Cassis harbour to the Calanque de Callelongue at les Goudes, south of Marseille, the 20km (12.5 miles) long coastline is criss-crossed with walking trails. This walk, from Cassis, takes around three hours for the round trip.

From Cassis, follow the signs for Les Calanques and park at the end of the road. Walk along the length of the Calanque de Port-Miou through the old quarry. Atypically, Port-Miou's entire length is taken up with yacht berths.

Climb up the terraces over a low ridge to reach the **Calanque de Port-Pin▶**, named after the *pins d'Alep* that once covered the Domaine de la Fontasse behind the inlet. The small shingle beach gets very crowded, since this *calanque* is the easiest to reach from Cassis, whether on foot or by water.

Continue up a narrow gully and climb up to the Plateau de Cadeiron. From here, there are wonderful views back to the magnificent cliffs of the Montagne de la Canaille rearing up above Cassis bay. In front of you, the ground starts to fall away until you reach a viewpoint over the **Calanque d'En-Vau▶▶**, one of the most spectacular of all the *calanques*. Beneath the dramatic, chalk-white cliffs and needle-like rocks, there is a small sandy beach, with rocky steps leading down.

Beyond En-Vau you can see the Riou archipelago (comprising the islands of Jarre, Jarron, Calseraigne and namesake Riou itself).

The cliffs continue down into the limpid depths, sheltering a rich profusion of marine life that makes their steep underwater slopes a favourite with local scuba divers.

From here, you can either continue along the GR98 all the way to les Goudes (at least a full day's walk), or turn back along En-Vau out towards the pinnacle known as *Doigt de Dieu* ("God's finger"), and then around the headland back to Port-au-Pin and Cassis. Note that in the summer months (15 June to 15 September) it is forbidden to stray off the GR98 because of the fire risk.

Walkers in the calanques

▶ Gémenos   97D2
This village outside Aubagne is worth a detour for the nearby **Abbaye de St.-Pons** (see page 166), or, if you are passing through on the way to Ste.-Baume, stop in the main square and look inside the courtyard of the unusual **Granges du Marquis d'Albertas**, a huge building designed to house agricultural workers, which was built in the second half of the 18th century. Bacchus astride a barrel over one of the four doorways (three are now closed off) attests to the function of what was essentially a huge barn with accommodation above.

▶ Graveson   96B3
Once surrounded by swamps, Graveson is part of the fertile Petite Crau. Difficult to find but worth the effort is the **Musée des Aromes et du Parfum▶▶**, south of the village on the back road to St.-Etienne-du-Grès (*Open* daily. *Admission: moderate*). Fragrant aromas permeate the whole of this converted farmhouse and barn, which houses a number of huge copper alembics (stills) as well as other traditional distilling equipment. Essential oils, soaps and perfumes made from the local herbs are on sale; the founder, Nelly Grosjean, also holds one-day aromatherapy courses (tel: 04 90 95 81 55 for details).

▶ Maillane   96B3
In the 14th century the village of Maillane was almost wiped out by the plague. Among those who repopulated it was a man from Tarascon called Mermet Mistral: several centuries later, Maillane was the birthplace of Frédéric Mistral (see pages 60–61), Provence's most famous literary figure. Mistral was brought up in the Mas de la Juge (no visits) just outside Maillane, but on the death of his father in 1855 he moved with his mother into Au Lezard, a house in the middle of the village at the junction of the D32/D5, just down from the café-edged place Mistral. In an alleyway alongside is the house Mistral moved into 20 years later when he married, and where he lived until his death in 1914. The house now contains the refurbished **Museon Mistral▶▶** (*Open* Tue–Sun. *Admission: inexpensive*), filled with the Nobel Prize-winning author's personal effects.

GASTRONOMY IN GÉMENOS
Every November the tourist office in Gémenos organizes a gastronomic festival that brings together some of the excellent local restaurants and vineyards around themes such as "Wine in Provençal Cuisine." As well as a two-day wine and food fair, there are special menus in participating restaurants (for details contact the Office de Tourisme, tel: 04 42 32 18 44; www.officedetourisme gemenos.com; e-mail: ot.gemenos@ visitprovence.com).

125

Gleaming copper stills at the Musée des Aromes et du Parfum in Graveson

Speedboats, yachts and fishing boats rub shoulders in Marseille harbour

Laid out in the 17th century, La Canebière is Marseille's main thoroughfare

Compared to the glittering resorts of the Côte d'Azur farther east or the historically rich inland cities of Provence, Marseille has never been a prime tourist destination and its image is certainly one of work not play. However, as France's second-biggest city (after Paris) and the Mediterranean's largest port, it has tremendous vitality and a cosmopolitan atmosphere that is difficult not to admire, even if you do not fall in love with the place.

Opening out to the sea from its niche between mountains and towering cliffs, Marseille's reputation precedes it, attracting all the worst labels—"the gangster capital of France," a "fascist hotbed," "a dirty, vulgar and noisy city"—and yet to the casual visitor none of this is necessarily apparent. Like any major city, there are areas to be avoided at night, but both Nice and Avignon have much higher crime rates per head of population than Marseille.

Marseille boasts over a dozen theatres, four times that many galleries, and art exhibition centres, numerous music venues with everything from world music to chamber music, and, of course, the renowned Marseille opera. It also has a carnival every March, which celebrates the story of Protis and Gyptis and the founding of the city by the Greeks (see panel on page 130).

The settlement, which they named Massalia, prospered very quickly. As a maritime people, the Massalians established a series of trading posts along the coast (notably at Nice, Hyères and Antibes) and their explorers ventured as far afield as Senegal, in Africa, and the Baltic.

For protection from the Celto-Ligurian tribes it allied itself with Rome, but *Massalia's* independent stance was irrevocably damaged when Caesar sacked the city in 49 BC in retaliation for its neutrality during the hostilities with Pompey (Caesar's great rival). Despite this, Massalia remained a stronghold of Hellenic civilization. Its port declined in importance until the crusades, when the city profited hugely by providing transport to the wars.

In 1720 a single ship, the *Grand Saint-Antoine*, slipped through the quarantine net around the port and unleashed the plague that was to devastate much of Provence; in Marseille alone, half the population died. But the town bounced back, benefiting particularly from the opening of the Suez Canal in 1869.

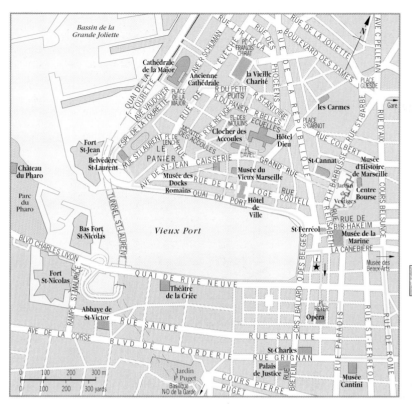

Marseille

This walk takes in many of the best museums of Marseille, as well as the interesting old quarter of Le Panier. Allow 3–4 hours.

Start the walk at the tourist office behind the quai des Belges. Take rue Beauvau down to place Reyer for the **Opéra▶▶**; the wonderful art deco interior dates from 1924. From here, head northeast for pedestrianized rue Paradis. Turn south, and on rue Grignan on your left is the **Musée Cantini**. Continue to the rue de Rome and turn left and keep going until you reach La Canebière.

Go through the Bourse shopping centre (entrance to the **Musée d'Histoire**). Exit through the **Jardin des Vestiges** and follow the Grand Rue across rue de la République to the place Daviel. Take the steps past **Clocher des Accoules** (all that remains of one of the city's older churches; parts date back to the 7th century) and follow the signs for the route through the old quarter of le Panier to la Vieille Charité. Continue down rue du Petits Puits; take the steps in the place des Treize Cantons to reach the **Cathédrale de la Major**.

Esplanade de la Tourette leads you to a belvedere, with a superb view over the old port. Go down the steps to the quay, and follow it along until place Jules Verne, for the **Musée des Docks Romains** and the remarkable **Maison Diamantée**, which houses temporary exhibitions. Finally, rejoin the quai du Port and walk back round to the quai des Belges.

PUGET'S BIRTHPLACE
Near the Centre de la Vieille Charité in the Le Panier quarter, a small plaque on the wall of No. 3 rue du Petits Puits, an unremarkable house, celebrates the birthplace of one of the 17th century's most remarkable sculptors, Pierre Puget.

Towering above the city, Notre-Dame de la Garde was used as a Nazi headquarters during World War II—bullet marks are still visible on the walls

THE BIG BLUE
First it was leading British architect Richard Rogers in Nîmes and now another Brit, Will Alsop, has joined the ranks of those who have designed controversial and prestigious buildings in Provence. Alsop's daring departmental headquarters (L'Hôtel du Département) in Marseille is unmistakable, a sculpted statement in bright blue that expresses the essence of post-high-tech architecture. Partially raised on stilts, it echoes one of the most famous architectural experiments in social housing—Le Corbusier's Unite d'Habitation, which still stands on the outskirts of Marseille.

With the loss of France's colonies in the 1950s the importance of trade again declined, but Marseille was left with the legacy of thousands of immigrants who had flocked here from North Africa in the 1960s (the population grew from 660,000 in 1955 to 960,000 in 1975); none of this was new to Marseille, which had welcomed refugees over the centuries. However, the downside has been a volatile combination of rising unemployment and poverty alongside bitter racial tensions enthusiastically fuelled by the xenophobic *Front National*, which occasionally explodes into violence.

WHAT TO SEE At the heart of the city is the **Vieux Port▶▶**, where a bronze plaque on the quai des Belges marks the spot where Protis first stepped ashore (see page 130). Fishing boats still pull in here every morning to unload their catches, which are sold straight to waiting customers. Alongside are the tourist boats for trips out to the **Frioul Archipelago** and the **Château d'If** (see page 131).

Leading up from the Vieux Port is the broad boulevard of **La Canebière**, Marseille's most famous street, though now full of banks and airline offices.

To the north is an area of steep streets and narrow alleyways known as **Le Panier▶**, Marseille's oldest district. Before World War II it housed fisherfolk and many Italian and Corsican refugees, and later gave shelter to hundreds of Jews hoping to escape the Nazis by catching a ship to America. In January 1943 the Nazis gave all 20,000 inhabitants one day's notice to quit and blew the whole lot up, rounding up 3,500 victims for the concentration camps in the process. The only buildings not destroyed were the Maison Diamantée and the 17th-century Hôtel de Ville on the quayside.

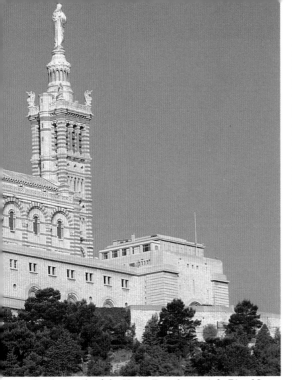

The first playing cards
reached Europe from
China via Venetian
merchants in the 13th
century, and this new-
found diversion soon
reached Marseille. The
first recorded mention of
cards in France occurs
here, in the minutes of a
public notary who, in
1381, was moved to ban
a merchant of the city
from playing a game
known as *naipi* or *nahipi*
(the forerunner of tarot).
By the 17th century it had
become a popular
pastime, and the first
cardmakers started up
in 1631. Marseille tarot
cards became classics
of the art.

129

The Tricolore *flies over
the entrance to the 17th-
century Hôtel de Ville*

On the south of the Vieux Port the quai de Rive Neuve
houses ship-chandlers' shops and the new Théâtre
National de Marseille de la Criée, with the **Abbaye de St.-
Victor** (see page 131) behind. From here, the road
continues around the walls of the Fort St.-Nicolas to the
Château de Pharo, built by Napoléon III as a gift for
Empress Éugenie.

Past the headland, the Corniche President John
Kennedy (with views over the offshore islands) leads past
several artificial beaches and a small yachting basin to the
popular sandy shore of **Parc du Prado**, the city's main
beach.

Farther on around the coast, in the suburb of
Montredon, the **Musée de la Faïence**, 157 avenue de
Montvedon (*Open* Tue–Sun. *Admission: inexpensive*) traces
the history of ceramics in a lovely 19th-century château.

MUSEUMS Marseille has numerous museums and it pays
to be selective. Starting on the north side of La Canebière,
across from the tourist office is the **Musée de la Marine et
de l'Economie de Marseille** (*Open* daily 10–6. *Admission:
inexpensive*), housed inside the Palais de la Bourse,
France's first stock exchange. Displays trace the maritime
history of Marseille from the 16th century onwards, with
models of old trading ships, paintings and engravings.

Just behind is the Bourse shopping centre, with the
Musée d'Histoire de Marseille▶▶ (*Open* Mon–Sat 12–7.
Admission: inexpensive) on the ground floor. Here is the
wreck of an ancient Roman merchant vessel, discovered
in 1974, which sank in one corner of the Roman port (now
unearthed in the **Jardin des Vestiges**▶, outside the
museum). Audiovisual displays explore the Greek
heritage of Massalia.

PROTIS AND GYPTIS
In 600 BC a shipload of Greek colonists from Ionia landed in what seemed like an ideal spot, the Lacydon inlet, and went to seek permission from Nann, the local king, to start a settlement. The king was throwing a banquet that day, during which, according to custom, his daughter Gyptis would choose her future husband. She went for Protis, the good-looking leader of the Ionian delegation, and as their wedding gift the king bequeathed them Lacydon (now the *vieux port*), where they founded a colony.

MASTER SCULPTOR
Born in Marseille, Pierre Puget (1620–1694) was one of the greatest French sculptors of the 17th century. He originally trained as a painter and later as a wood worker for the galley arsenal. Between 1638 and 1643, he studied art in Rome and Florence, and was taught decorative sculpture by Pietro de Cortone. Puget's first large commission was for the *Atlantes*, powerful mythological figures decorating the old town hall in Toulon. Thereafter his name was made and future commissions included statues for Louis XIV's Château de Versailles and also a brief to design the decorations for warships.

The gilded Madonna atop Notre-Dame de la Garde is the largest in France

An architectural curiosity of the historic le Panier district, the unusual **Maison Diamantée**▶ on rue de la Prison is so-called for the "diamond pointed" stones in the construction of its facade. Built in 1570, it now houses temporary exhibitions from the collections of the **Musée du Vieux Marseille**▶▶, which range from traditional Provençal *santons* and Arlesian furniture to the famous Marseille tarot cards (see panel, page 129).

Across the place Jules Verne is the **Musée des Docks Romains**▶ (*Open* Tue–Sun. *Admission: inexpensive*), built over the site where all the artefacts were recovered. Huge storage jars for oil, grain and wine sit on the 1st-century Roman quay.

Farther north in the Le Panier quarter is the **Centre de la Vieille Charité**▶▶, a wonderful building that was designed by Pierre Puget and built out of rose-coloured stone. The courtyard is surrounded by three floors with arcades of different heights, with a curious elliptical baroque chapel as the central focus. The hospice became a barracks in the early part of the 20th century, fell into disrepair, then was thoroughly renovated in the 1980s as a multimedia art and culture centre. It houses the excellent **Musée d'Archéologie Méditerranéenne**▶▶ (*Open* Tue–Sun. *Admission: inexpensive*), which features a number of revolving exhibits from around the Mediterranean basin.

Marseille's oldest art museum is the **Musée des Beaux-Arts**▶ (*Open* Tue–Sun. *Admission: inexpensive*) in a wing of the Palais Longchamp in the eastern quarter of the city. Much more centrally located is the interesting **Musée Cantini**▶▶▶ (*Open* Tue–Sun. *Admission: inexpensive*), the main focus for 20th-century art, with over 400 contemporary works of which only a small fraction is ever on display. Artists represented include Dufy, Bacon, Balthus, César, Max Ernst and Miró.

CHURCHES AND CATHEDRALS
The most prominent church in Marseille is **Notre-Dame de la Garde**▶▶ (*Open* daily), which stands sentinel

on an outcrop 162m (530ft) above the city. This huge Romano-Byzantine structure is surmounted by a 10m (33ft) high gilded Madonna and was built in the latter part of the 19th century. It is worth making the trek up here (or taking the bus or the tourist train) for the fabulous views below.

Constructed in a similar neo-Byzantine style, the **Cathédrale de la Nouvelle Major** ▶ (*Open* Tue–Sun) overlooks the modern docks on the north side of the *vieille ville*. With its 70m (230ft) high basilica and 444 marble columns supporting the roof, it is the largest church built in France since the Middle Ages. Despite its grandeur, it is not as interesting as the **Ancienne Cathédrale de la Major**▶▶ that it replaced and which sits alongside in its shadow. Although the older building was partially destroyed to make way for the new cathedral in the 19th century, what remains is a superb example of 11th-century Provençal Romanesque.

Across on the other side of the harbour is the **Abbaye de St.-Victor**▶▶, originally a powerful religious centre which spawned over 300 monasteries and priories throughout Provence and overseas. Founded in the 5th century, the abbey was damaged by the Saracens and later rebuilt with added fortifications; its walls are 3m (10ft) thick. Inside the basilica-church, you can descend into the **crypt**▶ (*Admission: inexpensive*), which has a series of sarcophagi hidden away in its ancient passageways. In the Chapelle Notre-Dame de Confession there is a black wooden statue of the Virgin, which is venerated in an ancient Candlemas ceremony (see panel).

THE ISLANDS No visit to Marseille is complete without a visit to the infamous **Château d'If**▶ ▶ (Boats from quai des Belges; journey 15 minutes, throughout the day, except in bad weather. *Admission: moderate*), perched on the rocky islet of the Île d'If. François I decided to build a fort here after visiting the island in 1516, and it was completed in 1531. However, it was soon turned into a prison and in the 17th century hundreds of Protestant prisoners perished within its gloomy walls. Novelist Alexandre Dumas used it as the setting for his book *The Count of Monte Cristo*.

The other islands in the Frioul archipelago are **Île Pomègues** and **Île Ratonneau**, where Julius Caesar anchored his fleet in preparation for the siege of Marseille in 49 BC. In the 17th century, the Île Ratonneau became a quarantine centre for plague victims, with the ruins of the old **Hôpital Caroline** on a hilltop attesting to the belief that the sea would sweep the sickness away. These barren-looking islands, alive with wild plants and flowers, can be visited on a round trip that also encompasses the Île d'If.

The massive Cathédrale de la Nouvelle Major

CANDLEMAS AT ST.-VICTOR
On Candlemas Day (2 February) a large procession gathers at the Abbaye de St.-Victor, where the Archbishop blesses green candles in front of the black statue of the Virgin. The faithful then take their candles back home, where they are lit to celebrate regeneration and rebirth. On the same day, small loaves are baked in the shape of boats, called *navettes*, to commemorate the arrival on Provençal shores of St. Lazarus and saints Mary Magdalene and Martha in les Saintes-Maries-de-la-Mer.

131

On the Roman quay

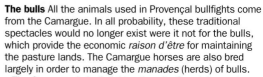

Summer is the season of bullfights in the Bouches-du-Rhône, with posters plastered on trees and billboards everywhere advertising Course de Taureau *in the nearest town with an* arène *worthy of the name. Unlike Spanish bullfights, the bulls are not put to death.*

RAMI
One well-known bull, Rami, who belonged to *manadier* Marcel Mailhan, died a natural death at 24 years old, a record that is celebrated by a monument over his tomb outside the hamlet of Villeneuve.

The bulls All the animals used in Provençal bullfights come from the Camargue. In all probability, these traditional spectacles would no longer exist were it not for the bulls, which provide the economic *raison d'être* for maintaining the pasture lands. The Camargue horses are also bred largely in order to manage the *manades* (herds) of bulls.

The Camarguais bull, lighter than its Spanish counterparts (some of which are also reared here), is a vigorous, agile and intelligent breed. It is not suited to agricultural work and were it not for the *course* it would probably exist only in zoos. The animals suffer no great hardship: Each bull spends a maximum of 15 minutes in the ring, appearing perhaps a dozen times in a year. At the end of its career, it retires to graze in the Camargue.

The game The *Course Camarguaise* (also known as the *Course à la Cocarde*) is more of a game than a fight, a contest of agility, courage and skill between the bulls and the participants. Dressed in white, the *razeteur* has a long hook (the *razet*) with which he has to snatch a *cocarde* (rosette) from between the horns of the bull. He is helped by a *tourneur*, whose role it is to distract the bull. He has to accomplish this within a 15-minute time limit, and if he does, he gains a prize. He risks being chased out of the ring by the bull, or forced to leap over

Young tourneurs *in the making?*

The Roman arena at Arles, packed to capacity

the barricades—and he hopes he doesn't fall back onto the bull's horns beneath him.

The round-up A tradition with more practical origins is that of the *ferrade*. At one year old, the young bulls are separated from the herd, chased on horseback and then grappled to the ground by the *manadier* (herdsman) in order to be branded. This too has evolved into a spectator sport, as has the *abrivado* (or *lacher des taureaux*, release of the bulls), during which the bulls are driven through the streets to the arena, chasing or being chased by the crowds.

Anyone can try Although the *Course Camarguaise* nowadays is organized on a professional basis (it became an official French sport in 1975) and the *razeteurs* train rigorously, most of the fun for the hundreds of people who flock down to their local ring on a Friday or Saturday night is in the *Course à la Vachette*. The local youth, and sometimes even children, leap into the ring to be chased by the *vachette* (which has capped horns) to try to tempt it to jump after them into a shallow pool in the middle. Cash prizes are the reward for this risky-looking game.

In the arena The most spectacular settings for local bullfights are in the old Roman arenas at Arles and Nîmes, where both *Course Camarguaise* and Spanish-style *corridas* (where the bulls are put to death) are held several times a year, notably at *feria* (festival) times such as Easter and the autumn rice festival. Details are available from local tourist offices; check schedules carefully if you want to avoid a *corrida*.

ORIGINS
The first recorded bullfights were held in honour of King Louis and Queen Yolands in Arles in 1405. The birth of the *Course Camarguaise* as it is today dates back to 1793, when a Commissaire called Fréron was welcomed into Arles with a spectacle that involved the now characteristic *cocarde,* in which the winner was awarded a prize. It was the Marquis de Baroncelli who stimulated the revival of this colourful tradition in the 19th century.

133

COMIC CAPERS
The *vachette* often vaults over the inner barrier around the ring, and as it chases round the outside everybody leaps to safety *inside* the ring. Just like a comedy cartoon, the bull's progress can be measured by the escaping bodies popping one by one back over the barrier. When it gets halfway round, the *vachette* is sent back in the ring again.

The serene cloisters of the Abbaye-de-Montmajour

The much-photographed and painted Miroir des Oiseaux, Martigues

▶ Martigues 97C2

Martigues is a pleasant base for exploring the Étang de Berre or for stopping over on the way to the Camargue, not least because of the picturesque canals that run through the centre between its three separate "villages."

On the southern side of the main canal is Jonquières, the busiest village if you are looking for a meal or a drink. In the middle is L'Isle, which has several restored 17th- and 18th-century houses as well as the splendid **Église de la Madeleine▶**. From the bridge next to the church is a celebrated view known as the **Miroir des Oiseaux▶** (the birds' mirror). This little cameo of fishing boats moored in a curve of the canal at the quai Brescon was painted by Corot, Ziem and several other artists of a century ago. Works by Ziem and others are on display in the **Musée Ziem** (*Open* Jul–Aug, Wed–Mon; Sep–Jun, Wed–Sun. *Admission free*) on the boulevard du 14 Juillet in the third village of Martigues, Ferrières.

▶ Maussane-les-Alpilles 96B3

Situated at the foot of the Alpilles with the fertile Plaine de la Crau stretching away to the south, Maussane-les-Alpilles is a prosperous village that made its fortunes from olive oil. At the beginning of the century it had over a dozen olive mills, but today only one survives, which still presses olives in the traditional way (*Open* Mon–Sat; follow the signs for the Cooperative des Baux down rue Charlour Rien on the north side of the main road).

▶ Miramas-le-Vieux 97C2

Miramas-le-Vieux has been restored (and the streets recobbled) to create the kind of medieval *village perché* which you are more likely to expect in the Vaucluse. The manicured ruins of the old château are the setting for music concerts on summer evenings.

Keep going on the D10 and you will reach **St.-Chamas**, a former fishing village now turning towards yachting and tourism to make its living. In the town centre, the **Église▶▶** has an impressive baroque facade attributed to the

17th-century Aixois architect Pierre Pavillon. Just outside is a well-preserved Roman bridge, the **Pont-Flavien▶**. Built in the 1st century AD, it is framed by two triumphal arches.

▶▶▶ Montmajour, Abbaye-de- 96B3

Route de Fontevieille (D17), 6km (4 miles) northeast of Arles (tel: 04 90 54 64 17)
Open: Apr daily 10–5; May–Sep daily 10–6.30; Oct–Mar Tue–Sun 10–5. Admission: moderate

Set on a hillock north of Arles, Montmajour was one of the most powerful monasteries of medieval Provence, and even in ruins it is still an impressive sight.

Montmajour owes its origins to one of the early Christian saints, St. Trophimus, who fled here from Arles to hide in a cave in the hillside. Later, a group of hermits took up residence to safeguard the site, which led to the founding of the monastery in the 10th century. Under Benedictine rule the abbey went from strength to strength, establishing numerous priories and starting on the Herculean task of reclaiming the surrounding marshlands. Thanks to these landholdings, the abbey became very wealthy—and decadent. In 1639 a group of reformed monks was sent in to sort it out, but those already in residence, reluctant to leave, sacked the abbey in revenge. In the 18th century Montmajour was partly rebuilt, but Louis XVI disbanded the abbey in 1786. Restoration began in 1907.

The incomplete 12th-century **upper church▶** is an impressive, austere structure. On the right of the nave is an interesting crypt, part-built into the side of the hill, with fine Romanesque vaulting. The **cloister▶▶▶** ranks among the most important in Provence, with finely detailed carvings of demons and beasts on the bases and capitals of the colonnades.

From the 26m (85ft) high **keep**, an impressive fortified structure built in 1369, there are spectacular views across to the Alpilles, Arles, Tarascon, and the Plaine de la Crau. From the keep, go down the hill to the wonderful little 11th-century **Ermitage St.-Pierre▶▶**, which is half carved out of the hillside in the caves where St. Trophimus sought refuge.

Montmajour was one of the most important medieval monasteries in Provence

135

OLIVE FESTIVAL

The annual harvest of green olives from Mouriès' 80,000 trees is around 1,200 tonnes. If you want to try out their famous olives (as well as a multitude of other olive products), the best time to come is in the middle of September, when there is an annual Olive Festival, which also features bullfights and Provençal dances.

One of the best-preserved Roman temples in Europe, the Maison Carrée in Nîmes was built in the 1st century BC

▶ Mouriès 96B3

Mouriès is well known for its peppery oils. The town is southeast of Maussane-les-Alpilles, and olive oil mills have been part of the landscape here for over 100 years. There were 18 mills in 1882; now there are only two (the *moulin cooperatif* and the *moulin moderne*), but they still produce 200,000 litres (44,000 gallons) of olive oil between them each year.

▶▶▶ Nîmes 96A3

Although situated 25km (15 miles) west of the Rhône and well outside the borders of present-day Provence, Nîmes shares much of the Provençal heritage, in particular, a glorious past as a Gallo-Roman city.

Nîmes first rose to prominence as the capital of the Celtic tribe of the Volcae-Arecomici, when it was known as Nemansus after a sacred and prolific spring that the Celts revered. The settlement was also strategically positioned on the main Spanish–Italian trade routes, and when the Romans forged through in the 1st century AD the inhabitants were quick to embrace their new overlords. Nemansus became Colonia Nemausensis.

Augustus reciprocated the Celtic welcome by heaping privileges on the town and encircling it with a monumental, 8km (5 miles) long wall; soon after, a large amphitheatre was added, as well as the celebrated Maison Carrée and the aqueduct of the Pont du Gard, which brought water to the city's baths and fountains.

After the decline of Rome, Nîmes fell into the hands of the Visigoths, followed by the Franks. In the 16th century the town sided with the Protestant Huguenots, which led to considerable bloodshed, but peace was restored with the Edict of Nantes in 1598. The 17th century saw further conflict, but after the troubles Nîmes concentrated on

building up its textile industry, and by the 18th century over 10,000 people and 300 looms were churning out silk fabric and serge for export. One of its best-selling lines was a hard-wearing blue serge that became known simply as *de Nîmes* ("from Nîmes"), and when some of this fabric found its way to California in 1848, Levi Strauss adopted it to create his famous denim jeans.

A quiet start to the 20th-century prompted one early guidebook to observe: "20th century Nîmes has stagnated…and it has been supplanted by Montpellier." Not for long, however. Enter, in 1983, the dynamic Jean Bousquet, former head of the locally based fashion empire of Cacherel, elected mayor on his promise to turn Nîmes' fortunes around.

By pouring money into arts and culture, and in particular by commissioning world-class architects to embellish the city with buildings and monuments, Bousquet sought to regain the crown from rival Montpellier and rejuvenate the city, and his ambitious blueprint for a thriving 21st-century city has put Nîmes firmly back on the map.

WHAT TO SEE Most of the sites are within easy walking distance of each other within the city centre. First stop is the spectacular **Arènes▶▶▶** (*Open* daily, Apr–Sep 9–7; Oct–Mar 10–5. *Admission: moderate*), one of the best-preserved Roman amphitheatres in existence. Dating from the turn of the 1st century AD, its mellow, honey-coloured sandstone exterior is now blackened by pollution.

A lapidary Cupid in the Jardin de la Fontaine

137

THE ARENA VILLAGE
After gladiator fights were banned in the 6th century under the influence of Christianity, the Nîmes arena was turned into a fortress by the Visigoths. Later, people started to move in and build houses inside it (a fate that also befell the arena at Arles and the theatre at Orange); by the 18th century this had grown into an entire village, with 2,000 inhabitants, 200 houses and even a couple of churches. It took over 30 years to clear the whole lot away in the early 19th century.

The place aux Herbes is the focal point of Nîmes' old quarter

Detail of one of the many statues in Nîmes' delightful Jardin de la Fontaine

Despite this the arena is in remarkable condition, and on the upper storeys you can still see the sockets for the posts that held the *velum*, an adjustable awning that sheltered spectators. Now the arena has the modern-day equivalent, a massive inflatable canopy weighing over 9 tonnes that is put up in the winter months: It takes a team of engineers over three weeks to erect. The canopy remains up from the end of October to April; during these months it may be closed for special events. In summer, it is a major bullfighting venue (see panel opposite).

The other "must" in Nîmes is the **Maison Carrée▶▶**, boulevard Victor-Hugo (*Open* summer, daily 9–7; winter, daily 10–5. *Admission free*), a delightful temple also in exceptional condition. Built in the 1st century AD and modelled on the Temple of Apollo in Rome, it was dedicated to Augustus' grandsons, Caius and Lucius. Surrounded by elegant Corinthian columns, it remains almost perfectly intact, despite having been used as a stable, among other things, in the Middle Ages.

Facing the Maison Carrée on the place du Forum is a high-profile reminder of Bousquet's commitment to modern architecture, the **Carrée d'Art▶▶**, which opened in 1993. With its name—"art square"—echoing the "square house" opposite, this beautifully designed Norman Foster building takes up the purity of line of the ancient temple and translates it into 20th-century idiom. Inside, light pours down a huge central well to the library on the basement floors; the upper levels house the **Musée d'Art Contemporain▶▶** (*Open* Tue–Sun 10–6. *Admission: moderate*). There is a café beneath the roof canopy with great views of Nîmes and the Maison Carrée below.

Just north of the Carrée d'Art is another Bousquet-inspired project, the **place d'Assas▶**, designed in 1989 by Martial Raysse. Water flows across the square between two figures representing Nemausa, deity of the original spring, and Nemansus.

Water also plays a central role in the wonderful **Jardin de la Fontaine▶▶**, off quai de la Fontaine. The late 18th-century gardens channel the waters of the Nemausus spring through a series of Roman-style pools beneath a maze of balustrades and statuary. On the left of the lower promenade are the remains of the **Temple of Diana**.

Follow the gardens uphill for the **Tour Magne▶** (*Open*

daily, summer 9–7; winter 10–5. *Admission: inexpensive*; or joint ticket with the Arènes) at the top of Mont Cavalier. This 30m (100ft) high tower was once part of the city walls built by Augustus; steps lead to a viewing platform at the top.

The heart of the city, old Nîmes, is almost entirely pedestrianized and is a pleasure to wander around. In the middle of the old quarter is the place aux Herbes, dominated by the **Cathédral Notre-Dame-et-St.-Castor**▶, which has been rebuilt many times over the centuries. Its west front (facing the square) is ornamented with a classical frieze illustrating Old Testament stories. In a corner is the **Musée de Vieux Nîmes**▶▶, which has a fine collection of Renaissance furniture and historical documents (*Admission free*). Nîmes' remaining museums are all *open* summer, Tue–Sun 10–6; winter, 11–6. *Admission: moderate*.

On the eastern side of the old quarter, the **Musée Archéologique** and **Musée d'Histoire Naturelle**▶, boulevard de l'Amiral-Courbet, are worth a look for the former's extensive collection of sculpted *menhirs* (dolmens) and Gallo-Roman bits and pieces such as jewellery and household items. A model shows the full extent of Augustus' amazing wall that once encircled the city.

South of the Arènes, the **Musée des Beaux Arts**▶, rue de la Cité-Foulc, has some significant Roman mosaics as well as other works spanning the 15th to the 20th centuries.

NEARBY Nîmes is inevitably associated with the **Pont du Gard**▶▶▶, and it is worth a detour to see what has always been considered "one of the wonders of the Ancient World."

The Pont du Gard owes its existence to the almost insatiable thirst for water of the average Roman city (for domestic use but also for the many fountains and public baths) and their desire for totally pure water. When the spring of Nemansus was deemed no longer sufficient, the city engineers began to carve out an aqueduct from the Source d'Eure near Uzès, some 50km (31 miles) away. Faced with the impetuous River Gard in their path, the Romans had this stunning masterpiece built out of masonry blocks weighing up to 6 tonnes each. Its three tiers of arches span the valley for 275m (900ft) and reach a height of 48m (160ft) above the river.

BLOOD GAMES
In Roman times the Nîmes arena enjoyed a reputation for particularly bloodthirsty games, and people would travel from far and wide to witness gladiators fight it out to the death, either with each other or with wild animals. Blood-lust continues even now, although it is nearly always the animals that die in the Spanish-style *corridas* held during festival times (*Ferias*). The main *Ferias* are during the Carnival in February; the *Feria de Pentêcote* (Whitsun) and the *Feria des Vendanges* (September).

139

The fountains of Nîmes are a constant reminder that the town owes its origins to the waters of the spring of Nemansus

VAN GOGH'S LANDSCAPES
There is a walking trail around some of the scenes that Van Gogh painted near St.-Rémy with placards showing which works were done where, along with Van Gogh's own comments. Details are available from the tourist office, place Jean Jaurès (tel: 04 90 92 05 22), which also offers guided walks.

Glanum's Mausoleum: inside there are statues of Caesar and Augustus

▶▶▶ St.-Rémy-de-Provence 96B3

St.-Rémy is undoubtedly one of the most delightful towns in all Provence. Encircled by a boulevard of plane trees, the centre of the town is a warren of fine old buildings, pretty squares, plant-filled alleyways, and cooling fountains. Its charms inspired many Provençal poets as well as novelist Gertrude Stein.

On the edge of the circular boulevard is the **place de la République**, with outdoor cafés and a lively market on Wednesday mornings. Facing the square is the neoclassical **Collegiale St.-Martin▶** with its famous organ. Built in 1983, it is said to be one of the finest contemporary organs in Europe. Regular recitals take place on Saturday evenings between July and September.

Behind St.-Martin in the shady place Favier, the 16th-century **Hôtel Mistral de Mondragon▶** houses the **Musée des Alpilles▶** (*Open* Mar–Dec, daily. *Admission: inexpensive*), with well-presented exhibits on local folklore, geology, ethnography and Nostradamus (see panel, page 144). Next door in another fine Renaissance palace, the **Hôtel de Sade▶**, is the **Musée Archéologique▶▶** (*Open* daily. *Admission: inexpensive*; or joint ticket with Glanum, below), devoted to finds from the Glanum excavations, including some well-preserved Roman temple decorations, statues of the gods, and everyday items such as jewellery and jars. Another old mansion, the **Hôtel Estrine**, contains the **Centre d'Art Présence Van Gogh▶** (*Open* mid-Mar to Oct and Dec Tue–Sun. *Admission: inexpensive*), with audiovisual displays and documentation on Van Gogh, and exhibitions of contemporary works.

NEARBY Within walking distance along the D5 (1km/0.5 miles outside St.-Rémy) are the ruins of **Glanum▶▶▶** and the remarkable Roman monuments known as **les Antiques▶▶▶**, which consist of a well-preserved mausoleum and a triumphal arch by the side of the road. The 18m (60ft) high mausoleum, with elaborate bas-reliefs on the podium, is thought to have been erected around AD 30. The triumphal arch, dating from around the same time, was one of the first of its kind in Provence.

Opposite les Antiques is the entrance to the site of **Glanum** itself (tel: 04 90 92 23 79. *Open* Apr–Sep, daily 9–7; Oct–Mar, daily 9–12, 2–5. *Admission: moderate*), where excavations since 1921 have uncovered many different layers of habitation from the Celto-Ligurian period through to its sacking in AD 270. There is an enormous amount to see, including the Forum, the *thermae* (baths), a sacred well from the Gallo-Greek period, several large private houses and the remains of various temples. One of these has been

partially reconstructed, with the mouldings, columns and elaborate capitals faithfully copied (using ancient tools and techniques) from the originals kept in the Musée Archéologique.

Just below the site is the former monastery of **St.-Paul-de-Mausole▶**, where Van Gogh was hospitalized (see page 112). It is still a private sanatorium, but you can walk down the main driveway and visit the church and the 12th-century cloisters.

The entrance to the Musée des Alpilles, housed in a 16th-century building

▶▶ les Saintes-Maries-de-la-Mer   96A2

This seaside resort is a popular base for visiting the Camargue and has plenty of things to do, including horse-riding, cycling, sailing, windsurfing and the beach.

The resort is at its busiest during the annual *Pèlerinage des Gitans,* a gypsy pilgrimage that takes place on the last weekend in May each year to honour the statue of Black Sarah, the Egyptian slave who was washed ashore along with the three Marys (see panel). Sarah's remains are interred in a reliquary in the crypt of the **Église▶▶** in the centre of the old town.

This stately Romanesque church, strengthened during the 12th century after a series of Saracen raids on the town, is one of the best examples of fortified churches in Provence; from its bell tower there is a panorama of the vast, open spaces of the Camargue.

Near the church is the **Musée Baroncelli** (*Open* Mar to mid-Nov 10–12, 2–6. *Admission: inexpensive*), with displays on local wildlife, Arlesian costumes and furniture, and a few mementos of Baroncelli's eccentric lifestyle (see panel, page 59).

Baroncelli's **tomb** is down on the waterfront next to the *arènes,* and although unmarked, it is unmistakable because it incorporates carvings of his two main interests, a horse and a bull.

THE LEGEND OF SARAH
According to legend, Sarah arrived here with Mary Magdalene, Mary Salome, Mary Jacobe and several disciples after they had been cast adrift from the Holy Land. Once they reached the Camargue in the "boat of Bethany," the disciples dispersed; the elderly Mary Salome, Mary Jacobe, and Sarah stayed and were eventually buried in the oratory that they had built here. Their tombs soon attracted pilgrims, particularly gypsies from all over Europe who had adopted Sarah as their patron saint. At the end of May, effigies of the saints are carried down to the sea to be blessed during the annual *Pèlerinage des Gitans.*

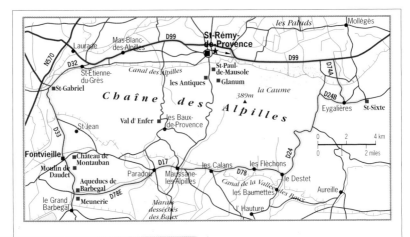

Drive

The Alpilles

An extension of the Luberon range, the Alpilles are one of the prime landmarks in the middle of the Crau plain. This tour goes through the heart of the range and encompasses interesting places around the base of the Alpilles (about half a day); you could also extend the tour to include les Baux (allow a full day).

From St.-Rémy take the D99 eastwards, turning right down the D74A across the Canal des Alpilles towards **Eygalières▶▶**, a charming little town with a long history. In the streets are

The remains of a Roman aqueduct at Barbegal

many fine old houses; there are the remains of the 12th-century castle keep of the old château, and below the ruins on the north side of the hill is the 17th-century **Chapelle des Penitents Blancs**.

Follow the D24B east towards Orgon, to see the charmingly simple, 12th-century **Chapelle de St.-Sixte▶▶** on a hillock to the right of the road. There is an annual pilgrimage from Eygalières at Easter (it is not otherwise open). Return via Eygalières and turn left down the D24, a lovely scenic road that winds through the heart of the Alpilles, surrounded on either side by pine forests and vineyards. Turn right at the hamlet of le Destet towards Maussane on the D78, which snakes around the south face of the Alpilles along an ancient route once used for the annual *transhumance*.

At **Maussane** (see page 134) you can either detour back up to **les Baux** (see pages 114–115) or continue on the D17 towards Paradou, where

outside the village a huge hangar houses **La Petite Provence du Paradou▶** (*Open* daily 10–6.30; Jul–Aug to 7. *Admission: inexpensive*). This "Provence-in-miniature" features over 300 figures—shepherds, gypsies, farmers, fishermen and so on—integrated into a vast, three-dimensional *village des santons* tableaux with working windmills and other careful touches. Turn off down the D78E until you see the **Aqueduct de Barbegal▶▶**. Park near the remains of the aqueduct and follow it between a

The impressive 12th-century Chapelle St.-Gabriel and (top) the Italianate rose window on its facade

cutting in the rocks to the edge of a small escarpment. Beneath you, the slope of the hill is covered with a series of ruins, one of the few surviving examples of a Roman flour mill. This interesting structure, the only one of its kind powered by hydraulics, consisted of no fewer than 16 mills,

143

linked up with two parallel series of paddlewheels in the middle. Turn right down the D33 towards **Fontvieille▶**. This attractive town owes its reputation largely to the link with novelist Alphonse Daudet, who wrote *Lettres de mon moulin*, a collection of Provençal short stories first published in 1869. An avenue lined with pines to the south of town leads to the rocky path clambering up the **Moulin de Daudet▶▶** (Daudet's windmill. *Open* Feb–Dec, daily. *Admission: inexpensive*), set on a hillock with views across to the Alpilles and the Tarascon plain. Just below the windmill there is a small museum containing first editions of his writings, portraits, manuscripts and other memorabilia.

From Daudet's windmill the path leads back to Fontvieille, past two other windmills, to the **Château de Montauban▶** (*Admission: joint ticket with* moulin), where Daudet actually stayed while in Fontvieille. The château now houses an exhibition, "Bonjour Monsieur Daudet," which focuses on Daudet's personal life. Take the D33 out of Fontvieille until you come to the lovely **Chapelle St.-Gabriel▶▶** just before the N570. This is nearly all that remains of a once thriving Gallo-Roman settlement, Ernaginum, which was a port for rafts that plied the surrounding marshes. The drying up of the marshes signalled the death knell for the town. From here, return to St.-Rémy on the D32 and the D99.

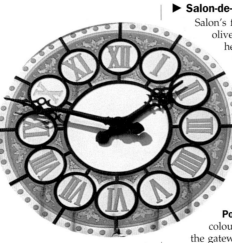

A decorative timepiece on the clock tower, Salon-de-Provence

144

▶ **Salon-de-Provence**   97C2

Salon's fortunes were founded on soapmaking and olive oil. The medieval seer Nostradamus moved here during the last years of his life (from 1547 to 1566), and his house in the old quarter is now a modern museum, **La Maison de Nostradamus** (*Open* daily afternoons. *Admission: inexpensive*). A series of waxwork tableaux depict scenes from his life, as well as key moments in the development of Renaissance philosophy. The town's dubious taste in waxworks extends to the historical displays of the **Musée Grévin de la Provence** (*Open* daily afternoons. *Admission: inexpensive*).

Near Nostradamus' house, the lovely old **Porte de l'Horloge**▶ was built of honey-coloured stone between 1626 and 1664. Opposite the gateway on place Crousillat is the beautiful 18th-century **Grand Fontaine**▶, which has become so encrusted with moss that it looks like a huge green mushroom cloud.

Within the "old" town centre, the 13th-century **Église St.-Michel**▶ has a noteworthy part-Gothic and part-Romanesque facade. At the top of the hideous new square is the imposing **Château de l'Emperi**▶▶ (*Open* Wed–Mon. *Admission: inexpensive*), a massive fortress dating back to the 10th century; it now houses the **Musée d'Art et d'Histoire Militaire**▶. The collection of over 10,000 items includes arms, uniforms, waxwork figures and flags, spanning the period from Louis XIV to World War I. Well worth a detour is the **Musée de Salon et de la Crau** (*Open* Mon, Wed–Fri 10–12, 2–6; Sat–Sun 2–6. *Admission: inexpensive*) for its displays dedicated to local crafts, industries and customs.

Just to the north of the town centre is the **Église St.-Laurent**, which houses the tomb of Nostradamus.

▶▶ **Silvacane, Abbaye de**   97C3

Set amid fertile fields on the south banks of the Durance, the Abbaye de Silvacane (*Open* Apr–Sep, daily; Oct–Mar, Wed–Mon. *Admission: moderate*) was the last of the three great Cistercian abbeys to be built in Provence (the other two being Sénanque and le Thoronet). Its name comes from *silva cana* ("forest of rushes"), which was all that was here before the monks set about draining the marshes to create farmland. Founded in the 12th century, the abbey prospered until pillaging and disastrous crops in the 14th century ruined it. It was turned into farm buildings before restoration began in the 19th century. As with its sister abbeys, the uncompromising austerity of Silvacane's architecture reflects the chaste lives of the Cistercians. The stark beauty of the clean-lined, pale stone church is echoed in a charming cloister with an old fountain.

▶▶ **Tarascon**   96B3

A former port on the banks of the Rhône, Tarascon is famous for its fabulous castle and the equally fantastic legends woven into its history, principally the story of Ste. Marthe and the Tarasque (see panel opposite).

THE TARASQUE MONSTER
After arriving in the "boat of Bethany," at les Saintes-Maries-de-la-Mer, Ste. Marthe came to Tarascon only to find the town terrorized by an amphibious monster, which devoured local children and cattle alike. Ste. Marthe tamed the beast by showing it her crucifix, after which it was captured and led away on a lead. To celebrate this miracle, in 1474 the Good King René organized an annual carnival, which still takes place on the last Sunday in June, with a ferocious, dragon-like Tarasque led through the streets snapping his mighty jaws at onlookers. Bonfires, fireworks, bullfights and dances precede the parade of the captive monster.

145

King René spent the last 10 years of his life surrounded by troubadours and artists in the fairytale **Château▶▶▶** (tel: 04 90 91 01 93. *Open* Apr–Sep, daily 9–7; Oct–Mar, 10.30–5. *Admission: moderate*) overlooking the Rhône. The building of the castle was initiated by Louis II of Anjou in 1400 and finished off by his son, the "Good King René," in 1449. It was used as a prison from 1800 right up until 1926.

Considered to be one of the finest fortified medieval châteaux in the whole of France, its massive walls and crenellated towers contrast markedly with the graceful and elegant interior architecture, particularly the flamboyant *cour d'honneur* where the royal apartments are linked by a spiral staircase.

Ste. Marthe's remains, discovered in 1187, lie in the **Collegiale Ste.-Marthe▶▶** just opposite the château. The church has suffered many indignities over the centuries, including having lost its best sculptures during the Revolution and being bombed in World War II.

Tarascon has another claim to fame in the contemporary legend of Tartarin, a comic figure invented by the novelist Alphonse Daudet in 1872, who bumbles through life bragging about his improbable adventures.

After shunning Daudet for many years because the ridiculous character, Tartarin, made them into a laughing stock, the people of Tarascon eventually forgave him to cash in on the fat man's fictional life in the **Maison de Tartarin** (*Open* Apr–Oct Mon–Tue, Thu–Fri; mid-Apr to mid-Sep also Sat. *Admission: inexpensive*) on the boulevard Itam.

Despite the march of modernization, country life in Provence still continues according to the cycle of the seasons, a calendar that alternates periods of intense work with equally intense festivities to celebrate the fruits of the earth.

Spring blossom (top) and autumn vines

146

Spring Spring unfolds quickly in Provence, and by February the mimosa is out and almonds start to bloom in March, soon followed by carpets of wild flowers. Olives and vines (if they have not been seen to in November) must be pruned, and cereal crops sown.

By April, plums, peaches, apples, apricots, pears and quinces are in blossom, and fires are lit in the orchards to stop frost killing the delicate buds. The sheep are sheared, and Easter celebrated with the first spring lamb. The first nightingales and swallows appear. In Arles, Pain de St.-Georges is baked to celebrate the feast day of the patron saint of the Camargue on 23 April.

Summer 1 May is considered the beginning of summer in Provence. *Primeurs* (early fruit and vegetables) brighten up market stalls, with asparagus, cherries, peas, apricots, melons and strawberries from the market gardens heralding a taste of sunshine. The flocks are shepherded back to the hill pastures, following the ancient traditions of the *transhumance*.

The autumn sowing of wheat is ready for harvesting in June, when migrant workers in their thousands descend from the mountains to cut the ripe sheaths. On the summer solstice, St. John's Day (24 June), bonfires are lit on hilltops to celebrate the end of the harvest. Other harvest festivals celebrate St. Eloi or St. Roch, and nearly all involve a great deal of wine and merriment, music and dancing, and huge banquets in village squares with grand *aïolis*.

As the summer progresses Spanish broom scents the *garrigue*, the lavender fields are resplendent with colour, and thyme, rosemary, marjoram and sage can be culled from the wild. Melons, peaches, and almonds are in abundance, and August is perfect for *ratatouille*, with courgettes, tomatoes, aubergines, garlic, onions and peppers overflowing in the markets. Honeysuckle, clematis and myrtle blossom decorates trellises and sunny walls.

Autumn September is dominated by the grape harvest, the *vendange*, a time when friends, neighbours and families

VAN GOGH ON SUMMER
"I keep remembering what I have seen of Cézanne, because he has exactly caught the harsh side of Provence. It has become very different from what it was in spring, and yet I certainly have no less love for this countryside burnt up as it begins to be from now on. Everywhere is old gold, bronze—copper, one might say—and this with the green azure of the sky blanched with heat: a delicious colour, extraordinarily harmonious, with the blended tones of Delacroix." Van Gogh, in a letter to his brother, Theo.

POPE-HENNESSY ON SPRING
"An April landscape, discovered at dawn from a moving train: Then, as I watched, the sun rose, and with it the whole panorama ceased looking like an underexposed photograph and came literally to light—the cabin roofs shone orange, the fields turned out to be scattered with poppies the colour of new blood, the long green grass was streaked with yellow flowers and cobalt flowers and round scabious flowers that were a hard, firm mauve. Over the distant crimson hills the sky was already blue, and the few people in the fields were a very dark walnut brown. Nothing I had expected of Provence equalled the harsh and yet mysterious quality of this flying landscape." James Pope-Hennessy, *Aspects of Provence*

get together to pick grapes and spend long evenings quaffing jugs of wine and relaxing after the day's arduous labour. The countryside is a patchwork of red, gold and rust-coloured tones as the leaves turn in the vineyards and forests. Mushrooms, particularly the much sought after *cèpes*, begin to spring up in woodlands and everybody is out at weekends with collecting bags and sticks for turning over leaves to seek them out. Figs are in season, and the rice harvest is in full swing in the Camargue.

The *vendange* continues through into October (depending on the region), and chestnuts are collected in the woods. A less peaceful harvest also gets under way as the hunting season opens, and shotguns obliterate the sound of birdsong on every hillside. Wild boar and walnuts appear in the markets.

Winter The last major harvest of the year, picking olives, starts in November (in his twilight years Mistral named his last work *Les Olivades* since he knew, too, that his season was over). The first bottles of heady young wines go on sale. The encroaching cold weather signals the *transhumance* of sheep back down from the mountains and hunting begins in earnest for the black diamonds known in Provençal as *rabasse* (truffles). While hardy souls are out hunting or truffling in the forests, the countryside seems to hibernate and many people only venture forth to warm themselves with hearty, nourishing soups and stews in the local tavern. Christmas is a major celebration in the depths of winter.

A tempting selection of olives on display at Carpentras' Friday market

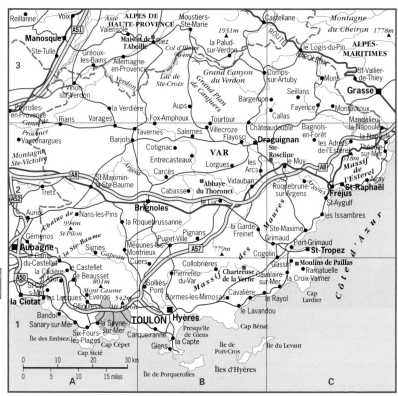

Var

Right: the gardens of the Parc Ste.-Claire in Hyères
Top right: a fountain in Cotignac

PROVENÇAL PINES
The Var's long coastline has numerous unspoilt beaches shaded, and scented, by the characteristic maritime pine (*Pinus pinaster*), with its dark blue-green foliage and reddish-coloured bark. Another species common along the coast is the Aleppo pine (*Pinus halepensis*), which has a lighter foliage and grey bark. Less common, and usually found growing in isolation, is the splendid umbrella pine (*Pinus pinea*), which owes its name to its easily recognizable shape.

Bordered by the hinterland of Marseille to the west and the Riviera to the east, the Var coastline stretches for 430km (270 miles) along the shores of the Mediterranean. It is, quite simply, the most affordable and accessible coastline in Provence. Affordable because you are not paying the over-inflated hotel and restaurant prices of the Riviera, and because the Var can boast more than twice as many campsites as its neighbouring *départements*. Accessible because it has over 150km (95 miles) of beaches, most of which are free, and because 177km (110 miles) of the coastline is open to the public thanks to the *Sentier du Littoral* (coastal path). The Var is also blessed with two unusual wilderness areas, the Massif des Maures and the Massif de l'Esterel.

THE COAST Tourism in the Var is orientated towards the sea, with plenty of opportunities for scuba-diving, windsurfing (notably L'Almanarre beach at Hyères and "Brutal" beach at Six-Fours), or just messing about in boats. The Var has around twice as many ports and marinas as the Côte d'Azur, and although some of the new marinas tend to be huge and characterless there are other, smaller ports which are perfectly charming.

And then there are the resorts: laid-back and friendly ports such as Sanary-sur-Mer or Bandol; simple beach resorts such as les Lecques or Cavalière; smarter spots such as le Lavandou or St.-Raphaël; and, of course, not forgetting flashy St.-Tropez (often mistaken for part of the Côte d'Azur, although in fact it is part of the Var).

INLAND With three-quarters of the population living in coastal areas (and 80 per cent of visitors spending their time there too), the inland expanses of the Var are sparsely populated and well worth exploring. From the coastal *massifs* the plains roll northwards, covered in a patchwork of vineyards (producing the renowned Côtes-de-Provence wines) and a smattering of villages and larger towns such as Draguignan and Brignoles. North of Draguignan, in the Haut Var, olives, truffles and honey still provide the mainstay of many small communities.

THE HISTORIC SITES The Var is not without its share of historic monuments, from the brooding mass of the Chartreuse de la Verne high up in the Massif des Maures to the Romanesque purity of the Abbaye du Thoronet in the valley of the Argens; other outstanding sights include the Collégiale St.-Pierre at Six-Fours and the Cité Épiscopal of Fréjus. One of the oldest pilgrimage sites is the cave where Mary Magdalene reputedly spent the last years of her life, in the mountains of Ste.-Baume on the western edges of the Var.

With all this, as well as plenty of appealing villages with welcoming bistros beside sun-dappled squares, it is perhaps not surprising that the tourism statistics show that on average people spend longer on holiday in the Var than they do in any other *département* of Provence.

149

Originally a watch-tower, Aups' Tour de l'Horloge now has a fine belfry

▶ **les Arcs** *148B2*

Les Arcs is an attractive medieval village in the Argens valley between Draguignan and Fréjus. The old quarter, known as le Parage, culminates in the ruins of a 13th-century castle, from where there is a view over the Massif des Maures and the surrounding vineyards that today provide les Arcs with its main source of income. Inside the **Église St.-Jean-Baptiste** there is a large Provençal pastoral tableau (*crèche*) depicting le Parage as it once was, and a 15th-century polyptych by Jean de Troyes.

In the opposite direction (4km/2.5 miles northeast on the D91), the **Chapelle Ste.-Roseline**▶ (*Open* Tue–Sun afternoons. *Admission free*) is worth a small detour. Originally part of the 11th-century Abbaye de la Celle-Roubaud, this Romanesque chapel was restored in 1970 and contains a bronze bas-relief by Giacometti, stained-glass windows by Ubac and a mosaic by Chagall.

▶ Aups   *148B3*

This small town in the middle of the woodlands of the Haut Var, dominated to the northeast by the Montagne des Espiguières, is famous for its honey and truffles (the truffle market is held every Thursday morning from November to mid-March). Although still mainly an agricultural town, it is becoming an increasingly popular base from which to tour the Haut Var or visit the Grand Canyon du Verdon (23km/14 miles to the north; see page 190). As well as the remains of its medieval ramparts, several fountains and a 16th-century tower with a fine wrought-iron belfry, Aups has an attractive Gothic church, the **Église St.-Pancrace▶**, entered through a restored Renaissance doorway.

▶▶ Bandol   *148A1*

Bandol is one of the busiest resorts west of the Côte d'Azur, with a pleasant, tree-lined promenade running the length of the port. It has all the trappings of the Riviera —discos, nightclubs, water sports and a casino—without the usual sky-high prices, which makes it a popular family resort.

Bandol has three beaches, the best of which is the Anse de Renecros, sheltered behind the headland on the west side of town. There is a lively Provençal market every Tuesday morning in the place de la Liberté, in the centre of town. The hills behind Bandol have been completely disfigured by a series of ugly, low-rise apartment blocks, but down in the town you can ignore them and concentrate instead on the yachts bobbing in the harbour and the palm trees along the port.

A hundred years ago Bandol was better known for the cultivation of flower bulbs (notably the *immortelle*, or straw flower), which were exported as far afield as Russia and America, and for its tuna fisheries. As the flower trade gradually died off at the beginning of the century, literature flourished in its place; Katherine Mansfield, Aldous Huxley and D. H. Lawrence were among the illustrious literati who descended on Bandol at the time.

The tuna fisheries are also long gone, but today the quayside is lined with boats offering deep-sea fishing, scuba-diving or simply *promenades en mer* ("boat tours"). A frequent ferry service links the port with the offshore island of **Île de Bendor▶**, which has several hotels, diving and windsurfing schools, an exhibition centre, an "artisans' village," and the **Exposition des Vins et Spiritueux▶** (*Open* by appointment until July 2008, when restoration begins). In a huge hall decorated with art students' frescoes, the museum contains over 8,000 bottles of wine and liqueurs from over 50 countries worldwide.

Back on the mainland, the tourist office can provide a map showing 50 *domaines-caves* of winegrowers offering tastings and sales of AOC Bandol wines. In town you can try the local vintages at the Maison des Vins and Caveau des Vins on Allée Alfred Vivien.

Just near Bandol on the D559B towards le Beausset is the **Jardin Exotique Zoo de Bandol-Sanary▶** (*Open* daily. *Admission: expensive*). The greenhouses and rock gardens display thousands of rare varieties of succulents, cacti and other tropical plants, while parrots, toucans, cockatoos, and other birds provide an exotic soundtrack.

WINE-TASTING
In the Argens valley, local wines can be sampled at the Maison des Vins des Côtes-de-Provence (*Open* daily in summer), around 3km (2 miles) south of les Arcs on the N7, where there is an exhibition on the history of Provençal wines and a restaurant specializing in regional food.

Bandol is one of Provence's best-known areas for wine, particularly the reds. The local winegrowers received their *appellation* AOC in 1941 (one of the first to do so) and the region spreads back from the coast to Ste.-Anne de Castellet.

151

Boats in the resort of Bandol, tied up alongside the promenade

A statue adorns the old palace which now houses Brignoles's Musée du Pays Brignolais

WHAT'S IN A NAME?
The cat's cradle of perilously steep alleys, passageways and steps that make up Bormes-les-Mimosas' *vieux village* offers up some evocative and entertaining names. Look out for rue des Amoureux (Lovers' Lane), conveniently leading off the square where village dances were held; the Montée du Paradis (Ascent to Heaven); and the pithy but expressive rue Rompi-Cuou (Bum-Breaker Street).

▶ **le Beausset**   *148A1*

Although the suburbs of le Beausset have expanded considerably in recent years, the old town centre retains much of the atmosphere of a typical Provençal town. Napoléon stayed in a house on the rue Pasteur for a month in 1793, but le Beausset's most recent claim to fame is being the home town of a gang that carried out one of the most successful bank robberies in French history, in Toulon in the late 1980s.

In the town square there is a lovely old fountain, which dates from 1832. There are three sculpted dolphins in the middle of the fountain (although the dolphins are entirely hidden beneath a mass of mossy vegetation). On the outskirts of the village, the Cave des Maîtres Vignerons du Beausset (tel: 04 94 98 70 17. *Open* Mon–Sat) sells *vin du pays*, Côtes-de-Provence AOC and Bandol wines.

On a hillside 400m (1,310ft) above le Beausset is the Romanesque **Chapelle Notre-Dame du Beausset-Vieux▶▶** (*Open* daily; afternoons only Mon, Thu, Fri. *Admission free*). Built on the site of a Celto-Ligurian settlement in 1164, the chapel was at the centre of the original settlement of le Beausset before the inhabitants moved down the hillside to the present location in 1506. Inside the chapel there is a gilded statue of the Virgin from the workshops of Pierre Puget and, on the right-hand side of the nave, an 18th-century wooden statue of Christ that once stood outside the chapel, where it was miraculously untouched by a fire in 1936, apart from the right hand, which is missing.

Alongside the chapel a gallery displays an interesting collection of around 80 *ex-votos*, including an unusual olive-wood group dating from the 15th century. An outbuilding houses a typical Provençal crib scene, or *crèche*.

From the tower atop the chapel there are sweeping views across to the Baie de la Ciotat.

▶▶ **Bormes-les-Mimosas**   *148B1*

Bormes would probably be just another *village perché* were it not for the bright yellow, vanilla-scented mimosas that it has adopted for its own and which flower throughout the village during the springtime. Winding up the road to the medieval village from its modern coastal annexe, the whole hillside is a puff of yellow blossom like dozens of plump Easter chicks arranged along neat terraces. The mimosa is not a native plant, however, but was introduced to the south coast from Mexico in the 1860s. During the summer, the mimosa is replaced with bougainvillaea, huge pots of geraniums and colourful window-boxes. As the most celebrated "floral village" in Provence, there are no fewer than three flower festivals (January, February and June).

Bormes-les-Mimosas has been "carefully" restored by artists and second-home owners and there is the usual plethora of potteries and galleries as well as the **Musée d'Arts et d'Histoire** (*Open* Mon, Wed–Sat 10–12, 2.30–7, Sun 10–12. *Admission free*), which traces the history of Bormes and boasts a Rodin statuette. The museum also holds regular exhibitions of contemporary works. There are lovely views of the coast from the courtyard of the medieval château.

▶ Brignoles   148B2

Brignoles, a large and lively town midway between the Haut Var and the Côte d'Azur, has an extensive and very attractive medieval quarter and is a good stopping point for a night or two if you are touring in the area. The heart of old Brignoles is best explored on foot (the tourist office provides a comprehensive leaflet, *Visite de la Vieille Ville*). The star attraction, not to be missed, is the fascinating **Musée du Pays Brignolais▶▶** (*Open* daily. *Admission: inexpensive*), housed in the 13th-century summer palace of the Counts of Provence.

The museum was started by a local doctor in 1947 and since then has expanded to include all sorts of curiosities, from an enormous 13th-century wine press and the world's first reinforced concrete boat, designed by local inventor Joseph Louis Lambot in 1849, to a Gayole sarcophagus dating from the 1st century AD. Discovered some 9km (5.5 miles) west of Brignoles, its incredibly well-preserved bas-reliefs depict both pagan and Christian figures.

The fairly dire collection of local paintings is somewhat less compelling but keep forging ahead for the outstanding collection of 18th- and 19th-century *ex-votos* and an automated Provençal *crèche*, or tableau.

153

Bormes' château is surrounded by pantiled houses

Var

The old church and adjoining château overlook the cobbled streets of le Castellet

154

SWEET CHESTNUTS
Collobrières was once an important centre for cork-making, but now it is sweet chestnuts from the surrounding forests that provide the economic mainstay. If you have a sweet tooth then you should visit the Confiserie Azuréenne, a seductively tempting shop selling everything imaginable made from chestnuts, from ice cream and nougat to *marrons glacés* and chestnut liqueur.

The place de la Mairie in the peaceful Haut Var village of Cotignac

▶ la Cadière d'Azur   148A1

Not as picturesque as neighbouring le Castellet across the valley, Cadière has far fewer tourists and is a much quieter, more genuine *village perché*. Three portals lead up into the old part of the village, where the 12th-century **Église St.-André** has a fine marble altarpiece. At the top of the village is the old **Chapelle Ste.-Madeleine** built by the Pénitents Gris (now a private house) and, farther down, the Chapelle Notre-Dame-de-la-Misericorde, which was built by the Pénitents Noirs and is now used for jazz concerts and other events in summer. On the D266 just outside the village, olive oil and other regional products can be bought at the excellent Moulin de St.-Côme (tel: 04 94 90 11 51).

▶▶ le Castellet   148A1

Surrounded by the terraced vineyards of Côte-de-Provence wines, le Castellet was one of the first *villages perchés* to be rejuvenated by artisans, who were encouraged to settle here in the 1950s. It now has a well-established mix of craft shops, art galleries, potteries, cafés and restaurants.

The delightful flower-filled streets lead up to the parish church (parts of which date from the 12th century) and the old château (rebuilt in the 15th century), which now houses the *mairie* (town hall) next door. To the left of the *mairie* is the so-called Trou de Madame, a gateway that leads onto a small balcony with magnificent views northwards across the vineyards in the valley and the foothills leading up to Ste.-Baume.

▶ Cogolin   148C2

On the edge of the Massif des Maures 6km (4 miles) inland from Port Grimaud, Cogolin does have the odd ruin, but most people come here for shopping rather than sight-seeing since it has a lively crafts-based tradition.

First and foremost are Cogolin's famous pipes, which are made at the workshops of La Fabrique de Pipes Courrieu (*Open* weekends) on the main street. Even if you are not a pipe-smoker it is worth glancing in their windows just to

FILM SET
Le Castellet's photogenic medieval streets have been used more than once for film sets, most notably by Marcel Pagnol, who shot *La Femme du Boulanger* here in the 1930s and returned more than 50 years later to film scenes from *Manon des Sources*. But the village's cinematic associations go back further, since it was here that the Lumière Brothers bought a house (now the Castel Lumière hotel) to use as a pre-production studio in 1895 for making France's first moving picture (see panel, page 123).

155

see the amazing variety of pipes made here: pipes with lids, pipes with faces, pipes with frills, inlaid, carved, long-stemmed, short-stemmed, even some with twin bowls.

Cogolin is also famous for its carpets, an industry that started up in the 1920s with the arrival of Armenian immigrants who brought with them a tradition of hand-knotted ancestral rugs; you can see them being produced in the workshops of La Manufacture de Tapis along the boulevard Louis Blanc (*Open* weekdays). Other crafts-men in the village specialize in pottery, ironwork, corks for the wine trade, cane furniture and top-quality reeds for wind instruments.

▶ Collobrières   148B1
Time seems to have passed by this large village in the heart of the Massif des Maures, where there are few concessions to modernity apart from a sweet chestnut factory.

Otherwise, Collobrières is a rest-stop on the long and winding road up to the **Chartreuse de la Verne**▶▶ (*Open* summer 11–6; winter Wed–Mon 11–5. *Closed* Jan. *Admission: moderate*), isolated among the forests of the Maures. Founded in 1170, this Carthusian monastery has been ransacked and rebuilt many times and is still under-going restoration. The rambling complex of cloisters, chapels and monks' cells (each of which has its own garden) is built from a combination of dark red schist and green-coloured serpentine, a local Maures stone.

The high walls that surround the monastery give it a dark, brooding presence, but it has uninterrupted views of the forested hills and the Gulf of St.-Tropez beyond.

▶ Cotignac   148B2
This dreamy Haut Var village is dominated by two ruined towers on top of an 80m (260ft) high cliff riddled with caves and grottoes. Behind the Romanesque parish church (with a facade rebuilt in the 19th century) is an enchanting Théâtre de Verdure where concerts are held in the summer. Wine, honey and olive oil are the village's main products.

Twin bells atop the medieval parish church in le Castellet

Provençal cuisine at its best bursts with the aromatic, sun-drenched flavours of the Mediterranean. The essential ingredients—olive oil, garlic, the ubiquitous tomato and herbs—are combined in many colourful dishes usually described as à la Provençale. An added bonus is that the Provençal style of cooking is good for your health!

APÉRITIFS

The locals like their *pastis* before a meal. *Pastis* is an amber-coloured spirit distilled with anis and other herbs, which goes cloudy when water is added. It is an acquired taste but hugely popular in Provence, perhaps due to its potency (at 45 per cent proof, its effects are quickly felt in the southern sun!). *Pastis* is usually accompanied by a dish of black or green olives, or canapés spread with a savoury paste called *tapènade*, an appetizing purée of capers, olives and anchovies.

Created in Provence, the potent apéritif pastis *was once illegal*

Soups *Soupe au pistou* (vegetable soup with a crushed paste made from olive oil, basil and garlic) is essentially a summer dish, but Provence's famous fish soups can be enjoyed year round. The most famous of these is *bouillabaisse*, which is more of a stew than a soup and usually served as a meal in its own right. Originating in Marseille, *bouillabaisse* can include a variety of fish such as *rascasse* (spiny hog fish), *loup* (sea bass), *rouget* (red mullet), eels, crabs and anything else pulled out of the sea that morning. The fish are cooked in a *bouillon* (stock) containing saffron, garlic, herbs, and fennel and are served up separately from the liquid at the table, accompanied by a spicy red pepper and garlic mayonnaise called *rouille*: You spread the *rouille* on croûtons, sprinkle them with cheese and dunk them in your soup, accompanied by bits of fish.

You will also find *rouille* being served with the less expensive (although no less tasty) *soupe de poissons*, while another classic fish soup-like stew, *bourride*, is more properly accompanied by *aïoli*.

Aïoli A delicious thick mayonnaise made with plenty of garlic and rich olive oil, *aïoli* is traditionally served alongside raw vegetables (*crudités*) as *hors d'oeuvres*. The more substantial version is an *aïoli garni*, with freshly cooked cod, potatoes and hard-boiled eggs that are dipped into it.

Salads and vegetables Artichokes, asparagus and aubergines (eggplants) are all locally grown in Provence, but the king of Provençal vegetables is probably the wonderfully full-flavoured and versatile sun-ripened tomato, which appears in numerous dishes or *au naturel* sprinkled with olive oil and basil. *Salade niçoise*, with its black olives, tuna, hard-boiled eggs and green beans, is a Provençal classic, as is *ratatouille*, a vegetable stew of tomatoes, aubergines, onions, peppers and courgettes. Precious truffles (*truffes*, or *rabasse* in Provençal) are gathered every winter in the north of the region and lend their distinctive flavour to the local culinary scene, as do *cèpes* mushrooms.

Meat The most common dish is lamb grilled with savoury herbs or served in a sauce *à la Provençale*. The best and tastiest lamb is the lean *agneau de Sisteron*, which has grazed on mountain pastures. Beef often comes braised in red wine and vegetables as a succulent *daube de boeuf*, or in the Camarguais version as *boeuf à la*

gardiane. Rabbit (*lapin*) and hare (*lièvre*) are also simmered in wine and herbs and more adventurous diners can sample *pieds et paquets* (a hearty trotter and tripe concoction made with mutton or pork).

Fish Naturally enough, fish features heavily on menus, some of the best choices being *loup de mer* (sea bass) grilled with fennel or vine shoots, *rouget* (red mullet), *St.-Pierre* (John Dory), sardines or *merlan* (hake). Up in the hills, *truite* (trout) often has a very short journey from a mountain stream to your table. The shellfish is usually excellent, and includes *moules* (mussels), *gambas* (giant prawns), *palourdes* (clams), *oursins* (sea urchins), crab and lobster.

Cheeses Local cheeses are usually made from the milk of goats (*chèvres*) or ewes (*brebis*). In any market you can find an enormous selection of goat's cheese, which is usually either very creamy and fresh (with a fairly mild flavour) or has been left to dry out, in which case it has a much stronger, sharper taste. *Petits chèvres* are small roundels of goat's cheese, often rolled in bay, thyme and other herbs. *Poivre d'âne* is a goat's cheese with a particularly peppery flavour, while *Banon* is a creamy sheep's cheese.

Desserts and fruit Desserts are always served after the cheese in France and the range of tempting flans and pastries can easily melt your resolutions about a light meal. However, Provençal markets are piled high with scrumptious fresh fruits throughout the summer, such as strawberries, cherries, figs, peaches, nectarines, apricots, pears and dessert grapes.

SNACKS
Apart from *baguette* sandwiches, pizza slices and the ubiquitous *frîtes* (french fries), a popular option is the *pan bagnat*, a monster bread bap spread with olive oil and filled with a *salade niçoise*-type mix. *Croque monsieurs* (toasted cheese and ham sandwiches) are not particularly Provençal, but *pissaladière* (a delicious onion, olive and anchovy flan, best eaten cold or just warm) is very much local. In Nice the delicacy is a slice of the extremely filling *socca*, a tasty pancake made from chick pea flour. Another Provençal delicacy is the *fougasse*, a baked slice containing olives, sausage, cheese and other goodies.

A salade niçoise—no two versions are the same

Market day in Draguignan, the Var's biggest inland town

▶ Draguignan *148B2*

As you descend from the isolated villages and sparsely populated countryside of the Haut Var, Draguignan comes as something of a shock. Spreading over the entire valley, the outskirts of the town are an unattractive conglomeration of commercial centres, hypermarkets and second-hand car lots. And yet, hidden away inside this ugly outer shell, Draguignan has a reasonably well-preserved *vieille ville* and one of the best ethnographic museums in the whole of Provence. The absorbing **Musée des Arts et Traditions Populaires de Moyenne Provence▶▶** (15 rue Roumanille, tel: 04 94 47 05 72. Open Tue–Sat 9–12, 2–6, Sun 2–6. *Admission: moderate*) displays the culture and heritage of the Var through a series of imaginative reconstructions of country life. Olive pressing, silk culture, winemaking, agriculture, cork-manufacturing, bee-keeping, hide-tanning and tilemaking are all faithfully covered. There are also Provençal costumes, musical instruments, religious art and temporary exhibitions on a variety of topics.

Above the old town stands the **Tour de l'Horloge▶**, on the site of the first settlement here. Built in 1663, it replaced an earlier keep that was part of the medieval fortifications.

The solid silhouette of the Tour de l'Horloge rises above Draguignan's spires and rooftops

Between the tower and the crumbling 13th-century **Chapelle de St.-Sauveur▶**, just below it on the hillside, is the charming **Théâtre de Verdure▶**, an open-air theatre artfully created with rocks, lawns and olive trees in perfect proportion. Ask the tourist office for details of concert performances in this lovely setting (tel: 04 98 10 51 05).

▶ Embiez, Île des   148A1

The Île des Embiez is owned by Paul Ricard. Ferries cross from le Brusc at regular intervals. Apart from a couple of small beaches, a summer season mini-train tour, and clifftop walks, the main attraction for visitors is the **Institut Océanographique Paul Ricard** (*Open* summer, daily 10–12.30, 1.30–5.30; winter Mon–Fri 10–12.30, 2–5.30, Sun, Sun 2–5.30. *Admission: moderate*), where there are several small aquarium tanks with around 100 species of Mediterranean fish and displays on marine ecology and local shipwrecks. The real seabed can also be viewed.

▶ Entrecasteaux   148B2

This small village is dominated by its 17th-century **Château▶** (*Open* for guided tours Easter–Oct Sun–Fri, tours at 4pm. Aug additional tour at 11.30, tel: 04 94 04 43 95. *Admission: expensive*), which was restored in the 1970s by an eccentric Scots painter, Ian McGarvie-Munn. The interior is rather bizarre, since parts are furnished in contemporary style (and decorated with McGarvie-Munn's own paintings), while others display period furnishings. Photographic and art exhibitions are also held inside the château, and there is a charming semi-formal garden, designed by Le Nôtre.

▶▶▶ Esterel, Massif de l'   148C2

Romantic travel posters in the past used to depict SNCF trains emerging from the tunnels in the Esterel *massif* to landscapes of brilliant red cliffs and bright blue seas: it is still so, but if you restrict yourself to the train or even the Corniche d'Or (the N98) alongside the railway line you will be missing one of the great splendours of Provence, an evocative wilderness hidden away behind the coast.

The Esterel (see page 171) is one of the Var's best-kept secrets. Most of the range (over three-quarters out of a total of 6,000ha/14,830 acres) is only accessible on foot or by mountain bicycle. There are numerous tracks throughout the Esterel (some of which may be closed off in summer due to the fire risk), for which the best source of information is a map produced by the Office National des Forêts (National Forests Office), available from the tourist offices in St.-Raphaël and Fréjus. There are also 42km (26 miles) of maintained roads, offering fabulous drives through parts of the *massif*.

▶ Evenos   148A1

High above the Gorges d'Ollioules loom the sombre walls of Evenos' 12th-century castle. It is worth the drive up the twisting road to walk around the outside of the walls (the interior is closed off). Huddled around the castle and a 13th-century church is the tiny village itself, where many of the crumbling houses have been restored. There is just one *auberge*, called, simply enough, *On Mange, On Boit* ("One Eats, One Drinks").

A square at the entrance to Evenos is dedicated to the Provençal writer Marie Mauron, who graphically describes the castle as "black and torn apart, standing tragically against the open sky," adding that "the approaching silhouette, the ruins of dark basalt, wring your heart." It is indeed a strange place, as is the Grès de Ste.-Anne outside the village of Ste.-Anne d'Evenos below the château. This weird moonscape of sandstone formations (reached via a path on the right of the road just to the south of Ste.-Anne) has many hidden grottoes and startling formations, and is at the base of the nearby Gros Cerveau (the "big brain") range.

159

The 1970s meet the 16th century in Entrecasteaux's château

THE ROMAN PORT

The port of Fréjus, or Forum Julii, was founded in 49 BC by Julius Caesar as a staging post on the coastal road that later became known as the Aurelian Way. It was the first Roman town in Gaul, and was soon turned into a major naval base by Octavian (later to become the Emperor Augustus), who used it to build a fleet of fast, light galleys with which he defeated Antony and Cleopatra in the Battle of Actium.

A palatial quayside residence in Port Grimaud

▶▶▶ Fréjus   148C2

Fréjus and its neighbour, St.-Raphaël, lie at the mouth of the Argens River between the Massif des Maures and Massif de l'Esterel. Now merged together into a somewhat characterless holiday conglomeration, Fréjus does have several relics that are worth investigating.

Founded by the Romans, Fréjus never recovered from Saracen attacks in the 10th century, nor the silting up of its harbour, leaving the port 3km (2 miles) inland. The sandy delta created by the Argens River is now Fréjus-Plage and adjacent St.-Aygulf, crowded, but handy for affordable campgrounds, assorted seaside family attractions and the Parc Zoologique Safari de Fréjus next to the A8 autoroute.

Compared with others in Provence, the Roman amphitheatre, **Les Arènes**, is not particularly impressive, although some of the upper tiers have been rebuilt. Most of the other **Roman remains**—the theatre and remnants of the aqueduct and harbour wall—are somewhat scattered, so hopping on the town's *petit train* is a good idea on a hot day. At the centre of the old town, Fréjus's real treasure is the **Groupe Épiscopal▶▶▶** (58 rue de Fleury, tel: 04 94 51 26 30. Cathedral *open* Jun–Sep daily 9–6.30; Oct–May Tue–Sun 9–12, 2–5. *Admission free*. Free guided tours to be booked in advance, tel: 04 94 51 26 30). Begun in the 10th century, the **cathedral▶▶** boasts a magnificent set of carved walnut doors from the Renaissance, protected by a set of shutters for the last 200 years. The octagonal **baptistery▶▶▶** dates

from the 4th or 5th century and is one of the best preserved of its era in France.

The final part of the cathedral complex is the charming **cloister▶▶▶**, with its slender columns and fantastic panoply of wood carvings on the ceiling; only 400 remain of the 1,200 panels. The **archaeological museum▶** contains finds from Forum Julii (see panel), including a copy of the famous double-headed bust of Hermes, discovered in 1970. The priceless Hellenistic original is kept in secure storage.

► **la Garde-Freinet**   *148B2*

Straddling a pass across the rolling hills of the Massif des Maures, this now peaceful village of narrow alleys, fountains and courtyards was one of the last Saracen strongholds in Provence during the 10th century, and France's main cork-producing town in the 19th century. The settlement is hedged in by a green sea of cork oaks, sweet chestnut groves and eucalyptus perched 360m (1,180ft) above the coast. You can take a 20-minute hike up to the **Fort Freinet►** to the west, from where there are extensive views back across to the le Luc plain and the foothills of the Alps beyond.

►► **Grimaud**   *148C2*

A picture-perfect *village perché* on the eastern flanks of the Massif des Maures, Grimaud is named after the Grimaldi family who owned it from the 10th century onwards. The rue des Templiers, with its arcades and Gothic doorways, leads up to the Hospice of the Knights Templars and the Romanesque **Église St.-Michel►**. Overlooking the village are the ruins of the Grimaldi **château►**, with views down to the Gulf of St.-Tropez and inland across the Maures.

Down on the coast is **Port Grimaud►►**. With its hundreds of pastel-shaded villas lining over 8km (5 miles) of quayside along the canals, it was designed by architect François Spoerry in the 1960s as a "seafaring" community where everyone could have their boats parked outside their own front doors. Inevitably this pastiche of a fishing village has become a visitor attraction in its own right, with most yacht-owning residents simply jetting in for their summer holidays.

Port Grimaud is worth a look, if you are passing by, just to experience this "Provençal Venice," although restaurants and cafés are absurdly overpriced and the compulsory parking outside the gates is expensive. View the whole ensemble from the top of the church tower. Boats leave regularly from beside the main square for trips around the canals.

Boats are the only way to get around in Port Grimaud

THE SARACENS
Apart from generally pillaging the surrounding countryside (until finally being expelled by Count William in AD 973), the Saracens also introduced the tambourine, flat roof tiles and the art of cork-making to Provence; the last was to become the economic mainstay of la Garde-Freinet until the 19th century.

Once a fashionable resort, Hyères thrives on local horticulture

MAD ABOUT PALMS
Palm trees were originally introduced to France from the Canary Islands in 1864 by an amateur horticulturalist, the Comte Vigier. He planted three trees in Nice in 1865, and in 1867 the first seeds found their way to Hyères. Hyères very quickly became the "palm tree capital" of the Riviera, sending 300,000 trees a year all over Europe. Some 12,000 majestic palms currently grace the streets of Hyères les Palmiers and there is even an association, the Fous des Palmiers ("mad about palms"), for enthusiasts to swap seeds, knowledge and growing tips.

▶▶ Hyères   148B1

The original Côte d'Azur resort, frequented by the likes of Robert Louis Stevenson, Tolstoy and Queen Victoria, Hyères' star faded with the development of Nice and Cannes. Since then the cultivation of fruit, flowers, and vegetables has provided a reliable economic mainstay and local horticulturalists are major growers of roses, marigolds, irises, tulips and gladioli.

Hyères is well known for its parks and also for its palm tree nurseries (see panel), hence the change of name to the more exotic Hyères les Palmiers. This embraces the old town of Vieux Hyères, the modern town centre, and the Port d'Hyères down on the seafront.

From the place Clemenceau in the centre of town, the 14th-century **Porte Massillon** leads into the old town, where all streets eventually converge on the spacious place Massillon, site of the daily market. At the top of the square is the half-rounded **Tour St.-Blaise▶**, built by the Knights Templar in the 12th century. Behind the square is the **Collégiale St.-Paul▶**, which houses over 400 *ex-votos* (dating from 1613 right up to 1985) and a large Provençal *crèche* (tableau) re-creating the Hyères of yesteryear.

To the right of the church a huge archway leads beneath a Renaissance house up to the **Parc St.-Bernard▶**, which culminates in the **Villa de Noailles** (*Open* Wed–Sun 10–12, 2–6) at the top of the hill. Now a private arts centre, the Cubist-inspired villa was designed by the architect Robert Mallet-Stevens for the arts patron Charles de Noailles in 1924. The park displays a wide variety of Mediterranean flowers and shrubs, with the pathways opening up to reveal delightful vistas where you least expect them. Follow the old walls westwards from the park to an insignificant-looking gateway that leads into the **Parc Ste.-Claire▶**, where the gardens of similar style, although far moreextensive, have a glorious profusion of Mediterranean flowering plants.

Back down in the main town, the **Musée Municipal** (*Open* Mon, Wed–Sat. *Admission free*) contains antiquities from the ancient port of Hyères, as well as two engraved menhirs found nearby.

More flowers, plants and exotic trees (as well as a small zoo and a tropical green-house) can be found in the 7ha (17-acre) **Jardin Olbius Riquier▶** (*Open* daily) on avenue Gambetta.

▶▶▶ Hyères, Îles d'   148B1

The three islands off the coast of Hyères have been known since the 17th century as the Îles d'Or thanks to the golden glint of the mica shale in their southernmost cliffs. They are scattered about with forts and the French military still maintains bases on two of them, but their wild, natural landscapes have been partially protected since the 1960s.

The islands are covered in dense vegetation—pine, eucalyptus, lavender, heather and rosemary scent the sea-swept air. Spring is the best time to come, when migrating birds pass through. The underwater flora is also protected as part of the Parc National de Port-Cros and spear-fishing is prohibited.

The islands can be reached by ferry from most nearby ports, including Toulon, la Tour-Fondue, Hyères-Plage and le Lavandou.

Porquerolles▶▶▶ is the most easily accessible, the largest of the three and the only one that is permanently inhabited. The village (also called Porquerolles) has cafés, restaurants and a handful of hotels, as well as bicycle rental shops. You can cycle or walk as far as the lighthouse on the south coast, or visit the gentle, sandy beach of Notre-Dame at the northeastern tip of the island.

Port-Cros▶▶ is the most hilly of the three, and its wealth of flora and fauna has been protected since 1963. France's smallest national park, it has marked walking trails (which you are forbidden to wander off) around the island or across the middle to the Vallon de la Solitude or the Vallon de la Fausse-Monnaie.

The third island, the **Île du Levant**, is mostly occupied by the military. The land that isn't claimed by them has been taken over by a nudist colony, which was originally set up in the 1930s, in the village of Héliopolis.

BIRTH OF THE "AZURE COAST"
A wealthy vineyard owner from Dijon, Stephen Liégeard, decided one day in 1887 to leave the rain and fog of the north behind and take a holiday in the South of France. Stopping at Hyères, he alighted on the beach to behold the luminous skies and translucent blue waters of the Mediterranean, at which point, so it is said, Liégeard cried "Côte d'Azur!" When Liégeard returned to Paris he published an illustrated book, *La Côte d'Azur 1888*, extolling the virtues of this wonderful coastline. Thus one of the most well-known tourism marketing slogans was born.

163

The Tour St.-Blaise is all that remains of a Knights Templar lodge

Hot, dry summers mean that fire is an ever-present menace in Provence and yet, contrary to popular belief, fires cause much less damage than they used to. In addition, tree-planting schemes mean that there is now a far greater area of woodland than there was a century ago.

REAFFORESTATION
The Foundation for the Protection of Mediterranean Forests replants an average of 60,000 trees every year. Just as you may see many burned-out areas in Provence, you will also see many others where signs proclaim "this area has been replanted by the schoolchildren of the village—please respect their work." In fact, through schemes such as these and natural regeneration, the forests of Provence have crept back up from 600,000ha (148,260 acres) just over a century ago to almost 1,107,000ha (2,735,400 acres) today. All is not yet lost for the woodland heritage of Provence.

The aftermath of a forest fire, an all too common sight

The forests The forests in Provence are dominated by conifers such as the maritime, umbrella, and Aleppo pines, as well as cedars. Around 60 per cent of existing woodland is coniferous, the rest comprising mostly deciduous trees such as chestnut, or evergreens, such as cork and dwarf scrub oaks. The majority of the forests are in the Var, with the Alpes-Maritime, Vaucluse and Hautes-Alpes accounting for less than half and the Bouches-du-Rhône with just under a third.

Setting the forest alight The Provençal forests are particularly susceptible to fires due to summer droughts and strong winds. During the long, hot summer months the dried-up forest floor, littered with leaves, twigs and resinous pine needles, can easily catch fire. If there is any wind, or, worse still, a *mistral*, the flames can be quickly fanned into an inferno, creating a wall of fire up to 30m (100ft) high that consumes all in its path.

Today the major causes of fire are carelessness on the part of walkers and picnickers, and the vandalistic acts of arsonists. Some of the worst fires since records have been kept were in 1764 (when the whole of the Esterel burned down), in 1864 (when vast areas of the Maures were destroyed) and in 1899 and 1964.

Devastation You don't have to drive far in Provence to witness blackened hillsides and stark slopes, littered with

the charred skeletons of trees, where fire has passed. The unprotected slopes are prone to erosion and a new flora soon takes over, that of the *maquis*, a sparse, low-lying cover of thistles, gorse, stunted downy oaks and hardy lavender, thyme and rosemary. Without help, the ancient forest cover seldom regenerates in this impoverished soil.

Prevention Since 1963 the various *départements* in Provence have co-ordinated their fire-prevention and fire-fighting efforts, and this was strengthened in 1989 with the creation of the Fondation pour la Forêt Méditerranéene (Foundation for the Mediterranean Forests).

Through research, public education and experiments with fire-prevention techniques, they have had considerable success in reducing forest fires. New laws require undergrowth to be cleared around houses and along roads in high-risk areas, and a vast network of cisterns (over 700 in the Var alone) has been installed in the forests to give firefighters access to water.

Whole areas of forest are now closed off during the summer in periods of drought, and if you try to venture past the barriers you will soon find there is a forest patrol warning you away.

Aerial attack Sunning yourself on a Riviera beach during the summer, it is quite likely you will witness the extraordinary sight of a plane descending to the sea and skimming the surface as it scoops up millions of litres of water, before taking off again and heading inland. You have just seen a Canadair, one of the main weapons in the fight against fire. There is now a fleet of these lumbering *bombardiers d'eau* (water bombers), based at Marignane airport at Marseille. They are guided and assisted by tracker aircraft that constantly patrol and monitor the hinterland. In 1986, the first helicopter water bombers (HBE) made their appearance, and a team of these are also now on permanent stand-by during the summer.

Thanks to better co-ordination and more water bombers, in recent years 95 per cent of fires have been extinguished before they covered 5ha (12 acres). However, it is strictly forbidden to introduce any form of fire into the national forests, including cigarettes.

"SHOOT THE ARSONISTS"
Arsonists are usually considered a latter-day phenomenon but this is not so, as evidenced by a letter from Napoléon to the Prefect of the Var, written on 21 August 1809: "I have learnt that several fires have broken out in the Department which I have entrusted to you," he wrote, "and I order you to shoot on the spot anyone convicted of the crime of having set them alight. If these fires break out again I shall be forced to replace you."

165

High-risk areas are now closed off during the summer

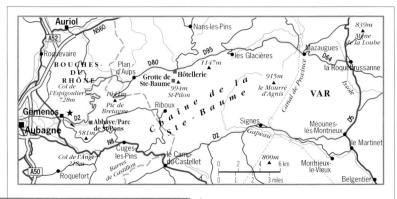

Drive
and country walk

Ste.-Baume

The Ste.-Baume massif is only 12km (7.5 miles) long, but it shelters one of the most unusual forests in Provence and also a shrine sacred to Mary Magdalene. This drive encircles the whole of the massif, and includes two

The summit of Ste.-Baume

walks, a short one up to a beautiful abbey and a longer one up to the sacred grotto itself. Allow 4–5 hours from Gémenos.

Take the D2 out of Gémenos until you see signs for the **Parc de St.-Pons▶▶** on the right. From the bridge, a delightful woodland path leads up through a valley, with the waters of the Frauge constantly burbling over cascades and rocks. After 15 minutes, you reach the **Abbaye de St.-Pons▶**, one of the best-preserved Cistercian convents in Provence. Established in 1205, it was a popular retreat for ladies of nobility. Just behind the abbey, the source itself gushes out of a small fissure in a rockface.

Continue on up the D2, which curves around the rock circle of the Pic de Bretagne before climbing up to the pass at the Col de l'Espigoulier. Here the view southwards suddenly opens out in front of you, with Marseille and the Chaîne de l'Etoile in the distance behind the Aubagne plain. Keep going through Plan d'Aups until you reach the Hôtellerie de la Ste.-Baume. From here, follow the signboards for the Grotte de Ste.-Baume. There are two paths up to the sanctuary. On the left is the Chemin des Rois (chosen by the kings of France, hence the name, who made pilgrimages here in the Middle Ages). The oratories were built in 1516 by Jean Ferrier, archbishop of Arles and Aix. The right-hand path, the Chemin des Canapés, follows broken-down, moss-covered stone steps. It is easier to take the Chemin des Rois on the way up and the Chemin des Canapés back down.

Both paths meander through a forest of ash, beech, aspen, holly, maple and ancient yew trees. On the forest floor lichens, moss and wild mushrooms flourish. This fantastic forest, one of few locally where Northern European tree species grow, is the last remnant of the woodlands that once covered Provence in the tertiary era. Covering around 130ha (320 acres), its survival is attributed to the shade created by the towering cliff faces above it. Always considered a sacred forest, it is now a Biological Reserve.

The two paths meet at the Carrefour de l'Oratoire (the oratory crossroads). Follow a flight of steps on the right up to the terrace, where there is a good view.

Behind you is the **Grotte de Ste.-Baume►►**, where Mary Magdalene is supposed to have spent the last years of her life. The cave is enormous, with stained-glass windows set in the rock, several statues of Mary Magdalene, and an altar with Bossan's *Rock of Penitence* behind it. Water drips constantly from the walls, and there is also a spring at the back of the sanctuary, which is open every day. There are services at Whitsun and on 21 July (Mary Magdalene's saint day) and midnight mass on Christmas Eve.

Return to the oratory crossroads and, if you are feeling energetic, take the GR9 zigzagging up to the **Col de St.-Pilon►**, half an hour farther on. From nearly 1,000m (3,280ft), the 360-degree view takes in Mont Ventoux, the Massif des Maures and the Alpilles. The small chapel at the summit stands on the site of the column (hence "St. Pilon") that once stood on the site.

Back down at the parking area, follow the D95 to Mazaugues, continuing to la Roquebrussanne. Turn down the D5, bearing right at Méounes-lès-Montrieux (with several fountains) towards Signes, with more fountains and a 16th-century Gothic church.

Continue parallel to the southern slopes of Ste.-Baume to reach the escarpment overlooking the Plan du Castellet and turn right on the N8 towards Gémenos.

In the lee of the cliffs, Ste.-Baume's forest is now designated a Biological Reserve

▶ le Lavandou 148B1

At the start of the smarter part of the coast, yachts now outnumber fishing boats in le Lavandou's harbour, and the prices in the numerous restaurants, boutiques and cafés in the pedestrianized streets behind the port are beginning to tip towards those on the Riviera. Le Lavandou's main attraction is a good selection of beaches. The town's own wide, sandy beach curves around the bay towards the west, and there are several smaller and more secluded retreats hidden away nearby.

Around 3km (2 miles) to the east, **la Fossette** is a small horseshoe-shaped beach with a handy café-restaurant,

An imposing town hall dominates the main square in Ollioules

168

while past here **Aiguebelle** has three beaches: the one on the sea front can get busy, but a short distance farther on a steep path leads down to a wonderful double bay, which is far less crowded. The east half is a nudist beach, as is the next beach along, the well-known **le Layet**, where *textiles* (people with clothes on), as French nudists call them, will be frowned upon. Finally, there is a superb beach at the pleasant little resort of **Cavalière▶** (not to be confused with the hideously built-up Cavalaire-sur-Mer farther on). Le Lavandou is a good base for exploring the Massif des Maures, where the wooded slopes come almost down to the sea behind the coast road (the Corniche des Maures).

COASTAL WALK
At the eastern end of the Baie des Lecques is la Madrague, from where a coastal path leads around the headlands to Bandol. The Sentier du Littoral winds around the unspoilt coastline for some 9km (5.5 miles), but it is an easy half-hour walk—scented with heathers, pine and sweet-smelling *salsepareille* (sarsaparilla)—out to the Pointe Grenier, where the Tour de Vigie (partially restored in 1993 under the auspices of APARE, see page 75) sits atop a headland with lovely views back down the coast to la Ciotat and eastwards along the cliffs.

▶ Les Lecques 148A1

The seaside suburb of the nearby town of St.-Cyr, les Lecques is a popular family resort largely due to its safe, sandy, gently shelving beach. The family appeal is further enhanced by a massive summer season water theme park, **Aqualand**, just outside St.-Cyr.

Les Lecques claims to be the site of the ancient Greek settlement of Tauroentum, although only Roman remains have been found so far. These are on display in the **Musée Tauroentum** (*Open* Wed–Mon afternoons in summer; weekends only in winter. *Admission: inexpensive*), with mosaics, frescoes, vases and household utensils.

▶▶▶ Maures, Massif des

148B1

Around 60km (38 miles) from end to end and 30km (18 miles) wide, the Massif des Maures stretches from Fréjus to Hyères, dipping down to the sea to form wide bays at Cavalière, Pampelonne (near St.-Tropez), and Bormes. The glittering mica cliffs of the Îles d'Hyères are an extension of the chain out into the sea.

The hills of the Maures, up to 760m (2,490ft) high, are thickly forested with chestnuts, cork oaks and Aleppo and umbrella pines. The forest's shaded depths gave rise to its name, which comes from *mauram* (Provençal for "dark"). In contrast to the wooded slopes, vineyards spread across sunlit valleys, where there are signs of human habitation. Much of the forest is impenetrable, except by forest fires, which have taken their toll here.

In the Dark Ages the Maures were ruled by the Saracens, who built their strongholds (*fraxinets*) on the hilltops and plundered the surrounding countryside for more than 100 years before Count Guillaume drove them out in AD 972. There are still very few settlements in the heart of the Maures, the main ones being Collobrières (see page 155) and la Garde-Freinet (see page 161).

▶ Ollioules

148A1

The southern outskirts of Ollioules, with their ever-multiplying superstores, have become practically a suburb of Toulon, but, in the town itself, traffic-calming measures, re-cobbling of streets and facelifts for many buildings have created an entirely different atmosphere.

Behind the church, the picturesque streets lead up to the ruined 11th-century **château▶**, which was once a stronghold ruled over by the Seigneurs de Signe et d'Evenos. A lone window punctuates the sole remaining full-height wall of the castle; for several years, volunteers have been slowly restoring the remaining rooms and doorways.

Ollioules has an active crafts community centred on small streets such as rue Gambetta, an arts exhibition centre, and a small amphitheatre with summer dance and drama.

Cork oak in the Massif des Maures

DRIVES AND WALKS
One of the most rewarding tours through the Maures is the 71km (44 mile) Routes des Crêtes, which starts in la Garde-Freinet and circles around via Collobrières and the D14 to Grimaud. You can also make a slightly longer tour (around 110km/68 miles) from le Lavandou, via Bormes-les-Mimosas, Collobrières, Grimaud and Cogolin.

For hikers, the GR9 from la Garde-Freinet skirts the highest points of the *massif* through the Forêt Domaniale des Mayons towards Pignans on the N97, while the GR51 takes a much longer, more southerly route from near Port Grimaud through to Pierrefeu-du-Var on the D12.

The neo-Byzantine Église-Notre-Dame de la Victoire rises up behind the Grand Casino in St.-Raphaël

►► Ramatuelle   148C1

In the heart of the St.-Tropez peninsula, Ramatuelle is a typical Provençal village with a typical influx of second-home owners, artisan workshops, art galleries and antiques shops, but very pretty and appealing. There is a Romanesque church with a 17th-century doorway carved from serpentine and the surrounding vineyards produce much sought-after Côtes-de-Provence wines.

NEARBY On the D89 heading out above Ramatuelle, three ancient windmills, **Les Moulins de Paillas►**, are perched on a hillside with fabulous views across the Presqu'Île de St.-Tropez and the Îles d'Hyères. There are also spectacular panoramas from the small village of **Gassin►►** farther up the same road. Gassin was built as a lookout point during the time of the Saracen invasions, and several restaurants now enjoy the same views, although you may well feel plundered yourself when presented with the bill.

► St.-Raphaël   148C2

St.-Raphaël is a popular family resort with a big sandy beach curving around the bay between its marinas. It was popularized in the mid-19th century by the writer Alphonse Karr, who lured Maupassant, Alexandre Dumas and Berlioz down for their winter holidays. Unfortunately all the grand hotels and *belle époque* villas were destroyed during World War II, although there are still remnants of the medieval village surrounding the Romanesque **Église St.-Pierre** on the other side of the railway line that runs through the centre of town.

Just beside the church, the **Musée Archéologique►** (*Open* Tue–Sat. *Admission: inexpensive*) has some interesting displays on underwater archaeology (as well as local terrestrial finds), including an enormous number of amphorae dating from the 1st century BC onwards, discovered in wrecks off the coast.

The town plays host to a lively New Orleans Jazz Competition during July, with outdoor performances along the promenade and around town.

BIKINI COVER-UP
Even in the summer heatwave of 1993, the Mayor of St.-Raphaël decided he had had enough of scantily clad visitors in the shops and streets of the resort. Dredging up an obscure municipal decree that forbids anyone to walk around the town in swimsuits, he sent out the *gendarmes* to enforce the law, warning people wearing bikinis and swimsuits that they were not on the beach and had better cover up. The only other place where this might happen is Ste.-Maxime, where there is a fine for anyone wearing less than a T-shirt.

The heart of the Esterel is one of the most captivating areas along the Riviera coastline, as unexpected and as wild as the Massif des Maures, yet more beautiful, more astonishing for its proximity to the built-up areas and its serenity and total lack of habitation.

The massif Like the neighbouring Massif des Maures, the Esterel is much older than the limestone that predominates in most of Provence, and presents a series of jagged profiles, rust-red canyons and dramatic rock formations. The vivid red porphyry (volcanic rock) has solidified in ridges and peaks that plunge into the sea, indented by small bays and inlets, creating a striking contrast with the deep blue of the Mediterranean. Elsewhere, the rocks have been mined for their blue tints, much favoured by the Romans for temple columns.

Flora and fauna The Esterel was originally heavily wooded with cork oaks and holm oaks, but forest fires have taken their toll. Over 120 fires have ravaged the hills and valleys since 1828, four of which (in 1838, 1918, 1943 and 1964) affected practically the whole of the *massif*.

The predominant vegetation is *maquis* (scrub), a dense covering of heathers, gorse, mimosa, lavender and other shrubs. Spring is one of the best times to be here, when wild flowers colour the landscape and scent the pure air.

The Esterel is home to wild boar, hares, partridges, pheasants, rabbits and a huge variety of birds. Deer, introduced here in 1988, are so far doing well.

Protection and access
Since 1984 the Esterel has been a protected area under the management of the National Forests Office, which maintains 114km (70 miles) of fire-roads through the *massif*. In addition, two areas have been designated Biological Reserves: the Ravin du Mal-infernet and the Ravin du Perthus. Both gorges have cold, humid conditions that have produced an exceptional flora unknown elsewhere on the Mediterranean coast. They are both spectacular, and easily reached.

DYING PINES
Large areas of the Esterel were once covered in maritime pines, but since 1958 the pines have succumbed to a plague of toxic, parasitic insects (*Matsucoccus feytaudi*). Considerable reafforestation has been taking place, but whether or not the new trees prove to be resistant to the insects and regenerate themselves has yet to be seen.

171

Rust-red rocks meet the sea on the Esterel's craggy coast

People-watching is the main pastime in "St.-Trop"

Pavement art in the old port

▶ ▶ ▶ St.-Tropez 148C2

For many years a byword for all that was chic on the Riviera, St.-Tropez is a summertime gridlock. The town's charms are not at all evident if you are stuck in a traffic jam trying to drive along the peninsula, or being jostled in the streets by all the other visitors (around 100,000 every year) who have come here to find out what it's all about.

Arrive by boat (from St.-Raphaël or Ste.-Maxime) or, better still, come in the spring or the autumn if you don't want to end up as red-faced and hot-tempered as St.-Tropez's traffic police.

The huge reputation of this surprisingly small resort (which has only 5,500 inhabitants) started with Roger Vadim's film *Et Dieu créa la Femme* (*And God Created Woman*) in 1956, starring the then-unknown Brigitte Bardot. The bandwagon of celebrity fun, fashion and sex has rolled on since then, with every *poseur* with a yacht worthy of the name wanting to be seen dining in exhibitionist elegance, stern to the quay, for all to see.

The French have always known it as "St. Trop" ("St. Too Much"), and as long as you are expecting just that (too much on the bills, too much posing, too much traffic...) then you can still have fun (excellent people-watching). The town parties until the small hours and sleeps late. In the early morning hours, when no one else is around, the port is pretty as a picture, recalling the works of the Fauvist artists who were so inspired by St.-Tropez at the beginning of the century.

St.-Tropez was founded by the Greeks from Marseille, when it was known as Athenopolis. Later destroyed by the Saracens, it was rebuilt by settlers from Genoa in the 15th century, who were granted indemnity from taxes by Good King René on condition that they defended the coastline from attack, which they did most notably when they fended off 22 Spanish galleons in 1637.

The first celebrity to breeze into St.-Tropez was Guy de Maupassant, who arrived in the harbour in the 1880s on board his yacht. He set the scene to come for another century or so with his eccentric behaviour (in his case, it was due to pre-syphilitic insanity). A decade or so later, the Impressionist painter Paul Signac was forced into port by bad weather and liked St.-Tropez so much he built a house here and invited all his friends down to take advantage of the wonderful southern light. Matisse was one of the first, followed by Dufy, Bonnard, Van Dongen, Vlaminck, Derain and others.

By the beginning of World War I, St.-Tropez had already established itself as the artists' colony in Provence. Between the wars it received an influx of literary talent with the arrival of writers such as Colette and Anaïs Nin, and became a home-from-home for the in-crowd from St.-Germain-des-Prés. Then, in the 1950s, it was the turn of film stars, starting with Vadim and Bardot.

WHAT TO SEE At the heart of St.-Tropez is the *vieux port*, chock-a-block with sleek yachts, pavement artists, ostentatious fashion victims and trendy bars such as Café Le Sénéquier. All is redeemed, however, by the superb **Musée de l'Annonciade**▶▶ (*Open* Dec–Oct, Wed–Mon. *Admission: moderate*) housed in the former chapel of the Annunciation on the south side of the port. The collection of paintings and sculptures features representative works by Paul Signac's circle and most of the other post-Impressionist and Fauvist artists who worked here a hundred years ago.

On the other side of the port, you can watch the boats coming back into harbour at dusk from the embankment of the Mole Jean Réveille. From behind the quai Jean-Jaurès the old streets lead up past the town hall, a massive tower (built by William I in AD 990) and the Italian–baroque church to the old **citadelle**▶. There are views back over the rooftops of the town and across the Gulf from this 16th-century fortress, which also houses a small **naval museum** (*Open* daily. Closed Tue in Nov. *Admission: moderate*) with maritime relics.

Apart from the port, St.-Tropez's other main focal point is the enormous **place Carnot** (often called by its old name, place des Lices), surrounded by cafés. There is nearly always a game of *pétanque* taking place here, except on Tuesday and Saturday, when the whole square is taken over by the local market. Between place Carnot and the port, endless designer-label shop windows display the latest items to tempt those with money to burn.

CHRISTMAS IN ST.-TROPEZ
By December, when summer's celebrities have migrated to warmer climes, St.-Tropez is illuminated by other stars as the town celebrates Christmas. From early December onwards the town and old port are festooned with lights as the festive schedule gets under way; annual events include a traditional Provençal pantomime, Christmas concerts, a children's film festival, an evening of Provençal storytelling, a sailing regatta and the arrival of Father Christmas by boat. (For information, tel: 04 94 97 45 21.)

173

Still a fishing port, despite the razzmatazz

THE ST.-TROPEZ *BRAVADES*

Every year the residents of St.-Tropez celebrate two *bravades* (literally, acts of bravado), the first of which coincides with the *fête* of their patron saint, St. Torpes (see panel opposite) on 16 May. In this colourful, noisy 400-year-old tradition the townspeople parade in historical costumes, armed with breech-loaded muskets, through the streets to the town hall and the church. St. Torpes is then paraded through the streets, with much noise and smoke from fusillades of muskets. The second *bravade* takes place on 15 June to commemorate the successful defence of the town against a Spanish fleet in 1637.

BEACHES With the exception of **Les Greniers** beach, below the *citadelle*, which can be reached on foot, the majority of St.-Tropez' fabled sandy beaches are around the headland to the south of the port. If you have not got your own speedboat then it is best to take the regular minibus from place Carnot, since parking charges are very high.

In fact the individual "beaches" are mostly private concessions (each with their own restaurants, bars, parasols and luxury beachchairs) along one huge, sandy strip bordering the Baie de Pampelonne. Some parts of the beach are free, but otherwise you will have to pay dearly for almost everything. Pampelonne has come a long way since the first bamboo-and-thatch beach hut was built here in 1952.

That first beach bar was at **Tahiti-Plage**, at the start of the bay, and stars like Errol Flynn, Lana Turner and Clark Gable would come here to relax after visiting the Cannes film festival. Tahiti is still considered the "movie stars' beach," although nowadays the neighbouring **Voile Rouge** attracts American celebrities such as De Niro, Eastwood, and Stallone when they are in town. The Voile Rouge was also the first beach where women ever dared to go topless, doing for St.-Tropez in the 1970s what one-piece bathing suits did for Juan-les-Pins in the 1930s.

Continuing down the 5km (3 mile) long strip next to the Voile Rouge is **Moorea**, best known for having launched the Gypsy Kings to stardom when they played in the bar. Following the South Pacific theme, other beaches on the northern section include **Bora Bora** (famous for its seafood) and **Pago Pago** (water sports and chocolate profiteroles). Farther down, **Club 55** is popular with Parisians, politicos and royalty (Gorbachev and several European and Middle Eastern monarchs have dropped by for lunch), whereas the **Aquaclub** is preferred by models and is a well-known gay rendezvous. **Tropezina** is more sporty, with a young crowd, whereas at **Le Blouch** or **Le Liberty** you won't even need to wear the minimum "string" to go and have an ice cream. Just your wallet will do.

NEARBY On the north shore of the Golfe de St.-Tropez, **Ste.-Maxime** has none of the glitz of its much-hyped

Not as smart as St.-Tropez, Ste.-Maxime is just across the bay

THE HEADLESS SAINT
St.-Tropez' name comes from the legend of a Roman soldier called Torpes who was beheaded by Nero for his Christian beliefs. His decapitated body was put in a boat, along with a cockerel and a dog, and set adrift in the Mediterranean. The animals were meant to eat the body but didn't, and the boat eventually drifted on to the shore here. A sanctuary was erected for the brave soldier, and in the 4th century the town adopted St. Torpes' name and localized the spelling.

175

Maritime trading in the 18th century is reflected in this statue of sea captain Pierre André de Suffren de St.-Tropez

neighbour and is happy enough in its role as a sedate family resort, with a casino thrown in for a bit of excitement. In front of the palm tree-lined promenade there is a big sandy beach with plenty of water sports (windsurfing, jet-skis and waterskiing) and seductive beachside bars.

Ste.-Maxime has several colourful markets, including a daily food and flower market, and regional produce on Thursdays. In the 16th-century **Tour Carrée▶** on the seafront there is a small **Musée des Traditions Locales** (*Open* daily 10–12, 3–6. *Admission: inexpensive*), which focuses on the history of the Golfe de St.-Tropez. More compelling is the **Musée du Phonographe et de la Musique Mécanique▶** (*Open* Easter to mid-Oct, Wed–Sun 10–noon, 3–6. *Admission: inexpensive*), 10km (6 miles) north of town on the road to le Muy. Treasures in this collection include one of Edison's phonographs from 1878, the first examples of recording machines, a language-teaching machine (the *"pathegraphe"*) from 1913 and an assemblage of barrel organs, musical boxes, pianolas, and the like.

▶▶ Sanary-sur-Mer *148A1*

Sheltered from the *mistral* by wooded hills to the north, Sanary is a charming resort to the west of Toulon with a small harbour surrounded by palm trees and pastel-coloured buildings. Although fishing is no longer of huge importance here, there is a small fleet (including several *pointus*, which are old-style boats with high curved prows) and every morning you can buy fish, *oursin* (black spiny sea urchins), lobster and other fresh seafood from the quayside. Every other year Sanary celebrates a fishermen's festival with a St. Peter's Day procession and giant *bouillabaise* feast on the last weekend in June.

The discovery nearby of amphorae for exporting wine, as well as ovens dating from the 2nd century, proves the antiquity of the port. In the 13th-century watchtower overlooking the port, a small scuba-diving museum displays equipment from the 1930s to 1950s, collected by diving pioneer Frédéric Dumas.

▶ Six-Fours-les-Plages *148A1*

The town of Six-Fours is a drab ribbon development stretching almost from la Seyne to Six-Fours-les-Plages across the neck of the Cap Sicié peninsula. Six-Fours itself is of limited interest but nearby are two churches worth navigating your way around the suburban streets to find. The old village of Six-Fours once topped a small hill inland from the present-day town but was totally demolished to make way for the **Fort** (still in use, no visits). Beneath the walls of the fort is the **Collégiale St.-Pierre-aux-Liens▶▶** (*Open* Jun–Sep Wed–Mon 10–12, 3–7; Oct–May 10–12, 2–6.

176

A 16th-century Flemish representation of the "Descent from the Cross" in the Collégiale Ste.-Pierre-aux-Liens

The Gothic-style nave of the Collégiale St.-Pierre-aux-Liens adjoins a much older chapel

Admission free), which is unusual in that it has two naves, one from the original Romanesque (5th-century) chapel and another, larger, Gothic-style nave added at right angles in the 17th century.

The older chapel has one or two curious features, the most striking of which is a niche on the right-hand side of the massive stone altar, which was known as the *reliquaire des morts*. Here, local people used to hang up coats, hats or the clothing of dead friends or relatives so that they could come and pray to them. This unique custom dates back to pagan times and, incredibly, was still being practised up to World War I (an old photo in the chapel shows the archway hung about with these reliquaries in 1909). Another niche inside the chapel contains beads and coins found during excavations of the 4th-century baptistery and a relic of Ste. Philomene.

At the other end of the Romanesque chapel (or at the back of the Gothic nave, depending on which way you look at it) there is a polyptych by Louis Bréa which features popular local saints; look out also for the marble statue of the Virgin and the Assumption attributed to Puget, which is in the Chapelle des Carmes on the right-hand side of the main church.

Also near Six-Fours is the **Chapelle Notre-Dame de Pépiole**▶ (*Open* afternoons. *Admission free*), which claims to be one of the oldest chapels in France, although little is known about it. It probably dates from the 3rd century (with a 10th-century nave added) and was restored from the 1950s onwards by a Belgian priest, M. Charlier.

It contains two massive palaeo-Christian altar stones and "stained-glass" windows that, as the *gardien* will explain, were made from old bottles because they had no money for the real thing. M. Charlier is buried outside the walls of this little old chapel to which he devoted his life.

The chapel can be hard to find. Take the D63 from Six-Fours towards Toulon-la Seyne and keep a careful watch for the turn left marked by an arrow.

The sheltered little port at Sanary-sur-Mer

THE TARGO
A plaque opposite the Six-Fours fort commemorates the founding on 20 October 1880 of the *Escolo de Targo* (the Targo School), to promote the Provençal language; the school still functions today. The *targo* is an old Provençal game similar to jousting, with teams of eight using boats instead of horses. The aim is to knock your opponents off the prow of their boat with a long wooden "lance." The player who knocks three of his opponents off without getting a drenching himself wins a prize. *Targo* games are usually held in ports such as Toulon, Marseille, la Ciotat and Martigues.

The cloisters in the Abbaye du Thoronet, echoing the clarity of its pure Romanesque style

IMPERIAL PURPLE
On the western side of the port is the Roman district known as the Quartier de Castigneau, where excavations have revealed the remains of the dye works upon which Toulon's economy was once based. The port was renowned for the production of purple dye, which was used to colour silk and wool clothing worn by the Roman emperor. It was obtained from the Murex molluscs that were once common along the coast; their glands were steeped in salt and boiled in leaden vats to obtain the distinctive, deep purple dye.

▶▶▶ **Thoronet, Abbaye du**   *148B2*
Off the D79 (tel: 04 94 60 43 90)
Open: Apr–Sep, Mon–Sat 10–6.30, Sun 10–12, 2–6.30;
Oct–Mar, Mon–Sat 10–1, 2–5, Sun 10–12, 2–5.
Admission: moderate
Hidden away in the forest of la Daboussière to the south of Entrecasteaux, the Abbaye du Thoronet is one of the most remarkable monasteries in Provence. It is the purest of the three great Cistercian monasteries (the other two are Sénanque and Silvacane) of the 12th century, and the first to be established. By the 14th century it had gone into decline; during the Wars of Religion the monks were chased out of the property, and it was finally abandoned in 1791. Restoration began in the 1850s.

The architecture of the complex (church, cloisters and chapterhouse) is in the purest Romanesque style, stripped of all decoration in accordance with the austere principles of the Cistercian order. The cloister is unusual in that it has been built on different levels and is one of very few to have a fountain-house in the middle, which fills the cloister with the gentle sound of running water. In the cellars there is a display documenting the restoration of the abbey over the last 150 years; indeed, some of the outbuildings are still propped up with massive beams to counter the damage from subsidence caused by bauxite mining in the surrounding hills.

▶▶ **Toulon**   *148B1*
Toulon, France's second-largest naval port, is often by-passed in favour of more glamorous locations farther to the east. One guidebook dismisses it as "a sprawling commercial and industrial city with many ugly buildings, dirty side streets and much of the sordid underworld which grows up around a large port." Grounds enough to keep going, you

THE SIEGE OF TOULON
Fiercely Royalist, Toulon accepted an offer of help from the English during the Revolution and welcomed their fleet into the bay in the summer of 1793. The British had built a seemingly impregnable fortress (on the site of the present Fort Napoléon), which they were so sure of they christened it "little Gibraltar." In the Siege of Toulon that followed, the Republicans set up a battery opposite the fort and it was here that the young Napoléon Bonaparte (then aged 24) distinguished himself as an artillery commander in the Republican forces.

might think. However, given the port's enviable surroundings (a huge natural harbour, backed by a ring of high hills) and its lively character, Toulon is worth a visit if you are nearby. In fact for many years drivers travelling along the coast have not had much choice about stopping here, since the streets of the town centre have been the only link between the A50 and A57 *autoroutes* on either side of Toulon. A tunnel is now being built which will take the *autoroute* beneath the town, but technical problems and cost overruns have delayed its completion.

Toulon's image as little more than a sleazy port is also fast disappearing as the city embarks on an imaginative transformation of the old parts of town. In what is possibly one of the largest architectural redevelopment schemes of its kind in Europe, over 20ha (50 acres) of the town centre have been smartened up and over 600 million francs were invested in the restoration of old houses and shops and the creation of gardens, fountains and pedestrian areas.

Most of the rebuilding has taken place in the lower town, which was Toulon's traditional red light district. The redevelopment has been boosted by the building of a huge Law Faculty and an Electronics Institute as well as the gleaming Centre Mayol, with conference centres and a mall with more than a hundred shops, boutiques, and restaurants.

Toulon became a naval base soon after Provence became part of France in 1481, with Louis XII building the first fortifications here. Under Louis XIV, Toulon was elevated to the strategic centre for the Mediterranean fleet, a role that it still maintains today. The town was partially destroyed by Allied bombings in World War II and the rest badly damaged by German troops before they surrendered on 26 August 1944. The story of the Allied victories in the South of France is recounted in a museum at the top of Mont Faron (see page 181).

One of sculptor Pierre Puget's famous Atlantes *propping up Toulon's old town hall doorway*

ST.-EXUPÉRY'S WRECK
Antoine de St.-Exupéry, author of *Le petit prince*, died in a plane crash while on a reconnaissance mission to survey German positions just before the Allied invasion of Provence in August 1944. Eyewitnesses reported seeing his Lightning P-38 go down in the Baie des Anges in Nice, but underwater soundings in 1992 found no wreckage. The search (led by those who discovered the *Titanic*) moved farther west after other witnesses reported seeing his plane crash offshore from Toulon. What appears to be St.-Exupéry's *Lightning* has now been found encased in sand in the Baie de Carquieranne.

WHAT TO SEE In the post-war reconstruction of Toulon some fairly hideous buildings were put up, most notably the austere-looking blocks of flats that now form a windswept wall along the back of rue de la République, the main waterfront thoroughfare. However, beneath these monstrosities are the famous **Atlantes**▶ by Pierre Puget on either side of the old town hall doorway. The powerful figures were some of Puget's first sculptures, their straining faces modelled on stevedores Puget had seen unloading ships in his native Marseille.

The quai Stalingrad is the embarkation point for trips around Toulon's **harbour**▶ and although modern catamarans have now replaced the old-style tourist boats, the boatmen's patter hasn't changed: *"depart en quelques minutes"* still means they will leave when there are enough passengers. So, choose a boat and relax in a quayside café until it really does look as if it is going to leave.

The majority of trips around the bay circle the inner roads (*la petite rade*) and the shipbuilding yards of neighbouring la Seyne. A lively commentary gives details of the frigates, aircraft carriers, and submarines of the Mediterranean fleet as well as visiting warships.

Toulon's maritime history is well documented in the **Musée National de la Marine**▶▶ (*Open* Wed–Mon 10–6. *Admission: moderate*) near the entrance to the Arsenal. The **Musée des Beaux Arts**▶▶ (*Open* afternoons daily. *Admission free*) has an extensive collection of Provençal paintings from the 17th century onwards, but displays a fairly meagre selection. However, the temporary exhibitions are often very good. On the other side of the building is the **Musée d'Histoire Naturelle**▶ (*Open* Mon–Fri 9–6, Sat–Sun 11–6. *Admission free*), which has an interesting room devoted to crystals and minerals, and an embarrassingly large collection of stuffed animals.

Sandwiched between shopfronts on the cours Lafayette is the **Musée du Vieux Toulon** (*Open* Mon–Sat afternoons. *Admission free*) with various historic documents and

Toulon's town centre is a maze of pedestrian streets and well-shaded cafés

memorabilia. The cours Lafayette itself is the setting for Toulon's well-known **Marché Provençal** (*Open* Tue–Sun mornings), a huge, lively market, selling the best and lowest-priced produce that Provence has to offer.

Within the network of pedestrian streets in the town centre, look out for the **Fontaine des Trois Dauphins▶** in place Puget. Toulon has no fewer than 17 fountains (probably more than Aix) and this is one of the best, with the three dolphins in the centre (sculpted in 1782) now completely obscured by a mini-jungle of fig trees, oleanders, ferns and ivy. Just nearby is the **Opéra▶**, which has a beautifully decorated interior inspired by Charles Garnier.

Toulon's old town tourist office (tel: 04 94 18 53 00), on place Raimu, offers guided tours of Vieux Toulon and plenty of suggestions for local excursions.

NEARBY The limestone *massif* of **Mont Faron▶▶** rises 542m (1,778ft) above the town and bay of Toulon, with wonderful views from the top that are worth the 9km (5.5 mile) drive to get there. A quicker way is via the *téléphérique* (funicular), which whisks you up in about 10 minutes from the terminus in boulevard Amiral Vence (*Open* Jul–Aug, daily; Sep–Jun, Tue–Sun. *Admission: moderate*).

At the top, a Sherman tank guards the entrance to the old Fort de la Tour Beaumont, which is now the **Mémorial du Débarquement en Provence▶** (*Open* Jul–Sep daily; Oct–Jun Tue–Sun. *Admission: inexpensive*); it commemorates the Allied landings of August 1944 in Provence. From the rooftop of the museum there is a panorama over the whole bay, with views that on a clear day can reach as far down the coast as the Bec l'Aigle at la Ciotat. In the surrounding wooded park are a couple of restaurants and a **Zoo** (*Open* summer, daily, unless it rains; hours vary in winter. *Admission: moderate*) that specializes in big cats (it also breeds wolves and snow leopards).

TOULON IN WORLD WAR II
The French navy lost a large proportion of its fleet in Toulon harbour when Hitler made a surprise attack on the free French zone in November 1942; the fleet had insufficient time to escape and as a result 60 ships were scuttled in the approaches on 27 November. Four days after the start of the Allied landings to liberate Provence on 15 August 1944, French troops attacked the German defences around Toulon; after a week of fighting the city was liberated.

NAVIGATING OR LOST?
At the western end of the quai Stalingrad is a statue by Daumas, *The Genius of Navigation*. Locals have it that the real story behind this is that the figure, naked except for a trailing loincloth, is in fact a drunken sailor emerging from the red light district (to which he has his back) in the early hours of the morning, having lost all his possessions. His pointing finger has nothing to do with navigation at all—the poor sailor is in fact desperately pointing in the direction of his ship, which is departing over the horizon.

The map shows the Alpes de Haute-Provence region with various locations including:

Col du Festre 1441m, St Bonnet, Orcières, Guillestre, Col du Longet 2616m, Lus-la-Croix-Haute, HAUTES-ALPES, Col Bayard 1248m, la Bâtie-Neuve, Embrun, Vars, 3410m, St Julien-en-Beauchêne, Gap, Chorges, Col de Vars 2109m, Fort de Tournoux, St-Paul, Aspres-sur-Buëch, Veynes, Lac de Serre-Ponçon, Savines-le-Lac, Grand Bérard 3042m, Larche, Col de Larche 1994m, ISÈRE, Tallard, le Lauzet-Ubaye, Jausiers, Serres, Durance, Barcelonnette, Ubaye, Rosans, ALPES DE, Laragne-Montéglin, HAUTE-PROVENCE, Seyne, Pra-Loup, le Sauze, Col de la Bonette 2802m, Buëch, Col de Maure 1347m, Parc National du Mercantour, St-Étienne-de-Tinée, DRÔME, Col d'Allos 2240m, Mt Pelat 3052m, Allos, Lac d'Allos, Auron, Séderon, Col du Labouret 1240m, Prads, Colmars-les-Alpes, Entraunes, Sisteron, A51, 1826m, Château-Arnoux, Musée Promenade, la Javie 2323m, Beauvezer, Var, Montagne de Lure, Cheval Blanc, Digne-les-Bains, Guillaumes, Valberg, Banon, Peyruis, Bléone, Rochers des Mées, St-André-les-Alpes, Annot, Puget-Théniers, Simiane-la-Rotonde, Prieuré de Ganagobie, les Mées, Mézel, Plateau de, Barrême, Entrevaux, N-D de Salagon, Lurs, Forcalquier, Col de Toutes Aures 1118m, Observatoire de Haute-Provence, Mane, Château de Sauvan, Oraison, Valensole, Col de Lèques 1146m, Castellane, Montagne du Chéron, 1778m, Reillanne, Voix, Asse, Moustiers-Ste-Marie, 1931m, ROUTE, le Logis-du-Pin, ALPES-MARITIMES, Saignon, 1125m, Manosque, Ste-Tulle, Gréoux-les-Bains, Allemagne-en-Provence, Riez, Lac de Ste-Croix, Col d'Illoire 964m, la Palud-sur-Verdon, NAPOLÉON, St-Vallier-de-Thiey, Ansouis, VAUCLUSE, A51, Musée de Préhistoire, Quinson, Verdon, Grand Canyon du Verdon, Grand Plan de Canjuers, Comps-sur-Artuby, Mons, Grasse, Pertuis, Vinon-sur-Verdon, la Verdière, VAR, Bargemon, Seillans, Montauroux, Aups, Callas, Fayence

The 14th-century Porte Saunerie leads into rue Grande in the heart of Manosque, one of the largest towns in the Alpes de Haute-Provence

▶▶▶ **REGION HIGHLIGHTS**

Barcelonnette
pages 186–187

Grand Canyon du Verdon
pages 190–193

Moustiers-Ste.-Marie
pages 196–197

Quinson *page 198*

The northernmost *département* in Provence, the Alpes de Haute-Provence is a land of wild open spaces and clear skies, of captivating mountain peaks, deep ravines and rushing rivers, of tiny hamlets and twisting mountain roads. If you are looking for action in the discos, this is the wrong place—most of the action here is in the great outdoors: racing down rugged hillsides on a mountain bicycle, hang-gliding above deserted valleys, sailing on massive lakes or simply walking peacefully amid the Alpine landscapes.

Covering some 5,548sq km (2,142sq miles), the Alpes de Haute-Provence is the most sparsely populated region in Provence: Its 121,000 inhabitants would fit into a city the size of Aix-en-Provence with room to spare. However, they prefer the comfortable ambience of their *"villages et cités de caractère."* It is also the least well-known area among visitors, though, significantly, the average length of stay here is just as long as it is on the coast. Those who have discovered the Alpes de Haute-Provence know a good thing when they see it and are prepared to take the time to unwind, to explore its hidden corners and to relax in the pure mountain air.

Although temperatures can drop below zero in winter, the climate in summer is a serendipitous balance between Provençal sunshine and cool Alpine weather. It is the perfect antidote to the insufferable summer heatwaves that sometimes grip the rest of Provence.

NATURAL ASSETS It is a region of great natural beauty, ranging from the superb Lac d'Allos (just one of 140 mountain lakes) to spectacular mountain passes (such as the Col d'Allos and the phenomenal Col de la Bonette) and the Grand Canyon du Verdon itself. This natural heritage is valued and protected, whether in the Réserve Géologique (the largest in Europe) around Digne, the Parc National du Mercantour (which is shared with the Alpes-Maritimes on the eastern boundaries of the *département*) or the innovative Conservatoire du Patrimoine Ethnologique de la Haute-Provence at the Prieuré de Notre-Dame Salagon just south of Mane.

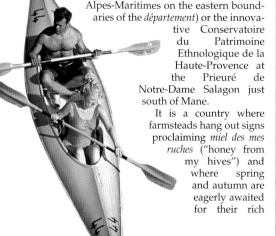

It is a country where farmsteads hang out signs proclaiming *miel des mes ruches* ("honey from my hives") and where spring and autumn are eagerly awaited for their rich

The Fort de France guards the mountain passes above Colmars in the Haut Verdon Valley

MOUNTAIN CHEESES
The Alpes de Haute-Provence is an important producer of goats' cheese, whose special flavour is attributed to the fact that the goats graze wild in the hills and *garrigue* (scrubland). Jean Giono conjures up the flavour in *Regain*, where he writes: "It seemed to him that he was kneading with his tongue a portion of the hill itself, with all its flowers." At the beginning of winter, when the goats are brought down from the hills, cheese production stops. To preserve those already made, they are either wrapped in fresh chestnut leaves (this is the famous Banon method) or left to marinate in olive oil, garlic, herbs and bay leaves.

harvest of *cèpes*, morels and other prize mushrooms, as well as truffles. This is the home of the delectable *agneau de Sisteron*, tender lamb cooked with fragrant herbs and garlic. Other gourmet treats include the renowned goats' cheeses of Banon and honey-and-almond nougat for the sweet-toothed.

Here, it is still possible to discover picturesque mountain villages (such as Lurs or Simiane-la-Rotonde) that have not yet been overrun by tourism, even though many villages are becoming increasingly popular as *residences secondaires* with city folk from Paris or Marseille.

This corner of the Alps has not always been so peaceful. The many wars which have been fought here have left a legacy of fortified towns and mountain strongholds that are visible everywhere, from the 14th-century walls of Colmars-les-Alpes to the 17th-century citadel of Entrevaux and the 20th-century pillboxes of the Maginot Line in the Vallée de l'Ubaye above Barcelonnette.

The Alpes de Haute-Provence is full of surprises: The unusual history of Barcelonnette, for instance, from where many impoverished inhabitants left for Mexico in the early 19th century and returned decades later to build themselves grand villas around the town, having made their fortunes. Another exotic connection is that of Alexandra David-Néel (see panel, page 189), who journeyed for decades in Tibet before settling in Digne, where her house is now a shrine to Buddhism and the spirit of adventure.

THE GREAT OUTDOORS But above all it is a part of Provence where the rewards are to be found in the wilderness. You can enjoy it from the air by hot-air balloon, helicopter, or glider, or by hang-gliding, parascending and motorized ultra-lights (ULM). A variety of water sports might appeal, with windsurfing, rowing and sailing on half a dozen major lakes. On the rapids, you can raft, kayak or white-water swim all the way down the Ubaye and the Verdon. You can choose from 900km (560 miles) of bridlepaths and a dozen or more riding centres, and there are over a hundred different mountain-bicycling routes, some of which take several days to explore. On two feet, routes range from one to ten days along 4,000km (2,485 miles) of marked paths. And, of course, you can choose any one of 10 main winter sports resorts.

THE LIE OF THE LAND The northwest of the Alpes de Haute-Provence is dominated by the Montagne de Lure: Its peaks have traditionally marked the gateway to this part of Provence from the north. Wedged into a narrow gap protecting these approaches is the old town of Sisteron, where a citadel stands high above the Durance as it flows southwards. This turbulent river, once the scourge of low-lying villages, has been tamed by a complex system of dams and now irrigates fertile agricultural land in the valley. To the west of the Durance and the Marseille–Grenoble *autoroute* that runs alongside it is the Pays de Forcalquier, a rugged area of valleys and plateaux with a patchwork of forests and pasture lands.

To the east of the Durance the central section of the *département* starts to rise into the pre-Alps, with the elegant spa town of Digne-les-Bains at its heart. To the south, the Plateau de Valensole is one of the main lavender-growing areas in Provence, with the old lavender-distilling centre of Riez now starting to re-orientate itself towards tourism and reclaim its architectural heritage in the quiet backstreets.

Below Riez, the magnificent Grand Canyon du Verdon is the biggest tourist attraction in the *département*, and one that is best visited out of the peak season. At either end of the canyon, Moustiers-Ste.-Marie and Castellane are often swamped by traffic but provide numerous facilities for exploring Europe's longest and deepest limestone rift.

Following the Verdon back to its source brings you to the dramatic Alpine landscapes of the Parc National du Mercantour and, high up in the Vallée de l'Ubaye, the charming town of Barcelonnette (see page 186). Surrounded by towering peaks, it is the northernmost town in the whole of Provence.

(see page 186)

PREHISTORY IN THE ALPS
Although the dramatic Grand Canyon du Verdon is the most famous of the Verdon gorges, the western section (*les moyennes gorges*) is equally fascinating for different reasons. Here, on the edge of the rugged Baume Bonne escarpment, a series of caves some 50m (165ft) above the river has yielded a rich seam of archaeological finds that covers every stage of human development in Europe from palaeolithic times to the Bronze Age. Over 80,000 artefacts from the site are displayed in the imaginative Musée de Préhistoire des Gorges du Verdon, designed by the internationally renowned architect Sir Norman Foster, and opened in Quinson (28km/17 miles south of Riez) in 2000.

185

Place Manuel, at the centre of Barcelonnette, a town with an unexpected past

Holiday chalets dot the countryside around Allos

VALLEY FORTIFICATIONS
Near Barcelonnette there is a series of remarkable fortresses spanning several centuries of military architecture. One of the most impressive is the Fort de Tournoux, built in 1843, on the D900 east of town; on the other side of the valley is the Fort de Roche-la-Croix, one of the most powerful batteries in the Maginot Line; further up the valley, the Fort de Haut de St.-Ours was part of the same defensive scheme. These and several other forts in the area can be visited on regular tours. For details contact the Communauté de Communes de la Vallée de l'Ubaye (tel: 04 92 81 03 68).

▶ **Allos**   *182C2*

Where sheep once grazed on the pastures surrounding Allos, the slopes of the valley are now a patchwork of ski chalets and summer holiday homes in this remote spot in the Haute Vallée du Verdon.

One of the main attractions in the vicinity is the dramatic **Lac d'Allos**▶▶ (14km/8.5 miles east along the D226), which is the largest high-altitude mountain lake in Europe. The road twists and turns as it climbs 800m (2,620ft) above Allos, stopping around 1km (0.5 miles) short of the lake itself. A 30- to 40-minute walk brings you to an immense amphitheatre encircling the glossy calm waters. The Lac d'Allos is so cold that nothing grows in it. Its pure colour reflects the surrounding peaks like a giant mirror.

The mountains around the lake are part of the Parc National du Mercantour (see page 236), and following the 3km (2 mile) long path around the waters' edge you may see ibex, chamois and other wildlife high up on the scree, with birds of prey circling overhead. Just outside Allos there is a large leisure park and, to the north, the ski resort of la Foux d'Allos. From Foux d'Allos the D908 leads up to the spectacular **Col d'Allos**▶ (2,240m/7,350ft), with views towards the Vallée de l'Ubaye and Barcelonnette.

▶▶▶ **Barcelonnette**   *182C3*

High up in the Vallée de l'Ubaye in the most northerly corner of the Alpes de Haute-Provence, Barcelonnette is a graceful, welcoming town. In the summer it is a good base for exploring the Parc National du Mercantour (see page 236), which extends into the valley at its northernmost boundaries. The **Maison du Parc** (tel: 04 92 81 21 31) near the town centre has details of guided tours, walks and the park's wildlife. From the Col du Longet at the head of the valley the River Ubaye flows for 90km (56 miles) down to the Lac de Serre-Ponçon, and downstream from Barcelonnette there are activity centres offering kayaking, canoeing and rafting. In the winter, when snow blankets the valley, ski resorts (such as Pra-Loup, le Sauze/Super-Sauz and Ste.-Anne La Condamine) come into their own.

Founded in 1231 by Count Raymond Berenger V, Barcelonnette ("little Barcelona") was named after the Catalan city where the count's family originated. But a more intriguing connection with the world outside the valley began in 1821 when three local men, the Arnaud brothers, emigrated to Mexico, via Amsterdam and New Orleans, to look for work (see panel). By the turn of the century, around 4,000 to 5,000 people from the region had emigrated and there may be around 40,000–50,000 of their descendants living in Mexico. The Arnaud brothers never returned, but many others came back to build sumptuous villas on the outskirts of town, mainly along the avenue des Trois Frères Arnaud and the avenue de la Libération.

The connection is presented in imaginative displays at the **Musée de la Vallée**▶▶ (*Open* Wed–Sat 2.30–6, also Tue during school holidays. *Admission: moderate*), on avenue de la Libération, laid out in one of the 19th-century villas. Here, too, is an ethnographic section and a room devoted to the fantastic travels of writer Émile Chabrand, who journeyed from Barcelonnette to Mexico via the Far East in the 1880s. At the heart of Barcelonnette is the **place Manuel**▶, where you can sip coffee and gaze at the snow-capped peaks.

SPORTS D'HIVER

In winter, the Val d'Allos is one of the busiest winter sports centres in the Alpes de Haute Provence. The alpine village of la Foux d'Allos is linked by lifts and trails to neighbouring Pra-Loup across the mountain and between them they can offer some 230km (143 miles) of alpine pistes and another 100km (62 miles) of cross-country trails. Alternative daredevil pursuits include paragliding, parachuting, flying microlights, ice-climbing and snow scooters. For information, contact the Office du Tourisme du Val d'Allos (tel: 04 92 83 02 81).

187

Alpine peaks rise up above the streets of Barcelonnette

THE "MEXICANS" FROM BARCELONNETTE

In 1821, the three Arnaud brothers emigrated to Mexico. In 1830 they were joined by two of their compatriots, Éugene Caire and Alphonse Jauffred. It was these two men who opened the floodgates when they returned to Barcelonnette 15 years later with 250,000 francs apiece—a large fortune in those times—and precipitated a mass emigration that lasted for over a century as hundreds of people from the valley (and eventually the surrounding valleys as well) left to seek their fortunes. Some thrived in commerce; others simply managed to survive; and many ended their days in poverty.

The modernized thermal baths in Digne offer all sorts of different cures

▶ Castellane
182C1

The eastern gateway to the Canyon du Verdon, Castellane is inevitably overrun during the summer season. It is a useful place for stocking up on supplies (with plenty of camping and outdoor shops) and for arranging activities such as rafting, climbing, walking or riding mountain bicycles in the gorges. There is a choice of simple hotels and more than a dozen campsites nearby.

The most striking aspect of the town is the sheer pinnacle rising up behind it, topped by the **Chapelle Notre-Dame du Roc**. If you are feeling energetic you can climb up to the chapel via a path to the left of the church (it takes around 30 minutes). Back on the village square, the **Musée des Sirènes et Fossils** (*Open* May–Sep, daily; Oct–Apr, Mon–Fri. *Admission: inexpensive*) tackles the connection between legendary mermaids and marine mammals whose skeletons (similar to manatees) have been discovered at the Col des Leques, 6km (4 miles) northwest.

▶▶ Colmars-les-Alpes
182C2

Just down the Haut Verdon Valley from Allos (see page 186), Colmars is a lovely old fortified town in a picturesque position amid the surrounding woodlands and peaks. It acquired its first defences in the late 14th century, and remained an important frontier town until 1713.

At the end of the 17th century two forts were added to protect the town from constant attacks by the Savoyards. To the south is the **Fort de France**, with the much larger and more imposing **Fort de Savoie**▶ to the north.

▶ Digne-les-Bains
182B2

Digne is a placid, genteel town that has built its reputation on the seven springs to the south of town which supply its

It is a steep climb up to the Chapelle Notre-Dame du Roc, which dominates the skyline above Castellane

GETTING WET
Local tour operators in Castellane offer a mind-boggling number of adventurous methods for descending the Grand Canyon. These include rafting (in specially adapted Zodiacs); white-water swimming (wetsuits, helmets and a special type of surfboard provided); "hot dogging" (two-person inflatable canoes); canyoning (a combination of rappelling down into the canyon and white-water swimming); aquatic walks (*through* rather than *on* the water); "flotting" (floating feet-first with a specially designed inflatable back-pack); and kayaking. (Contact Aqua Verdon, tel: 04 92 83 72 75; Montagne et Rivière, tel: 04 92 83 67 24; Bureau des Guides, tel: 04 92 77 30 50.)

189

renowned spa; *"les cures anti-stress"* are now offered here alongside the more traditional rheumatism treatments. It is also the main centre for lavender production in the mountains of Haute Provence, which it celebrates with the *Corso de la Lavande*, running for five days around the first weekend in August.

The town centre is bisected by the boulevard Gassendi, at the eastern end of which is the place du Général-de-Gaulle, where the Wednesday and Saturday markets are held (good value if you are looking for *miel de lavande* or other lavender products). On the south side of the boulevard is the old town, with the crumbling **Cathédrale St.-Jérôme**. Farther up the boulevard is the **Musée Gassendi▶** (Open Apr–Sep Wed–Mon 11–7; Oct–Mar Wed–Mon 1.30–5.30), with various archaeological finds and 19th-century Provençal paintings, as well as an extensive collection of 19th-century scientific instruments and a model for the first Channel tunnel, conceived by local engineer Alex du Breton in 1880. To the north the **Cathédrale Notre-Dame-du-Bourg▶** is a good, if neglected, example of the Provençal Romanesque.

Digne's star attraction is the **Musée Alexandra David-Néel▶▶** (*Open* daily; guided tours only. Jul–Sep, 10, 2, 3.30, 5; Oct–Jun, 10.30, 2, 4. *Admission free*). In 1928 David-Néel (see panel) bought this house, which she called *Samten Dzong* ("the castle of meditation"), although then it was in the countryside and not next to a busy main road. It houses a fascinating collection of Buddhas, prayer-wheels, other Tibetan mementoes and many of David-Néel's personal effects. The museum (20 minutes' walk from the town centre) also contains a Tibetan shop.

AN INTREPID TRAVELLER
Born in Paris in 1868, Alexandra David-Néel studied Oriental languages at the Sorbonne and then spent many years in Tibet, travelling across the country on foot and living in the forbidden city of Lhasa in disguise. On her return she published several books, becoming one of the top Tibetan scholars in the West. From the age of 69, a decade after moving to Digne, she spent a further nine years in Central Asia. In 1968, aged over 100, she renewed her passport because she wanted to visit China. She died in Digne on 8 September 1969, having just started to write another four books.

THE FIRST EXPLORERS

Early inhabitants of the Verdon gorges were Ithe Ligurians; several centuries later, shepherds fleeing the Saracens converted caves near the Circque de l'Escales into farmhouses and haylofts. In the Middle Ages the gorges were reputed to be the home of "wild men" and other assorted devils. The first scientific expedition was carried out in August 1905 by the speleologist E. A. Martel and several companions equipped with ropes, cameras and collapsible canoes. It took them three and a half days to get from one end of the canyon to the other.

Carving on the Chapelle Notre-Dame-de-Provence, Forcalquier

▶ Entrevaux   182C1

Approaching Entrevaux from either direction along the Var Valley it is easy to see why it was such an important town in the 17th century. The gorges here narrow to just a few hundred metres across—plug this, and you block a major route between France and Savoy.

On the west bank of the Var a jagged curtain of rock makes the hillside impassable. On the east bank, this natural barrier is reflected in the grand fortifications, built by Vauban, Louis XIV's military architect, which zigzag up to La Citadelle (*Open* daily. *Admission: inexpensive*) perched 135m (440ft) above the *vieille ville*.

The main access to the old town is a fortified **bridge▶**, another of Vauban's works. After a couple of centuries of quiet neglect a steady trickle of visitors drawn by Vauban's handiwork is injecting much-needed life back into Entrevaux's medieval streets. Some restoration is under way and there are concerts and festivals in the summer.

▶ Forcalquier   182A1

From a simple village on the Domitian Way in Roman times, Forcalquier rose to become an independent state in the 12th century. The Counts of Forcalquier held sway over Sisteron, Apt and Gap from their citadel, and the town became the centre of cultural and commercial life in Haute-Provence.

Only the ruins of one tower remain of the Counts' château on the **citadel** above the town. However, it is worth the walk for the view over the surrounding Pays de Forcalquier, and the 19th-century **Chapelle Notre-Dame-de-Provence**.

The spacious place du Bourguet is dominated by the austere, Gothic facade of the **Cathédrale Notre-Dame du Marché**. On Mondays, the *place* and the surrounding streets are transformed into a vast market, overflowing with local produce. South of the cathedral are the narrow streets of the **vieille ville▶** (*Tours* from the tourist office, tel: 04 92 75 10 02), with many 13th- and 15th-century houses. You can skip the stuffy old **municipal museum**, but the **Couvent des Cordeliers▶▶** (*Guided tours* daily in summer; Sun in winter. *Admission: inexpensive*) befits a visit. Built in the 12th to 14th centuries, it is one of the oldest Franciscan monasteries in France.

▶▶▶ Grand Canyon du Verdon   182B1

Rising just above la Foux d'Allos in the Mont des Trois Evêchés, the Verdon river flows south before looping west just above Castellane to carve its way through the limestone plateau of Haute Provence on its journey towards the Durance.

Between Castellane and Moustiers-Ste.-Marie the river has hewn a deep crevice in the plateau—the spectacular, 21km (13 mile) long Grand Canyon du Verdon. From sheer cliffs some 700m (2,295ft) above the rushing torrent there are

Taking to the water through the Grand Canyon

THE HAUTE-PROVENCE OBSERVATORY
After considerable research to find the location with the clearest atmosphere in Provence, the Observatoire de Haute-Provence was eventually built on a plateau just to the southwest of Forcalquier in 1936, near the village of St.-Michel-l'Observatoire. Its 14 domes house a number of telescopes, the largest of which has a diameter of 1.93m (6.3ft). Tours of the observatory take place on Wednesday afternoons at 3PM (tel: 04 92 70 64 00. *Admission: inexpensive*), but since they take place in daytime they are not particularly enlightening.

WALKING THE CANYON
The canyon is best appreciated on foot. On the right bank the Sentier Martel runs from Mayreste to Rougon following the GR4, but this takes about two days: A section of this route, from la Maline to Point Sublime, can be accomplished in about 7 to 8 hours. The Sentier Imbut follows the GR99 for part of the way on the left bank, crossing over at the Passerelle de l'Estellié to reach the refuge at la Maline (around 2.5 hours one way). Always take a torch, sweater, water and provisions, and beware of sudden changes in water-levels due to upstream power stations. A detailed colour booklet of the routes, *Canyon du Verdon*, is widely available (in several languages) in Moustiers or Castellane.

panoramic views down the length of this corridor, with the emerald green waters of the river (which was named after its unusual colour) sparkling in the sunshine below.

The first survey of the canyon was not carried out until 1905, when the eminent speleologist E. A. Martel charted its course (see panel opposite). His report that it was "a marvel without parallel in Europe" prompted the Touring Club de France to build the first tracks and belvederes in 1928. In 1947 the first road, known as the Corniche Sublime, was built on the southern side of the canyon, and the northern half opened up in 1973 with the Route des Crêtes (see Drive, pages 192–193).

Since then traffic volumes have been inexorably increasing; in high season you are likely to find yourself in a slow-moving convoy of campervans and cars.

In 1997, the Grand Canyon became a Parc Naturel Régional, which gives greater protection to this unique area, but that is certainly difficult to appreciate at the height of summer.

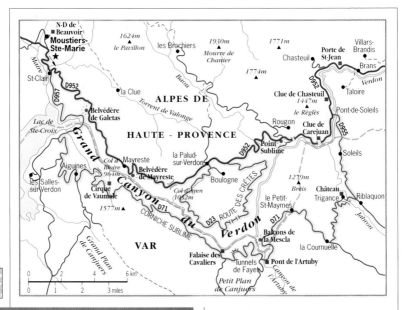

Drive

Grand Canyon du Verdon

One of the classic tourist routes in Provence, and best undertaken outside the peak months of July and August. Allow at least the whole day for the entire circuit, departing from and returning to Moustiers.

From Moustiers take the D952 to the Belvédère de Galetas, the first of many viewpoints, and take in the view of the impressive canyon mouth as the River Verdon pours out into the vast Lac de Ste.-Croix.

From here, the road starts to climb upwards and shortly you arrive at the Mayreste Belvédère, which involves a 10-minute scramble over the rocks to the cliff edge. This vantage point offers the first overall view of the canyon upstream. After passing through the Col d'Ayen, the road temporarily leaves the gorge and descends to the plateau of la-Palud-sur-Verdon, now a major centre for mountain bicycling, climbing, trekking, canoeing, and rafting.

Just after La Palud take a right turn down the D23, signposted *Route des Crêtes*. This loop returns after a nerve-racking 23km (14 miles) to La Palud. It passes several dramatic viewpoints, most notably the Trescaïre Belvédère, the Escales Belvédère (the view rendered even more dramatic by the climbers usually seen clinging to the cliff face—this is an internationally renowned rockclimbing site), the Baou Pass Belvédère (with a drop of 715m/2,345ft into the canyon), the Tilleul Belvédère (fabulous panorama back across the Plan de Canjuers) and the Imbut Belvédère.

Back in La Palud, continue on the D952 towards Castellane. After around 7km (4 miles) you will come to a large parking area for the Point Sublime. Walk up to the viewpoint to see the meeting of the Verdon and the Baou rivers and the openings into the Couloir Samson and the Grand Canyon itself.

The route follows the Verdon through the Clue de Carejuan until it reaches the Pont-de-Soleils, the crossover point between the right and left banks. Take the D955 on the other side of the bridge and then turn right into the village of Trigance. Turn right again onto the D71 and you soon reach the Balcons de la Mescla, a series of impressive belvederes almost directly opposite the Route des Crêtes on the north bank. Down below, the Verdon meets the equally turbulent Artuby River in the middle of the bend.

From the Balcons de la Mescla you cross the Artuby canyon on the impressive, single-span Pont de l'Artuby before arriving at the Tunnels de Fayet; between the tunnels, there are views of the Falaise des Cavaliers. The road follows these cliffs and then continues on the edge of the precipice past the Falaise de Baucher and the Imbut Pass before leaving the canyon and climbing up to the Cirque de Vaumale. At this lookout there are views extending over to the north bank and downstream to the opening into the lake.

At the Col d'Illoire the road finally leaves the gorges behind; stop at the belvedere for a last look back before continuing to the village of Aiguines. From here, a series of hairpin bends downhill gives lovely views across the whole Valensole plateau and the Lac de Ste.-Croix. Cross the Pont du Galetas (with a panorama of the lake on one side and the entrance to the gorges on the other) before joining the D952 into Moustiers.

The Grand Canyon is one of the natural wonders of Provence

GRÉOUX'S SPA BATHS
In the 2nd century the Romans built the first spa here. The baths then fell into disuse until being reopened in the 17th century. They became fashionable at the start of the 19th century when Napoléon's sister visited, but fell out of favour once again until being entirely rebuilt in 1962. Now popular with *curistes* from all over France, they pump out around three million litres (660,000 gallons) a day at an average temperature of 36°C (97°F).

► **Gréoux-les-Bains**   *182A1*

Dominated by the ruins of a 12th-century castle built by the Knights Templars, Gréoux has relied since antiquity on making a living from the warm, sulphurous springs that rise just to the south of this small town (see panel).

Gréoux's Grand Rue has several excellent *traiteurs* for stocking up on picnic supplies, as well as plenty of cafés, inviting restaurants and bars. There are many craft galleries and exhibitions, among them the **Maison de Pauline** (*Open* May–Oct, Mon–Fri. *Admission free*), an old Provençal house furnished in traditional style. Farther down the Grand Rue is the **Atelier Musée du Vitrail et de la Mosaïque** (*Open* Mon–Fri. *Admission: moderate*), which has extensive displays of stained-glass and mosaics in several showrooms. Just outside town at 36 avenue des Alpes is the **Petit Monde d'Emilie** (*Open* Mar–Nov Mon–Fri 3.30–7), an exhibition of dolls and costumes from 1832 to the present day.

A ruined Knights Templar castle stands guard over the town of Gréoux-les-Bains

►► **Lurs**   *182A1*

From its position high above the west bank of the Durance, Lurs commands a wonderful view across the surrounding countryside. The neatly kept streets and attractive houses amply justify the sobriquet of *village de caractère*, and the whole village is now classified as a historical site.

During the Middle Ages, Lurs thrived when the Bishops of Sisteron had their summer residence here, but the population fell to zero early in the 20th century when it was abandoned due to the lack of electricity and running water. The village was saved from oblivion by a group of graphic artists and printers (led by the typographer Maximilian Vox) who moved in after World War II.

Lurs now plays host every year to the prestigious *Rencontre Internationale de Lure*, which brings together graphic artists, photographers, designers, and printers during the last two weeks in August.

NEARBY The narrow D30 north of Lurs leads to the **Prieuré de Ganagobie**, a Benedictine monastery founded in the 10th century. The 12th-century **church**►► (*Open* Tue–Sun 3–5. *Admission free*) has an unusual decorative doorway and an even more striking set of mosaics composed solely of white, black and red tiles: Carefully restored in the 1960s, the mosaics combine geometric motifs with wonderful representations of fantasy beasts and animals.

▶ Mane   *182A1*

This small village 4km (2.5 miles) south of Forcalquier has a well-preserved old quarter, a château (private property) and a 16th-century church, but the chief attraction in the vicinity is the **Prieuré Notre-Dame de Salagon▶▶**, just outside Mane on the N100. Established at the end of the 11th century by Benedictine monks from Villeneuve-lès-Avignon, the priory complex includes a 12th-century Romanesque church, a small lodging house for the Abbot, and barns and farm buildings that date from the time the priory was deconsecrated after the Revolution.

Since 1981 Salagon has been home to the Conservatoire du Patrimoine Ethnologique de la Haute-Provence, a conservation organization actively involved in local heritage issues. As well as a museum dedicated to ethnography of the region there are also revolving exhibitions on traditional lifestyles. The centre (*Open* Feb–Apr, Oct daily 2–5; May daily 10–12.30, 2–6.30; Jun–Aug daily 10–7.30; Sep daily 10–12.30, 2–6.30; Nov–Dec Sun 2–5. *Admission: moderate*) also has an excellent bookshop with titles on regional culture. Outside, there are four small gardens, including a re-created medieval monastery garden and a medicinal herb garden.

Farther down the same road you will find the 18th-century **Château de Sauvan▶** (*Guided tours* Jul–Aug Sun–Fri 3.30pm; Sep–Jun Thu and Sun. *Admission: moderate*). The architecture of this classical mansion echoes that of the Petit Trianon at Versailles and is all the more surprising for being in Haute-Provence, especially as it overlooks lawns and a lake with geese. The interior style matches the palatial ambitions of the château's facade.

▶ Manosque   *182A1*

"Certain towns can show you their proud cathedrals, their medieval ramparts or the guts of martyrs but Manosque has only its beauty." Thus wrote author Jean Giono (1895–1970), who lived nearly all his life in Manosque and wrote evocative poems and stories about the surrounding countryside of Haute-Provence and its inhabitants. His myopia can perhaps be forgiven but he certainly would not have appreciated the sprawling, ugly industrial suburbs that surround Manosque today, nor the Cadarache Nuclear Research Centre on the banks of the Durance.

Once you have penetrated the core of the old town via the 14th-century **Porte Saunerie**, Manosque takes on a more pleasing aspect. The pedestrianized **rue Grande** is the central axis of the old town, lined with shops (a plaque above a shoe shop at No. 13 marks Giono's birthplace) and leads to the lively **place Hôtel-de-Ville**. Market days in the rue Grande are Monday, Wednesday, Friday and Saturday.

Manosque may not have a cathedral, but it has two churches. The **Église St.-Sauveur** combines a Gothic doorway with a Romanesque nave and an intricate wrought-iron belfry from the 18th century; on place Hôtel-de-Ville, **Notre-Dame-de-Romigier** has a finely carved Renaissance doorway and a 12th-century black-wood Virgin.

THE PERSISTENT MADONNA
The black Madonna in Manosque's Église St.-Sauveur is said to be the oldest in France. Found in a nearby pine wood in the 6th century, it was then mysteriously lost again for two centuries. After being rediscovered, it was presented to the monks building the church, but they thought it too ugly and left it outside the door. The Madonna, so the story goes, made its own way to the altar. It was once more put outside, and again found its way back to the altar. The sceptical Manosquais finally decided it was a miracle, and the Madonna remained. Today, supplicants pray to her for rain in times of drought.

195

Flowers and plants to go, in the old town of Manosque

Modern-day faience for sale in Moustiers

►►► Moustiers-Ste.-Marie   182B1

Moustiers, the western gateway to the Grand Canyon du Verdon, suffers badly in the summer months from traffic jams and overcrowding, and like the Grand Canyon itself, the village is best visited out of season. The old, tile-hung houses of the village cling precariously to the banks on either side of the Rioul, a torrent which descends from the craggy cliffs above Moustiers. Suspended across the gorge is a 220m (720ft) long chain with the famous star of Moustiers (see panel opposite) hanging down in the middle.

As well as being one of the principal access points for the Grand Canyon, the village is famous for its glazed ceramics (faience), examples of which can be seen in numerous museums throughout Provence. This centuries-old tradition (see panel) died out in the 1870s but was revived by Marcel Provence in 1927 and there are now a dozen or so studios doing a thriving trade. However, do not expect any bargains (prices range from around €15 for the smallest butter dish up to €1,500 for a large, decorative wall-plate) and be prepared to look hard to find something really special.

If you want to see what the classic designs should look like you can take a stroll around the **Musée de la**

MOUSTIERS FAIENCE
According to local tradition, it was an Italian monk who passed the secret of the glaze on to local potter Pierre Clérissy in 1668; his luminous blue designs on a brilliant white background became hugely popular during the reign of Louis XIV. Multicoloured designs were introduced around 1740, and by the end of the century there were a dozen or more workshops in the village. The potteries thrived until the Revolution but with many of their clients lost to the guillotine the industry declined, and the last kiln closed down in 1874.

Faïence►► (*Open* Apr–Oct, Wed–Mon 10–12.30, 2–6; Nov–Dec, Feb–Mar Sat–Sun 2–5. *Admission: inexpensive*), founded by Marcel Provence in 1929. The museum has a superb collection of faience by potters such as Clérissy, Olérys, Laugier, Ferrat and many others who made Moustiers' reputation in the 17th and 18th centuries.

In the town centre, the 12th-century **Église**► is dominated by a three-tiered Romanesque bell tower; inside you can watch the rushing waters of the torrent beneath through a glass panel in the floor.

Moustiers was settled in AD 433 by monks from the Îles de Lérins, who moved into the caves high up in the rock face above the village and founded a monastery: In the 12th century the **Chapelle Notre-Dame de Beauvoir**► was built on this site. The 20-minute walk up to the chapel, via a winding path lined with oratories, is a popular way of escaping the pottery shops. The chapel was rebuilt in the 16th century and has an unusual Romanesque porch with carved wooden doors.

A pilgrimage to the chapel takes place on the first weekend after Easter, when villagers wearing 18th-century costumes climb the path for Mass. There is also a procession to the chapel during the *Fête de la Nativité de la Vierge* on 8 September.

An ancient bell tower looms above the tiled roofs of Moustiers

THE CHAINE DE L'ÉTOILE
The origins of the chain with its five-pointed star that hangs high above Moustiers date back to the 12th century, when one was placed here by a seigneur of the Blacas family. Imprisoned during the Crusades, he vowed to make an offering to Notre-Dame de Beauvoir if he was released. The star on the chain was originally made from silver, but it was supposedly stolen during the Wars of Religion. It was replaced with a metal chain and star, although the chain is in such an exposed, windy position that it has frequently fallen down and been renewed.

The Rocher de la Baume, with its all but vertical strata, faces Sisteron's equally impressive citadel across the River Durance

ROMAN RIEZ
Built at the confluence of two rivers (the Colostre and the Aivestre), Riez was an important colony of the Roman empire. Once known as Colonia Julia Augusta Reiorum Apollinaris, it guarded the borderline between Roman-occupied territory to the south and the unruly Alpine domain to the north. Archaeological excavations have uncovered the ancient bed of the Colostre (to the south of the present river) and a monumental doorway, near four Corinthian columns, which are all that remains of a temple standing in a field by the road to Aix.

MUSIC IN THE ROUND
The circular tower in Simiane-la-Rotonde has very pure acoustics and concerts have been staged here since 1986. There is a popular summer concert season, *Les Riches Heures Musicales de la Rotonde*, and although this tiny venue can seat only 150 people it has attracted musicians of considerable calibre. As befits the setting, the repertoire is mostly medieval music. Concerts take place from mid-July to mid-August (for details, tel: 04 92 75 90 14).

▶▶▶ **Quinson**   182B1

Quinson is at the head of the lower Verdon gorges where its position close to the Grand Canyon and the Baume Bonne cave site has secured it a major tourism coup as home to the **Musée de Préhistoire des Gorges du Verdon** (*Open* Jul–Aug daily 10–8; Apr–Jun, Sep Wed–Mon 10–7; Feb–Mar, Oct to mid-Dec Wed–Mon 10–6. Closed mid-Dec to Jan. *Admission: moderate*). Europe's largest prehistory museum combines cutting-edge architecture with state-of-the-art facilities, and its 19 themed galleries trace a million years of history in Provence, from humankind's arrival in Europe through to the Iron Age. In the grounds is a reconstructed prehistoric village and garden demonstrating neolithic agricultural techniques, plus a path through the *garrigue* to the Grotte de la Bonne Baume where the original Provençaux lived 500,000 years ago.

▶ **Riez**   182B1

Riez lies at the centre of the **Plateau de Valensole**, which extends west from the Gorges du Verdon. The plateau is one of the largest lavender-growing areas in Provence, and, if you want to capture the rolling vista of lavender flowers at its best, the time to come is July.

As well as being a centre for traditional lavender-distilling, Riez has a long history as a market town on the crossroads of the Roman route through Provence from Fréjus to Aix. In the 5th century it became a bishopric and a **baptistery**▶ was erected over the ruins of the Roman baths by the cathedral (check opening times with tourist office).

At the heart of the old town the **Grand Rue** has preserved several fine Renaissance houses and in the streets and alleyways off to either side are a number of craft workshops, *santonniers* and potteries.

NEARBY On the D953 towards Digne, the intriguing **Maison de l'Abeille►** (House of the Bee) presents displays on the old-fashioned production of honey, the life cycle of the bee, and other aspects of beekeeping. There is an insect museum (*Open* daily. *Admission free*) and a shop.

►► Simiane-la-Rotonde   *182A1*

Spiralling around a hillock on the edge of the plateau that marks the boundary between Haute-Provence and the Vaucluse, Simiane-la-Rotonde is a charming *village de caractère* surrounded by farmland and lavender fields.

At the summit of the village is the **Rotonde►►** (*Open* summer, daily; *closed* Tue off-season and Oct–Mar. *Admission: inexpensive*) from which it gets its name. Built in the 12th century, this curious, truncated structure is one of the few remaining examples of non-religious Romanesque architecture in Provence. The main feature of the Rotonde is the extraordinary domed ceiling with a series of finely detailed carved masks and figures on the columns supporting the cupola. Most of the buildings around the Rotonde have long since gone, except for part of the seigneurial manor linked to it on the south side.

►► Sisteron   *182A2*

Strategically situated where the Durance valley narrows down to less than a kilometre (0.5 miles) wide, Sisteron guards the mountain gateway between Provence and Dauphiné. This ancient fortified site is capped by a **citadel►** (*Open* Mar to mid-Nov. *Admission: moderate*) standing 500m (1,640ft) above the waters of the Durance, which has a 12th-century keep. The citadel was badly damaged (as was much of the town) during Allied bombing raids in August 1944.

At the centre of town is the place de la République, with three huge towers (remnants from the medieval ramparts) and the **Cathédrale Notre-Dame►** to the east. Behind here is the *vieille ville►►*, a maze of steps and alleyways between tall houses linked by covered archways (known locally as *andrônes*). A signposted route leads past some fine houses in the old quarter, ending up in the place de l'Horloge on the north side, where there is a lively market in the mornings on Wednesday and Saturday.

Ramparts in Sisteron's old citadel

Close-up on the scant remains of Roman Riez

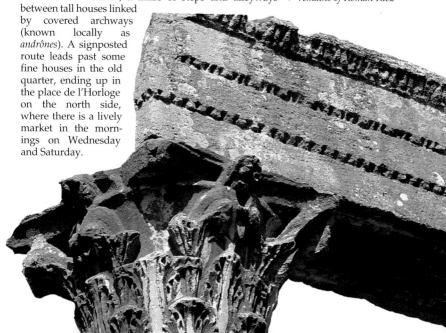

Côte d'Azur and Alpes-Maritimes

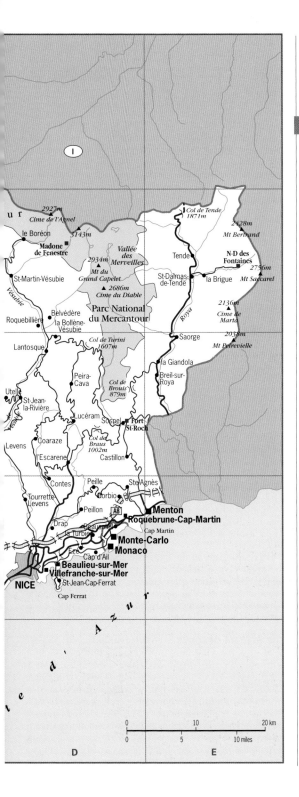

Côte d'Azur and Alpes-Maritimes

A year-round reminder of Cannes' international film festival

The most famous corner of Provence, the southeastern coastline known as the Côte d'Azur, often seems like part of another country: a glitzy, high-rise, ostentatiously wealthy sunshine state where pampered poodles and their equally immaculately manicured owners stroll the palm-lined boulevards and enjoy shopping sprees in Parisian couture boutiques. Nothing symbolizes the real wealth on display here better than a marina. With several dozen to choose from between Menton and la Napoule, they seem to encapsulate the image of this glamorous playground: conspicuous riches, the jet-set lifestyle and the joys of a sensual holiday next to the warm, blue Mediterranean.

The pleasures promised by the hyperbole surrounding the Riviera, as this 70km (44 mile) long stretch of coastline is also called, can seem like a distant dream when you are stuck in a traffic jam along one of the *corniches*, contemplating a beach down below packed to overflowing, with the sea a mass of pedal boats, bobbing bodies, jet-skis and sailboards. And the glories of the *belle époque* hotels on the seafront have been eclipsed in many places by a contagious rash of houses and apartment blocks spreading up every available sea-facing hillside.

INLAND PEAKS Fortunately, the real Provence is never far away, with the mountains of the Alpes-Maritimes forming a splendid backdrop to the glittering coastline. Just an hour or so from the beach the *arrières-pays* (the backcountry) shelters dramatic hill villages, linked by twisting mountain roads where signs warn of multiple *lacets* (hairpin bends).

Some of the better known of these *villages perchés* (such as Èze and St.-Paul-de-Vence) are sadly over-commercialized, but there are still plenty of others (such as Peille, Peillon, Coaraze and Gorbio) where the narrow streets retain more of an authentic flavour.

Behind Cannes the rolling hills culminate in the pre-Alps of Grasse. Behind Nice the narrow river valleys lead up to the wilderness of the Parc National du Mercantour. Farther east, the remote Roya valley displays characteristic Italianate architecture and many fine works of art in the old border towns of Tende, Sospel, Saorge and Breil.

In the summer you can hike and mountain bike beneath the snow-clad peaks of the Alpes-Maritimes, while in winter the ski resorts come into their own. For the budget-conscious it can make sense to stay in the *arrière-pays*, where hotel prices are more reasonable, descending to the coast for a taste of the high life when the bright lights call.

THE RIVIERA RESORTS Nice is the capital of the *département* of Alpes-Maritimes and France's fifth-largest city, with over 350,000 inhabitants. Some 4 million visitors a year come to Nice, drawn partly by its lovely setting and 7.5km (4.5 miles) of beaches on the big, blue Baie des Anges (Bay of Angels). Nice has a well-preserved *vieille ville*, as has the charming port of Antibes, which houses the remarkable Picasso museum—just one of an extraordinary number of first-class modern art museums along the coast, a legacy of the contemporary artists who settled here from the end of the 19th century onwards. The beaches at Antibes are mostly shingle and those on the neighbouring Cap d'Antibes largely private, but neighbouring Juan-les-Pins has a fine sandy beach.

Cannes is perhaps the most elitist of the Riviera resorts, a place to see and be seen, but avoid it during the Film Festival in May. It is, though, the jumping-off point for the lovely, unspoilt Îles de Lérins, the only islands off this part of the coast.

East of Nice, the picturesque port of Villefranche and the old resort of Menton, with its sedate charms, both have their devotees. In between is the independent principality of Monaco, where the harbour, with its massive yachts moored below the famous Monte-Carlo casino, has to be seen at least once.

The "perched village" of Gourdon, with its bird's-eye view into the gorge of the River Loup

FROM FORTS TO FLOWERS

Like so many ports along the coast, Antibes started out as a Greek trading post and was known as Antipolis ("the city opposite"), referring to Nice. The town was destroyed by the Saracens but took on a new role as a frontier outpost when Nice became part of Savoy in 1388. Over the centuries the fortifications were improved upon, culminating in the solid ramparts built by Vauban in the 17th century. When Nice became reunited with France in 1860, Antibes lost its military functions and, strangely enough, turned to growing flowers instead.

Porte de l'Olivette, a small bay on the Cap d'Antibes

▶▶ Antibes   200C1

For Riviera regulars, Antibes holds a special place, not just because of its setting but for the ambience of a lively town that does not rely solely on tourism for a living.

Across the Baie des Anges from Nice, the old town of Antibes is protected from the sea by stout ramparts. Inside the ramparts the narrow, bustling streets evoke another world, but step through an old gateway and you are immediately on a quay alongside the multi-million-dollar yachts of movie moguls and megastars. Antibes has its share of ugly modern flats on the outskirts, one of which was home to Graham Greene until his death in 1991.

Antibes is the largest horticultural centre in the Alpes-Maritimes *département* and is well known for its roses (which are exported worldwide), tulips and carnations. Baskets of flowers brighten the produce market (*Open* Tue–Sun mornings) in the cobbled **cours Masséna▶**, the main street of the old town. Barrels of herb-flavoured olives, little roundels of goat's cheese, melons, asparagus, figs and Provençal *primeurs* (early vegetables) offer a treat for the eyes and nose.

Wander southwards from the cours Masséna between the tall 17th- and 18th-century houses ("climbing on top of each other for a view of the sea," as one writer put it) until you come to the **Château Grimaldi▶** at a strategic point overlooking the ramparts. Converted into a museum of local history in the 1920s, the château was in a fairly run-down state in the 1940s when the curator offered Picasso (then living in a cramped flat in Juan-les-Pins) the use of it as a studio. When Picasso moved to Vallauris, in thanks he left behind the majority of the work that he had done on permanent loan. This *oeuvre* now forms the core of the **Musée Picasso▶▶▶** (tel: 04 92 90 54 20. *Open* Jun–Sep, Tue–Sun 10–6; Oct–May, Tue–Sun 10–12, 2–6. *Admission: moderate*).

Alongside the astonishing Picasso collection are works by Nicolas de Staël, Léger, Modigliani, Max Ernst and many others, as well as photographs of Picasso by Bill Brandt and Man Ray.

Interior of the Chapelle Notre-Dame-du-Bon Port

PICASSO IN ANTIBES
During the six months from July to December 1946 that Picasso was in Antibes, his work achieved new heights of creative genius, an outpouring of Mediterranean exuberance and fantasy. Picasso was in high spirits. The war was over, and he had a new lover, Françoise Gilot. His pleasure at life's prospects (despite a post-war shortage of materials that meant he sometimes had to use boat paint instead of oils) is reflected in the uncomplicated geniality of the still lifes, the aptly titled *Joie de vivre*, the mythologically inspired *faunes musiciens*, and *Ulysse et les Sirènes*.

205

Housed in Vaubon's 16th-century Bastion St.-André to the south of the Grimaldi château, the **Musée d'Archéologie** (*Open* Tue–Sun. *Admission: inexpensive*) draws together Etruscan, Greek, Roman and medieval finds from the vicinity, as well as *objets trouvés* from shipwrecks. Just next to the château the old cathedral, the **Église de l'Immaculée Conception**, is worth a look inside for the 16th-century altarpiece, the *Retable du Rosaire*, attributed to Louis Bréa.

To the east of the huge marina are boat-building yards and a stadium, behind which stands the massive **Fort Carré▶** (*Open* guided tours Tue–Sun. *Admission: inexpensive*). This impressive, geometric structure was started in the 16th century and finished by Vauban.

Children will enjoy **Marineland** and **Aquasplash** on the road towards Biot.

▶ Antibes, Cap d'   *200C1*

Between Antibes and Juan-les-Pins the **Cap d'Antibes** is dotted with sumptuous villas and private beaches; on the eastern side of the peninsula there is a huge sandy public beach, la Salis, and farther round the Plage de la Garoupe and the Plage Joseph are also both free. From Plage Joseph a coastal path meanders for 3km (2 miles) around the shoreline to Cap Gros.

Most of the Cap d'Antibes is cordoned off into millionaires' estates and you can but glimpse some of the palatial houses behind their massive gates and electric fences. However, it is possible to visit the **Chapelle Notre-Dame-du-Bon Port** at the top of the Garoupe plateau, where there is an extensive collection of sailors' *ex-votos*.

Just beneath the Garoupe plateau, the **Jardin Thuret▶**, 1 boulevard du Cap (Visits by appointment, tel: 04 93 67 88 88) covers 7ha (17 acres) with collections of rare exotic and tropical plants. The gardens were established by botanist Gustave Thuret in the mid-19th century.

At the westernmost point of Cap d'Antibes there is the **Musée Naval et Napoléonien** (*Open* mid-Jun to mid-Sep Tue–Sat 10–6; mid-Sep to mid-Jun 10–4.30. *Admission: inexpensive*). As well as model ships and cannons there are all sorts of items relating to Napoléon's return from exile in Elba and his connections with Antibes.

Naturalized palms in the Jardin Thuret

THE MACABRE DANCE
The *Danse Macabre* is a mysterious 15th-century tableau, which some say is an invocation against the plague, while others claim it is a sort of collective exorcism. The most likely explanation is that it illustrates the legend of the Count of Bar, who insisted on throwing a grand ball in his château during Lent: Several of the "sinners" who took part died as a result, and the painting shows the dancing couples being struck by Death's arrows and dragged off to hell.

▶ **le Bar-sur-Loup**   200B2

High above the river, le Bar-sur-Loup has been a military encampment under the Celts, the Gauls, the Ligurians and the Romans. From the Roman period the only traces that remain are two tombstones (one set in the base of the church clock tower) and from medieval times, the château's cylindrical towers in the town centre. In the main square is the château's dungeon, once seven storeys high, reduced to just a single floor during the Revolution.

The **Église St.-Jacques▶** has a fine Renaissance doorway with carved wooden panels, but the strangest sight in the village is the curious painting of the *Danse Macabre* (see panel) at the back of the church.

▶ **Beaulieu-sur-Mer**   201D2

Like nearby Menton, Beaulieu has an exceptionally mild climate (they claim a mere four nights of frost per year, and even bananas are grown here) and was a fashionable resort during the late 19th century. The town's name is due to a visit made here by Napoléon, who, not at his most eloquent, exclaimed in Corsican *"O qual bel luogo!"* ("Oh what a lovely place!").

In contrast to the sedate, palm-fringed seafront on the Baie des Fourmis, fantasy takes over completely in the extraordinary **Villa Kerylos▶▶** (*Open* daily; mid-Nov to mid-Feb weekends and Mon–Fri afternoons only. *Admission: expensive*), past the casino on the northern headland. Designed in 1908 by archaeologist Theodore Reinach, it is a faithful reproduction of an Athenian villa and was built using lavish amounts of Carrara marble, alabaster and rare woods and decorated with reproduction frescoes, furniture, vases and bronze statues. The only concessions that Reinach made to the 20th century were modern plumbing, glass windows and a hidden piano. For the last 20 years of his life Reinach lived here in emulation of Greek society, exercising and bathing with his male friends; women were banished to separate suites.

The old dungeon of le Bar-sur-Loup's château, now a tourist information centre

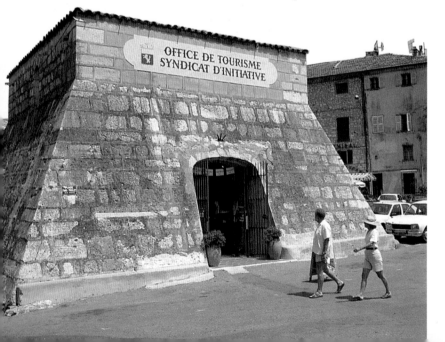

A glass-blower at work in one of the many glass workshops in Biot

►► Biot   200C1

As you approach Biot there is little doubt as to the village's main industry, with signboards at every corner of the road announcing *verrerie*—glassware. Biot started out in Roman times producing huge clay storage jars but this trade ended in the 19th century. Biot's conversion to glass and ceramics is largely due to the brief sojourn here of artist and sculptor Fernand Léger, who bought a plot of land to build a ceramics museum in 1955. Sadly he died soon afterwards, but his inspiration led to the opening of the Biot Glassworks, and in 1960 the **Musée National Fernand Léger**►► (*Open* Jul–Sep Wed–Mon 10.30–6; Apr–Jun Wed–Mon 10–12.30, 2–6; Oct–Mar Wed–Mon 10–12.30, 2–5.30. *Closed* Tue. *Admission: inexpensive*).

The museum was later expanded to include nearly 400 of his works such as ceramics, tapestries, stained glass and mosaics. On the facade is a monumental mosaic designed for the entrance of the Olympic stadium in Hanover, while the galleries trace Léger's artistic development through Cubism (he was a fellow pioneer alongside Picasso) to his obsession with machinery and the bright, geometric tableaux that became his trademark.

Fernand Léger's mosaics embellish the exterior of a museum in Biot devoted to his works

On the outskirts of the village, the **Verrerie de Biot**►► (*Open* daily. *Admission moderate*) has grown into a mini-commercial centre with several galleries, shops, the glass works itself (where you can watch the glassblowers), a museum (relabelled as the Éco-Musée du Verre) and an exhibition centre with extraordinary glass art exhibits.

Biot is a delight, especially the **place des Arcades**► at the heart of the village. At the south end of place des Arcades is the tiny place l'Église, where a doorway in a crumbling bell tower leads into a capacious **church** hidden behind the houses. On the left is a red-and-gold altarpiece, the 16th-century *Retable de Rosaire*, from the Bréa school; on the right, *Christ aux Plaies*, also 16th-century, attributed to Canavesio.

In the **Musée de Biot**► (*Open* Wed–Sun. *Admission: inexpensive*) are photographs, documents, pottery and *objets trouvé*s from Biot's past.

La Brigue's situation, well off the beaten track, belies its remarkable artistic heritage

KAYAKING ON THE ROYA
By the time it reaches Breil the River Roya has broadened out enough after its sinuous passage through the gorges to justify a hydroelectric station and to provide enough open water for kayaking. This can be arranged (as can trekking and mountain bicycling in the surrounding hills) through a small agency in the village, Roya Evasion (tel: 04 93 04 91 46).

▶▶ **Breil-sur-Roya**   *201E3*

Breil, the first major town you meet when travelling up the Roya valley from the border with Italy, straddles the River Roya with the old quarter on the eastern bank. At the centre of the narrow streets in the *vieille ville* is the 18th-century church of **Sancta-Maria-in-Albis**, with an altarpiece by Bréa hidden away somewhere inside its gloomy baroque interior. Far more cheerful are the two bell towers with their jolly caps of colourful Niçois tiles. Next door, the pastel-coloured, Renaissance **Chapelle Ste.-Catherine** is literally falling apart.

Just outside Breil, the quaint **Ecomusée du Haut Pays** (*Open* 1–2 days per week; check with the tourist office for details, tel: 04 93 04 99 76) occupies three old railway carriages in the station sidings. On display are the flora and fauna, agricultural activities and history of the valley.

▶▶ **la Brigue**   *201E4*

La Brigue is an attractive and welcoming village set amid the lovely landscapes of the Levenza valley, 6km (4 miles) southeast of Tende. The Levenza burbles past the main square in the village, from where the snow-capped peak of Mont Bégo is visible to the west. The old houses of the village are built from the local grey-green schist, as is the Romanesque **Église St.-Martin▶▶**, which contains an astonishing collection of primitive paintings by Louis Bréa and his followers from the Niçois school of the late 15th and early 16th century. There is a notable contrast between the nobility of Bréa's wonderful nativity altarpiece and his gruesome painting of St. Elmo having his intestines pulled out with a rope, which shows a degree of cruel realism unusual for Bréa.

But the most macabre paintings are the truly remarkable frescoes in the **Chapelle Notre-Dame des Fontaines▶▶** (*Open* daily; Oct–May afternoons only. Check with the tourist office in place St.-Martin, tel: 04 93 04 60 04), 4km (2.5 miles) up the valley to the east. The chapel is reached via a winding road that passes a pretty zigzag bridge, the Pont du Coq, which dates back to the

15th century. Perched above a mountain stream in the middle of a woodland valley, the chapel is all the more extraordinary for being in such a remote location. The compelling 15th-century frescoes, painted by Giovanni Baleison and Giovanni Canavesio, depict the life of Christ in a series of 38 episodes culminating in a grisly Last Judgment on the back wall, where the tortures of the damned are shown in gory, violent detail.

A mural in la Brigue

▶▶ Cagnes-sur-Mer   *200C2*

The seaside section of Cagnes (known as Cros-de-Cagnes) has none of the charm of other towns along this coast, but there are two compelling reasons to slow down and turn inland. The first of these, in Cagnes-Ville, is the **Musée Renoir▶▶** (*Open* Wed–Mon. *Closed* 2 weeks in Nov. *Admission: inexpensive* or joint ticket with Château-Musée) in the Domaine des Collettes. The house and gardens, where Renoir lived and worked (see panel), contain works by the artist as well as portraits and sketches by visitors such as Bonnard, Dufy and Albert André.

The medieval streets of **Haut-de-Cagnes▶▶**, with their vaulted passageways and steep steps, are crowned by a crenellated castle built by Rainier Grimaldi in 1309 and which now houses the **Château-Musée▶** (*Open* Dec–Oct, Wed–Mon. *Admission: inexpensive*). Spanning several centuries of culture, the château not only houses an olive museum on the ground floor but also a display of over 40 paintings of the cabaret star Suzy Solidor by well-known names such as Dufy, Cocteau and Van Dongen. In one section is the **Musée d'Art Méditerranéen Moderne,** which embraces a wide assortment of painters including Chagall, Matisse, Brayer and many more who have worked on the coast. In the summer, the château hosts the prestigious *Festival Internationale de la Peinture.*

The Genoese who worked on the château also created the frescoes in the **Chapelle Notre-Dame-de-Protection**, which can be visited on guided tours of the old town organized by the tourist office (tel: 04 93 20 61 64).

RENOIR IN CAGNES
Renoir moved to Cagnes in 1907 in the hopes that the warm weather would alleviate his arthritis. He built the Domaine des Collettes amid luxuriant gardens which also included a grove of 100-year-old olive trees. His talent flourished in this setting, despite the crippling disease that forced him to strap paintbrushes to his fingers in order to work. His north-facing studio has been preserved just the way the artist left it, with his palette, easel, and wheelchair in place. He died here in 1919.

The vieille ville *of la Brigue*

209

The Côte d'Azur has long been one of Europe's glitziest holiday destinations, and curiosity about the lifestyles of the rich and famous has no doubt contributed to its popularity in the past. Today, however, superstars and the ultra-rich are more likely to be hidden behind the security fences of private villas than spotted speeding along the corniche in an open-top sports car.

Above: The Monte-Carlo Story

BARDOT'S WOES
Once the icon of St.-Tropez, Brigitte Bardot famously retired from the world of show business at her 40th birthday party. Having turned her back on the limelight and sold all her jewels to set up an animal sanctuary, she flounced out of St.-Trop, leaving it to "the invaders" in 1989, then caused a further furore by marrying a right-wing politician on board the yacht of National Front leader Jean-Marie Le Pen. Since then she has returned to St.-Tropez to check on her animals and been accused of being too political—millions of euros in donations have been withheld from her sanctuary.

Bardot burst on the scene in 1957

210

Early decadence In the early days of tourism the Côte d'Azur was principally a sedate winter resort for the English and Russian nobility, but the pace changed in the late 1800s when the first casino was opened in Monte-Carlo, and the Riviera began to acquire its racy image. Stories of the *fin-de-siècle* decadence that followed abound. A Russian princess, for instance, was celebrating a big casino win in a hired villa one night, but when the owners decided that the revelry had gone on too long, she simply bought the house rather than stop the party.

Yachtsmen had already begun to frequent the coastal ports, when the writer Guy de Maupassant put in to St.-Tropez in the 1880s, followed by the painter Paul Signac in 1892, who stepped ashore and liked the place so much he bought a house and started the initial wave of contemporary artists to settle there.

The American influx After World War I the Riviera got back into the swing again with a new wave of clients, mostly wealthy Americans and stage and opera stars. Jazz clubs sprang up everywhere and Zelda and F. Scott Fitzgerald arrived to document the revelry (Gertrude Stein and Cole Porter were among the famous guests who stayed at the Antibes villa of rich Bostonians Sara and Gerald Murphy, a couple who served as role models for Dick and Nicole Driver in Fitzgerald's novel *Tender is the Night*).

Noel Coward, Ernest Hemingway, Katherine Mansfield (who adored Menton, and now has a street named after her there) and Colette (who preferred St.-Tropez) were among those descending for the season, which had now become a summer rather than a winter phenomenon, prompted by Coco Chanel, who made suntans fashionable in the late 1920s. The American dancer Isadora Duncan came to a tragic end in Cannes in 1927 when her scarf caught in a wheel of her Bugatti and strangled her.

The American influx came to an abrupt end with the stock market crash of 1929, although royalty (the Prince of Wales and King Faisal of Saudi Arabia) and the rich (such as the Aga Khan) remained faithful to the Riviera up until World War II.

Star turns The first Cannes Film Festival was planned for 1939, although it did not take off properly until 1947 (which was also the year that Picasso moved into his

studio in Antibes). The Festival soon became a compulsory stop on the itinerary of international movie stars, and by the 1950s the likes of Clark Gable, Errol Flynn, Lana Turner and Kirk Douglas were to be seen taking a post-Festival break on the beaches of St.-Tropez. It was at the Cannes Festival in 1955 that Prince Rainier of Monaco fell in love with the American movie star Grace Kelly, whom he later married.

In 1957 the Riviera took on a whole new dimension when Roger Vadim filmed Brigitte Bardot in St.-Tropez in the film *Et Dieu Créa la Femme* (*And God Created Woman*, also known as *And Woman Was Created*). The coast again became a byword for all that was chic and sexy. More recently, celebrities such as Mick Jagger, George Michael and Elton John, plus a whole host of French cinema and media figures, have owned houses in St.-Tropez.

The beaches of St.-Tropez continue to attract megastars (see page 174) but although you might see the occasional television celebrity shopping in Monaco or lunching in Mougins, today's beautiful people are keeping a much lower profile, and not necessarily staying on the coast.

CAP D'ANTIBES
This exclusive forested peninsula is one of the last true bastions of the Riviera's rich and famous. Luxurious villas nestle behind discreet veils of pine trees and flowering shrubs, and a star-studded cast of famous names from Guy de Maupassant and Hemingway to the Duke and Duchess of Windsor have stayed here over the years. Today, the likes of Robert de Niro and Madonna prefer a fleeting visit to the glorious Victorian *palais* of the Hôtel du Cap Eden Roc, at the tip of the peninsula.

211

Luxury yachts line the Riviera's many marinas

*Franco Zeffirelli is one of
many showbiz talents to
have left his mark on la
Croisette at Cannes*

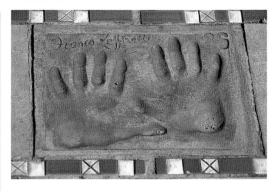

THE FILM FESTIVAL

It will come as no surprise
to discover that Cannes is
twinned with Beverly Hills.
Even if the outrageous
cost of hotel rooms does
not give you a clue then
the snobbery and hype
associated with the
International Film Festival
certainly will. With over
12,000 movie moguls,
directors and celebrities,
a press contingent of
around 3,000 journalists,
hundreds of films
screened around the
clock, wheeler-dealers
wining and dining with
fat wallets at the ready,
aspiring starlets posing
on the beach for the
photographers—yes, the
best place to be in May
is…somewhere else.

*Golden aspirations, or
just too many movies?*

▶ Cannes   200C1

"Closed for the summer"—a signboard on Cannes' casino
long ago, when winter holidays on the Riviera were all
the rage—would not be tolerated today during the high
season, with visitors arriving in their thousands to catch a
glimpse of the glitter and glamour for which Cannes is
now famous. That glitzy reputation is, of course, largely
due to the International Film Festival (see panel) held in
May each year, when thousands of agents, producers,
distributors and stars descend for a two-week expense-
account binge of celluloid consumption.

It was in December 1834 that the Lord Chancellor of
England, Lord Brougham, arrived here by accident, on his
way to Italy, but prevented from going farther due to an
outbreak of cholera. Cannes was then a sleepy fishing
village of some 4,000 souls. Brougham slept so well in the
one and only *auberge* (and enjoyed the innkeeper's *bouillabaisse* so much) that he decided to stay, and built a house,
the Château Eleonore behind avenue du Docteur Picaud,
where he spent the next 34 winters up until his death.

The seafront promenade, **la Croisette▶**, is bordered by
elegant hotels with big reputations, such as the Carlton, the
Martinez and the Majestic. A seam of terrace cafés with
brightly-covered parasols line the pavement and offer
excellent people-watching—at a not inconsiderable price.
Across the street, the beach itself is divided up into the
colour-coded concessions where you will not have to
budge from your sun-lounger for a cocktail or a snack.
The only free section is in front of the hideous, orange-
coloured **Palais des Festivals**, where all the real
work goes on during the film festival. Known as
"The Bunker" to regulars, its basement screenings
represent the real *marché du film*, where options
change hands at astronomical prices. Beside the
Palais is the **allée des stars**, where you can look
for your favourite film star's handprints. To the
west, luxury yachts crowd into the confines of
the **Vieux Port** alongside local fishing boats.
Behind la Croisette the streets around rue
d'Antibes have window displays that look
like colour spreads for glossy magazines,
but for mere mortals the shops in rue
Meynadier two blocks farther back
might be more useful, with excellent
charcuteries, pasta shops, *pâtisseries* and
cheese shops. At the western end of rue

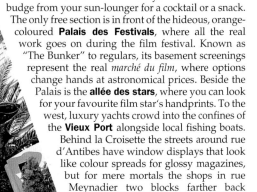

Meynadier there is a great food market in the Forville covered market (*Open* summer, daily; winter, Tue–Sun).

On a small hill above the port is Cannes' oldest quarter, **le Suquet**. In the 11th century it belonged to the monks from the Îles de Lérins (see below), who fled here after Saracen raids on their island retreat. The monks built a watchtower to warn of coastal raids, and fortifications, remnants of which are behind the Gothic **Notre-Dame de l'Espérance** on the hilltop. The monks' fortified priory now houses the **Musée de la Castre▶** (*Open* Jul–Aug daily; Sep–Jun Tue–Sun. *Admission: inexpensive*), which has an eclectic archaeological and ethnographic collection covering five continents. Admission includes the **Tour du Suquet**, the monks' watchtower; the platform at the top has views down the coast and out to the Îles de Lérins.

As an antidote to the traffic and crowds in Cannes there can be no better place than the **Îles de Lérins▶▶**, just 15 minutes away on a ferry from the *gare maritime* in the port (more than a dozen departures daily in summer).

The smaller of the two, **St.-Honorat▶▶**, is completely unspoiled and has been the property of monks since the 4th century, when Honoratus first landed here. Today it is Cistercian monks who cultivate the vineyards, olive groves and lavender fields around the abbey, which was rebuilt in the 19th century. Apart from visiting the remains of a fortified 11th-century **abbey** (*Open* daily; guided tours in summer. *Admission: inexpensive*) on the cliff tops, there is little to do except wander among the eucalyptus and pine trees and enjoy the peaceful atmosphere of this haven.

Ste.-Marguerite▶▶ is nearly twice as big (although it still takes only two hours to walk around), has some good beaches on the southern shores, and walking trails through the woods. The **Fort Royal** (*Open* daily. *Closed* Oct–Mar Mon. *Admission: inexpensive*) was built by Richelieu and reinforced by Vauban; the Man in the Iron Mask (see panel) is supposed to have been held prisoner here. On the ground floor is the **Musée de la Mer**, with archaeology exhibits and finds from shipwrecks.

"THE MAN IN THE IRON MASK"
In 1687, a prisoner was brought to one of the cells in the Fort Royal on Ste.-Marguerite who was later immortalized by Alexander Dumas as *The Man in the Iron Mask*. He was held here for over 10 years, but the question of his identity has never been fully resolved. Was he the illegitimate brother (or the twin) of Louis XIV? Or a loose-mouthed relative of the doctor who performed an autopsy on Louis XIII? That autopsy showed that the King was incapable of fathering children, and when the doctor's son-in-law inherited his papers, he couldn't keep this secret to himself.

213

The monks' watchtower rises high above Cannes harbour

SUNNY CERAMICS
The sunshine theme in Coaraze, the *village du soleil*, inspired a clutch of artists to create a series of massive and colourful ceramic sundials throughout the village in the 1960s. Those by Henri Goetz and Ponce de Léon are in the place Félix Giordan in front of the church, while others by Cocteau, Mona-Christie, Douking and Valentin are less happily placed on the pink facade of the town hall/post office building.

A curious fountain in the village square, Èze

▶▶ Clues de Haute-Provence · 200B3

As the River Var changes course in Haute-Provence and heads down towards the sea it encircles a sparsely populated region cut through with rifts known as *clues*. Forged by torrential streams, the valleys traverse limestone mountains where small, isolated villages hang on to a precarious existence. In the middle of this region is the 1,777m (5,830ft) high Montagne du Cheiron, to which skiers from the Riviera resorts flock in the winter months.

At the centre of the *clues* on the northern slopes of the mountain is **Roquestéron**, a fortified village that is separated in two by the River Esteron (prior to 1860 this river formed the frontier between France and Savoy, so each half of the village was in a different country).

Leaving the village westwards on the D17, the **Clue du Riolan▶** opens up on your right; farther past here on the D10 is the **Clue d'Aiglun▶**, which is perhaps the most spectacular of these narrow gorges, with a vertical torrent pouring down from the mountains above. To the west, the village of St.-Auban perches on a hillside at the opening to the **Clue de St.-Auban▶**, where the steep sides are riddled with grottoes and caves.

▶▶ Coaraze · 201D3

This little circular village perched atop a peak in the hills behind Nice has a sunny reputation (signboards proclaiming *Village du Soleil* mark the entrances to Coaraze) which obviously proved inspirational for the artists' colony first established here in the 1950s (see panel). The village still boasts its fair share of cobbled stairways and vaulted passageways, as well as a handful of *artisans d'art* and second homes for Niçois trendies.

On the outskirts of the village, the **Chapelle Notre-Dame des Sept Douleurs▶** (Our Lady of the Seven Sorrows) took on a much more cheerful character and a new name, the Blue Chapel, when Ponce de Léon (see panel) redecorated the interior in 1965 with bright murals and a vivid green stained-glass window. To reach the chapel, take the small road beside the Bar Tabac Les Arts either by car or on foot (20 minutes return).

▶ Contes · 201D2

This old town warrants a mention for its numerous legends, which may possibly account for its name, *conte* meaning story. The most famous fable is that of the caterpillar plague (see panel opposite), and there are several others revolving around appearances by the devil, who has his tail glued down by villagers and is forced to shed it and flee. Contes' myths are far more colourful than the village itself, which is now surrounded by suburbs, factories and an enormous cement works.

▶▶ Èze · 201D2

Along the Moyenne Corniche between Nice and Monte-Carlo, the dramatic location of Èze, 430m (1,410ft) above the

A quiet day in picturesque Èze

NIETZSCHE'S PATH
An old mule path which wends its way down to the seaside at Èze-sur-Mer from just outside the village of Èze is now known as the Sentier Frédéric-Nietzsche. This is in recognition of the fact that Nietzsche is supposed to have conceived the third part of *Thus Spake Zarathustra* while walking through the countryside here.

sea, making it the highest perched village you will find anywhere in Provence, has contributed to its popularity, with amateur snappers keen to capture the extraordinary sight of this settlement clinging to a cone of rock.

Entering the village through a crenellated 14th-century gateway, you find yourself in a maze of narrow streets and stepped alleys, a labyrinth designed to be easily defended. The *bijou* flower-filled passageways are now chock-a-block with boutiques, antiques-dealers and artisans; in the summer, the crowds can be insufferable.

Some respite can be gained in either the **Chapelle des Pénitents Blancs** (which has an unusual 13th-century Catalan crucifix with Christ smiling down from the cross) or in the **Jardin Exotique** (*Open* daily. *Admission: moderate*) surrounding the ruins of the château at the top of the village; the château itself was dismantled in 1706 on the orders of Louis XIV.

► Golfe-Juan 200C1

This rather bland resort does at least have the merit of a long sandy beach, sheltered by the headlands of Cap d'Antibes and the Pointe de la Croisette on either side. Unless you are stopping for a swim, though, it has little else to detain you except for a glance at the mosaic on the **quai du Port** marking the spot where Napoléon stepped ashore on 1 March 1815 after escaping from Elba.

PLAGUES OF CATERPILLARS
In 1508 Contes was inundated by hordes of large caterpillars—nasty, hungry beasties that defoliated the woods by munching their way through massive amounts of pine needles, secreting a poison that causes painful rashes and allergies in humans. The villagers were so desperate they called in the Bishop of Nice, who performed an exorcism to banish the creatures. Faced with a similar dilemma in 1993, the municipality of Villefranche, evidently with more faith in germ warfare than in prayer, brought in helicopters to spray the district with bacteria which, when eaten by the caterpillars, results in certain death.

MAGICAL PROCESSION

The *Procession dai limaca* is a pagan ritual giving thanks for the previous winter's olive harvest and exorcizing any demons that might damage the next crop. The whole village of Gorbio is illuminated by little flickering lamps made from snail shells (*limaca* in Provençal; snails are also a pagan symbol of renewal) set in beds of sand and filled with olive oil. Dabs of plaster fix the shells on walls, doorways, windowsills and on the pavements; a night-time procession makes its way from the church through the magically lit streets for the blessing.

▶ **Gorbio**   *201D2*

An attractive *village perché* 10km (6 miles) northwest of Menton, remarkable for being practically a souvenir-free zone, Gorbio is often swept by clouds and mists, which has led to the locals being nicknamed *les nebuleux* ("the cloudy ones"). Although it has at least half a dozen chapels and churches in or near the village, the most arresting spectacle in Gorbio is the annual *Procession dai limaca* (see panel), which takes place during the *Fête Dieu* (Corpus Christi) in May–June.

▶▶ **Gourdon**   *200B2*

Situated in a remarkable position some 500m (1,640ft) above the River Loup, Gourdon merits the description *nid d'aigles* (eagles' nest) with its stunning views embracing 80km (50 miles) of the coastline on a clear day. A fort was built on this dizzying site in the 9th century to keep watch for Saracen invaders; the vast rectangular **château**▶▶ (*Open Guided tours* Jun–Sep, daily; Oct–May, Wed–Mon afternoons. *Admission: moderate*) that stands at the heart of the village today dates from between 1607 and 1654, when it was entirely rebuilt by the Lombard family.

This immaculately preserved building contains a pair of museums, the better of which is the **Musée Historique**▶▶. A veritable treasure house on the ground floor of the château, the museum displays a large collection of antique armaments and suits of armour, 16th- and 17th-century furnishings, which range from Marie-Antoinette's writing desk to an Aubusson tapestry, and religious works of art in the chapel (including a rare sculpture of St. Sebastian by El Greco and a *Descent from the Cross* by Rubens).

On the first floor, the **Musée des Arts Décoratifs et de la Modernité** displays collections of art nouveau, art deco and works by the Union of Modern Artists (*Admission: moderate*). Outside the château the curved stone balconies of the lovely Le Nôtre-designed gardens jut out over the hillside, where you can admire the beautiful view while waiting for the next guided tour.

Apart from the château, Gourdon has several fountains and the usual clutch of shops with Provençal souvenirs such as olive-wood carvings, honey, nougat and scented soap.

Santons (*Provençal dolls*) on sale in Gourdon

Demonstrating the art of perfumery in Grasse

THE SALT SEAT
One of the curiosities in the château at Gourdon is a small *fauteuil à sel* (salt chair), which dates from the time when there were heavy taxes on salt: The family's salt supplies were hidden under the seat and granny promptly sat down on top when the taxmen called—a crafty solution, since it was also forbidden to force old people to stand up!

HEADY BLOOMS
In the valleys surrounding Grasse, lavender, jasmine, mimosa, roses and other sweet-scented plants are cultivated before being harvested (always at dawn, when the dew is still upon them) to undergo the alchemical process of extracting their essences. It takes 900,000 rose buds or 8 million jasmine blooms to render just one kilo of the heady elixir that is the essence of the flower.

▶▶▶ Grasse   *200B2*

On a still day the scent in the air as you enter Grasse is probably a lot more appealing than first impressions of the town itself, which sprawls untidily along the lower slopes of the Provençal Alps and down across the valley. But in addition to the famous *parfumeries*, which are the main lure for tourists, Grasse has a quaint old quarter and several sights worth seeking out once you have done the obligatory tour of the perfume factories.

Grasse started out in the Middle Ages by specializing in the less-than-fragrant industry of tanning sheep skins from Alpine pastures and hides imported from Spain and Sicily. In the middle of the 17th century many of the tanneries abruptly switched over to glovemaking to meet demand from Parisian society for perfumed gloves, which had become a hot fashion item since being adopted by Italian aristocracy during the Renaissance. The Grassois became *gantiers parfumeurs* until gloves ceased to be a status symbol after the Revolution, at which point they became simple *parfumeurs*.

With the rise of the big perfume companies in Paris at the beginning of the 19th century, the Grassois abandoned making the finished product and decided to specialize instead on what they did best, the distillation of raw materials into concentrated fragrances for perfume-making. The ancient techniques of *enfleurage* (flowers are placed in trays of fat, which are then washed in ethyl alcohol to extract the scent) and *maceration* (hot fat is saturated with blooms) and subsequent distillation will all be explained if you take a factory tour at one of the *parfumeries*.

Up to 300 different essences may go into a single fragrance

THE SMELL OF SUCCESS
There are currently around 30 *parfumeries* surrounding Grasse, each of which employs a head perfumer known as *le nez* (the nose). He has his own laboratory where he performs a sort of olfactory orchestration to select and blend different essences to create a fragrance. He has around 3,000 different essences to choose from, and may include anything up to 300 of these in a single fragrance. There are only 300 "noses" worldwide with a good enough olfactory memory of the raw materials to be able to do this: Out of the 150 "noses" in France, 50 of them work in Grasse.

The narrow streets of Grasse lead to the old town square

The main *parfumeries* in the centre of town are Galimard (73 route de Cannes), Molinard (60 boulevard Victor Hugo) and Fragonard (20 boulevard Fragonard). Tours in English and French are free, and naturally enough end up in the factory shop (although there is no pressure to buy).

The Fragonard *parfumerie* also has an enchanting **musée▶▶** (*Open* daily) in the same building, which covers over 5,000 years of perfume-making and has a beautiful collection of over 3,000 rare perfumery objects, with many exquisite antique *flacons* from Egypt, the Orient, Rome and Greece. Above the Fragonard shop across the street is another treat in the **Musée Provençal du Costume et du Bijou** (*Admission free*), with its pretty traditional local costumes and jewellery from the 18th and 19th centuries. Fragonard's collections make it difficult for the **Musée International de la Parfumerie** to compete, but it has teamed up with the **Villa-Musée Fragonard**, housing works by the rococo artist and scion of a leading local family, Jean-Honoré Fragonard. There is also the **Musée d'Art et d'Histoire de Provence▶**, which displays a good cross-section of Provençal decorative arts and furniture in an 18th-century mansion that once belonged to Count Mirabeau's sister. (Museums open Jun–Sep, daily; Oct and Dec–May, Wed–Mon. *Admission: moderate.*)

Grasse's *vieille ville* was at the core of the city when it declared itself an independent republic in the Middle Ages, allying itself with Pisa and Genoa, and the influence of Grasse's trading partners is evident in the Italianate architecture of the old town. At the centre of

the old town is the **place aux Aires▶▶**, which is best seen in the early mornings when there is a colourful fruit and vegetable market; by late morning, the square has been taken over by tables from the cafés and restaurants underneath the surrounding arcades. Above the arcades are the old mansions of the 18th-century tanning magnates, including at one end the grand Hôtel Isnard, which has a wrought-iron Provençal balcony typical of the area.

To the south of the old quarter is the **Cathédrale Notre-Dame-du-Puy▶**, where the plain 12th-century interior contains several interesting works including three paintings by Rubens, a rare religious painting by Fragonard, and an altarpiece from the Bréa school. Also of note are the splendid 18th-century carved wooden doors at the entrance.

Drive

Gorges du Loup

The River Loup, on its short journey from its source on Montagne de l'Audibergue down to the sea, cuts a spectacular path through the mountains. Allow 3–4 hours for this round trip from Grasse.

Take the N85 northwest out of Grasse, which climbs up to the Col du Pilon. In St.-Vallier-de-Thiey (see pages 240–241) turn right along the scenic D5, which soon climbs up to the Col de Ferrier. Beyond the Col de la Sine, follow the road down into the valley and across the Pont-du-Loup.

At the les 4 Chemins crossroads, turn right towards Gréolières, crossing the Plan-du-Peyron, bordered by pine forests and pastureland. The road starts to descend down the Clue de Gréolières, and, as the rift opens out, there is a series of tunnels through the rock face and a belvedere for a view of the river a dizzying 400m (1,310ft) below you. After crossing a small stone bridge outside Gréolières, the road divides: the eastern, left-hand fork, the D2, ends up in Vence (see page 247); the western side of the gorge is just as spectacular, ending up in Gourdon (see page 216).

Continue through Gourdon to return to Grasse.

PERFUMERY MUSEUM

THE CÔTE DE SWING

In Juan-les-Pins during the interwar "Années Folles" (Mad Years), Scott and Zelda Fitzgerald painted the town red, Rudolph Valentino lived in the Château de Juan, and Gloria Swanson became engaged to the Marquis de Falaise. Cole Porter made Douglas Fairbanks, Mary Pickford, Maurice Chevalier and the King of Montenegro dance, and at night everybody drank and caroused in the clubs and casinos. After World War II, the American Sixth Fleet, stationed in the Mediterranean, came to Juan to party. Sidney Bechet married here in 1951, amid wild celebrations and Dixieland bands playing in the streets. He returned annually, bringing other jazz musicians with him, and by his death in 1959 Juan-les-Pins was established as the jazz capital of Europe.

Enjoying the sun, sea and silvery sands on the beach at Juan-les-Pins

▶ Guillaumes 200B4

Dominated by the ruins of a château and perched some 800m (2,625ft) above the confluence of the Var and the Tuébi, Guillaumes is one of the largest villages in the Upper Var valley. At its entrance is the chapel of **Notre-Dame-du-Buyei▶**, which houses a remarkable painting showing the village in flames during the terrible fire of 1682.

From Guillaumes the D2202 leads southwards through the spectacular **Gorges de Daluis▶▶** (named after the village of Daluis), which cut through the red schist down towards Entrevaux. There are dramatic views of the Var below from the serpentine road on the west bank.

▶ Isola 2000 200C5

A popular ski resort due to its proximity to Nice (90 minutes away), Isola 2000 was purpose-built in the 1970s. Its name derives from the altitude (at 2,000m/6,560ft it is the highest ski resort in the Sud-Alpes) and the old village of **Isola**, 17km (10.5 miles) away back down the valley.

▶▶ Juan-les-Pins 200C1

Protected by the headland of Cap d'Antibes on one side and la Croisette on the other, Juan-les-Pins has a fine sandy beach in front of what used to be a magnificent pine forest.

Although a resort had been established amid the pines as early as 1881 (by the Duke of Albany, Queen Victoria's son, who coined its name), it did not really take off until the 1920s when a restaurateur from Nice, M. Baudoin, bought up the old wooden casino and opened a cabaret restaurant. On honeymoon nearby with his third wife, American railway heir Frank Jay Gould (who already owned two hotels on the coast) decided to go into partnership with Baudoin, and together they launched

the first summer season on the Riviera; at the time, it was still only a winter holiday destination.

By the 1930s Juan-les-Pins had become a huge success, helped along by scandalized publicity—here was the first beach in France where young women dared to bathe in one-piece swimsuits.

Outside the jazz festival (see panel), Juan-les-Pins' reputation for nightlife remains undiminished, with live bands competing on decibel levels in cafés, bars and discos. Not a place to stay, unless you have a pair of earplugs, but tons of fun to visit late at night and people-watch over an exotic cocktail in a plush, streetside bar.

▶ **Lantosque** *201D3*

There can be few other villages in Provence that have suffered quite so many landslides and earthquakes as Lantosque, with almost the entire village having been sent hurtling down into the ravine below on numerous occasions during the 15th, 16th and 17th centuries. It was rebuilt so many times because it was an important staging post on the *route du sel* (the salt route), which was followed by caravans of pack animals carrying this precious commodity from the *salines* of Hyères up to the Sud-Alpes and beyond into Piedmont.

Lantosque still looks as if it is about to slide down the hillside from its perch on a rocky spur overlooking the Vésubie valley, but beyond here the valley itself opens out onto richer, greener pastures. When covered in snow, these slopes are much appreciated by skiers from the coast, who flock here in winter to the small but trendy ski resort of **la Bollène-Vésubie**, northeast of Lantosque along the D70.

▶ **Levens** *200C3*

This large village (unusual because it once had two rows of encircling medieval ramparts) dominates the plains at the mouth of the **Gorges de la Vésubie▶▶**, leading back up into the Vésubie valley. From Levens, the D19 on the east bank and the D2565 on the west bank snake round the scenic gorges before meeting up at **St.-Jean-la-Rivière**. A hair-raising, 6km (4 mile) detour from here leads up to one of the most isolated sanctuaries in the mountains, the **Madone d'Utelle▶▶**. The panorama down towards the sea from the peak just past the chapel is outstanding; the chapel itself is still an active pilgrimage centre, with processions on Easter Monday, Whit Monday, 15 August and 8 September.

DYING FOR A HOLIDAY

As early as 1861, Menton was put on the map of international tourism thanks to a book written by an English doctor, J. Henry Bennett, which lauded the virtues of its climate for invalids. By 1870 Menton had become a chic seaside resort with sumptuous villas and luxury hotels financed by aristocratic English, German and Russian tourists. Many more people came in the hopes that Menton's warmth and sunshine would alleviate the symptoms of consumption (tuberculosis): Among the better known, whose graves can be found in the hilltop cemetery, were Katherine Mansfield, Aubrey Beardsley, and the Spanish writer Blasco Ibáñez.

►►► Menton 201E2

Hemmed in by a chain of mountains behind the bay, which protects it from the cold north winds, Menton is known for its unusually warm climate. No doubt this is what prompted the first ever visitors to the Riviera to settle here: The 30,000-year-old skull of "Menton man," discovered nearby in 1884, is one of the oldest palaeolithic relics in France.

The name Menton was first mentioned in the 13th century, and the town was acquired by Charles Grimaldi of Monaco in 1346. In 1793 it became part of France, then reverted to the Grimaldi family in 1814. In 1848 Menton revolted against high taxes and opted for independence under the protection of Sardinia, then rejoined France in 1860, when Napoléon III bought Menton and its neighbour, Roquebrune, from Charles III of Monaco for 4 million gold francs.

Today Menton is a charming resort that tries hard to counter its image as a retirement haven with a lively schedule of arts, culture and festivals. The most celebrated event is the 60-year-old *Fête du Citron* (Menton has been famous for its lemons for more than 500 years), which lasts for 10 days from Shrove Tuesday onwards. Now equally well known is the Chamber Music Festival in August, which is held in the **Parvis St.-Michel** overlooking the harbour. Another Menton delight is its glorious gardens, which flourish in the microclimate. Garden tours are available from the tourist office (tel: 04 92 41 76 76).

The most important museum in Menton is the excellent **Musée Cocteau►►** (*Open* Wed–Mon. *Admission: inexpensive*), housed in a truncated watchtower on the seafront. The museum contains mosaics and tapestries, and Cocteau's portrayal of love affairs in the *Inamorati* series as well as photographs, poems and ceramics. Another must is the Cocteau-decorated **Salle des Mariages►** (*Open* Mon–Fri. *Admission: inexpensive*) on the right-hand side of the town hall. The skull of "Menton man" can be found in the **Musée Municipal de Préhistoire Régionale** (*Open* Wed–Mon. *Admission free*), which also houses rock carvings from the Vallée des Merveilles (see page 246) and thousands of prehistoric exhibits.

Menton, a resort that enjoys a particularly favourable climate

Rare is the Provençal market that does not have at least one stall groaning under the weight of colourful vats or baskets of olives, with as many different herb flavourings as there are days in the month.

Top: olive trees are planted with enough space between them for a mechanical harvester to operate
Left: a scene typical of any Provençal market

All thanks to the Greeks Wild olive trees grow naturally in Provence but their fruit is sour and produces very little oil. The cultivation of more productive varieties (and the art of grafting) was introduced by the Greeks some time around 600 BC.

Olives grow equally well in limestone or sandy soil and, provided their roots do not get too wet, they can live for hundreds of years. What *will* kill them is a late, hard frost, such as the one in 1956 that destroyed hundreds of olive groves.

A young tree starts to bear fruit in its fifth or sixth year and attains its full yield when around 25 to 30 years old. Wild trees can reach heights of 15 to 20m (50 to 65ft), but modern varieties are pruned, making them easier to harvest.

The harvest Olives are usually harvested from the beginning of November through to January. At first the olives are green, but they ripen on the tree, turning brown and then black. Harvesting is traditionally a family affair, with friends and neighbours joining in. The old method was for someone to climb up the tree and shake the fruit loose on to mats spread on the ground beneath, although green olives have to be picked by hand because they do not dislodge so easily. Nowadays mechanical harvesters do the work, grasping the tree trunk and shaking it until the olives tumble down.

Olive oil A mature tree can produce up to 30kg (65 pounds) of olives, yielding between 5 and 6 litres (just over a gallon) of oil. Even if you only have one or two trees in your garden, the nearest *moulin à huile* (olive mill) will process your olives to give the appropriate amount of oil. The first pressing produces the best olive oil, sold as *premier pression à froide vierge extra*, or simply *vierge extra* (extra virgin). The residue (the *grignon*, or pulp) is pressed again with more cold water added, and labelled *fine* or *extra fine*. The third pressing, with warm water, produces an oil that is used commercially.

CRACKED OLIVES
Raw olives are inedible unless properly cured, and one of the most popular ways of doing this at home is to make *olives cassées*, or cracked olives. The recipe is simple: The olives are broken with a mallet and then mixed with water and equal amounts of wood ash (preferably olive or vine wood). This mixture is left for two days (with frequent stirrings) and the olives are then rinsed in cold water and left to soak for another week. Finally, they are covered in brine flavoured with coriander, fennel and orange peel, and put into storage jars.

223

SCOURTINS
Before the advent of modern hydraulic presses, the olive paste was spread on flat, densely woven mats called *scourtins* before the oil was squeezed out in a hand mill. The first *scourtins* were made from straw, but later sisal or coconut fibre was used instead. *Scourtins* are still produced in Provence, and you can sometimes find them in souvenir shops.

Musée
d'Anthropologie
Préhistorique
Grotte de
l'Observatoire
Jardin
Exotique
St-Martin
Gare
Casino de Monte-Carlo
Musée de Poupées
et Automates
RUE GRIMALDI
R PRINCESSE CAROLINE
BOULEVARD RAINIER III
BOULEVARD CHARLES III
PLACE
D'ARMES
Port de Monaco
La
Condamine
Stade
Zoo
Palais
Princier
AVE DU PRINCE HÉRÉDITAIRE ALBERT
AVE DU PRINCE
FONTVIEILLE
Stade
Louis II
St-Nicolas
Port de
Fontvieille
PLACE DU
PALAIS
Musée
Historial des
Princes de Monaco
Musée du
Vieux
Monaco
Palais
de Justice
RUE ÉMILE DE LOTH
Chapelle de
la Miséricorde
PL DE LA
VISITATION
Cathédrale
AVE
DES PINS
QUAI ANTOINE 1er
PORTE NEUVE
Yacht
Club
Fort
Antoine
AVENUE SAINT-MARTIN
Jardins St-Martin
Musée
Océanographique
BOULEVARD ALBERT
AVENUE DE LA PORTE
AVENUE DU PORT
N
0   100   200 m
0   100   200 yards

SAFE ON THE STREETS
Monaco likes to portray an image of stability and safety, and is said to have more remote-controlled cameras and police on the streets than practically anywhere else in Europe (yes, you can walk around wearing jewellery at night). Crime (apart from the white-collar variety) and delinquency are virtually non-existent: apparently if it were not for a steady stream of divorce cases, the Law Courts could have shut up shop long ago.

The view from old Monaco down to a modern marina

►►► Monaco and Monte-Carlo   201D2

Monaco conjures up images of glamour and wealth, of high-rollers winning or losing fortunes in the casino, high-octane Formula One racing cars screeching through the streets during the annual Grand Prix, high society cavorting in nightclubs until dawn. Yet Monaco is a surprisingly sedate place. In the lobby of the Hôtel de Paris you are more likely to see bored-looking businessmen hammering out deals. In the gaming room built on the side of the Café de Paris, gambling has been reduced to the unglamorous level of ranks of one-armed bandits. The sanitized streets of the old town hold about as much allure as a tawdry souvenir shop, of which it has plenty.

But Monaco is still worth visiting for the day, if only to gaze at the wonderful *belle époque* casino and the lavish hotel lobbies, and to marvel at the justly famed Musée Océanographique, probably one of the best in Europe, which alone justifies the trip.

The principality of Monaco covers a mere 195ha (just under 1sq mile, much of which has been reclaimed from the sea), making it Europe's second-smallest independent state after the Vatican.

After they had seized Monaco, the Grimaldis (see panel) continued to expand along the coast, eventually taking control of Menton, Roquebrune, Antibes and Grimaud. In 1848 Menton and Roquebrune declared themselves independent republics, fed up with the high taxes imposed by the Grimaldis on their lemons and olives. Facing bankruptcy, Charles III decided to take advantage of his independence from France and open a casino, since gambling was still illegal in France at the time. But the venture failed, and it was not until 1863, when he called in François Blanc, director of the hugely successful casino in Bad Homburg, that it began to take off. The royal coffers were so flush that Charles decided to abolish all taxes, a situation that still holds today.

His successor Albert I lavished money on the arts and sciences and commissioned Charles Garnier (architect of the Paris Opéra) to rebuild the Casino, incorporating an opera house, which became the home of Diaghilev's Ballet Russe. He initiated the first Monte-Carlo rally in 1911, but spent most of his vast inherited wealth roaming the oceans on a series of fabulous yachts collecting scientific data for his beloved Oceanographic Institute.

These halcyon days came to an abrupt end in 1933 when France legitimized gambling, and by the time Rainier III came to the throne in 1949 Monaco was relatively down on its luck. However, this tax-free zone still attracted offshore finance and Rainier tried to build on this as well as encourage business tourism, conferences (a state-of-the-art convention centre was opened in the 1990s), and diversification into light industry. Even though Monte-Carlo now has four casinos, gambling today only brings in 4 per cent of revenues, compared to 95 per cent in the golden days at the turn of the last century.

The principality continues to attract numerous anonymous tax exiles, not to mention more well-known faces such as Boris Becker, Claudia Schiffer, Karl Lagerfeld and several Formula One racing drivers.

Guarding the Grimaldi home, the Palais Princier, in Monaco-Ville

225

FRANÇOIS THE SPITEFUL

In the 12th century Monaco became the property of the Genoese, who were split between the Guelfs (allied to the Pope) and the Ghibellines (allied to the German emperor). Legend has it that in 1297 the chief of the Guelf faction, a Grimaldi known as François the Spiteful, disguised himself and his men as monks and knocked on the door of the Ghibelline garrison in Monaco asking for help. Having been admitted, they pulled out their swords and massacred the garrison. This is the origin of the two monks brandishing swords on the crest of the Grimaldi family, who have (apart from a couple of hiccups) ruled Monaco ever since.

The Jardin Exotique, overlooking the sea

LES TERRACES DE FONTVIELLE
On the hillside above the Port de Fontvielle and Monaco-Ville, the Terrasses de Fontvielle have been developed to house a clutch of low-key attractions. On the Esplanade Rainer III, the Jardin Animalier is home to white tigers, hippos, rhinoceroses and reptiles (*Open* daily. *Admission: moderate*). A short walk away, Prince Rainier's private classic car collection features Bugattis, Rolls Royces and Lamborghinis (*Open* daily. *Admission: moderate*). Farther west is the outdoor Chemin des Sculptures, displaying works by contemporary artists (*Open* daily. *Admission free*).

Monaco-Ville►► Across the harbour from 19th-century Monte-Carlo, the old town is home to the **Palais Princier**► (*Guided tours* Jun–Sep, daily. *Admission: moderate*), with its Court of Honour, Hercules Gallery (with 17th-century frescoes), Throne Room and various plushly decorated state apartments. The ornate facade of the palace overlooks the **place du Palais**►, where the rows of cannons (a donation from Louis XIV) are complemented by neatly stacked piles of cannon balls. The Toytown impression is further reinforced by the changing of the guard, which takes place at 11.55am sharp every day.

The **old town** stretches south from the palace; it is immaculately kept but about as stimulating as the endless Prince Rainier mugs, tea towels and ashtrays on sale. The **Musée Historial des Princes de Monaco** (*Open* daily. *Admission: moderate*), which promises 40 "bigger than life" waxworks tracing the history of the Grimaldi family, is equally dull.

At the heart of the old town is the **cathédrale**, a neo-Romanesque structure inside which is one of Louis Bréa's masterpieces, the **retable de St.-Nicolas**, as well as his *Pietà de curé Teste*. Here too are the tombs of all the Grimaldi family, including that of Princess Grace, which is often smothered in bouquets.

The highlight of the old town is the splendid **Musée Océanographique**►►► (tel: 377 93 15 36 00; *Open* Jul–Aug, daily 9.30–7.30; Apr–Jun, Sep, daily 9.30–7; Oct–Mar, daily 10–6. *Admission: expensive*) on the headland. Founded in 1910 by Prince Albert I, this huge edifice was built into the cliff face to hold the specimens he collected on his many voyages and to house marine research laboratories (under the direction of Jacques Cousteau 1957–1988). The excellent aquarium features the weirdest and most wonderful fish from the world's oceans, including the spectacular giant groupers and jacks, piranha and black-tipped sharks swarming over a small, sunken boat. There are also beautifully lit displays of living corals. Try not to come on a Sunday (particularly a wet one), when the crowds will be three or four deep around every tank.

The first floor has a bit of everything, from natural history to displays on the atmosphere and deep-sea trenches. It also has the world's first submarine (powered by pedals, it was built in 1774 and used against English ships during the American War of Independence) and models of all the magnificent ships that Albert had built for his voyages.

If the museum prompts your curiosity about the underwater world you can take a glass-bottomed boat trip with **Aquavision** (tel: 377 92 16 15 15; *open* Jun–Sep. *Admission: expensive*), who operate 55-minute tours departing from the quai des États-Unis in the port.

Moneghetti Just off the **Moyenne Corniche** is the fabulously surreal **Jardin Exotique▶** (*Open* end Dec to mid-Nov, daily. *Admission: moderate*), which has an extensive collection of some 7,000 succulents and cacti. Guided tours of the **Grotte de l'Observatoire**, an ancient cave and an anthropology museum, are included in the ticket.

Monte-Carlo▶▶▶ No visit here is complete without a look (let alone a flutter) inside the **Casino de Monte-Carlo▶▶**, for many years the chief income-earner of the principality and still its main showpiece. You have to be over 21 (with passport as proof) to enter the American Room, where slot machines line the walls around the crap, roulette and blackjack tables; the gilded rococo ceilings have to be seen to be believed. The stakes get higher and the decor more extravagant once you reach the European rooms, which you will have to pay to enter.

Flanking the casino on either side are the **Café de Paris** and the **Hôtel de Paris**, both worth a look: the Café de Paris for the clientele and the Hôtel de Paris for its sumptuous lobby.

"THE MAN WHO BROKE THE BANK"
When Garnier's casino first opened in 1878 the clientèle were almost entirely wealthy, visiting several times a week from the other resorts for a bit of fun. But the passion for gambling spread and people began to believe they could make their fortunes, partly inspired by Charles Deville Wells, who turned $400 into $40,000 in a three-day gambling spree in 1891, later immortalized in the song *The Man Who Broke The Bank At Monte-Carlo*. Other gamblers were not so lucky, and the growing number of suicides was covered up by the casino for fear of bad publicity.

227

Founded in 1910, the Musée Océanographique is one of France's most popular museums

On the other side of Monte-Carlo heading east are the artificial sandy strands of the Larvotto beaches (most of which charge a moderate daily rate). Nearby, the appealing **Musée National** (*Open* daily. *Admission: moderate*) displays over 400 dolls, dolls' houses and working automata from the 18th and 19th centuries.

Pavement space is at a premium during the annual Monaco Grand Prix (May–Jun). Tickets can be hard to obtain (they are often sold out months in advance), but you may be able to purchase one for standing space in the old town, from where there is a bird's-eye view of parts of the circuit. The Monte-Carlo rally takes place in January. There is an International Fireworks Festival in July and August, and early September's Classic Week yachting regatta attracts an impressive field.

Faites vos jeux—
Monaco's famous Casino

SKY-HIGH GASTRONOMY
A foothills village turned foodie pilgrimage centre, 7km (4.5 miles) above Cannes, Mougins' gastronomic reputation has extended far and wide, largely due to the presence of Roger Vergé, one of France's most celebrated and charismatic chefs, who owns two of the restaurants and also runs an expensive gourmet food shop. Critics say that the exorbitant prices (up to €125 per person in some restaurants) are not matched by the quality of the food and that it is all just hype. Nonetheless, Mougins continues to be popular, although anyone on a tight budget will have a hard time finding an affordable meal.

▶▶ Mougins   200C1

It makes a change to find a *village perché* behind the coast that has not been overrun with souvenir shops, but then such downmarket commercialism probably would not be allowed to spoil the tasteful medieval streets of Mougins, where the much more serious art of gastronomy holds sway (see panel).

If you are not here to eat, Mougins is still worth a visit, if only to wander around the immaculate streets with their carefully restored houses. There is also an interesting **Musée de la Photographie▶** (*Open* Jul–Aug, daily 2–8; Sep–Jun daily 10–6. *Admission: inexpensive*) just next to the Porte Sarrazine. Art exhibitions are also held in the old washhouse, **la Lavoir**, on the picturesque place de le Mairie.

Just outside Mougins (2km/1 mile southeast on the D3) is the charming **Chapelle de Notre-Dame de Vie▶▶** on a hilltop flanked by ancient cypress trees. This 12th-century retreat was largely rebuilt in 1646 and used to be a popular place of pilgrimage. Stillborn babies were brought here and it was believed that they came back to life during Mass just long enough to be baptized. Picasso spent the last years of his life in a villa hidden away behind the trees just opposite the chapel.

Back down towards Cannes at the *Aire des Bréguières* turn-off from the A8 *autoroute* is the huge **Musée de l'Automobiliste▶▶** (*Open* daily. *Admission: moderate*), which has a vast collection of vehicles, from vintage Bugattis, rally and racing cars to armoured cars.

▶ la Napoule   200B1

At the western end of the Golfe de Napoule opposite Cannes, la Napoule (full name Mandelieu-la Napoule) marks the start of the Riviera. On the road above the marina is the extraordinary **château▶**, a folly rebuilt on the site of a medieval castle in 1918 by the American sculptor and millionaire Henry Clews. The gateway is ornamented with a series of mythical beasts and creatures, a theme that is carried through to the interior (*Guided tours* early Feb–early Nov daily 10–6 rest of year Mon–Fri 2–5, Sat–Sun 10–5. *Admission: moderate*). The château also houses the Napoule Art Foundation.

The traditional outdoor game of **boules** *is as Provençal as* pastis *and is a familiar sight in every town and village during daylight hours—sometimes even at night too, if there is a floodlit* **boules** *court.*

The game *Boules* looks like a fairly easy game; certainly anyone can take part and enjoy it from the first throw. However, for serious players there is a great deal of gamesmanship involved, not to mention plenty of noisy exclamations and dramatic gesticulation.

The game starts with a small wooden ball, the *cochonnet*, being thrown some distance up the court, which is usually a reasonably flat, hard area of gravel or sand—or even a tarmac parking area or road. Each player has three steel balls (they were once made from wood, studded with tacks), usually etched with different patterns or colours for identification. The winner is the person who throws the ball closest to the *cochonnet*.

Tactics Although it sounds straightforward enough, the skill (and the fun) of *boules* is in choosing the right tactic to get your ball next to the marker. For instance, you can simply roll your ball along the ground until it gently comes to rest (you hope) next to the *cochonnet*. But your opponent (who becomes the *tireur*) can "fire" his ball at yours, knocking it out of the way. Or he can "fire" at the *cochonnet*, knocking it towards his other balls on the court, a tactic called *faire le carreau*. At the conclusion of the round, there will be much careful scrutiny of the positioning of the balls to see who has won, often involving a tape measure to check distances to the millimetre.

Pétanque The original game of *boules* was known as *la longue*—that is, over a long distance (usually 15–20m/50–65ft)—in which players would take a running start and make three short hops from a marker before throwing their balls. Nowadays, *la longue* has been overtaken in popularity by *pétanque*, a variation which originated in la Ciotat. The game starts off *pieds tanques* ("feet together") and the balls are thrown over a shorter distance.

229

Boules is part of the fabric of life in Provence

UP AND DOWN THE HILL

Around 1000 BC the Ligurians built two forts straddling the site of present-day Nice, one near the mouth of the Paillon River and the other farther up the valley. The Phoenicians set up a small trading post, Nikaia, from the 6th century BC. Plagued by Ligurian pirates, they asked the Romans for help, who arrived in 200 BC, founding a town near the old *oppidum*, which they named Cemenelum (now the district of Cimiez). Cemenelum became the capital of the Roman Alpes-Maritime, with 20,000 inhabitants by the 3rd century AD. It was destroyed during the barbarian invasions, and the inhabitants moved down to the more easily defended site of Nikaia on the bay.

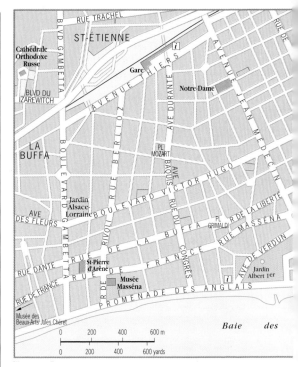

▶▶▶ Nice   201D2

Like the bubbling fountains in the place Masséna, Nice sparkles by day and by night, confident of its position as Queen of the Riviera. It might not attract celebrities in the way that Monaco or St.-Tropez do, but it is far more interesting for that, a lively, energetic city with an independent character that is not at all swayed by tourism.

After the fall of the Roman town of Cemenelum, the port of Nikaia was the main medieval settlement (see panel). The city prospered under the Counts of Provence but in the 14th century it passed into the hands of the Counts of Savoy, and mostly remained under Italian control for the next 400 years. In 1860 Napoléon III signed a secret treaty with the House of Savoy by which Nice would revert to France in return for helping Vittorio Emanuele II of Savoy drive the Austrians out of northern Italy.

By this time the first visitors had begun to arrive, and in 1864 the building of the railway station sealed Nice's future as a Riviera resort. In 1827 around 600 visitors descended on Nice for the winter season, and by the end of the century the number had risen to 20,000. Construction began of the many *belle époque* mansions and follies so beloved of the aristocracy. Queen Victoria and other heads of state added to the allure of the resort, and by the start of World War I the city was welcoming 150,000 visitors per year.

With the advent of the "summer holiday" in the 1920s, Nice switched seasons. Today, the emphasis is on year-round tourism, with the development of such facilities as the Acropolis convention centre.

NIÇOIS TRADITIONS

Nice even has its own language, "Nissart" (derived from the ancient Occitan dialect), which is still spoken and kept very much alive through language courses, theatre productions and traditional songs. The songs are often performed at *fêtes*, when girls wear the traditional costumes of a *bouquetière* (red-and-white striped cotton skirt, blouse and black velvet waistcoat) and boys don fishermen's costume (red-and-white striped corsaire trousers, a broad belt of red wool and white cotton shirt).

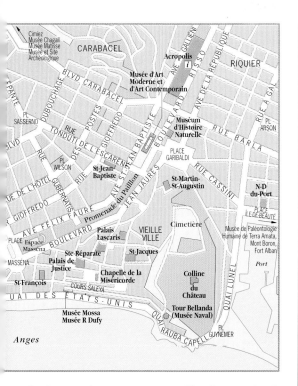

Anges

THE RIVIERA *CORNICHES*
The three famous *corniches* ("cliff roads") of the Riviera run between Menton and Nice along a dizzying stretch of coastline overlooking the resorts and beaches. The most spectacular views are from the Grande Corniche (D2564), built by Napoléon along the route of the old Roman road, Via Julia Augustus; the route passes through la Turbie (see page 243) and some of the most sweeping panoramas are found above Èze. The Moyenne Corniche (N7) also has good views and is the only way to reach Èze itself (see page 214) by car. The lowest of the three is the Corniche Inférieure (N98), which gives access to all the coastal resorts and is the most prone to traffic jams during summer. The top two *corniches* are notoriously accident-prone, so if you are in a hurry it is better to take the A8 *autoroute*, which carves its way through the mountains behind the three coast roads from Nice as far as the Italian border.

Seafront and town centre▶▶ The **Promenade des Anglais▶▶** (see panel, page 234) has been widened many times since the 1820s and has since been extended right out to the Nice–Côte d'Azur airport, becoming fairly traffic-clogged as a result. About midway along the promenade, the **Hôtel Negresco** still stands facing the Mediterranean in all its domed splendour. Behind the Negresco in the Palais Masséna is the **Musée d'Art et d'Histoire** (tel: 04 93 88 11 34; *temporarily closed*) , which contains a couple of fine 15th-century paintings by Jacques Durandi and a Bréa polyptych, as well as all-too-predictable Napoléonic souvenirs and dusty First Empire mementoes.

West of the Palais Masséna is the **Musée des Beaux-Arts** (*Open* Tue–Sun 10–6. *Admission: moderate*), with 17th-century Italian works through to the Impressionists and contemporary works, including oddities such as Kess Van Dongen's entertaining paintings of bejewelled and/or completely naked *belles dames* of the roaring twenties.

It is worth the trek north up boulevard Gambetta to the **Cathédrale Orthodoxe Russe▶▶** (*Open* Jun–Sep daily 9–12, 2.30–6; Oct–May 9.30–12, 2.30–5. *Admission: inexpensive*), beyond the flyover and railway tracks. Inaugurated in 1912, this monument was financed by Tsar Nicolas I in memory of his son Nicolas, who died in Nice.

At its eastern end, the Promenade des Anglais stops at the Jardin Albert 1er, where there is a small Théâtre de Verdure (it offers concerts in the summer months). Behind here is the **place Masséna▶**, with its gardens, fountains and *belle époque* facades, such as that of the Hôtel Plaza.

Crowds enjoying the Mardi Gras in Nice

From the place Masséna a broad concourse runs northeast, following the course of the River Paillon, now buried underground. This boulevard was the site chosen for Jacques Médecin's grand civic projects such as the enormous **Musée d'Art Moderne et d'Art Contemporain►►** (*Open* Tue–Sun 10–6. *Admission: moderate*), known as MAMAC; four octagonal marble towers linked by glassed-in walkways. The museum concentrates on the Second Nice School, with Pop Art and New Realist works, as well as other influential figures from the 1960s and 1970s such as Lichtenstein, Warhol and Niki de St.-Phalle. Most of the displays were conceived as a send-up of not just consumer society but the whole art world. Next to it is a huge conference centre. Cunningly disguised as a gigantic air-conditioning vent, the **Acropolis** could not be more inappropriately named.

West of the Paillon is the central district of Nice, bisected by the city's main thoroughfare, the avenue Jean Médecin, busy with cafés, cinemas, banks, department stores and the large Nice–Etoile shopping centre.

Cimiez►►► To the north the streets start to climb up to the smart residential district of Cimiez, and the intriguing **Musée National Message Biblique Marc Chagall►►►** (tel: 04 93 53 87 20. *Open* Jul–Sep, Wed–Mon 10–6; Oct–Jun, Wed–Mon 10–5. *Admission: moderate*), devoted to Chagall's canvases on Old Testament themes. The austere lines and light-filled rooms of the purpose-built museum building by André Hermaut (a follower of Auguste Perret) provide a perfect backdrop to the 17 vivid panels of the *message biblique*. Chagall himself directed the layout and also designed the three limpid blue stained-glass windows entitled *Creation of the World* that illuminate the auditorium. In addition to the biblical series, the museum boasts the largest public collection of Chagall's work ,including sculpture, drawings, engravings, a tapestry, and (outside) a mosaic.

Farther up the hill is the **Musée Matisse▶▶▶** (tel: 04 93 81 08 08. *Open* Apr–Sep, Wed–Mon 10–6; Oct–Mar, Wed–Mon 10–5. *Admission: moderate*). Matisse came to live in Nice in 1917, and the museum contains a good cross-section of his works, from the early experiments with Fauvism through to the cut-out compositions done just before he died here in 1954, aged 85. The museum holds the world's largest collection of his drawings (238), etchings (218), and nearly all the bronze sculptures he ever made. Next to the museum is the **Musée Archéologique de Nice-Cimiez▶** (*Open* Wed–Mon 10–6. *Admission: moderate*), which stands on the site of Roman *Cemenelum* (see panel, page 230). The ancient city enjoyed its heyday between the 1st and 5th centuries, as illustrated by the scope and interest of the collections, from coins and jewellery to sculpture and ceramics.

Vieille ville▶▶▶ The *vieille ville* is beneath the Colline du Château at the eastern end of the Baie des Anges. You might once have risked losing your wallet in these alleyways, but since the 1980s massive redevelopment has turned it into one of the trendiest areas in the city, an admirable mix of bistros and boutiques alongside shops serving residents' needs, and no-nonsense cafés.

In the backstreets you will come across the 17th-century **Cathédrale de Ste.-Réparate▶**, a baroque extravaganza topped by a roof of colourful Niçois tiles. One block north is the Genoese-style **Palais Lascaris▶** (*Open* Wed–Mon. *Admission free*), a baroque museum housing collections of sumptuous 17th- and 18th-century paintings, furnishings and tapestries. On one corner of the **cours Saleya▶▶**, site of the daily market, is the **Chapelle de la Miséricorde▶**, with a distinctive baroque facade. It overlooks the famous **flower market** and close-packed fruit and vegetable stalls massed on the square daily except Monday morning when the antique-dealers take over.

233

One of many processions during the famous Nice Carnival

THE PROMENADE

One of the first celebrities to visit Nice was the English writer Tobias Smollett, who lived here for 10 months in 1763. He was soon followed by a bevy of English milords and ladies attracted by the climate and the casino. In the 1820s they clubbed together to build a promenade (later named the Promenade des Anglais) so that they could stroll along the shoreline. It also provided work for the local unemployed to help them through the harsh winter of 1820 and 1821, though it has been suggested that a rather less altruistic motive was to keep bothersome beggars off the streets.

PARKS AND GARDENS

The city's oldest garden is the Jardin Albert 1er, which leads into the Espace Massena and the Promenade de Paillon in the town centre. The Jardin des Arènes de Cimiez in the northern districts (near to the Musée Matisse) is a lovely old olive grove often used for traditional festivities, and in the nearby Jardin du Monastère de Cimiez, masses of roses climb over pergolas. In neighbouring St.-Maurice, the Parc Chambrun features a delightful "temple of love" at its summit. Out to the west the Jardin Botanique, 78 avenue de la Corniche Fleurie (*Open* daily. *Admission free*), displays a classic collection of Mediterranean flora. Near the airport the spectacular Parc Flora Phoenix, 408 Promenade des Anglais (*Open* daily. *Admission: moderate*) has a vast conservatory with tropical plants, palms and orchids as well as fish, birds and butterflies.

A wedding ceremony in Nice's cathedral

Eastern hills and the port► Above the *vieille ville* is the **Colline du Château►**, where from the belvedere an artificial cascade draws the eye down to the rooftops of Vieux Nice. On the other side of the hill is the **port►►**. Nice's first "port" was simply an anchorage on the other side of the Colline du Château; the present harbour, excavated in the late 18th century and named Port Lympnia, was enlarged a hundred years later.

At the back of the port is the **Musée de Paléontologie Humaine de Terra Amata►** (*Open* Tue–Sun), which occupies the ground floor of a block of flats. The explanation for this rather bizarre location is that when excavations were started to build the flats they discovered traces of the very first settlements in the area, dating back 400,000 years: these now form the core of the museum.

The road continues beyond the port up to **Mont Boron►**. The 60ha (150 acre) Mount Boron forest was planted in the 1860s and now has about 11km (7 miles) of walking trails around the hilltop. The best of the several forts around the hill is **Fort Alban►**, a rare example of French military architecture of the 16th century. Its four turrets, adorned with glazed Niçois tiles, give it a sort of toytown look, but as a watchtower its position is superb.

Ever since The French Connection *hit cinema screens, Marseille's reputation as an international drug-trafficking centre has been well known, and the local papers are never short of copy on shoot-outs between members of the local mafia (known as the* milieu*) or arrests of leading gang members. But that's Marseille, and the Riviera is a different matter...or is it?*

'Azur

Dimanch

assins du ministre

rchés sur la Côte

r Hugues Chevallier
t Tomas Maréchal

mais parce qu'il ne ma
d'aller à Montpelier à
types qui ressemble à
les témoins.'

a 'Yann d'Arc' comme tout le monde

Graham Greene's *bête noir* Nice likes to portray an image of the *grande dame* of the Riviera but beneath the surface the murky currents of civic corruption run deep. As long ago as 1982 the author Graham Greene published a booklet entitled *J'Accuse: The Dark Side of Nice*, which pilloried the city's long serving mayor, Jacques Médecin, for his links with the *milieu* and for siphoning off public money for his private use. The Médecin dynasty had been in power in Nice since 1928: Jacques, who took over the post from his father in 1966, vehemently denied Greene's accusations. However, the author's prophecies proved correct when Jacques fled to Uruguay in 1990 after the Justice Department uncovered a swindle involving funds for the Nice Opéra. He was arrested by Interpol in 1993, but his misuse of millions of francs of public money resulted in only the briefest prison sentence.

Jewel-heists and bombs Outside Nice the *milieu* continues to operate with impunity. Kickbacks on big projects are a way of life (see panel). A popular and successful nightclub in Hyères was destroyed by a bomb, attributed to Mafia rivals. The Mafia were also suspected when Hollywood mogul Marvin Davis's gold Cadillac was hijacked in 1993 and he was robbed of $10 million worth of jewels at Cap d'Antibes. But worse was to come...

Death of a "saint" In February 1994 Yann Piat, dubbed "Yann d'Arc" by the French press for her relentless campaign against Mafia corruption, was murdered near her home in Hyères. Two masked gunmen shot Mme. Piat from a motorcycle as she was being driven home; the murder bore all the hallmarks of a classic contract killing and shocked the nation not just for its brutality but because the assassination of a prominent member of the National Assembly was seen as a direct challenge to the French state. Just prior to her death, Mme. Piat claimed to have uncovered evidence of Mafia money being laundered through Hyères's casino and various real estate projects.

Unanswered allegations Three months after Yann Piat's death an employee of the right-wing PACA administration was found dead just before he was due to hand over to a magistrate documents naming politicians involved in corruption along the coast. Fernand Saincène, who claimed trade tax exemptions were being traded for political favours, had apparently "committed suicide."

MAFIA-SUR-MER
The naval dockyards of la Seyne near Toulon have been derelict since 1985, but a recent attempt to revitalise 30ha (75 acres) of docks have been scuppered by greedy local *milieu* bosses. A British consortium had spent three years planning an innovative maritime and business complex, the World Sea Centre, but the £120 million Franco–British deal was called off after demands for £1 million in bribes were turned down by the project's backers. Now the dockyards will remain empty in la Seyne, which has been dubbed Mafia-sur-Mer by the French media.

Gene Hackman in French Connection II

REUNITED RESERVE

The Mercantour was originally a hunting reserve, created by Italian royalty in 1859; it remained an Italian enclave until after World War II. In 1946 it was split, with Italy gaining the major part and France the rest. The two were symbolically joined together again with the creation of the Aregentera National Park in Piedmont in 1980, forming a huge and unique protected area for Alpine flora and fauna.

PARK RULES

Picking flowers is forbidden in the park as are camping, fires, and dogs. There are park information centres at Allos, Barcelonnette, Entraunes, St.-Dalmas-de-Tende, St.-Étienne-de-Tinée, St.-Martin-Vésubie and St.-Sauveur-sur-Tinée. Any of these bureaux can provide information on walking and ATB (All Terrain Bike) trails, as well as guided tours.

The Parc National du Mercantour is a region of unspoilt wilderness and imposing peaks

▶▶▶ Parc National du Mercantour   *200C4*

Covering the highest peaks and the most dramatic scenery of the region, the Parc National du Mercantour stretches for over 128km (80 miles) along the Italian border. Established in 1979, it has no permanent inhabitants, but basic *refuges* provide shelter for hikers and climbers.

Covering over 68,000ha (168,000 acres), the park lies mostly in the *département* of the Alpes-Maritimes (53,000ha/130,960 acres), with the rest in the Alpes de Haute-Provence. It is divided between a central protected zone (a core strip of the most inaccessible areas, including the Vallée des Merveilles, see page 246) and the peripheral access zone surrounding it.

The landscapes of the Mercantour are highly varied, ranging from pastureland and Alpine forests to glacial lakes, canyons, and peaks. The park starts at an altitude of 490m (1,605ft), and as you climb upwards the pines and larches of the lower slopes give way to beautiful Alpine meadows and rock-strewn scree, before reaching permanent snow on peaks around 3,000m (9,845ft) high.

Above these wild landscapes circle birds of prey such as golden eagles, kestrels and falcons, and the rare lammergeyer vulture, successfully reintroduced after becoming extinct here. Other feathered fauna include the ptarmigan, which changes its summer plumage of mottled brown for a winter plumage of pure white, the great spotted woodpecker, hoopoe, citril finch, ortolan, and rock bunting.

The small Alpine marmot can be seen sitting on its haunches in meadowlands, until it spots a predator, and disappears in a flash down its burrow. Mouflons (wild mountain sheep) were reintroduced from Italy in the 1950s, and the chamois, ibex and boar populations are all now increasing. There are also foxes, stoats and hares, including the mountain hare which, like the ptarmigan, changes colour to white in winter.

The flora of the park is equally remarkable, with around 2,000 of the 4,200 species found in France represented, including 40 which are endemic to the region. In springtime the meadows are ablaze with bellflowers and blue gentians. There is also the elusive edelweiss, and, rarest of all, the big, spiky saxifrage (*Saxifraga florulenta*), which has become the symbol of the park.

►► Peille 201D2

This unspoiled *village perché* has a great deal of character; there are several lovely old buildings in the cobbled alleys and passageways. Inside the **Église Ste.-Mairie►** (ask at the hospice for the key) is an interesting painting of the village in medieval times, with its castle (now in ruins), which once belonged to the Counts of Provence, and a fine 16th-century *Polyptych of the Rosary* by Honoré Bertone, of the Niçois school.

► Peillon 201D2

Peille's twin and neighbour, Peillon enjoys a spectacular setting high above the Peillon valley. The vaulted alleys and steep steps that climb up through the village are lined by carefully restored houses, many looking older than their 16th-century origins. The **Chapelle des Pénitents Blancs►** is decorated with dramatic frescoes depicting *The Passion of Christ*, painted in 1485 by Giovanni Canavesio.

► Puget-Théniers 200B3

This attractive old town straddles the confluence of the Var and the Roudoule rivers and is dominated by the ruins of the Château des Trainières, which belonged to the Grimaldis until it was pulled down in 1691.

On the west bank of the Roudoule the old town, centred around the place A-Conil, was once the Templars' quarter and features many fine old doorways with carved shields on the lintels. On the other side of the river the parish church of **Notre-Dame-de-l'Assumption►** contains a couple of remarkable 16th-century altarpieces, the *Polyptyque de Notre-Dame-de-Secours* by Antoine Ronzen, and the carvings of the *Passion* by Mathieu d'Anvers.

NEARBY A detour from Puget-Théniers (5.5km/3.5 miles along the D116) brings you to the small village of Puget-Rostang, where the main attraction is the excellent **Écomusée du Pays de la Roudoule►►**. Unlike many "ecomuseums," which have simply jumped on the bandwagon by adding the eco tag to their names, this *écomusée* plays an active role in the surrounding area and runs guided tours based on themes such as architecture, geology, and botany (tel: 04 93 05 07 38 for details). In the *Maison de l'Écomusée* (*Open* Apr–Sep, daily; Oct–Mar, Mon–Fri. *Admission: moderate*) itself there is a series of exhibitions on local heritage topics.

A typical medieval street in the village perché *of Peille*

AUGUSTE BLANQUI
A monument in the town square of Puget-Théniers (*L'Action enchaînée* by Aristide Maillol) commemorates the town's most famous son, Auguste Blanqui. Born in 1805, Blanqui was one of the leaders of the Paris Commune of 1871.

Cap Ferrat, crowned by the Italianate Villa Ephrussi de Rothschild

▶ Roquebrune-Cap-Martin   201D2

Sandwiched between Menton and Monte-Carlo, **Cap Martin** and the village of **Roquebrune** seem to have merged into one big suburb of Menton. The medieval village of Roquebrune is a maze of steps and passageways, covered by arches and vaults, culminating at the **château** (*Open* daily. *Admission: inexpensive*).

Cap Martin, an exclusive enclave of fenced-off villas among the cypresses, pines and mimosa, had its heyday towards the end of the 19th century when aristocrats fluttered like moths around the socialites Empress Eugenie and Elizabeth, Empress of Austria. Le Corbusier, who died while swimming off the cape in 1965, has a superb coastal path among the rocks and battered pine trees named in his honour.

▶▶ St.-Jean-Cap-Ferrat   201D2

Like the Cap d'Antibes and Cap Martin, Cap Ferrat was long ago taken over by luxurious mansions and villas hidden away behind tall gates and impenetrable hedges. The peninsula's past residents have included Leopold II of Belgium, Otto Preminger, Somerset Maugham and David Niven. It is, however, a little more welcoming than some of the other privacy-obsessed enclaves, with a tourist office of its own which is happy to point you in the direction of the little harbour area, or the marked walking trails around its 14km (9 miles) of coastline.

The highlight of Cap Ferrat is the amazing **Villa Ephrussi de Rothschild**▶▶ (tel: 04 93 01 33 09. *Open* mid-Feb to mid-Nov daily 10–6; Jul–Aug, daily 10–7; mid-Nov to mid-Feb Mon–Fri 2–6, Sat–Sun 10–6; first week of Jan 10–6. *Admission: expensive*) set in fabulous gardens. An avid art collector, Beatrice de Rothschild built this Italianate-style villa after marrying the banker Baron Ephrussi. The choice of site was influenced by his love of gambling at nearby Monte-Carlo.

The villa was built over a period of seven years. Around 40 different architects worked on it (some did not last more than a few hours, thanks to the Baroness's capriciousness), and it contains something in the region of 5,000 art treasures. Critics say that the Baroness had more money than taste but this is not borne out by the many exquisite pieces she assembled here, ranging from Beauvais tapestries to Sèvres porcelain, Renaissance furniture, rare Chinese chests and vases, frescoes, paintings…the list goes on. Don't miss the lovely tearoom, with its huge bay windows framing the Bay of Villefranche. The villa was bequeathed to the Académie des Beaux-Arts on the death of the Baroness in 1934.

Visits to the villa are by guided tour only, but you are free to wander around the extraordinary gardens (see page 245) on your own.

▶▶ St.-Martin-Vésubie   201D4

This cool mountain retreat at the head of the Vésubie valley, the only substantial town in the area, is a popular base for excursions into the Parc National du Mercantour (see page 236). From the Mercantour, the streams of le Boréon and la Madone de Fenestre descend and meet at St.-Martin to form the Vésubie itself.

Chalet-style houses overhang the main street of rue Dr.-Cagnoli, where another torrent is channelled through a conduit between the cobbles creating a lovely effect—not the original intention, since the channel once carried the village sewage.

Descending rue Dr.-Cagnoli from place Félix-Faure, the main square, you pass the **Chapelle des Pénitents-Blancs** with its bulb-shaped bell tower, the **Église** (which has an altarpiece from the Bréa school) and a massive Gothic mansion, the **Maison des Contes de Gubernatis**.

The polychrome wooden statue of the Madone de Fenestre (see panel) stays in the parish church for part of the year, but at the beginning of July it is carried in procession up to the **Sanctuaire de la Madone de Fenestre▶**, 12km (7.5 miles) northeast of St.-Martin, and is brought back in September. The procession and the monthly summer pilgrimages are good reasons to make the steep trip. An ancient refuge, the chapel gets its name from a natural window in the rocks above it, through which you can see the sky.

NEARBY WALKS Following the Boréon 8km (5 miles) upstream from St.-Martin-Vésubie you come to the charming resort village of **le Boréon**, where the local delicacy is fresh trout from the mountain streams (the season is from mid-March to early September). Some of the wild and beautiful landscapes of the Parc National can be explored on a four-hour circular walking tour of the Haut-Boréon area above the village, skirting isolated Lac de Trecoulpes.

MASSACRE OF THE TEMPLIERS
The origins of the Madone de Fenestre are obscure, but it is thought to have been brought to St.-Martin-Vésubie in the 12th century by the Templiers (Knights Templar) when they acquired this territory. In the 14th century, the sanctuary (then half-ruined) was pillaged by brigands, who slit the throats of the Templiers; their bodies remained slumped under the snow in the ruined eaves, and when the chapel was later restored, 15 skeletons were found. Their ghosts are said to haunt the sanctuary, walking ceaselessly in procession around it on dark nights, howling and wailing like the glacial winds that sweep down the mountain.

239

St.-Martin-Vésubie is a popular base for exploring the neighbouring mountains

Sculpture is just one of the strengths of the Fondation Maeght. Above: a Giacometti piece

THE COLOMBE D'OR
St-Paul-de-Vence was no doubt a much more peaceful place in the 1920s when a clutch of artists settled here after World War I and ended up paying their bills at the famous *La Colombe d'Or* restaurant with paintings that are now priceless. The walls are hung with works by Picasso, Matisse, Vlaminck, Léger, Dufy, Bonnard, Derain, and Modigliani, but you will have to stump up a small fortune to eat or stay in these rarified surroundings.

The baroque interior of the Église-St.-Sauveur in Saorge

▶ **St.-Paul-de-Vence**   *200C2*

Probably the only medieval village in the country with a compulsory underground parking area, St.-Paul-de-Vence is another of those tourist haunts that have become so overrun with boutiques that their identity has been totally swamped. Packed with *ateliers*, art galleries, antiques and gift shops, it is a wonder that St.-Paul does not come to a complete standstill with shoppers clogging the narrow streets in the summer months.

There is a small but interesting **Musée d'Histoire▶** (*Open* Mon, Wed–Sat. *Admission: inexpensive*) housed in a 12th-century keep next to the town hall. At the exit, hundreds of photographs record the numerous celebrities who have visited or lived in this overblown village.

Unmissable is the **Fondation Maeght▶▶▶** (see panel opposite. Tel: 04 93 32 81 63; *open* Jul–Sep, daily 10–7; Oct–Jun, daily 10–12.30, 2.30–6. *Admission: moderate*), set on a wooded hill just outside St-Paul-de-Vence. The vast permanent collection includes major works by the most important artists of the latter 20th century, as well as temporary exhibitions of young artists and retrospectives. Incorporated into the grounds and the outside of the building are mosaics by Braque and Chagall, a moving tubular fountain by Pol Bury, a stick-like cat by Giacometti, and a Calder mobile. Also within the grounds is the small Chapelle St.-Bernard, with stained-glass windows by Braque.

The complex includes a huge arts library, a bookshop, workshops and studios, and a cinema screening films (at 3PM daily) on the lives of artists represented here.

▶ **St.-Vallier-de-Thiey**   *200B2*

This small town in wooded hills 12km (7.5 miles) above Grasse has few attractions of its own, but nearby are three of the best cave systems in Provence (see map, page 219).

The **Grotte de Baume Obscure▶▶** (*Open* Jul–Aug daily; Sep–Jun Tue–Sun. *Admission: moderate*) is signposted off the D5 west of town. Inside, a 700m (2,300ft) long path climbs and winds up and down through vast galleries and caverns draped with stalagmites and stalactites; the caves descend to around 60m (200ft) and are beautifully lit, with fluorescence fed in for added effect.

Continue down the same road and turn left onto the D613 for the **Grottes de St.-Cézaire▶** (*Open* Jun–Sep, daily; Oct and Feb–May, afternoons only; Nov and Jan Sun afternoons only. *Closed* Dec *Admission: moderate*). The circuit here is only 200m (655ft) long, but is known for the unusual red colouring of its stalactites and stalagmites.

Finally, there is the **Grotte des Audides▶** (tel: 04 93 42 64 15; *open* Jul–Aug, daily 11–6. Closed Mon mornings; Sep–Jun by appointment. *Admission: moderate*). The cave descends almost vertically (with 279 steps) to a depth of 60m (200ft), and has some unusual and very beautiful formations. There is also a **Parc Prehistorique** (*Admission: moderate*) in the woodland setting around the cave mouth, with life-size mock-ups of the prehistoric settlements.

Modern art at the Fondation Maeght

▶▶ Saorge 201E3

The next village up the Roya valley after Breil-sur-Roya (see page 208), Saorge is set on a steep slope high above the river. The tortuous drive up to the village is well worth it to see how this peculiar place has been built, with houses piled one on top of the other and connected by obscure stairways and alleys where daylight never penetrates.

In this semi-troglodytic world, the inhabitants of Saorge have retained some of their own, ancient dialect, which contains elements of Provençal and Ligurian Italian. The site was an important defensive post in the Middle Ages, guarding the approach to the Col de Tende, but the fort was destroyed by Napoléon. At the centre of the village the **Église St.-Sauveur** contains *trompe l'oeil* frescoes and an organ built in Genoa and brought here by pack-mules. From the village a track leads across the terraces to a 17th-century **Franciscan convent** and the adjoining 11th-century chapel of **la Madone del Poggio▶**, containing some fine 15th-century works.

PLAYFUL RHYTHMS
The Maeght foundation was established by collectors Aimé and Marguerite Maeght, who commissioned the building from Spanish architect Jose-Luis Sert (a protégé of Le Corbusier) in the 1960s, with numerous contemporary artists contributing to the ornamentation. The result is an extraordinary temple to modern art where the structure is "a play between the rhythms of the interior and exterior spaces," as described by Sert himself.

241

SILICON VALLEY
Dubbed "France's answer to Silicon Valley", Sophia-Antipolis was the nation's first Science Park and now covers a huge area behind Vallauris and Antibes on the Plateau de Valbonne. Created in the 1970s, this thriving futuristic complex amid rolling hills has attracted a wide spectrum of businesses working in information technology, life sciences, pharmaceuticals, robotics and other high-tech areas.

The lovely old medieval bridge and tollgate spanning the River Bévéra at Sospel

▶▶ Sospel 201D3

Sospel, a charming Alpine-Italianate town on the banks of the River Bévéra, thrived from the Middle Ages to the 18th century, when it was an important crossroads on the trade routes between Haute-Provence, the coast, and Piedmont via the Col de Tende.

The tollgate through which travellers then had to pass sits in the middle of an 11th-century **bridge▶▶** connecting the two halves of the town. Damaged during the war, it was restored in 1947 and now houses a small tourist office. From the road bridge downstream, there is a fabulous view of the medieval/Italianate houses on the right bank, with the tollgate and mountains behind.

In the western half of the town, the narrow streets unexpectedly open up into the **place St.-Michel▶▶**, a large square surrounded by magnificent, colourful baroque facades. The main building is the vast Église St.-Michel, built in the 17th century and incorporating, somewhat incongruously, the Romanesque bell tower of the 12th-century church that it replaced. Inside, there is a magnificent Bréa altarpiece, the *Annunciation*.

To the left of St.-Michel are the chapels of the Pénitents Gris and Pénitents Rouges and, to the right, the Palais Ricci with *trompe l'oeil* windows.

Just outside Sospel on the D2204 there is an old Maginot Line fortress, the Fort St.-Roch. Built in 1932 against the threat of an Italian invasion, it was put to effective use towards the end of the war and has more than 1km (0.5 miles) of underground tunnels. It now houses the **Musée des Fortifications Alpines** (*Open* Jun–Sep Tue–Sun 2–6; Apr–May & Oct Sat–Sun 2–6. *Admission: inexpensive*).

▶ Tende 201E4

The former capital of the Upper Roya, Tende is the last town before the Col de Tende and once played an important role guarding the route across to Piedmont. Tende's tall, gaunt houses and bell towers cling to the side of the valley, in the shadow of a terraced cemetery set high above the town.

Many of the houses are roofed with stone slabs (*lauzes*) in the local green schist, with door lintels dating back to the 15th century and bearing coats of arms and the symbols of old trades. The **Collégiale Ste.-Marie des Bois** has a handsome Renaissance doorway and a 17th-century organ.

The tourist office in Tende (tel: 04 93 04 73 71) is able to provide information and help with bookings for tours to the Vallée des Merveilles (see page 246). An easier option is to visit the striking **Musée des Merveilles▶** (*Open* Wed–Mon. *Admission: moderate*), which has dioramas and models that explain the history of the valley and the rock engravings.

▶▶ la Turbie   *201D2*

The chunky silhouette of the monument for which this village is famous, the **Trophée des Alpes▶▶▶** (tel: 04 93 41 20 84; *open* mid-May to mid-Sep, daily 9.30–6; mid-Sep to mid-May Tue–Sun 10–1.30, 2.30–5. *Admission: moderate*) is an unmistakable landmark. Situated at the loftiest point of the main Roman highway (the Via Julia) between Cimiez and Italy, 480m (1,575ft) above sea level, the trophy was built in the 6th century BC to commemorate Augustus' triumphs over the Alpine tribes. Originally topped off with a statue of Augustus, it stood 50m (165ft) high and 38m (125ft) wide. Despite being vandalized, turned into a fortress in the Middle Ages, partly dismantled on the orders of Louis XIV in 1705, and then finally quarried to build the neighbouring church in the 19th century, enough of it survived to make partial restoration feasible, even though it is now "only" 35m (115ft) high. The long inscription on its base, listing all 44 tribes conquered by Augustus, has also been restored.

In the gardens surrounding the trophy there is a small museum documenting its restoration, financed by an American, Edward Tuck, and from the terrace behind there is a wonderful panorama of Monaco and the coastline from Italy to the Esterel.

Next to the trophy, the baroque **Église St.-Michel-Archange** contains works attributed to the schools of Veronese, Raphael, Bréa, Ribera and Murillo.

Intricate paintwork on Sospel's riverside houses

The Roman monument that put la Turbie on the map, the Trophée des Alpes

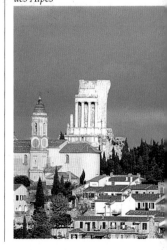

Water gardens, stone gardens, secret gardens, kitchen gardens, perfumed gardens—you can find so many different types of garden in Provence. Here is a selection of just a few, all of which can be visited.

A PERFUMED GARDEN
One of the most charming books ever written about Provençal gardens is the classic *Perfume from Provence* by Lady Winifred Fortescue, first published in 1935. Lady Fortescue and her husband, Sir John, settled in a small stone house outside Grasse between the wars and set about trying to tame the terraced landscape of vines, roses, lavender and wild flowers that surrounded them. The book's patronizing attitude to Provençals now seems very dated, but this warm-hearted account (it was an instant best-seller) conveys the magic of Provençal gardens very convincingly.

Cacti (below and right) flourish in the hot, dry climate

244

Châteaux gardens The castles of Provence have not always had a great deal of space surrounding them in which to plant gardens. The garden was often an after-thought, squeezed onto a terrace between the castle and the village streets surrounding it.

Such is the case with the Château de Sabran at Ansouis, where the stone-walled terraces were filled in during the 17th century (the castle itself dates back to the 10th century): On the west side of the château, hemmed in by the adjoining chapel, the Paradise garden displays an elegant pattern of clipped box hedges in the northern French style.

At Entrecasteaux, the castle sits on a small knoll with its garden (featuring magnolias, box hedges and eucalyptus surrounding a small pool) some way beneath. The garden was designed by Le Nôtre, who created the gardens of Versailles; he also designed the gardens at the château of Gourdon (spectacularly perched on the edge of the hillside) and those at the **Château de la Barben▶** (*Open* Apr–Oct daily 10–6; Nov–Mar daily 11–12, 2–5.30. Closed Dec–Jan except school holidays. *Admission: moderate*) outside Salon. Rebuilt many times over the centuries, the château is remarkable for its elegant 18th-century ceilings; Pauline Borghese, Napoléon's sister, once lived here. The formality of the flower borders, statues and basins is emphasized by the untamed woodland that surrounds them. Adjacent to the château there is a large zoo and a children's playground.

Herb gardens Although herbs are a vital part of Provençal cuisine and folk medicine, herb gardens are rare for the good reason that most herbs grow wild. But there are two exceptions: The first is at the Ethnological Conservatory of Haute-Provence (Conservatoire du Patrimoine Ethnologique de la Haute-Provence) in the old Prieuré de Salagon near Mane, where they have planted a medicinal herb garden with over 100 of the most commonly used species. There is also a medieval monastery garden with ornamental, edible, and herbal plants.

The second is the Harmas of the entomologist J-H Fabre at Sérignan-du-Comtat, a little wilderness that Fabre allowed to grow untended

simply so that he could study the insect inhabitants. This leafy botanic garden contains over 800 plant species.

Exotic gardens In the 18th century the first botanic gardens were opened in Aix and Salon to nurture exotic plants brought back from Africa and the Orient. Palm trees arrived in Hyères in 1867, and palms, along with a multitude of other exotic species, form an important part of the huge Jardin Olbius Riquier on the outskirts of Hyères. In contrast, thousands of species of succulents, such as cacti, are the main feature of the Jardin Exotique in Monaco, and papyrus, ferns and pineapple plants are interspersed with thousands of orchids in Parc Floral Tropical Provence Orchidées, just outside Barbentane. The Parc Naturel de Mugel at la Ciotat is predominantly Mediterranean, with *garrigue* species and wild flowers, but it also contains cacti and thickets of wild bamboo.

City gardens Framed by monumental ruins or grand buildings, city gardens often have a dramatic setting. The Rocher des Doms in Avignon, for example, is perched above the Rhône with the Palais des Papes rising up beside it. Its leafy paths, rock gardens, lawns, and splashing fountains offer a respite from the hurly-burly below. In Nîmes, the best-loved public park is the Jardin de la Fontaine, which incorporates not only the Temple of Diana but also the old Roman baths and the spring itself, landscaped into a series of balustrades and monumental steps beneath the shade of chestnuts and hackberries. Aix has its French-style gardens in the Pavillon de Vendôme and Arles its charming Jardin d'Été on the boulevard des Lices with enormous cedars backing onto the Théâtre.

Unusual gardens One of the most extraordinary gardens is that of the Villa Ephrussi de Rothschild on St.-Jean-Cap-Ferrat, created by Baroness Ephrussi de Rothschild from 1905 onwards. The Île de France garden in the centre, styled in the form of a boat, is flanked on either side by a series of smaller gardens designed in Japanese, Spanish, Florentine, Oriental and Provençal styles: an instant tour of the world's gardens, completely mad and great fun.

245

Pottery is one of the mainstays of Vallauris

▶ Vallauris

200C1

Vallauris is a fairly hideous town—the modern part, at least—that is full of pottery and ceramic shops of variable quality that owe their popularity (if not their style) to Picasso's stay here in the 1940s and 1950s. He got hooked on a new passion when he started working with clay in the Poterie Madoura, giving fresh impetus to an industry that has existed here since Roman times. Pottery-making thrived in Vallauris during the Middle Ages, was knocked out by the plague, and then re-invigorated by the arrival of Genoese potters in the 16th century. After World War II the industry suffered badly, only to take off again thanks to Picasso's 10-year sojourn.

Picasso-inspired designs can be purchased at the Poterie Madoura (off rue 19 Mars 1962) and several of his originals are on view at the **Musée de la Céramique▶** (*Open Wed–Mon. Admission: inexpensive*), housed in a Renaissance château on place de la Libération. The ticket also covers the **Musée National Picasso▶▶** in the same complex, which is in fact a small, deconsecrated chapel that Picasso decorated in 1952 with his seminal paintings *La Guerre et La Paix.*

▶▶▶ Vallée des Merveilles

201D4

Part of the Mercantour National Park (see page 236), the Vallée des Merveilles contains one of the richest collections of open-air petroglyphs (rock carvings) in Europe. Lying on the western flank of Mont Bégo between Lac du Basto and Lac Long, the valley covers over 30sq km (11.5sq miles) and contains an estimated 30,000 carvings.

The carvings may be the work of pilgrims (see panel) but since latter-day visitors with less reverential attitudes have also left their mark, the two most important areas are now protected and you must stick to the marked paths unless accompanied by an official guide.

Although there are thousands of symbols, they are not easily visible to the untrained eye, which is another good reason for visiting with a guide. Destination Merveilles (tel: 04 93 73 09 07) organizes regular guided visits from

MYSTERIOUS MARKINGS
Little is known about the purpose of the carvings of the Vallée des Merveilles, which represent human figures, animals, and tools, and include many mysterious symbols, but they are thought to date from between 1500 and 1800 BC. It is possible that the valley was an ancient sacred site, and that the symbols were made by pilgrims. However, the tools which were used to carve them have never been found and it has even been whispered that they may be fake. The first systematic investigation of the site was carried out in the arly 20th century century by an Englishman, Clarence Bicknell.

June to October, with the main access point being St.-Dalmas-de-Tende south of Tende (see page 242).

▶▶▶ Vence   *200C2*

Although only 10km (6 miles) from the coast, this lively town has more in common with its counterparts in inland Provence than with the frenetic resorts of the Riviera. Vence was popular with artists and the intelligentsia during the 1920s (including the likes of Dufy, André Gide, Paul Valéry, and D. H. Lawrence). Matisse moved here in 1941 to escape the bombings on the coast but fell dangerously ill; he was nursed back to health by the Dominican sisters and in thanks to them he started work in 1946 on his famous **Chapelle du Rosaire▶▶▶** (avenue Henri-Matisse, tel: 04 93 58 03 26; *open* Dec–Oct Tue and Thu 10–11.30, 2–5.30, Mon, Wed, Fri, Sat, 2–5.30. *Admission: inexpensive*).

Above: detail on a church in Vence's vieille ville

247

"I think it is my masterpiece" declared Matisse after five years of work. The white tiled walls of the chapel are covered in black line drawings of the Stations of the Cross, the Virgin and Child, the Crucifixion and St. Dominic; the only colour to intrude on the simple, stark interior comes from the stained-glass windows, which throw delicate patterns of yellow, green and blue.

The *vieille ville* of Vence is an enjoyable place to wander, starting off at the **place du Peyra**, where mineral-rich waters gush from an urn-shaped fountain. From here, head down **rue du Marché**, which is crammed with mouth-watering food shops—little *pâtisseries*, fish-mongers offering sacks of *moules* and mounds of fresh-cooked *crevettes*, *charcuteries*, cheese shops and *poulet grillé à la flame* wafting tempting aromas down the narrow street.

The rue du Marché leads to the central place Clemenceau, where you can see Roman tombstones incorporated into the walls of the **cathédrale▶**. As well as a mosaic by Chagall (in the baptistery at the back) there are all sorts of odds and ends inside including finely carved Gothic choirstalls, the sarcophagus of St. Veran and stone reliefs from the 5th-century church that it replaced.

A Picasso ceramic (1953) from his Vallauris period

Villefranche harbour and fishing boats

248

THE HARBOUR
Protected by the Cap Ferrat peninsula, Villefranche harbour has a long history. Its deep waters (over 60m/200ft in places) sheltered galleys in Roman times, when it was known as Olivula. In the 14th century the Comte de Provence, Charles II of Anjou, declared it a duty-free port, Villam-Francam, hence its name today. In the 16th century Charles V moored his imperial galley here: One tale has it that when the King's sister (then Queen of France) came to visit, the entire entourage, dukes, Queen and all, was plunged into the sea when the gangplank collapsed.

Cocteau's chapel

▶▶▶ **Villefranche-sur-Mer**   *201D2*

Just around the Boron headland east of Nice, Villefranche is a small "fishing village" that the Niçois visit at the slightest opportunity for a meal out in one of the harbour-side restaurants. It is indeed one of the most delightful spots on the Riviera to spend a summer's evening dining on the quayside, with fishing boats and yachts bobbing about in the harbour.

Villefranche has been a military port for many centuries and although warships sometimes still put in to the deep, sheltered harbour, it was the small fishing community that inspired Villefranche's most famous resident, Jean Cocteau, when he lived here.

In homage to them he decorated the **Chapelle St.-Pierre**▶▶▶ (Port de Villefranche, tel: 04 93 76 90 70; *open* summer, Tue–Sun 10–12, 4–8; winter, Tue–Sun 9.30–12, 2.30–5; spring, Tue–Sun 10–12, 3–7; *closed* mid-Nov to mid-Dec. *Admission: inexpensive*) near the waterfront. Depicting the fisherwomen of Villefranche, gypsies and the life of St. Peter, these extraordinary, luminous frescoes are suffused with Cocteauesque symbolism.

Behind the port is the **rue Obscure**▶, a vaulted passage-way that has altered little since the 13th century; this dark, cavernous alleyway has sheltered the inhabitants of the port from bombardments throughout history, including during World War II.

Within the massive walls of the **Citadelle St.-Elme**▶▶ above the port is the *mairie* (town hall) and, tucked away in various corners, an open-air theatre and two museums. The **Fondation-Musée Volti**▶ (*Open* Dec–Oct Mon–Sat ; Jul–Aug daily. *Admission free*) is dedicated to the provocative sculptures of local artist Volti. The **Musée Goetz-Boumeester** (*Open* as above) contains two works by Picasso and one by Miró, as well as various displays of ceramics. Once you have visited these, take time for a stroll around the brightly painted buildings, looking out for a scattering of contemporary sculptures, while at the entrance to the citadel there is a display of maritime archaeological finds from the wreck of a Genoese trading ship that went down in the harbour in a violent storm in 1516.

Visitors to Provence have a choice of international airports

Arriving and departing

By air Nice and Marseille are Provence's two main international gateways. Montpellier and Lyon are two other options slightly to the west and north of the region. There are also regular air connections from Paris to Toulon and the smaller regional airports of Avignon and Nîmes. During the summer months, the best deals are on charter flights to Nice from London and elsewhere. If you are heading primarily for the Vaucluse, the Bouches-du-Rhône, or the Var it is more convenient to fly into Marseille–Provence airport (previously Marseille–Marignane). Marseille caters mostly for business traffic and is France's fifth-busiest airport.

By sea The classiest way to arrive on the coast is on your own yacht, and with over 125 marinas and ports and 57,000 berths there is no shortage of mooring space. Coastal Provence also features on many a cruise ship itinerary, with the principal ports of call being Cannes, Marseille, Nice, Toulon, St.-Tropez and Villefranche. Regular ferry services operate between Marseille and Tunisia and Algeria.

By train French National Railways (SNCF) operates probably the most efficient rail service in Europe with easy connections to Eurostar services from London to Paris and Lille.

The fastest option is the high-speed TGV (Train à Grande Vitesse), which plunges southwards at 270kph (170mph), achieving Paris–Avignon, Paris–Arles, Paris–Marseille and Paris–Toulon in 2.5–4 hours. There

are also direct TGV services from Lille–Avignon (4 hours) and Lille–Marseille (4.5 hours). Heading east along the coast, the TGV Mediterranéen from Paris also serves St.-Raphaël (4.5 hours), Nice (5.5 hours) and Monaco (6 hours). TGV tickets are slightly more expensive than normal tickets, and you will need to reserve a seat in advance or before boarding the train. If you are travelling to northeast Provence you can take the TGV to Grenoble, Lyon or Valence and change to local trains from there.

Another option is an overnight sleeper train from Paris, which is one of the most relaxing and evocative ways to arrive as the Provençal landscapes unfold outside your window in the early morning hours.

If you are taking your own car or motorcycle, the Motorail service operates from Calais to Avignon, Fréjus/St.-Raphaël and Nice, and from Paris to the same stations plus Marseille and Toulon. Again, these are overnight trains with *couchettes* (berths) for sleeping, and although ticket prices are fairly exorbitant, it is safer and more relaxing than driving all the way there.

For further information and bookings, contact the overseas branches of SNCF in European capitals or major US or Canadian cities. Discounts on rail tickets are available (for students and senior citizens) and also on rail passes (see box on page 255).

Coach Long-distance coach services connect Provence with European cities such as London, Paris, Brussels, Madrid, Geneva and elsewhere.

Car Travelling down from Paris the quickest route is on the Autoroute du Soleil (the A6 from Paris, then the A7 from Lyon), which goes to Marseille.

❏ Although the *autoroute* is fast it is not cheap: toll charges from Calais to Menton add up to around €80. An alternative is to take the N7 south from Paris to Lyon. Both will be very busy in July and August. ❏

❏ **Duty-free allowances**
These allowances apply to goods brought into France from outside the EU:

Cigarettes	200
or Cigars	50
or Tobacco	250g
(non-EU residents should check their allowances)	
Table wine	2 litres
Alcohol over 22 proof	1 litre
or	
Alcohol under 22 proof	2 litres
or Additional table wine	2 litres
Perfume	60ml
Eau de toilette	250ml

However, if you are continuing down the coast you will need to branch off at Aix along the Autoroute la Provençale (A8), which runs all the way to the Italian border. If you are coming from the UK, the quickest route is via the A26 to Reims and Troyes, followed by the A5 and A31 to Dijon, after which you join up again with the Autoroute du Soleil. This completely avoids the nightmare of the Boulevard Périphérique around Paris.

Customs There are no limits on the import or export of tax-paid goods between EU countries (provided they are for personal use). For duty-free goods, see table.

Insurance Travel insurance should cover medical expenses, loss of luggage or money, cancellation of your holiday or flight, delayed departure and delayed baggage. If you intend to take your own car,

breakdown and accident insurance is recommended (third-party insurance is compulsory).

Visas A valid passport is sufficient for citizens of the EU and permits US and Canadian citizens a stay of up to 90 days. Visa requirements can vary so it is vital that you check with a travel agent or the French Government Tourist Office.

Departing Airport departure taxes are included in ticket prices.

Made in Provence

Essential Facts

Climate and when to go Although renowned for its temperate weather and sunshine, Provence is a land of climatic extremes, veering between blistering hot summers and freezing winters during which the *mistral* can blow for several days. What's more, normal weather patterns are no longer as predictable as they once were, with extensive flooding of some coastal areas over recent years.

Spring A delightful time to be in Provence, with wild flowers in profusion and mimosa and almonds blossoming on the coast from February onwards. In April and May it is warm enough to sit out in the sunshine in restaurants and cafés, although the sea is still a bit chilly for swimming.

Summer Peak season throughout Provence, hot and dry with minimal rainfall and temperatures that rarely drop below 20°C (68°F) between June and September (summer heatwaves can push temperatures even higher). The sea is warm enough for swimming from June onwards, and the crowds not yet unbearable.

Dining alfresco

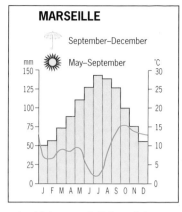

MARSEILLE

September–December

May–September

Avoid the coast in July and August. It is at its worst then, with overcrowding, traffic jams, over-inflated prices and short-tempered service. Festivals, however, are in full swing.

If you are planning on walking (particularly on any of the long-distance paths), wooded areas and sometimes entire hill ranges are closed off from 1 July through to 12 September if they are in a high-risk Red Fire Zone. Summer is the ideal time to be in the Alpes de Haute-Provence, where cooler temperatures favour outdoor activities.

Autumn September and October can be extremely pleasant; you can still

252

Harvesting grapes in the autumn

sunbathe although there are occasional rainstorms. The vineyards and forests take on their mantle of autumn colours and, after early September, resorts start to empty when the French school holidays end.

Winter In November colder weather settles in and most of the small local museums (and many hotels and restaurants) close. Snow starts to settle on the Alps from late November onwards, with the skiing season in the high altitude resorts lasting through to March/April.

A predominant feature of the winter months is the dreaded *mistral*, which whips down the Rhône valley and can make life unpleasant for days on end. However, it can be avoided by moving farther east down to the Côte d'Azur.

National holidays (*jours fériés*)
1 January, Easter Sunday, Easter Monday, 1 May (Labour Day), 8 May (VE Day), Ascension Day (40 days after Easter), Pentecost (7th Sunday after Easter) and the following Monday, 14 July (Bastille Day), 15 August (Assumption Day), 1 November (All Saints' Day), 11 November (Armistice Day) and Christmas Day. Banks, businesses and most shops and museums are closed.

Time differences France is on Central European Time, which is one hour ahead of Greenwich Mean Time from the end of October to the end of March, and two hours ahead the rest of the year.

Money matters The unit of currency in France is the euro (€). Bank notes are issued in denominations of 5, 10, 20, 50, 100, 200 and 500 euros; coins are issued in denominations of 1, 2, 5, 10, 20, and 50 cents, and 1 and 2 euros. The French franc ceased to be legal tender in 2002.

Euro currency, whatever the country of origin, is valid throughout the 12-country Euro zone.

Travellers' cheques are a safe way of carrying holiday money. Foreign currency and travellers' cheques can be changed at banks and bureaux de change, as well as some hotels and tourist offices.

Exchange rates can vary, as do commissions on changing travellers' cheques. If you are changing large amounts, it makes sense for you to shop around.

Banks generally open Monday to Friday 9–12, 2–4 or 5, and some open on Saturday mornings. They close Sundays, public holidays and in some cases Mondays.

Bureaux de change (in airports, main railway stations and town centres) stay open for longer hours and sometimes on holidays.

Credit cards such as Visa/Barclaycard (Carte Bleue in France), Access/MasterCard (Eurocard), American Express, and Diners Club are widely accepted. In remote places or small restaurants cards may not be accepted.

253

You will need a car if you wish to seek out the best of Provence

Getting around

Driving Provence lends itself to gentle exploration by car, with many unexpected sights and delightful corners of the countryside that are accessible only with your own transport. Unfortunately the public transport network is just not extensive enough to cater to the needs of most visitors unless you are planning on staying put in a coastal resort with just the occasional excursion to major sights. Over 70 per cent of overseas visitors (and nearly 80 per cent of French tourists) travel around by car.

Driving documents If you are taking a car to France, it is compulsory to carry a full driving licence, current insurance certificate and the original vehicle registration document (plus a letter of authorization from the owner of the vehicle if it is not registered in your name). You should also display a nationality sticker and your headlights must be adjusted with beam deflectors. As long as your lights are properly adjusted, tinting them yellow is not required. A spare set of headlight bulbs is a good idea, since driving with faulty lights is illegal. A red warning triangle is compulsory if your car is fitted with hazard warning lights.

Car rental There are plenty of rental agencies but the major drawback is price, with costs that exceed most other European countries. Renting a car locally is the most expensive option. Usually the best deals are fly-drive packages arranged by a travel agent or tour operator in your home country, or train/car rental arrangements with SNCF. Sometimes competitive rates can be obtained by booking in advance through major car rental companies (such as Hertz, Avis, Budget or Europcar, all of whom are represented in Provence). Motorists requiring automatic transmission should make arrangements as far in advance as possible, as very few rental cars offer this facility.

The minimum age for renting a car ranges from 21 to 25 years old (with the national licence having been held for at least a year). Many companies levy an additional surcharge on drivers under the age of 25. A valid licence and credit card are required for local bookings.

Car breakdown On *autoroutes* emergency telephones are located every 2km (1 mile), with breakdown services provided by nearby garages 24 hours a day, seven days a week (including holidays). Tow and repair rates are fixed by the government, and carry a 25 per cent surcharge at night and on Saturdays, Sundays, and holidays. These rates are shown on the emergency telephones.

❑ SNCF discount rail passes offering savings of 25–50 per cent include:

Euro Domino: Coupons for 3 up to 8 days' travel within one month, must be bought outside France.

Découverte 12–25: For young travellers aged 12 to 26 years.

Découverte Senior: For over-60-year-olds, half-price on some trains.

Découverte Enfant and Enfant+: Family cards with discounts for up to four non-family members. ❑

Public transport

Air Air Inter, the French domestic airline, has frequent flights connecting Paris with local airports such as Hyères–Toulon, Avignon and Nîmes, as well as the international airport gateways of Nice–Côte d'Azur and Marseille–Provence. Information from Air France or travel agents.

Rail The main SNCF line links towns in the Rhône valley with Marseille and coastal resorts. Trains are an excellent way of avoiding summer traffic along the coast. All tickets must be date stamped in the orange

Parking can be a problem in the coastal resorts

machines on station platforms, and you will face a surcharge if you forget to *compostez votre billet* (validate your ticket). Information from tourist offices or SNCF stations (general rail information, tel: 08 36 35 35 35).

There is a wonderful narrow-gauge railway that winds up through mountain scenery from Nice to Digne. The *train des Pignes* makes the three-and-a-quarter hour (each way) journey several times a day (tel: 04 97 03 80 80).

Bus The bus network is not brilliant. Where they exist at all, buses in rural areas are geared to school runs and market days. Between towns and cities, they tend to duplicate the rail services and are not necessarily cheaper or faster. Most large towns have a *gare routière* (coach station), usually near the railway station. SNCF also operates buses to various places on the rail routes where trains no longer stop.

❑ The most efficient bus network in Provence is in Nice. Pick up a route map and a 1-, 5- or 7-day pass from the Sunbus office at 10 avenue Félix Fauré. ❑

Driving tips

Keep to the right (*serrez à droite*). The most common cause of confusion (and accidents) is the rule of giving priority to traffic coming from the right (*priorité à droite*) at any intersection unless indicated otherwise. It does not matter how small the side-turning is, you must give way. In any town, treat junctions with the utmost caution. On main roads outside towns main roads usually have priority, which is indicated by roadsigns with a yellow diamond or marked *passage protégé*. Beware a yellow diamond crossed-out, which signals that you do not have right of way. On roundabouts (rotaries) traffic already on the roundabout has priority.

In rural areas driving behaviour is normally fairly sedate; the main

Old-style road markers even give the altitude

hazard in small villages is locals suddenly stopping their cars in the middle of the road to lean out of the window and chat to friends travelling in cars coming the other way. On the Côte d'Azur different standards apply, with tempers and the blare of car horns reaching a crescendo in July and August, which probably equals Parisian driving conditions (possibly because many of them are Parisians).

In villages and small towns many streets are now closed off to cars *sauf riverains* (except for residents). Although these restrictions may not appear to be enforced so strictly out of season, during the peak season only foolish drivers would ignore them. Pay attention to signs in village centres indicating market days; you will not be popular if you leave your car overnight and block stallholders setting up in the early hours.

Parking Finding somewhere to park can be a headache in peak months, although most large towns have sufficient underground car parking (follow the blue "P" signs). If you lose your car parking ticket be warned that you will need to produce your vehicle registration document in order to exit the parking area, as well as having to pay the full day price. If you can find a space, on-street parking is cheaper for short periods in *stationement payant* zones (you will need change for the ticket machines).

Fuel stations These are plentiful, and sell unleaded fuel (*sans plomb*) and diesel Be careful on weekends (many are closed on Sundays) and in mountainous areas, where there are far fewer of them.

Rules and regulations Speed limits are 130kph (80mph) on the *autoroutes*, 110kph (68mph) on dual carriageways, 90kph (56mph) on other roads, and 50kph (31mph) in urban areas. These limits are lower in poor weather conditions. Seat belts must be worn and children under 10 cannot travel in the front of the vehicle.

Fines for speeding or other violations are levied on the spot, with only cash or a cheque drawn on a French bank account accepted. The minimum fine for speeding is €137, and the same for using a mobile phone. Drink-driving means an automatic court appearance.

Accidents If you are involved in an accident take the registration number of the other car and exchange insurance details with the other driver: Try and take the names and addresses of witnesses. Once you have contacted the police, you will be required to fill in a statement (a *constant aimable*), but if your written French is not good enough to do this you will have to find someone to translate.

Autoroutes The *autoroutes à péage* generally offer safe, hassle-free driving (at a price, except for limited stretches near urban areas, which are free). Service stations are plentiful, and are obliged to provide free tyre checks, oil checks, and windscreen

❑ French car licence plates carry a *départemental* identification number. In Provence they are as follows:
Vaucluse: 84
Bouches-du-Rhône: 13
Var: 83
Alpes de Haute-Provence: 04
Alpes-Maritimes: 06 ❑

washes in the interests of motorway safety. Most have small supermarkets (where you can buy everything from snacks to souvenirs) and usually also a café/restaurant; some provide free showers (ask for the key at the cash desk), great for freshening up during a long drive.

Payments at *autoroute* toll booths can be made by credit card and they do add up over a long drive. Speeding drivers should also be aware that they may be timed between *péages* and fined for exceeding the speed limit over the distance.

To avoid holiday weekends and traffic jams the *Bison Futé* leaflet, obtainable from *autoroute* tollbooths, lists seasonal blockages and suggests alternative non-motorway routes.

Tollbooths (péages) on an autoroute

Communications

Media Local newspapers such as *La Marseillaise* and *Nice-Matin* supply details of local events and entertainment, while hotels usually carry copies of freesheets and local tourist offices bring out regular events bulletins. The *International Herald Tribune* is widely available, as are British newspapers and other foreign publications, in most large towns and holiday resorts.

French television relies heavily on game shows and foreign films. There is a wide selection of radio stations, including the English-language stations Riviera Radio on 106.3 and 106.5FM, and Radio International on 100.5 and 100.9FM with BBC World Service news bulletins.

Post offices Formerly the PTT (Poste, Télégraphes et Téléphones), post offices are simply known as *La Poste*, though they still deal with both mail and telecommunications services. Well-signed with a stylized bluebird symbol on a yellow background, they are usually open 9–7 weekdays, 9–noon Saturdays in large towns; in villages they may have shorter hours and close for lunch. The range of services includes selling stamps and phonecards, *poste restante* and in some cases fax-sending and cheque-cashing facilities. Stamps (*timbres de poste*) can

The post is usually efficient

also be bought in tobacconists' kiosks (*tabacs*).

Telephone and fax The country code

for France is 33. All French numbers have 10 digits, and there are five telephone regions in the country. All numbers in Paris and the Île de France begin with 01; all the areas covered in this book (with the exception of Monaco) start with 04.

Monaco has its own international code (00 377), followed by the eight-digit number.

Most public phone booths (*cabines*) are now card-operated. Phonecards (*télécartes*) can be bought in post offices, *tabacs* and newspaper shops.

For international calls, invest in a €15 Kertel card, which offers heavily disounted calls to a nominated destination. For instance, a single €15 card will cover two hours of calls to anywhere in North America or within Western Europe. Once you have bought your card, you will need to make a simple call to an operator to select the destination of your choice and activate the card.

Major hotels have internet facilities and there are internet cafés in the larger cities.

Language guide

English is spoken by many people involved in tourism (at campsites, hotels and so on) and in the smarter shops and restaurants, but less so in rural areas. Your attempts at French will be appreciated, even if you master only *"Bonjour," "monsieur," "madame"* and *"s'il vous plaît."*

Basic vocabulary

yes	*oui*
no	*non*
hello/good morning	*bonjour*
good evening	*bonsoir*
goodbye	*au revoir*
please	*s'il vous plaît*
how are you?	*comment allez-vous?*
thank you (very much)	*merci (beaucoup)*
sorry	*pardon/excusez moi*
I understand	*je comprends*
I do not understand	*je ne comprends pas*
I don't know	*je ne sais pas*
please help me	*aidez-moi, s'il vous plaît*
help!	*au secours!*
toilets	*les toilettes*
no smoking	*défense de fumer*
entrance	*entrée*

exit	*sortie*
at what time?	*à quelle heure?*
today	*aujourd'hui*
tomorrow	*demain*
yesterday	*hier*
the morning	*le matin*
the afternoon	*l'après midi*
the evening	*le soir*
the night	*le nuit*
now	*maintenant*
later	*plus tard*
closed	*fermé*
open	*ouvert*
prohibited	*interdit*
when?	*quand?*
why?	*pourquoi?*
with	*avec*
without	*sans*
big	*grand*
small	*petit*
hot	*chaud*
cold	*froid*
cheap	*bon marché*
expensive	*cher*

Shopping

shops	*les magasins*
market	*le marché*
bakery	*la boulangerie*
food shop	*l'alimentation*
butcher	*la boucherie*
newspaper shop/stationers	*la libraire*
supermarket	*le supermarché*
I would like…	*je voudrais…*
this one	*ceci*
that one	*cela*
that's enough	*ça suffit*
how much…?	*combien...?*

Eating and drinking

to eat	*manger*
to drink	*boire*
breakfast	*le petit déjeuner*
lunch	*le déjeuner*
dinner	*le diner*
coffee/tea	*café/thé*
beer (draught)	*une bière (pression)*
wine (white/red)	*le vin (rouge/blanc)*
wine list	*la carte des vins*
the bill, please	*l'addition, s'il vous plaît*

Directions

where is...?	*où se trouve...?*
left	*à gauche*
right	*à droite*
near/not far	*près/pas loin*
far	*loin*
straight on/ahead	*tout droit*

there	*là*
behind	*derrière*
in front of	*devant*
before	*avant*
after	*après*

Numbers

one	*un/une*
two	*deux*
three	*trois*
four	*quatre*
five	*cinq*
six	*six*
seven	*sept*
eight	*huit*
nine	*neuf*
ten	*dix*
eleven	*onze*
twelve	*douze*
twenty	*vingt*
fifty	*cinquante*
one hundred	*cent*
one thousand	*mille*

Days of the week

Monday	*lundi*
Tuesday	*mardi*
Wednesday	*mercredi*
Thursday	*jeudi*
Friday	*vendredi*
Saturday	*samedi*
Sunday	*dimanche*

A public cardphone box

259

Shopping

Provence offers an enormous variety of things to buy, ranging from local produce such as olives and garlic to handicrafts and colourful textiles. Provençal markets are not to be missed (local tourist offices can provide lists of nearby market days) and often feature crafts alongside traditional products such as honey, cheeses and olive oil.

For the serious shopper in western Provence, there is a handful of really excellent shopping destinations in Arles, Aix-en-Provence, and the little town of St.-Rémy-de-Provence where the pint-sized old town centre has been transformed into a warren of crafts shops and boutiques yielding up every imaginable Provençal objet d'art.

Clothes and fabrics Block-print fabrics were first produced in Provence in the 17th century after the import of inexpensive Indian prints was banned: Provençals responded by producing their own cotton prints, still known today as *indiennes*. These colourful fabrics can either be bought by the length or ready-made into skirts, tops, scarves or furnishing items. The two most famous retail chains for traditional prints are Souleiado and Les Olivades, both of which have numerous outlets throughout Provence.

Beautifully worked traditional costumes, flamboyant waistcoats, *gardians'* jackets and hats, and other items can be found in Aigues-Mortes, the unofficial Camarguais capital.

At the other end of the clothing spectrum, haute-couture boutiques are thick on the ground in Monte-Carlo and Cannes, with a fair smattering in Nice and St.-Tropez. Many of the Riviera hill villages also have designer boutiques hidden away down their narrow streets.

Crafts Small clay figurines known as *santons* are one of the most traditional Provençal crafts. Most *santons* originate from workshops in and around Marseille, Aubagne, Aix-en-Provence and Arles, and local tourist offices can provide addresses of *santonniers* who are open to the public.

Olive-wood carvings can be found in most souvenir shops and basketry, cork bowls and handwoven woollen garments are also popular. Hundreds of different kinds of pipes are sold in Cogolin, and traditional handmade paper products in Fontaine-de-Vaucluse.

Souvenirs of Provence

Herbs, scents and soaps Small sachets of *herbes de Provence*, lavender bags packaged in pretty Provençal fabric and pot-pourri are wonderfully evocative of a Provençal holiday, and easy and light to pack. The scents of Provence are also captured in floral perfumes and essences. All the perfume factories in Grasse have boutiques offering retail sales; the main *parfumeries* are Fragonard, Galimard and Molinard (see page 218).

Marseille olive oil soap was once exported worldwide, with the industry reaching its peak in the 17th century. With the advent of washing powders manufacturing declined, but it is now enjoying a revival thanks to the pure, biodegradable properties of the soaps (which are often scented with mountain herbs). Beautifully packaged Marseille soaps (as well as bath oils, perfumes and herbal essences) are widely available.

Pottery, ceramics and glassware
Practically every *village perché* has its share of pottery shops, with the quality varying widely and prices that are in many cases unjustified. However, you can often find original pieces that are well worth the investment. In the pottery town of Vallauris, made famous by Picasso in the 1940s, the Galerie Madoura (tel: 04 93 64 66 39) still produces beautiful reproductions of Picasso's original

Local produce

designs. Visitors often comment on the number of ceramic cicadas gracing the souvenir stores. The cicadas were first produced in Marseille in 1895 and traditionally perch on an olive branch with a Provençal quotation from Frédéric Mistral: "*Lou souleù mi fa canta*" (the sun makes me sing).

Moustiers-Ste.-Marie is the Provençal capital for faience (fine, glazed ceramics) with a reputation dating back to the 17th century. Among the more reputable establishments are Atelier Michèle Blanc and Atelier Lallier in the village centre.

Finally, an extensive range of handblown glassware, with its distinctive air-bubbled appearance, is on sale at the Verrerie de Biot (chemin des Combes, Biot), situated just outside Antibes.

> ❑ Provence is a great place for the sweet toothed, with candied fruits in Apt, *calissons* (almond biscuits) in Aix, nougat in Vence, *berlingots* (mint-flavoured caramels) in Carpentras and *marrons glacés* (glazed chestnuts) in Collobrières. The best jam in Provence is the sensational Les Merveilles range, which includes bilberry, black fig, apricot and plum. ❑

Sports

Provence has a well-developed infrastructure providing first-rate facilities for outdoor activities and sports. As well as the sports listed here, you can also find places for hang-gliding, gliding, waterskiing, scuba-diving and skiing.

Canoeing and kayaking There are numerous locations for canoeing and kayaking, the two most spectacular of which are the Grand Canyon du Verdon and the Ubaye valley in the Alpes de Haute-Provence, where they also organize "hydrospeed" (white-water swimming with wetsuit and floats). Canoeing is also possible on the Durance and the Sorgue.

Many rivers in Provence are harnessed to hydroelectric power schemes and are subject to sudden changes in water level as barrages are opened or closed: Always seek local advice before setting off on your own.

Climbing The top climbing regions are the Grand Canyon du Verdon in the Alpes de Haute-Provence, the seacliffs

Bicycles can be hired in many areas

(*calanques*) of Cassis in the Bouches-du-Rhône and the Dentelles of Montmirail, as well as the cliffs at Buoux in the Vaucluse. Contact the *comités départementals* (see pages 269–270) for further details.

Cycling The French have always been keen cyclists and they have taken to mountain bicycles (called VTT – *velo touts terrains*) with enthusiasm. Daily or weekly rental deals are available in coastal resorts as well as the more spectacular (and demanding) mountain areas. Local tourist offices can supply details of bicycle rental shops. Many long-distance hiking paths (see below) have now been waymarked with a VTT logo indicating permitted routes (although in some forestry areas and fragile environments VTT is prohibited).

One of the most stunning areas near the coast is the Esterel *massif*; there are also extensive trails in the Alpes de Haute-Provence. A colour brochure in English detailing cycling tours of several days' duration, plus guides and rental shops, is available from the Comité Départemental du Tourisme, Immeuble François Mitterand, BP 170, 04005 Digne-les-Bains (tel: 04 92 31 57 29).

Golf Golfers are spoiled for choice in Provence with dozens of courses to play on, particularly on the coast. Some of the best are the Golf de Fregate near Bandol, the Golf d'Esterel near Fréjus (designed by Robert Trent Jones), Golf de Ste.-Maxime (a challenging course), the Golf de Fuveau in the Bouches-du-Rhône (one of the biggest courses in Europe) and the prestigious Pont Royal at Mallemort in the Luberon.

Other good courses include those at Cannes, Mandelieu, Ste.-Baume, and Barbaroux.

Full details are obtainable from the Ligue de Golf de Provence-Alpes-Côte d'Azur, Relais du Griffon, 439 route de la Seds, 13127 Vitrolles (tel: 04 42 76 35 22).

Hiking There is a comprehensive network of hiking trails throughout Provence, starting with the long-distance footpaths, the *sentiers de grande randonnée* (known as GRs for short), which criss-cross the mountains and coastal hinterland. Each GR is described in a detailed *Topoguide*, which should be available in local bookshops and park information centres, or contact the Fédération Française de la Randonnée Pédestre, 64 rue du Dessous des Berges, Paris 75013 (tel: 01 44 89 93 93).

National and regional parks also have their own signposted trails, and guides can usually be hired if required (details from local tourist offices).

Horse-riding Explorations on horseback are particularly popular in the Camargue, although there are many short- and long-distance trails throughout Provence and numerous *centres équestres* where you can rent horses. For details of excursions into the marshes, contact the Association Camarguaise de Tourisme Équestre, Centre de Ginès, Pont de Gau, Stes.-Maries-de-la-Mer (tel: 04 90 97 86 32).

Sailing With 125 ports and marinas along 833km (518 miles) of coastline, Provence offers plenty of opportunities for the nautically inclined. Most ports and marinas have sailing schools and boats for rent and tourist offices can provide lists of tour and charter operators, or contact the regional tourist boards (see pages 269–270) in advance.

Sailing, waterskiing and windsurfing are also popular on the big mountain lakes of the Alpes de Haute-Provence, such as Lac de Castillon, Lac d'Esparron, Lac de Ste.-Croix and Lac de Serre-Ponçon. Lakes and reservoirs provide opportunities for water-based activities among mountain scenery.

Windsurfing With the benefit of the *mistral*, which gusts at over 100km (62 miles) an hour, it is perhaps not surprising that world windsurfing records have been broken here; but beginners will also find plenty of gentler spots along the coast. Two world-class locations are les Stes.-Maries-de-la-Mer and l'Almanarre near Hyères, both of which have staged championship events. Boards can be hired in many resorts and there is tuition available by the day or week.

263

Emergencies

Crime and police Although Marseille and the Côte d'Azur have a near-legendary reputation for organized crime, you are unlikely to be affected unless you are in the seriously rich category and a target for a jewel-heist. The most common causes of theft from unfortunate visitors are pick-pockets and car break-ins.

Always leave valuables locked up or in the hotel safe, and be particularly careful when parking at remote tourist spots where car leave valuables on the back seat, and keep doors locked.

Make sure you have adequate travel insurance and carry travellers' cheques rather than cash. It is a good idea to keep a separate record of all credit card numbers, cheque numbers and emergency phone numbers for cancelling credit cards and travellers' cheques.

If you are the victim of a theft report it to the nearest *gendarmerie* and keep a copy of the statement if you intend to claim on your insurance.

Pharmacists will give first aid

break-ins are common; never leave cameras or valuables in your car. Burglars tend to target rented villas: Always secure the house at night or if going out, and do not leave anything on the terrace overnight. Thieves are known to terrace-hop between villas to see what they can grab.

In the big cities, thefts from cars waiting at traffic lights are becoming common (the thieves escape at high speed on their motorcycles). Don't

Police In cities and towns police duties are the responsibility of the Police Municipale, while the Gendarmes (part of the national police force) cover smaller places and the countryside.

You are unlikely to encounter the fearsome CRS (Compagnies Républicains de Securité), a flying squad who deal with riot situations and civil unrest, although strangely enough they also look after security on public beaches. The Garde Mobile or Police de la Route look after highway security.

Embassies and consulates

Embassies in Paris
UK: 35 rue de Faubourg St-Honoré, 75383 (tel: 01 44 51 31 00).
US: 2 rue St.-Florentin, 75001 (tel: 01 43 12 22 22; emergencies: 01 43 12 23 47).
Canada: 35 avenue Montaigne, 75008 (tel: 01 44 43 29 00).

Consulates in Provence
UK: 24 avenue du Prado, 13006 Marseille (tel: 04 91 15 72 10).
US: place Varian Fry, 13006 Marseille (tel: 04 91 54 92 00).

Emergency telephone numbers
Emergencies 112
Police: 17
Fire (*sapeurs pompiers*): 18
Ambulance: 15

❏ The French passion for wild mushrooms means that inevitably dozens of people fall ill or die every year after eating poisonous varieties. During the autumn, pharmacists' windows display mushroom identification data to help prevent this, and anyone can take in a mushroom so that the pharmacist can check if it is an edible variety. ❏

Lost property
Serious losses should be reported to the police (copy the statement for your insurance). Report lost passports to the nearest embassy or consulate (see left). Report loss of credit cards and travellers' cheques to the relevant company immediately.

Health and pharmacies
France does not require any vaccinations, and health care standards are high. Water is safe everywhere except for taps marked *eau non potable*.

EU citizens are entitled to reciprocal health care (British citizens should bring their European Health Insurance Card. Apply at UK post offices or online at www.dh.gov.uk).

If you need a doctor urgently, contact SOS Médecins (telephone numbers are in the directory under *Urgences* or call directory enquiries, tel: 12) or ask in a pharmacy.

Pharmacists (marked by a green cross) are trained to administer first aid and can also dispense advice on minor ailments. On weekends or holidays, pharmacies operate on a rota basis (addresses are posted in the window or in local papers) or you can call the *gendarmerie* for the nearest *pharmacie de garde* (duty chemist).

A local resident finds time to pause in the sunshine

265

Campsites in popular areas can be crowded

Other information

Camping Camping is extremely popular in Provence, particularly among the French themselves. Campsites are well organized and graded from one to four stars depending on the facilities provided. The best have swimming pools, sports facilities, supermarkets or shops and a restaurant/bar.

Camping municipals are the most basic, run by local authorities and found in nearly every town; other possibilities include *camping à la ferme*, where you can pitch your tent on farmland, although generally there will be no facilities. Camping outside recognized sites (*camping sauvage*) is sometimes possible but often forbidden (*interdit*) by local authorities (always check with the town hall first). Never camp in the forests in summer because of the fire risk.

In July and August campsites on the Côte d'Azur are notoriously over-crowded (and can be insanitary).

Always phone ahead to check space availability.

Lists of campsites (state the region) are available from local tourist offices or French Government Tourist Offices. For information in advance of travel from the UK, contact the Maison de la France, 178 Piccadilly, London W1J 9AL or call the France Information Line, tel: 09068 244123).

Pre-booked camping packages are a popular option for budget holidays. UK holiday firms include: Eurocamp Independent (tel: 0870 9019 410; www.eurocamp.co.uk); Canvas Holidays (tel: 0870 192 1154; www.canvasholidays.com); Select France (tel: 01873 859876; www.select-site.com).

Villa rentals There are numerous options for renting in Provence. Good value rentals in or near small country villages are offered by the Gîtes de France organization, with properties ranging from village houses to converted farm outbuildings or country cottages. For information, contact Gîtes de France, 59 rue St.-Lazare, 75439 Paris (tel: 01 49 70 75

❑ There are more than 925 campsites in Provence, providing a whole range of options from farmers' fields with fewer than 10 pitches to vast tented cities offering 450-plus *emplacements*. The majority are in the coastal regions of the Var, while the *département* with the fewest sites is Vaucluse. ❑

75; www.gites-de-france.fr).

Discounts on flights or ferries can sometimes also be arranged through specialized accommodation agencies in the UK such as:
Great Escapes (tel: 0845 330 2084; www.greatescapes.co.uk).
French Life Holidays (tel: 0870 336 2877; www.frenchlife.co.uk).
Individual Travellers Company (tel: 0870 0780189; www.indiv-travellers.com).
VFB Holidays (tel:01452 716830; www.vfbholidays.co.uk).

Agencies in the US include:
At Home Abroad, 163 3rd Avenue, No, 19, New York, NY 10003, tel: 212/421 9165; www.athomeabroad.com.
Interhome, 1131 South State Road 7, Fort Lauderdale, FL33317, Tel: 954/791 8282; www.interhome.com.
Vacation Home Rentals Worldwide, 235 Kensington Ave., Norwood, NJ 07648,tel: 201/767-9393 or 1-800-633 3284 toll-free; www.vhr.ww.com.

Student and youth accommodation
Budget accommodation is available in dormitory rooms in youth hostels (*Auberges de Jeunesse*) in most towns; contact your home branch of the International Youth Hostel Federation (IYHF) or the Fédération Unie des Auberges de Jeunesse (27 rue Pajol, 75018 Paris, tel: 01 44 89 87 27). Some places also have more comfortable accommodation in Foyers des Jeunes Travailleurs/euses, which usually provide individual rooms.

Visitors with disabilities France is no better or worse than other EU countries in providing access facilities for travellers with disabilities, although the situation is gradually improving and ramps and other forms of access are now provided at many museums and tourist sites (nearly all new museums and public buildings are wheelchair-friendly). Public transport is difficult, but there are accessible hotels in most major towns and resorts. Not surprisingly, these tend to be newer properties. However, it is worth asking whether ground-floor rooms with reasonable access are available in older properties. Also, the red *Guide Michelin* lists hotels with facilities for people with disabilities.

In the UK, information on all aspects of disabled travel is available from RADAR (The Royal Association for Disability and Rehabilitation), Unit 12, City Forum, 250 City Road, London EC1V 8AF (tel: 0207 250 3222; www.radar.org.uk).

In the US: SATH 347 5th Avenue, Suite 610, New York City, NY 10016; tel: 212/447-7284; www.sath.org.

Opening times Lunch is a serious business in Provence, and almost everything closes for two hours at midday. Normal working hours are 8–12, 2–6. Food shops are usually

Nice-Côte d'Azur Airport is one of the busiest in France

open at 7.30, closing at lunchtime and not reopening in some cases until 3 or 4, but they then stay open until 7.30 or 8. Shops and supermarkets in large towns and resorts often don't close in the lunch hour, but may not open until 10. Sunday and Monday (or sometimes Tuesday) are the standard closing days, although food shops are usually open on Sunday mornings until noon. Food markets (weekly in small villages, daily in the cities) operate mornings only.

Museums and monuments usually open from 9 or 10 to noon, then 2 or 3 to 5 or 6 depending on the season. The longer hours are during the summer (around early June until September), when some also remain open over lunchtime. Closing days are usually Monday (for municipal museums) or Tuesday (national museums and monuments), sometimes both. Many sights close during November, with some of the smaller ones staying closed throughout the winter.

Churches and cathedrals are usually open for visitors all day except during services, although a handful spurn visitors altogether and are only open during Mass (sometimes you can request the key from the priest's house, the *presbytère*, nearby).

On national holidays (see page 253) shops, banks and businesses are closed; some museums stay open (apart from Christmas Day and New Year's Day) and you can be sure that restaurants will usually be open.

Places of worship Nearly every town or village has a Catholic church, with the times of Mass usually pinned on the door. Protestant churches with English-language services are found in Nice, St.-Raphaël and Menton. There are synagogues in Avignon, Carpentras, Nice and Cavaillon, and Greek and Russian Orthodox churches in Nice.

Toilets There are coin-operated, self-cleansing public toilets, found on the streets, or buy a drink to use the facilities in a bar or café; you are not obliged to, but signs indicating that the WC is *strictement réserve pour la clientèle* indicate that it's frowned on not to do so. Public toilets (other than the automatic ones) usually have a dish for small change. Women's are labelled *Dames*, men's *Hommes* or *Messieurs*. If you have to ask, request the WC (pronounced vey-sey).

Electricity Usually 220V, with double, round-pin wall sockets; adaptors are necessary for foreign appliances. In some remote areas the supply is still 110V.

Women travellers Women travellers should take the normal precautions if they are travelling alone, and hitchhiking is not recommended.

You will probably find the French courteous and charming and it is quite normal to be offered a drink without the expectation that it will lead any further than a pleasant chat.

Topless bathing is perfectly acceptable and doesn't provoke harassment.

Tourist offices

Overseas

French Government Tourist Offices can provide a vast range of information on every aspect of travelling in France. Also try the website (www.franceguide.com).

● Australia: Maison de la France, 25 Bligh Street, Level 22, Sydney, NSW 2000 (tel: 02 9231 5244).

● Canada: Maison de la France, 1981 Avenue McGill College, Suite 490, Montreal, Quebec H3A 2W9 (tel: 514 288 4264).

● Ireland: Maison de la France, 10 Suffolk Street, Dublin 2 (tel: 01 635 1008).

● UK: Maison de la France, 178 Piccadilly, London W1V 0AL (tel: 09068 244123, premium rate service).

● USA: Maison de la France, 444 Madison Avenue, New York NY 10022 (tel: 212/838-7800).

Local information

Local information can also be obtained in advance from the various Comités Départemental/Régional de Tourisme (CDT/CRT; departmental or regional tourist offices), which can supply brochures covering accommodation, attractions, sports and events in their area:

CDT Alpes de Haute-Provence: 1 Immeuble François Mitterrand, BP 170, 04005 Dignes-les-Bains (tel: 04 92 31 57 29; fax: 04 92 32 24 94; e-mail: info@alpes-haute-provence.com; www.alpes-haute-provence.com).

CDT Bouches-du-Rhône: Le Montesquieu, 13 rue Roux de Brignoles, 13006 Marseille (tel: 04 91 13 84 13; fax: 04 91 33 01 82; e-mail: cdt13@visitprovence.com; www.visitprovence.com).

CRT Riviera–Côte d'Azur: BP 3126,

CONVERSION CHARTS

FROM	TO	MULTIPLY BY
Inches	Centimetres	2.54
Centimetres	Inches	0.3937
Feet	Metres	0.3048
Metres	Feet	3.2810
Yards	Metres	0.9144
Metres	Yards	1.0940
Miles	Kilometres	1.6090
Kilometres	Miles	0.6214
Acres	Hectares	0.4047
Hectares	Acres	2.4710
Gallons	Litres	4.5460
Litres	Gallons	0.2200
Ounces	Grams	28.35
Grams	Ounces	0.0353
Pounds	Grams	453.6
Grams	Pounds	0.0022
Pounds	Kilograms	0.4536
Kilograms	Pounds	2.205
Tons	Tonnes	1.0160
Tonnes	Tons	0.9842

269

MEN'S SUITS							
UK	36	38	40	42	44	46	48
Rest of Europe	46	48	50	52	54	56	58
US	36	38	40	42	44	46	48

DRESS SIZES						
UK	8	10	12	14	16	18
France	36	38	40	42	44	46
Italy	38	40	42	44	46	48
Rest of Europe	34	36	38	40	42	44
US	6	8	10	12	14	16

MEN'S SHIRTS						
UK	14	14.5	15	15.5	16	16.5 17
Rest of Europe	36	37	38 39/40	41	42	43
US	14	14.5	15	15.5	16	16.5 17

MEN'S SHOES						
UK	7	7.5	8.5	9.5	10.5	11
Rest of Europe	41	42	43	44	45	46
US	8	8.5	9.5	10.5	11.5	12

WOMEN'S SHOES						
UK	4.5	5	5.5	6	6.5	7
Rest of Europe	38	38	39	39	40	41
US	6	6.5	7	7.5	8	8.5

06203 Nice (tel: 04 93 37 78 78;
fax: 04 93 86 01 06; email:
info@guideriviera.com).
CDT Var: BP 99, 83003 Draguignan
(tel: 04 94 50 55 50;
fax: 04 94 50 55 51; e-mail:
info@cdtvar.com;
www.tourismevar.com).
CDT Vaucluse: BP 147, 84008
Avignon (tel: 04 90 80 47 00;
fax: 04 90 86 86 08;
e-mail: info@provenceguide.com;
www.provenceguide.com).

In Provence Tourist offices are called
Offices du Tourisme or Syndicats
d'Initiatives (which are smaller and
may not open daily). Larger towns
have tourist offices called Accueil de
France (which help with hotel bookings for personal callers on the same
day or up to eight days in advance).
  Provence's main tourist offices are:
Aix-en-Provence: 2 place du Général

*A Provençal view, with Mont Ventoux
in the background*

de Gaulle (tel: 04 42 16 11 61;
fax: 04 42 16 11 62)
Arles: boulevard des Lices
(tel: 04 90 18 41 20; fax: 04 90 18 41 29)
Avignon: 41 cours Jean-Jaurès (tel: 04
32 74 32 74; fax: 04 90 82 95 03)
Cannes: Palais des Festivals,
La Croisette (tel: 04 93 39 24 53;
fax: 04 92 99 84 23)
Digne-les-Bains: place du Tampinet
(tel: 04 92 36 62 62; fax: 04 92 32 27 24)
Fréjus: 325 rue Jean-Jaurès (tel: 04 94 51
83 83; fax: 04 94 51 00 26)
Marseille: 4 la Canebière (tel: 04 91 13
89 00; fax: 04 91 13 89 20)
Nice: 5 promenade des Anglais (tel: 08
92 70 74 07; 34 cents per minute)
Nîmes: 6 rue Auguste (tel: 04 66 58 38
00; fax: 04 66 58 38 01)
Toulon: place Raimu (tel: 04 94 18 53
00; fax: 04 94 18 53 09).

Hotels & Restaurants

HOTELS

The following recommended hotels have been divided into three price categories:

budget (€) a double room for up to €60
moderate (€€) a double room for €60–130
expensive (€€€) expect to pay more than €130 for a double room

VAUCLUSE

Apt
Auberge de Luberon (€€)
8 place du Faubourg du Ballet, 84000
tel: 04 90 74 12 50 fax: 04 90 04 79 49
www.auberge-luberon-peuzin.com
A charming Logis overlooking the north bank of the river and the town centre. Comfortable and attractive rooms make the best of limited space; friendly staff and good food. (Closed Nov.)

Avignon
de Blauvac (€€)
11 rue de la Bancasse, 84000
tel: 04 90 86 34 11; www.hotel-blauvac.com
email: blauvac@aol.com
Hemmed in by the old town, this lovely 17th-century mansion was once owned by the Marquis de Blauvac. Sixteen rooms with pretty fabrics to relieve the bare stonework. Friendly reception.
d'Europe (€€€)
12 place Crillon, 84000 tel: 04 90 14 76 76
fax: 04 90 14 76 71 www.heurope.com
Elegant, welcoming, and central. Royalty and celebrities alike enjoy the first-class service and antique-furnished rooms at Avignon's smartest hotel, arranged around a flower-decked courtyard.
de Mons (€)
5 rue de Mons tel: 04 90 82 57 16
fax: 04 90 85 19 15
email: hotel.mons@wanadoo.fr
Higgledy-piggledy small hotel fashioned out of a 13th-century chapel just off place de l'Horloge. Creaky wooden floors and twisting stairs; fairly basic but very friendly and full of quirky character.
Provençal (€)
13 rue Joseph Vernet tel: 04 90 85 25 24
fax: 04 90 82 75 81
Modest, well-priced hotel in a flat-fronted town house minutes from all the museums and town centre. Each modern room has a shower and bath, TV and telephone.

Bonnieux
Hostellerie du Prieuré (€€–€€€)
rue J-B Aurard, 84480 tel: 04 90 75 80 78
fax: 04 90 75 96 00
Lovely 18th-century former abbey building at the foot of the ramparts with 10 antique-furnished rooms. Roaring fires in autumn and a pretty garden terrace. Meals in summer. (Closed Nov–Feb.)

Carpentras
Le Fiacre (€€)
153 rue Vigne, 84200 tel: 04 90 63 03 15
www.hotel-du-fiacre.com
Delightful accommodation within an 18th-century

hotel. An interior courtyard is hidden behind a discreet street-front facade. Antique furnishings and tapestries, plus a relaxing family atmosphere.

Cavaillon
du Parc (€)
183 place François-Tourel, 84300
tel: 04 90 71 57 78
www.hotelduparccavaillon.com
Old-fashioned but hospitable establishment opposite the Roman arch. The rooms are nothing special but clean and very quiet on the park side. The sunny terrace is a bonus in summer.

Fontaine de Vaucluse
Du Poete (€€–€€€)
Le Village, 84800
tel: 04 90 20 34 05
An atmosphere of elegant simplicity surrounds this charming hotel, set in an old mill beside the River Sorgue and surrounded by shady gardens. Each lovely room is named after a muse. Facilities are good with a pool, Jacuzzi, breakfast room and riverside terrace bar.

Gordes
Auberge de Carcarille (€€)
Les Gervais, 84220 tel: 04 90 72 02 63
www.auberge-carcarille.com
A modern *mas* 3km (2 miles) south of the village with rooms at very reasonable prices, a swimming pool, and nearby restaurant. A useful option for families. (Closed end-Nov to end-Jan.)
Les Romarins (€€)
Route de Sénanque tel: 04 90 72 12 13
fax: 04 90 72 13 13
Enchanting 10-room inn occupying an 18th-century *bastide* on the ridge-top road to Sénanque. Simple light-filled rooms (go for one at the rear with gorgeous views over the valley) and a pool terrace you won't want to leave. (Closed Nov to mid-Dec and Jan to mid-Mar.)

L'Isle-sur-la-Sorgue
Araxe (€€)
Route d'Apt (N100), 84800
tel: 04 90 38 40 00 fax: 04 90 20 84 74
Smart and well-run modern hotel complex with apartments and bungalows in extensive grounds leading down to the river. Family-friendly base with gardens, two pools, tennis and play area.

Orange
Arène (€€)
place des Langes, 84100 tel: 04 90 11 40 40
www.hotel-arene.fr
Overlooking a quiet square in the heart of town, the Arène enjoys a long-standing reputation as the best hotel in town. Public rooms verge on the kitsch, but it is comfortable and welcoming.
L'Herbier d'Orange (€)
8 place aux Herbes, 84100
tel: 04 90 34 09 23 fax: 04 90 51 61 12
www.lherbierdorange.com
A clean and friendly budget option close to the Théâtre Antique and main shopping area, popular with business people. A more lively clientele takes over during the summer festival season.

272

Vaison-la-Romaine
Burrhus (€–€€)
place Montfort, 84110 tel: 04 90 36 00 11
fax: 04 90 36 39 05 www.burrhus.com
e-mail: info@burrhus.com
Not very promising from the outside, but this is a
real find. The welcoming patrons have redecorated
every room, the bathrooms are smartly tiled and
there is an upstairs terrace over the square.
Hostellerie Le Beffroi (€€)
rue de l'Évêché, Cité Médiévale, 84110
tel: 04 90 36 04 71 fax: 04 90 36 24 78
www.le-beffroi.com
Two handsome 16th- to 17th-century seigneurial
mansions have been joined to create this interesting hostelry decorated with Provençal antiques
and paintings. Pool, restaurant, and courtyard.

BOUCHES-DU-RHÔNE

Aigues-Mortes
St. Louis (€€)
10 rue Amiral Courbet, 30220
tel: 04 66 53 72 68 www.lesaintlouis.fr
email: hotel.saint-louis@wanadoo.fr
22 comfortable rooms in a wonderful old building
right in the heart of town. Good local cooking in the
restaurant; terrace dining in summer.

Aix-en-Provence
L'Hôtel des Augustins (€€–€€€)
3 rue de la Masse, 13100 tel: 04 42 27 28 59
www.hotel-augustins.com
Luxurious hotel housed in the vaulted precincts of
the 12th- to 15th-century Convent des Grands
Augustins just off Cours Mirabeau. Spacious, well-
appointed rooms and delightfully helpful staff.
Cardinal (€€)
24 rue Cardinale tel: 04 42 38 32 30
fax: 04 42 26 39 05
email: hotel-cardinale@wanadoo.fr
Charming family-run hotel in the Quartier Mazarin.
Large rooms in an 18th-century house furnished
with an eclectic mix of antiques, chintz and
unusual items collected by the owners.
Le Manoir (€€)
8 rue d'Entrecasteaux tel: 04 42 26 27 20
fax: 04 42 27 17 97 www.hotelmanoir.com
e-mail: msg@hotelmanoir.com
Quiet, spotless, comfortable and quaintly traditional
(busy wallpapers, brocade chairs, heavy wooden
armoirs). Breakfast is served in the 14th-century
cloister of a former convent. (Closed Jan.)
Des Quatre Dauphins (€€)
54 rue Roux-Alphéran tel: 04 42 38 16 39
fax: 04 42 38 60 19
A peaceful oasis in a handsome Quartier Mazarin
town house, decorated with traditional Provençal
prints and hand-painted furnishings. A little tight
on space, but oodles of charm.

Arles
d'Arlatan (€€–€€€)
26 rue du Sauvage, 13200 tel: 04 90 93 56 66
fax: 04 90 49 68 45 www.hotel-arlatan.fr
e-mail: hotel-arlatan@wanadoo.fr
Chic and delightful lodgings in a converted 15th-
century mansion built over Roman baths, which

can be seen through a glass floor in reception.
Beautifully and individually furnished rooms; patio
and peaceful walled garden.
Le Calendal (€€)
5 rue de Laure tel: 04 90 96 11 89
fax: 04 90 96 05 84 www.lecalendal.com
Behind the Théâtre Antique, this is a lovely spot
with a shady garden for relaxing over a book, afternoon tea or a light meal. The interior is cheerily
Provençal and the rooms have air-conditioning.
Hotel du Forum (€€)
10 place du Forum, 13200
tel: 04 90 93 48 95
In the center of town opposite the Van Gogh cafe,
this friendly, family-run hotel has a lot of charm,
with shuttered windows, large airy rooms, well-
appointed bathrooms, courtyard and pool.

les Baux-de Provence
Mas d'Aigret (€€–€€€)
Col de la Vayède, 13520 tel: 04 90 54 20 00
fax: 04 90 54 44 00 www.masdaigret.com
This charming hotel has wonderful views across
the Crau Plain and most of the pretty rooms have a
balcony or terrace. Pool, gardens and a very good
restaurant carved out of the rock.

Cassis
Le Jardin d'Émile (€€)
23 avenue Amiral Ganteaume, 13260
tel: 04 42 01 80 55 fax: 04 42 01 80 70
Just seven rooms in a stylishly furnished Provençal
mas set back from the water at Plage du
Bestouan. Pine-shaded terrace and views of Cap
Canaille; good regional cooking. (Closed Jan.)

Marseille
New Hotel Vieux-Port (€€)
3 bis rue Reine Elisabeth tel: 04 91 99 23 23
fax: 04 91 90 76 24 www.new-hotel.com
e-mail: marseillevieux-port@new-hotel.com
In the pedestrianized zone, a few minutes' walk
from the old port with attractive, air-conditioned
rooms overlooking the harbour.
Le Petit Nice-Passédat (€€€)
Anse de Maldormé, Corniche J-F Kennedy
tel: 04 91 59 25 92 fax: 04 91 59 28 08
www.petitnice-passedat.com
e-mail: passedat@relaischateaux.com
The Passédat family's gorgeous villa hotel is the
height of restrained good taste, offering 10 chic
rooms and 6 apartments, saltwater pool and an
excellent restaurant.
Tonic (€€–€€€)
43 quai des Belges
tel: 04 91 55 67 46 www.tonichotel.com
This chic hotel is ideally placed, on the western
end of the Vieux Port. The comfortable rooms have
modern decor and are sound-proofed and air-
conditioned. It's worth paying more for a room with
a view to watch the action on the quayside.

Nîmes
Impérator Concorde (€€–€€€)
quai de la Fontaine, 30900
tel: 04 66 21 90 30 fax: 04 66 67 70 25
e-mail: hotel.imperator@wanadoo.fr
Nîmes' long-standing top hotel is within walking

273

distance of all the sights. Floral window dressings hang in the comfortable rooms; there is a fine restaurant (see page 280), one of Hemingway's favourite bars and a shady terrace.

Kyriad Nîmes-Centre (€€)
10 rue Roussy tel: 04 66 76 16 20
www.hotel-kyriad-nimes.com
Small, modern and very friendly, a few minutes' walk from the *vieille ville*. Refurbished with bright fabrics and good bathrooms; some rooms have terraces or balconies.

St.-Rémy-de-Provence
Auberge de la Reine Jeanne (€–€€)
12 boulevard Mirabeau, 13210
tel: 04 90 92 15 33 fax: 04 90 92 49 65
Charming Logis in a 17th-century building ranged around a courtyard off the road which encircles the old town. Eleven well-priced and comfortable rooms, plus a restaurant serving good local cooking.
Villa Glanum (€€)
46 avenue Van Gogh tel: 04 90 92 03 59
www.villaglanum.com
At the gates of Glanum, this welcoming hotel nestles in tree-shaded gardens with a pool. Some of the newer rooms have exposed beams, and tile floors open onto the lawns.

Saintes-Maries-de-la-Mer
L'Etrier Camarguais (€€)
Chemin Bas des Launes, 13460
tel: 04 90 97 81 14 www.letrier.com
A popular place to stay outside town with large rooms in bungalows decked out in Provençal fabrics. Rustic dining room, decoy ducks and the tools of the trade at every turn. Pool, tennis, riding.

Salon-de-Provence
Abbaye de Sainte-Croix (€€€)
Route du Val-de-Cuech, 13300
tel: 04 90 56 24 55 www.hotels-provence.com
Set in woodlands 5km (3 miles) east of Salon, this converted 12th-century abbey is one of the region's top hotels. Small but charming rooms in former monks' cells, sweeping views from the garden terraces; pool, restaurant.

VAR

Bandol
Master Ker-Mocotte (€€)
103 rue Raimu, 83150 tel: 04 94 29 46 53
fax: 04 94 32 53 54
A lovely old Provençal house in a prime position above the water, where the actor Jean Raimu once spent his holidays. Access to the beach below, pine-shaded garden, restaurant.

la Cadière d'Azur
Hostellerie Bérard (€€–€€€)
avenue Gabriel-Péri, 83740
tel: 04 94 90 11 43 fax: 04 94 90 01 94
www.hotel-berard.com
e-mail: berard@hotel-berard.com
Perched above terraced vineyards, this elegant country inn, set in a part of an 11th-century monastery, is run by the second generation of chef-hotelier Bérards. Appealing mix of traditional

Provençal antiques and modern comforts, pool, plus a wonderful restaurant.

le Castellet
Castel Lumière (€€)
2 rue Douce, 83330 tel: 04 94 32 62 20
www.castellumiere.fr
This handsome creeper-covered 17th-century house by the village gates has six comfortable rooms, a popular restaurant and a terrace.

Draguignan
du Parc (€–€€)
21 boulevard de la Liberté, 83300
tel: 04 98 10 14 50 www.hotel-duparc.fr
e-mail: hotelduparc93@wanadoo.fr
Five minutes' walk from the town centre, in a fine old house with jaunty blue shutters and a garden. Simply but thoughtfully furnished rooms (the quietest are at the back), plus a good regional restaurant downstairs.

Fréjus
L'Arena (€€)
145 rue de Général de Gaulle, 83600
tel: 04 94 17 09 40 fax: 04 94 52 01 52
www.arena-hotel.com
e-mail: info@arena-hotel.com
A cheerful modern hotel in the centre of town, run by charming staff. The rooms are decorated with bright prints and pottery, and stripey loungers await guests on the garden pool deck.

Hyères
du Soleil (€–€€)
rue du Rempart, 83400 tel: 04 94 65 16 26
fax: 04 94 35 46 00 www.hotel-du-soleil.fr
e-mail: soleil@hotel-du-soleil.fr
Very cosy and welcoming little hotel, redolent with the scent of the lavender bags kept in reception. Simple, quiet rooms with shutters overlook the hillside above the town centre. Parking can be a problem.

le Lavandou
Belle-Vue (€€–€€€)
chemin du Four des Maures, St.-Clair, 83980
tel: 04 94 00 45 00 fax: 04 94 00 45 25
e-mail: hotelbellevue@wanadoo.fr
Tranquil Logis set in flowery gardens with lovely views on the Corniche des Maures just east of the town centre. There is a sandy beach 100m (330ft) below the hotel. (Open Apr–Oct.)

St.-Raphaël
Golf de Valescure (€€€)
avenue Paul L'Hermite, 83700
tel: 04 94 52 85 00 fax: 04 94 82 41 88
www.golf-hotel-provence.com
e-mail: info@valescure.com
Golfer's haven 5km (3 miles) out of town surrounded by parasol pines and bordering the 100-year-old golf course. Comfortable, modern and well-equipped rooms with terrace-verandas. Pool, tennis, restaurant.
Hotel Excelsior (€€–€€€)
Promenade Rene Coty, 83700
tel: 04 94 95 02 42 www.excelsior-hotel.com

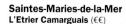

Set along the seafront promenade in central St-Raphael, this family-run hotel has beautiful sea views and is opposite the beach. The 40 rooms have modern decor. There's a shady terrace, an English pub and a gastronomic restaurant serving Provencal specialities with a good selection of local wines.

St.-Tropez
Le Byblos (€€€)
avenue Paul Signac, 83990
tel: 04 94 56 68 00 www.byblos.com
e-mail: saint-tropez@byblos.com
A deluxe Provençal village in miniature with artfully arranged groups of brightly painted and shuttered cottages in landscaped grounds. Fabulous pool, gym and restaurant. (Open Apr–Oct.)
Ermitage (€€–€€€)
avenue Paul Signac, 83990
tel: 04 94 97 52 33
This unpretentious hotel above the village is like a breath of fresh air. Grand views from the gardens and some of the 26 rooms. Open fire in winter and a genuine welcome.
Lou Cagnard (€€)
18 avenue Paul Roussel, 83990
tel: 04 94 97 04 24
www.hotel-lou-cagnard.com
Large and attractive house not far from the town centre. The 19 rooms have light, bright decor and country-style furniture, the nicest ones open directly onto the garden terrace. (Open New Year–Oct.)

Ste.-Maxime
de la Poste (€€–€€€)
11 boulevard Frédéric Mistral, 83120
tel: 04 94 55 58 63
www.hotelleriedusoleil.com
A symphony in cream and brown, this modern hotel, centrally located, looks rather uninspiring, but its rooms are very pleasant and good value. Gardens and pool.

Toulon
New Hotel La Tour Blanche (€€)
boulevard Amiral-Vence, 83000
tel: 04 94 24 41 57
www.new-hotel.com/TourBlanche
e-mail: toulontourblanche@new-hotel.com
Popular with the conference trade, this modern hotel has thoughtfully equipped rooms, a garden and pool. There are fantastic views over the city from the restaurant.

ALPES DE HAUTE-PROVENCE

Allos
Les Gentianes (€–€€)
Grand'Rue, 04260 tel: 04 92 83 03 50
Small and cosy Logis with nine rooms and a good restaurant (see page 281) that caters to hikers in the summer and skiers in the winter.

Annot
de l'Avenue (€–€€)
avenue de la Gare, 04240
tel: 04 92 83 22 07 www.hotel-avenue.com
Small but comfortable rooms at the right price in this modest hotel. The charm here is in the family atmosphere and the excellent restaurant. (Closed Nov–Mar.)

Barcelonnette
du Cheval Blanc (€–€€)
12 rue Grenette, 04400 tel: 04 92 81 00 19
fax: 04 92 81 15 39
Welcoming auberge that seems to attract a sporty clientele who park their bicycles in the old stables at night and dash off clutching a packed lunch by day. There are 20 rooms and a restaurant serving hearty food. (Closed Nov and 1–20 Apr.)
La Grande Epervière (€€)
18 boulevard des 3 Frères Arnaud
tel: 04 92 81 00 70
www.hotel-grande-eperviere.com
In a peaceful spot surrounded by its own park, this value-for-money low-key hotel-restaurant is extremely comfortable and has mountain views from every room. Children are welcome.

Castellane
La Forge (€)
place de l'Église, 04120 tel: 04 92 83 62 61
fax: 04 92 83 65 81
www.perso.orange.fr/forge
Pleasant little family-run hotel at the back of the main square. Simple but spotless rooms in an old house full of strange angles. Friendly restaurant frequented by locals. Good budget find at the eastern end of the Canyon du Verdon.

Château-Arnoux
La Bonne Étape (€€€)
chemin du Lac, 04160 tel: 04 92 64 00 09
fax: 04 92 64 37 36 www.bonneetape.com
Gorgeous waterfront Relais et Châteaux property set in an elegantly renovated 18th-century coaching inn. Lovely bedrooms in warm Provençal colours with antique furnishings and every comfort. Gardens, heated pool and famous restaurant (see page 282). (Closed Jan.)

Digne-les-Bains
Le Grand Paris (€€)
19 boulevard Thiers, 04000
tel: 04 92 31 11 15
www.hotel-grand-paris.com
Attractive rooms and apartments in a splendidly converted 17th-century convent building painted in shades of peach and terracotta. This friendly family-run hotel has a pretty, flowery terrace and a good restaurant.
Le Petit St.-Jean (€)
14 cours des Arès, 04000
tel: 04 92 31 30 04
An old-fashioned but quaint restaurant, with rooms to let, makes a useful stop for travellers on a budget. All rather creaky, but clean.

Forcalquier
Hostellerie des Deux Lions (€€)
place du Bourguet, 04300
tel: 04 92 75 25 30 www.lesdeuxlions.com
A welcoming provincial hotel in a 17th-century coaching house with pleasant rooms and a worthy restaurant.

275

Hotels and Restaurants

Gréoux-les Bains

Villa Borghese (€€€)
avenue des Thermes, 04800
tel: 04 92 78 00 91 www.villa-borghese.com
e-mail: villa.borghese@wanadoo.fr
Relaxing hotel with flower-filled balconies and
delightful rooms, pool, tennis and gardens. There
is a Health and Beauty centre and diet-conscious
dishes are also served in the restaurant. (Open
mid-Mar to early Dec.)

Moustiers-Ste.-Marie

La Bastide de Moustiers (€€€)
chemin de Quinson, 04360
tel: 04 92 70 47 47
www.bastide-moustiers.com
Alain Ducasse (Monaco and Paris) goes country in
this fabulous 17th-century farmhouse surrounded
by gardens and lavender fields. There are 11
delightful rooms and an apartment decorated with
antiques. The excellent young chef is following in
his master's footsteps.
Le Relais (€–€€)
place du Couvert, 04360 tel: 04 92 74 66 10
www.provenceweb.fr/04/uk.relais.htm
Very popular village centre inn, much in demand.
The old building and rooms are charming and the
restaurant serves good local dishes. (Closed
Nov–Feb.)

Sisteron

Grand Hôtel du Cours (€€)
place de l'Église (allée de Verdun), 04200
tel: 04 92 61 04 51 www.hotel-lecours.com
e-mail: hotelducours@wanadoo.fr
Traditional town centre hotel with 50 comfortable
and pleasant rooms; ask for a room facing the
cathedral and citadel. Helpful staff and a rather
pricey restaurant. (Open Mar–Oct.)
Hôtel-Restaurant La Citadelle (€–€€)
126 rue Saunerie, 04200 tel: 04 92 61 13 52
Well-run budget establishment on the far side of
the tunnel under Sisteron's mid-town cliff. Some of
the rooms have spectacular views over the
Durance valley or the mountains (well worth paying
a little extra for). Good restaurant (see page 282).

CÔTE D'AZUR/ALPES-MARITIMES

Antibes

Auberge Provençale (€€–€€€)
61 place Nationale, 06600
tel: 04 93 34 13 24
www.aubergeprovencale.com
Super small hotel in a former abbey building in the
heart of the old town. Seven delightful rooms with
antique furnishings and some four-poster beds.
Shady garden with tables spilling out from the
restaurant.
Hôtel du Cap Eden Roc (€€€)
boulevard J-F Kennedy, Cap d'Antibes, 06601
tel: 04 93 61 39 01 www.edenroc-hotel.fr
e-mail: reservations@hdcer.com
Glorious belle époque palace-hotel set in a park on
the tip of the Cap. Exquisite rooms containing
every conceivable luxury, elegant public spaces
and gourmet dining; pool, tennis, beach. (Open
mid-Apr to mid-Oct.)

Mas Djoliba (€€)
29 avenue de Provence, 06600, Cap d'Antibes
Juan-les-Pins tel: 04 93 34 02 48
www.hotel-djoliba.com
e-mail: contact@hotel-djoliba.com
Lovely old farmhouse within walking distance of
town and the beach. Pretty, romantic rooms; tree-
shaded gardens with pool and vine-covered terrace
for al fresco evening meals. Half-board obligatory
in season. (Open Feb–Oct.)

Beaulieu-sur-Mer

La Réserve de Beaulieu (€€€)
5 boulevard Maréchal Leclerc, 06310
tel: 04 93 01 00 01
www.reservebeaulieu.com
One of the classic seafront palace-hotels for which
Beaulieu and the Riviera are famous. Sumptuous
Florentine-Renaissance-style decor, fine dining,
gardens, heated saltwater pool, loyal clientele.
Le Select (€–€€)
1 place du Général-de-Gaulle
tel: 04 93 01 05 42
This is an absolute bargain for trendy Beaulieu.
Here, the friendly patron welcomes guests like
long-lost friends to his unpretentious domain.

Biot

Les Arcades (€–€€)
16 place des Arcades, 06410
tel: 04 93 65 01 04
This entertainingly eccentric bar/hotel/restaurant
is set in an ancient house (with more recent additions) and also boasts an art gallery. There are
three wacky grandes chambres (fireplaces, four-
posters and modern art), plus a handful of less
expensive creations.

Breil-sur-Roya

Le Castel du Roy (€€)
146 route de l"Aigara, 06540
tel: 04 93 04 43 66
www.castelduroy.com
Excellent base for exploring the mountainous backcountry that borders Italy. Fine modern hotel with
impeccable rooms and a restaurant set in gardens
by the river. There is a heated pool, games and
bicycles for guests to borrow.(Open Apr to mid-
Oct.)

Cagnes-sur-Mer

Le Val Duchesse (€–€€)
11 rue de Paris, 06800 tel: 04 92 13 40 00
www.levalduchesse.com
Cute and very reasonably priced Provençal-style
studios (2 persons) and apartments (4 persons) in
a quiet street two minutes from the seafront.
Basic kitchen facilities, sunny verandas, garden
pool, child-friendly.

Cannes

Carlton Inter-Continental (€€€)
58 La Croisette, 06400 tel: 04 93 06 40 06
www.intercontinental.com
The magnificent facade of this grand hotel is a
familiar Riviera landmark. Inside, the keynote is
luxury on a palatial scale. Private beach, fitness
club, casino, gourmet restaurant.

Le Chanteclair (€€)
12 rue Forville
tel: 04 93 39 68 88
Great budget find a few streets back from the
Vieux Port and close to all the action, offering
simple yet comfortable rooms. (Closed mid-Nov to
mid-Feb.)
Le Provence (€€)
9 rue Molière, 06400
tel: 04 93 38 44 35
fax: 04 93 39 63 14
www.hotel-de-provence.com
e-mail: contact@hotel-de-provence.com
Delightful little oasis of tranquillity close to La
Croisette. Tree-shaded gardens out front and all the
attractive double rooms have verandas with window
boxes, as well as air-conditioning.

Èze

Château de la Chèvre d'Or (€€€)
rue du Barri, Moyenne Corniche, 06360
tel: 04 92 10 66 66
www.relaisetchateaux.fr/chevredor
e-mail: reservation@chevredor.com
Gorgeous collection of old stone buildings with
flower-filled terraces, pool and stunning sea views
from the *village perché*. Elegant antique-filled
rooms and suites. Three restaurants with superb
service. (Closed Nov to mid-Mar.)

Grasse

Le Patti (€€)
place du Patti, 06130
tel: 04 93 36 01 00
www.hotelpatti.com
Right in the heart of the old town, the Patti offers
bright modern rooms and slightly more expensive
chambres de charme decorated with pretty fabrics.
Restaurant with summer terrace.

Juan-les-Pins

Sainte-Valérie (€€€)
rue de l'Oratoire, 06160 tel: 04 93 61 07 15
ww.juanlespins.net
e-mail: saintevalerie@juanlespins.net
Bijou little hotel with 30 romantic rooms, in a quiet
spot a short walk from the beach, behind the
Pinède Gould. Shady garden brightened up by
colourful bougainvillaea and a pool. (Open late Apr
to mid-Oct.)

Menton

Aiglon (€€–€€€)
7 avenue de la Madone, 06500
tel: 04 93 57 55 55
www.hotelaiglon.net
A gracious and romantic 1880s garden villa perfectly in tune with Menton's Victorian heyday. 29
rooms with little balconies, poolside seafood
restaurant, a 3-minute stroll from the beach.
Beauregard (€)
10 rue Albert-1er, 06500
tel: 04 93 28 63 63
email: beauregard.menton@wanadoo.fr
A real old-fashioned budget option in a quiet
backstreet near the seafront. Tall town house
fronted by a terrace, with simple bedrooms and
a restaurant. (Closed Oct–Jan.)

Monaco/Monte-Carlo

France (€€)
6 rue de la Turbie, Monaco tel: 377 93 30 24
64 www.monte-carlo.mc/france
Comfortable, modern rooms with showers in a flat-
fronted town house on a quiet street above the
port in La Condamine.
Hôtel de Paris (€€€)
place du Casino, Monte-Carlo, 98000
tel: 377 98 06 25 25
www.montecarloresort.com
e-mail: hp@sbm.mc
The most prestigious address in Monte-Carlo, frequented by royalty and rakes for almost 150 years.
Plush Louis XV-style rooms (sea views at a premium), opulent public areas and a lucky statue of
Louis XIV for gamblers.

Nice

La Belle Meunière (€)
21 avenue Durante, 06000
tel: 04 93 88 66 15 www.bellemeuniere.com
email: hotel.belle.meuniere@cegetel.net
A budget hotel close to the station, but very hospitable, clean and comfortable. A big plus here is
the shady garden, which provides a welcome
retreat from the city bustle. (Open Feb–Nov.)

277

Negresco (€€€)
37 promenade des Anglais, 06000
tel: 04 93 16 64 00
www.hotel-negresco-nice.com
Nice's flagship hotel is one of the great (though a
little faded) landmarks of the Riviera. Opulent *belle
époque* architecture, luxurious rooms decorated
with original artworks, and impeccable service.
Villa La Tour Hotel (€–€€)
4 rue de la Tour, 06300
tel: 04 93 80 08 15 www.villa-la-tour.com
Set in a former convent, this small hotel has 16
charmingly decorated rooms, a cosy roof garden
and a great location in the heart of the old town.
Windsor (€€–€€€)
11 rue Dalpozzo, 06000 tel: 04 93 88 59 35
www.hotel/windsornice.com
This characterful hotel is set in a fantastic city
garden and each room is decorated with murals or
styled by a particular designer. *Al fresco* dining,
pool, sauna, Turkish bath, massage.

Vence

La Roseraie (€€–€€€)
128 avenue Henri Giraud, 06140
tel: 04 93 58 02 20
A delightful little hotel situated on the edge of
Vence with a pretty terrace and pool. The rooms
are warm, light and full of thoughtful touches,
and the owners go to great lengths to make all
their guests welcome. (Open mid-Feb to mid-Nov.)

Villefranche-sur-Mer

Welcome (€€–€€€)
1 quai Courbet, 06230 tel: 04 93 76 27 62
www.welcomehotel.com
Famous hotel that can count artists and writers
such as Jean Cocteau and Somerset Maugham
among its past guests. It enjoys a grand position
on the seafront, with well-furnished and equipped
rooms, and two restaurants.

RESTAURANTS

The following restaurants have been divided into three price categories based on a three-course meal (this can be a set menu) exclusive of wine and service:

budget (€) up to €20
moderate (€€) €21–45
expensive (€€€) over €45

VAUCLUSE

Apt
Auberge du Luberon (€)
8 place du Faubourg du Ballet, 84400
tel: 04 90 74 12 50
Maître Cuisinier de France, Serge Peuzin, is in charge of the kitchen behind this sunny dining room and summer terrace. Luberon lamb (lamb's tongue salad and a delicous basil-flavoured daube) are popular, as are local crystallized fruits.

Avignon
Hiély (€€)

5 rue de la République, 84000
tel: 04 90 86 17 07
With its long-standing reputation for fine dining, this unassuming restaurant rarely disappoints. Memorable salt cod roasted in olive oil with slivers of lemon and juniper berries, plus a wine list pleasingly heavy on Côtes du Rhone reds.
Rose au Petit Bedon (€€)
70 rue Joseph-Vernet tel: 04 90 82 33 98
Generous portions of Provençal cooking with innovative touches served in a country chic dining-room. *Coq à la royale* marinated with onions, rosemary, and thyme; lambs' kidneys with Camarguais salt.
Le Venaissin (€)
place de l'Horloge tel: 04 90 86 20 99
The best-value (and busiest) brasserie-restaurant on the square, so be sure to arrive early for a table. Grilled sole, salads, crêpes and regional fried aubergine (eggplant) provençale are popular.
Le Vernet (€€)
58 rue Joseph-Vernet tel: 04 90 86 64 53
The perfect setting on a summer's day with tree-shaded tables in the walled garden of a handsome town house. Creamy soup of Puy lentils and smoked duck, fillet of sea bass with stewed fennel.
Woolloomooloo (€)
16 bis rue des Teinturiers tel: 04 90 85 28 44
Funky spot set in the middle of a miniature "restaurant row" on this pretty street. World cuisine (Oriental lamb, Greek salad, Moroccan chicken tajine) served in a candlelit den of bric-à-brac.

Carpentras
Le Marijo (€)
73 rue Raspail, 84200 tel: 04 90 60 42 65
Cheerful, intimate restaurant in the town centre. Provençal fabrics adorn the tables and the waitresses. Regional menu includes pickled artichokes with tapenade and *filet de dorade Mistral* (bream).
Le Vert Galant (€€)
12 rue Clapiès tel: 04 90 67 15 50
A hand-painted facade fronts this attractive little

dining-room. Imaginative cuisine, known for its seafood and a *Menu Découverte aux Truffes.*

Cavaillon
Fin de Siècle (€€)
46 place du Clos, 84300 tel: 04 90 71 12 27
Café-restaurant with brass and glass in *fin de siècle* style serving tempting dishes such as delicately spiced scallops, at very reasonable prices.

Fontaine de Vaucluse
Restaurant Philip (€–€€)
Chemin de la Fontaine, 84800
tel: 04 90 20 31 81
Follow the footpath along the river to the foot of the soothing cascades and find a table on the terrace for a mixed bag of seafood and grills or snacks and sandwiches from the bar.

Gigondas
Les Florets (€€)
route des Dentelles, 84190
tel: 04 90 65 85 01
In a pine forest 1.5km (1 mile) outside the wine village of Gigondas, this popular hotel-restaurant is excellent value for money. House special dishes include *noisettes d'agneau à la crème d'ail.* 15 rustic rooms (€€€).

Gordes
La Bastide de Gordes (€€€)
Le Village, 84220 tel: 04 90 72 12 12
Set on a hilltop in a 16th-century manor house, this elegant hotel and spa has a superb restaurant. Mediterranean cuisine is complemented by an extensive wine cellar, and there are stunning views from the veranda and terrace.
Comptoir du Victuailler (€€–€€€)
place du Château tel: 04 90 72 01 31
Sophisticated bistro with a fine reputation for Provençal cuisine. The "must have" here is the *grand aïoli de morue fraîche,* a heroic platter of cod and seasonal vegetables topped with garlic mayonnaise.

L'Isle-sur-la-Sorgue
Le Carré d'Herbes (€)
13 avenue des Quatre-Otages, 84800
tel: 04 90 38 62 95
Tucked into a courtyard surrounded by an eclectic collection of *objets de hasard* (antique bathtubs, iron gates, statuary), this is a great lunch stop. Fresh and tasty soups, salads, *tartes* and puds.
Le Pescador (€–€€)
le Partage des Eaux tel: 04 90 38 09 69
Pick a sunny day for the Hôtel Le Pescador's shady terrace overlooking the "parting of the waters" as the Sorgue divides around town. Fresh trout (naturally) and *bouillabaisse* are favourites.

Malaucène
Hostellerie La Chevalerie (€€)
place de l'Église, 84340 tel: 04 90 65 11 19
In a charming location with a garden terrace enclosed by the ancient ramparts, this Logis (with six rooms) offers a choice of regional menus. Hare terrine with an onion confit, kid with rosemary and garlic; also wild boar.

Orange

Le Parvis (€€)
3 cours Pourtoules, 84100 tel: 04 90 34 82 00
Smart little restaurant widely recommended for its
Provençal cooking with innovative touches. Dishes
range from seafood—*escalope de loup* (bass) with
fennel—to lamb.

Le Yaca (€)
24 place Sylvain (rue de la Tourre)
tel: 04 90 34 70 03
Cheery tablecloths, fresh flowers and home-cooking create a warm ambience. A variety of terrines
Provençale followed by grilled herbed lamb.

Roussillon

Mincka's (€)
place de la Mairie, 84220 tel: 04 90 05 66 22
Squirrelled into a tiny square and surrounded by
old pink and ochre buildings, this is a relaxing spot
with a delicious and unusual choice of salads and
other dishes dictated by what's best and fresh in
the market.

Vaison-la-Romaine

Le Bateleur (€–€€)
1 place Théodore-Aubanel, 84110
tel: 04 90 36 28 04
Small, friendly restaurant with lace curtains near
the Roman bridge. Traditional cooking, from a
terrine aux poissons or a leek and onion tart to
veal fricassé with celery and green olives.

Le Moulin à Huile (€€€)
quai Marechal Foch, 84110
tel: 04 90 36 20 67
An old oil mill beside the river makes a charming
setting for enjoying this impressive regional cuisine prepared with creative modern accents. Dine
on the veranda overlooking the lovely garden terrace or in the vaulted cellar.

BOUCHES-DU-RHÔNE

Aix-en-Provence

Le Bistro Latin (€–€€)
18 rue de la Couronne, 13100
tel: 04 42 38 22 88
Busy little apricot-coloured dining room serving
excellent *menus du marché* and pricier options.
Green lentil terrine with *saucisses vinaigrette au
parmesan, pot au feu.*

La Brocherie (€€)
5 rue Fernand Dol tel: 04 42 38 33 21
Sedate atmosphere and a rustic feel with game
spit-roasted beneath a large chimney. Also fish
dishes such as stuffed mussels and salmon fillet
with basil.

Le Grillon (€–€€)
49 cours Mirabeau tel: 04 42 27 58 81
Green-and-white striped awnings spread over the
pavement and bustling waiters serving up chicken
and chips, steaks, omelettes, pasta, club sandwiches and other bistro-type fare.

L'Hacienda (€)
7 rue Mérindol tel: 04 42 27 00 35
Pint-sized restaurant with tables on a shady square
in summer. Crab gratin, Roquefort salad, grilled
lamb *aux herbes de Provence*, paella au aïoli (Fri),
or chili, and brownies for homesick Americans!

Arles

Brasserie Nord-Pinus (€€)
place du Forum, 13200 tel: 04 90 93 44 44
Fashionable diners flock to this busy brasserie
which overflows onto the square. Light but assured
Provençal cooking: aubergine (eggplant)
millefeuille, bream in a herb crust.

Lou Marquès (€€€)
Hôtel Jules César, 9 boulevard des Lices
tel: 04 90 52 52 52
Gourmet restaurant in Arles' smartest hotel (€€€).
Wood panelling and restful shades of brown and
green set the scene for fine classic cuisine: lobster consommé with scallops, veal with tarragon
and red Camarguais rice flavoured with *cèpes.*

La Gueule du Loup (€€)
39 rue des Arènes tel: 04 90 96 96 69
Swags of creepers swathe the shuttered facade of
this small but seriously good restaurant. Provençal
flavours, from the lamb *en croûte* with its pastry
jacket spread with pungent olive tapenade, to
nougat ice cream.

Le 16 (€)
16 rue du Docteur-Fanton tel: 04 90 93 77 36
This restaurant offers an extensive choice of
imaginative salads and other healthy eats such as
plates of Provençal- or Greek-style crudités, pasta
dishes and fresh fruit and vegetable juices (as well
as wine).

Les Baux-de-Provence

La Reine Jeanne (€–€€)
rue Porte Mage, 13520 tel: 04 90 54 32 06
Very pleasant hotel (€€) dining room at the
entrance to the village. Large picture windows, a
summer terrace, good home-cooking and attentive,
friendly service.

L'Oustau de Baumanière (€€€)
Val d'Enfer tel: 04 90 54 33 07
fax: 04 90 54 40 46
www.oustaudebaumaniere.com
Garlanded with awards, this renowned hotel-
restaurant occupies a gorgeous old farmhouse
with tree-shaded terraces. Jean-André Charial's
exquisite ravioli with truffles and leeks and lamb
"cooked for seven hours" are legendary.

Cassis

Chez César (€–€€)
21 quai des Baux, 13260 tel: 04 42 01 75 47
Cassis' waterfront restaurants are not renowned
for their budget prices, however this is one of the
few where you can enjoy the port's famous fresh
seafood without breaking the bank.

Marseille

Les Arcenaulx (€€)
25 cours d'Estienne d'Orves, 13000
tel: 04 91 59 80 30
Housed in an ancient arsenal with massive book-
lined stone walls, this atmospheric regional
restaurant serves a delicious fish soup, artichoke
barigoule and stews. Excellent value lunch menu.

Chez Etienne (€–€€)
43 rue de Lorette
tel: 04 91 73 31 55
It's a favourite with sports stars and actors, but
the genial Etienne welcomes everyone alike to this

279

warm, homely Italian restaurant tucked away in the Panier quarter. Enjoy seafood pasta, pizza from the wood-fired oven or more adventurous specialities such as lamb's foot

Chez Fonfon (€€–€€€)
140 Vallon des Auffes tel: 04 91 52 14 38
The *bouillabaisse* at Chez Fonfon is legendary. This famous seafood establishment overlooks the waterfront in a small fishing harbour east of the city centre.

Chez Madie (€€)
138 quai du Port
tel: 04 91 90 40 87
Escape the bustle of the city at this friendly restaurant at the far end of the quai du Port. Tables are set along the pavement to catch the sea breeze. The menu of fresh modern cuisine features such delectable dishes as duck breast with figs and red mullet tart.

Restaurant Miramar (€€–€€€)
12 quai du Port
tel: 04 91 91 10 40
Try *bouillabaisse* at its best in this elegant restaurant beside the Vieux Port. Whether you dine on the outdoor terrace or the formal dining room, Chef Christian Buffa's seafood dishes are inspired and the service is impeccable.

Maussane-les-Alpilles
Ou Ravi Provençau (€€)
34 avenue de la Vallée-des-Baux, 13520
tel: 04 90 54 31 11
A small restaurant with a big reputation for simply prepared but flavoursome local cooking. A popular dish is *pieds et paquets* (pigs' trotters and tripe) but there are plenty of less adventurous options.

Nîmes
Chez Jacotte (€€€)
15 rue Fresque, 30000 tel: 04 66 21 64 59
Snug little spot tucked down a dead-end alley, but there is nothing dead-end about the warm welcome and great food. Duck breast with peaches, ravioli with basil, mouthwatering home-made pastries.

L'Enclos de la Fontaine (€€–€€€)
Hôtel Impérator Concorde, quai de la Fontaine
tel: 04 66 21 90 30
Light glass-fronted dining room opening onto a pretty garden terrace. The equally light, classic and appealing menu might offer a lobster salad followed by red mullet flavoured with anchovy paste.

Le Paradis du Couvent (€)
21 rue du Grand Couvent tel: 04 66 76 26 30
Five different budget menus, salads, fresh pasta, seafood, and *specialités nîmoises* served up in an historic stone-walled and beamed dining-room or outside on the terrace.

St.-Rémy-de-Provence
La Gousse d'Ail (€–€€)
25 rue Carnot, 13210 tel: 04 90 92 16 87
An intimate old town dining room, where strong flavours of Provence emanate from the stove: escargots, lamb with creamed garlic (*ail*), *bouillabaisse* on Tuesdays. There is a jazz evening on Thursdays.

Le Marceau–Alain Assaud (€€)
13 boulevard Marceau tel: 04 90 92 37 11
Bare stone walls and antique-rustic chic, plus a chef who has paid his dues in some smart kitchens. Dishes include a *galette* of fresh tomatoes and basil, cod *aïoli*, and pigeon with lentils.

Salon-de-Provence
Mas de Soleil (€€–€€€)
38 chemin St.-Côme, 13300
tel: 04 90 56 06 53
François Robin's cuisine is *la gastronomie provençale*, and he brings a light, assured hand to a fragrant mussel soup, chicken and artichokes flavoured with thyme, and red mullet with basil and red pepper butter.

VAR

Bandol
Auberge du Port (€€)
9 allée Jean-Moulin, 83150 tel: 04 94 29 42 63
Across the street from the marina, this big and busy seafood restaurant spreads out onto the pavement. *Bouillabaisse*, *bourride* (fish soup-like stew), seafood paella and fish couscous all appear on the huge menu.

Le Clocher (€€)
1 rue Paroisse, 83150
tel: 04 94 32 47 65
It's a good idea to book ahead for this small but highly rated restaurant in the old quarter. Simple, stylish decor complements the delicious modern dishes, and guests are warmly welcomed.

Le Beausset
La Grange (€–€€)
34 boulevard Chanzy, 83330
tel: 04 94 90 40 22
Busy local restaurant with open-spit fire. Try Bandol wines with regional favourites such as rabbit terrine or smoked duck, *foie gras* and chicken livers, omelettes or fresh fish from the coast.

Bormes-les-Mimosas
La Tonnelle des Délices (€–€€)
place Gambetta, 83230 tel: 04 94 71 34 84
Among a clutch of café-restaurants, the Tonnelle is the nicest and most interesting. Roast cod with tapenade and pistou, aubergine (eggplant) compôte with tomatoes, leeks and parmesan, homemade nougat ice cream.

La Cadière d'Azur
Hostellerie Bérard (€€–€€€)
avenue Gabriel-Péri, 83740 tel: 04 94 90 11 43
Panoramic views play second fiddle to René Bérard's outstanding Provençal cooking. Truffles from Aups, lasagne of purple artichokes, fennel, tomatoes and roasted prawns, fillet of beef with a fondue of shallots may make you want to sign up for a cooking course.

Fréjus
Cadet Rousselle (€)
25 place Agricola, 83600 tel: 04 94 53 36 92
Handy *crêperie* for a light lunch. Ham or warm

goats' cheese *galettes*, a wide choice of salads, and sweet chestnut *crêpes* with vanilla ice cream and piles of chantilly to finish.

Les Potiers (€–€€)
135 rue des Potiers tel: 04 94 51 33 74
Diminutive little dining room on a quiet backstreet with a long-standing reputation for straightforward classic cooking. Duck with seasonal fruits, rabbit flavoured with *herbes de Provence*.

Grimaud
Café de France (€–€€)
place Neuve, 83310 tel: 04 94 43 20 05
The large, vine-covered terrace is a lovely spot for lunch in the hills behind the coast. A well-priced menu features the likes of rabbit with mustard, salad and steaks.

Hyères
Les Jardins de Bacchus (€€–€€€)
32 avenue Gambetta, 83400
tel: 04 94 65 77 63
The "gardens" are hand-painted or potted in this elegant dining room, which has a long-standing reputation for stylish regional cuisine. Baked tomato tart with quail breasts, stuffed chicken in a basil sauce.

La Reine Jane (€–€€)
Port de l'Ayguade tel: 04 94 66 32 64
Dine on the waterfront terrace of this popular hotel-restaurant overlooking the port. The menu features plenty of fresh seafood and *bouillabaisse* at very reasonable prices.

Le Lavandou
Auberge Provençale (€–€€)
11 rue Patron Ravello, 83980
tel: 04 94 71 00 44
Conveniently situated on a pedestrianized street one back from the waterfront, this rustic auberge cooks up regional favourites, from rabbit baked with prunes and fresh herbs to *la fameuse aïoli* and *bourride*.

St.-Tropez
Bistro des Lices (€€)
3 place des Lices, 83990
tel: 04 94 55 82 82
This fashionable bistro flourishes well away from the port. Robust flavours combined with a rare gentle touch create risotto with *cèpes* and dried tomatoes, delicious sea bream with anchovies, and lamb with basil.

Le Girelier (€€–€€€)
quai Jean-Jaurès tel: 04 94 97 03 87
A long-time favourite for excellent Mediterranean seafood and notable poseurs' paradise right on the harbourfront. However, the classic *bouillabaisse* and plain grilled seafood plus the view probably justify the prices.

Spoon Byblos (€€€)
avenue Pal-Signac
tel: 04 94 56 68 20
Hotel Byblos is the setting for the St-Trop branch of masterchef Alain Ducasse's trendy Spoon restaurants. The multi-cultural cuisine ranges from inspired seafood dishes to regional Spanish and Moroccan specialities, accompanied by an extensive wine list. The chic decor and fashionable background music add to the occasion.

La Table du Marché (€€–€€€)
38 rue Georges Clemenceau
tel: 04 94 97 85 20
Provençal specialities from Chef Christophe Leroy are at the heart of this delightful bistro. Comfy armchairs, bookshelves and warm regional hues create a relaxed setting in the dining room. You can have a light snack or a set menu, and there's an afternoon tearoom and a sushi bar in summer.

Toulon
Le Cellier (€)
52 rue Jean-Jaurès, 83000
tel: 04 94 92 64 35
Tiled floor and beams set the basic scene for good home-cooking and a warm welcome. Skate with a green olive cream sauce, *coq au vin*, spiced fillet of wild boar.

Le Gros Ventre (€€)
Littoral Frédéric Mistral, Le Mourillon
tel: 04 94 42 15 42
Alain Audibert's *restaurant gastronomique* to the east of the city with a waterfront terrace overlooking Port St.-Louis. Seasonal cuisine with a noticeable seafood bias: fish in puff pastry is a favourite.

ALPES DE HAUTE-PROVENCE

Allos
Les Gentianes (€–€€)
Grand'Rue, 04260
tel: 04 92 83 03 50
Madame Millou ensures her guests and other diners set out to hike or take advantage of Allos' winter sports scene fully fuelled with good home-cooking, from generous stews and pasta dishes to steak and chips.

Annot
L'Avenue (€–€€)
avenue de la Gare, 04240
tel/fax: 04 92 83 22 07
A family-run concern with a well-deserved reputation for good, honest regional food served up in generous quantities. Memorable red mullet tartlet with ratatouille and summery poached figs in local wine.

Barcelonnette
La Mangeoire (€€)
place des Quatre-Vents, 04400
tel: 04 92 81 01 61
Popular restaurant in an old sheep barn where young chef Loïc Balanec is busy creating quite a name for himself. Delicous tartlet of assorted cheeses with tomato and basil sauce, pigeon with Provençal vegetable ratatouille. Reservations advised.

Le Passe Montagne (€€–€€€)
Route du Col de la Cayolle
tel: 04 92 81 08 58
Take the D902 a short distance south of town to this friendly chalet-restaurant. Generous mountain cooking such as marinated roast lamb with bilberries. Roaring fire to warm diners on cold days and a terrace for the sun.

Hotels and Restaurants

Castellane
Auberge du Teillon (€–€€)
Route Napoléon, 04120 (5km/3 miles south on the N85) tel: 04 92 83 60 88
A great little restaurant with rooms (€–€€). Rustic dining room serving regional dishes such as rack of lamb provençal. Summer terrace. (Open mid-Mar to mid-Nov.)

Château-Arnoux
Au Goût du Jour (€)
chemin du Lac, 04160 tel: 04 92 64 48 48
If you cannot afford the Bonne Étape's prices (see below), then check out Jany Gleize's bistro next door. Attractive dining room and even more attractive prices for a marinated fish salad with Camarguais rice or duck with olives.
La Bonne Étape (€€€)
chemin du Lac tel: 04 92 64 00 09
Chef Jany Gleize's copiously garlanded restaurant is a highlight on any gourmet pilgrimage to Provence. Local ingredients prepared with subtle flair: pigeon *en cocotte* with shallots and baby potatoes flavoured with tapenade, roast lamb on the bone with a truffle *jus*.

Digne-les-Bains
Le Grand Paris (€€–€€€)
19 boulevard Thiers tel: 04 92 31 11 15
Set in a 17th-century convent that has been converted into a hotel, this pleasant restaurant has a gorgeous terrace set around a fountain and shaded by tall trees. It specializes in traditional French and Provençal cuisine, accompanied by a good selection of regional wines.
L'Origan (€–€€)
6 rue Pied de Ville, 04000 tel: 04 92 31 62 13
In the pedestrianized town centre, this local restaurant offers a good value *formule provençale* (set menu) and more elaborate choices. Classic dishes include a hearty *pieds et paquets* (trotters and tripe), scallops poached in olive-tapenade butter, and a chestnut tart.

Forcalquier
Le Lapin Tant Pis (€–€€)
place Vieille, 04300 tel: 04 92 75 38 88
Tucked behind its delicatessen, this sunny Provençal dining room is a great find. Market-fresh produce is used to create equally sunny flavours, from a mozarella pastry with sun-dried tomatoes to lamb with polenta and black olive *jus*.

Gréoux-les Bains
La Crémaillère (€–€€)
Route de Riez, 04800 tel: 04 92 70 40 04
Delightful bright and sunny hotel (€€, open Mar to mid-Dec) dining room in yellows and blues with sprouting potted greenery and French windows. Light and flavoursome Provençal dishes.

Moustiers-Ste.-Marie
Jadis (€)
rue Courtil, 04360 tel: 04 92 74 63 01
Tucked away on the corner of a cobbled backstreet, Jadis is the acceptable (and affordable) face of this tourist-trap village. Pizzas from the wood-fired oven, pasta dishes and hearty stews in winter.

Prads-Haute-Bléone
L'Auberge des Trois Évêchés (€)
04420 tel: 04 92 34 92 42
One for the adventurous, this welcoming *auberge* is so far up the Bléone valley, north of Digne, that you almost run out of road. Unpretentious, hearty and delicious regional cooking; the quail stuffed with prunes comes highly recommended. (Open Apr–Sep.)

Sisteron
Les Becs Fins (€–€€)
16 rue Saunerie, 04200 tel: 04 92 61 12 04
Sisteron lamb is the best-known dish of the region and this accomplished restaurant is a good place to try it. Also duck with Provençal herbs, prawns flamed in *pastis*, and a gourmet menu featuring a cassoulette of *escargots au champagne*.
Hôtel-Restaurant de la Citadelle (€)
126 rue Saunerie, 04200 tel: 04 92 61 13 52
There are wonderful views from the terrace of this touristy traditional restaurant decorated with copper pots and dodgy landscape paintings. The *marmite du pêcheur* (fish stew) is a house favourite, also omelettes, salads and pizzas.

CÔTE D'AZUR/ALPES-MARITIMES

Antibes
La Bonne Auberge (€€–€€€)
Route de Nice, 06600 (N7; 4km/2.5 miles east of town) tel: 04 93 33 36 65
This smart villa looks rather out of place beside the busy N7. However, all is peace and elegance within and Philip Rostang's superb lobster salad with ravioli, pike quenelles and seven-hour lamb are things of classic beauty.
Le Clafoutis (€€)
18 rue Thuret tel: 04 93 34 66 70
Small and simple dining room with plain wooden tables and posters on the wall. However, Gérard Montaron's regional menu keeps diners happy with veal and artichokes, fresh fish in pistou, and crayfish tails in niçoise butter.
La Marmite (€)
20 rue James-Close tel: 04 93 34 56 79
Seafood heads the menu at this friendly place down a narrow pedestrian alley in the old town. The house special is a *cassoulet* of mussels and prawns Provençal, or sample the fresh sea bass with basil butter.

Cagnes-sur-Mer
Fleur de Sel (€€)
85 Montée de la Bourgade tel: 04 93 20 33 33
In an old stone house next to the church, this charming, rustic restaurant features an open kitchen hung with copper utensils, two dining rooms with Provençal colours, furniture and paintings, and delicious contemporary cuisine.

Cannes
Au Bec Fin (€)
12 rue du 24-Août, 06400 tel: 04 93 38 35 86
The decor may not inspire but almost every dish is appetizing and well-presented. Generous portions

of classic home-cooking and interesting *plats du jour*, fresh fish straight from the port.

Lou Souléou (€€)
16 boulevard Jean-Hibert tel: 04 93 39 85 55
Dining room with a nautical theme somewhat off the tourist track, with views of the sea and Esterel *massif*. Fish is king here; try a hearty *bourride* (chunky fish soup) laden with croutons and cheese.

La Palme d'Or (€€€)
Hôtel Martinez, 73 boulevard de la Croisette tel: 04 92 98 74 14
Stylish and inventive Mediterranean cuisine served in wonderfully ornate surroundings. Lamb with almonds and lemon thyme; John Dory flavoured with parsley and olives on a bed of grilled vegetables. Huge wine list.

Èze

Auberge du Troubadour (€€)
4 rue Brec, 06360 tel: 04 93 41 19 03
Antique house near the medieval village entrance, a warm welcome, and a Provençal menu featuring the likes of stuffed courgette flowers with truffle butter and *millefeuille* of escargots with pistou.

Grasse

Auberge le Vieux Château (€€)
place du Panorama, Cabris (5km/3 miles west via D4 or D11, 06530 tel: 04 93 60 50 12
By the château ruins in this glorious *village perché* just outside Grasse, the *auberge* offers stunning views from its terrace, a rustic dining-room, traditional dishes such as mountain lamb with a herb crust, and four attractive rooms.

Juan-les-Pins

Le Capitole (€)
26 avenue Amiral-Courbet, 06160 tel: 04 93 61 22 44
The menu offered at Le Capitole represents remarkably good value for this neck of the woods. Seafood specials include fish soup with croutons and *rouille* (a spiced garlic mayonnaise) and fresh scallops, also homemade nougat ice cream.

La Juana Terrasse (€€€)
avenue Georges Gallice tel: 04 93 61 20 37
Overlooking the pine trees at La Pinède, this is one of the top gourmet spots along the Riviera coast. Sample impeccable scampi raviolis or roast sea bass accompanied by pumpkin poached with thyme and a delicate seafood sauce in amazing 1930s surroundings.

Menton

L'Exocet (€–€€)
3 rue Trenca, 06500 tel: 04 93 28 80 24
Traditional seafood establishment with rather a formal table arrangement but a good line in platters of fresh *fruits de mer*, *bouillabaisse* (for two) and a few pasta dishes. Near to the seafront, rue Trenca is something of a mini-restaurant row.

Monaco/Monte-Carlo

Castelroc (€€)
place du Palais, Monaco-Ville, MC 98000 tel: 377 93 30 36 68
A busy pine-shaded terrace opposite the palace and a traditional menu make this a favourite stop

on the tourist trail. Try the *Monegasque stocafi* (stockfish) cooked with garlic, white wine, tomatoes and olives.

Le Louis XV (€€€)
Hôtel de Paris, place du Casino tel: 377 92 16 30 01
Alain Ducasse's gastronomic shrine basks in rather unsuitably lavish and gilded surroundings for his deceptively simple creations. Tender young pigeon breast stuffed with *foie gras* or sautéed sole with baby fennel are, in reality, unforgettable taste sensations.

Polpetta (€€)
2 rue Paradis, Monte-Carlo tel: 377 93 50 67 84
Bustling rustic-style Italian trattoria, ever-popular with locals and visitors alike. Tuck into a tempting array of antipasti, steaming plates of homemade pastas, seafood risotto or veal. Lengthy Italian wine list.

Nice

Acchiardo (€)
38 rue Droite, 06000 tel: 04 93 85 51 16
Popular and busy little local restaurant serving a variety of excellent regional and Italian dishes, such as steaming bowls of pasta, at incredibly reasonable prices (no credit cards).

L'Âne Rouge (€€–€€€)
7 quai des Deux Emmanuel tel: 04 93 89 49 63
This is a highly rated Niçois establishment with a leaning towards seafood, and where better to sample the catch of the day simmered *à la niçoise* (tomatoes, onions and garlic) than on the terrace overlooking the port?

Atmosphère (€–€€)
36 cours Saleya tel: 04 93 80 52 50
Long-established seafood restaurant with a delightful ambience and classic cooking plus Niçois delicacies at affordable prices in the colourful market district.

La Zucca Magica (€€)
4 bis quai Papacino tel: 04 93 56 25 27
The "magic pumpkin" is a local rarity, a decidedly eccentric but very good vegetarian restaurant run by a cousin of opera giant Luciano Pavarotti. No-choice menu, but everything is fresh and delicious from Roman-inspired lentil dishes to tasty pasta creations.

Vence

La Farigoule (€–€€)
15 rue Henri-Isnard, 06140 tel: 04 93 58 01 27
La Farigoule specializes in genuine Provençal country cooking of a consistently high standard. The shady patio-garden at the back is a lovely place for a relaxed, light lunch, such as an omelette with fresh herbs; more weighty dishes in the evening.

Villefranche-sur-Mer

La Mère Germaine (€€)
9 quai Courbet, 06230 tel: 04 93 01 71 39
One of the largest and most popular waterfront seafood restaurants, serving *bouillabaisse* and a well-priced set menu based on the catch of the day.

Index

Index

Picture credits

The Automobile Association would like to thank the following photographers, libraries and associations for their assistance in the preparation of this book.
ART DIRECTORS & TRIP PHOTO LIBRARY 218
THE BRIDGEMAN ART LIBRARY St.-Tropez, Pinewood, 1896 by Paul Signac (1863–1935), Musée de l'Annonciade, St.-Tropez, France © ADAGP, Paris and DACS, London 2007 24; Self portrait c.1879–85 (oil on canvas) by Paul Cézanne (1839–1906), Pushkin Museum, Moscow, Russia 25
COURTAULD GALLERIES 107 Cézanne "Still Life with Apples, Bottle and Chairback," 112b Vincent Van Gogh "Self Portrait with Bandaged Ear"
DACS© ADAGP Paris and DACS, London 2000 Ile Prophete Elie, 1970 (Il Rois, 11–13), Detail, Marc Chagall
MARY EVANS PICTURE LIBRARY 28 Greek heptareme, 32 Troubadour, 36/7 Louis XIV, 37 Bishop of Marseille, 39a Execution of Robespierre, 40 Somerset Maugham
FOOTPRINTS COLOUR PICTURE LIBRARY 13b Cassis, 14/5, 15 Farmhouse, 116 Gardian's cabane, Camargue, 117a Trees, Camargue, 124 Walkers (N. Hanna)
RONALD GRANT ARCHIVES 210/1 The Monte Carlo Story, 210b And Woman was Created, 235 French Connection II
GETTY IMAGES 35, 38/39, 60/61
PICASSO MUSEUM "Nature Morte" (A. Ramie)
PICTURES COLOUR LIBRARY LTD Front cover c, 17 Lavender, 18/9 Gypsy festival, 117 Horses
BARRIE SMITH 133 Bullfight
SPECTRUM COLOUR LIBRARY 19 Procession of Gardians, 20/1 St.-Raphaël, 132 Bullfight, 170 St.-Raphaël

The remaining photographs are held in the Automobile Association's own library (AA PHOTO LIBRARY). Adrian Baker took all the pictures except pages 22, 112a (P. Kenward), 157 (E. Meacher), 23, 182, 184, 185, 186, 187, 195, 207a, 207b, 208, 209b, 234, 236, 239, 240/1, 242, 243a, 246, 258, 259, 264, 266 (R. Moss), 49a, 93, 220 (T. Oliver), 18, 211, 232, 232/3 (N. Ray), 12/13, 42/3, 146/7, 147, 160, 196/7, 213, 256 (B. Smith), 4b, 5b, 6/7, 10/1, 10, 11, 13a, 16/7, 24/25, 27, 28/9, 30/1, 30b, 33, 34/5, 40/1, 41, 44, 45, 46, 47, 49b, 73a, 74a, 78, 80/1, 81, 92a, 95, 96, 97, 98/9, 104a, 104b, 105, 106, 107, 114/5, 115, 119, 120/1, 121, 122, 123, 132b, 138, 140, 149, 151, 153, 156, 158b, 164, 168, 169, 172a, 172b, 175b, 183, 201, 202, 212a, 212b, 222, 223a, 225, 229b, 238, 243b, 247a, 248a, 248b, 250, 253, 261, 265 (R. Strange).

Contributors

Revision verifier: Donna Dailey
Revision edit and design: Bookwork Creative Associates Ltd